THE PATH TO A
MODERN SOUTH

*Northeast Texas between Reconstruction
and the Great Depression*

WALTER L. BUENGER

UNIVERSITY OF TEXAS PRESS

AUSTIN

Copyright © 2001 by the University of Texas Press

First edition, 2001

Requests for permission to reproduce material from this work should be
sent to Permissions, University of Texas Press, Box 7819, Austin, TX
78713-7819.

⊗ The paper used in this book meets the minimum requirements of
ANSI/NISO Z39.48-1992 (R1997) (Permanence of Paper).

Library of Congress Cataloging-in-Publication Data
Buenger, Walter L. (Walter Louis), 1951–
The path to a modern South : northeast Texas between reconstruction
and the great depression / Walter L. Buenger.— 1st ed.
p.   cm.
Includes bibliographical references (p.   ) and index.
ISBN 0-292-70887-4 (cloth : alk. paper) —
ISBN 0-292-70888-2 (pbk. : alk. paper)
1. Texas—History—1846-1950. 2. Texas—Social conditions. 3. Texas—
Economic conditions. 4. New Deal, 1933-1939—Texas. 5. World War,
1939-1945—Texas. 6. World War, 1939-1945—Influence. 7. Social
change—Texas—History. I. Title.
F391 .B878   2001
976.4'8061—dc21   00-061517

For Vickie

CONTENTS

ILLUSTRATIONS

FIGURES

TABLES

PREFACE

On one level this work concerns connections and disconnections. It is a linear study of how the relationship between regions of Texas, the state as a whole, and the South changed over time. It examines how politics, economics, culture, religion, and race entwined in Northeast Texas from the point in the 1880s when the post-Reconstruction order began breaking down to the eve of the Great Depression. In a less linear way it examines how the connection and disconnection between memory and reality, between the past and the present, shaped the modernization of a region. Throughout it probes what these connections and disconnections meant and, in particular, explores linkages between the lead-up to the New Deal and the results of the New Deal and World War II.

On another level then, this book is a reexamination of the "self-evident" truth that significant transformation of Texas and the South into a more prosperous region that fit more closely into the American mainstream awaited federal intervention during the New Deal and World War II. This study examines that truth by looking at the years 1887 to 1930 and by focusing on the eleven counties that made up the First Congressional District of Texas. Located in the state's northeast corner and bordered by Louisiana, Arkansas, and Oklahoma, the First District closely resembled—on the surface—any other cotton-growing region of the South. The history of Northeast Texas, one of the most southern regions of the state, provides an opportunity to identify the level, nature, and implications of change in the pre–New Deal South. Beyond that the region's history offers a chance to systematically gauge just how much being Texan affected modernization.

While working on this project over the past decade, I incurred many debts. Early in the process several colleagues in the profession proved essential. At the start, Worth Robert Miller provided precinct-level voting returns for several counties and educated me on the intricacies of county-level politics in the 1890s. Randolph B. Campbell read early drafts of several chapters and helped work out the direction this study finally took. In frequent emails he probed the weak spots of my arguments while encouraging me to continue. Ty Cashion located research assistants in Northeast Texas, read early drafts of some chapters, and tracked down photographs. He went out of his way to help time and time again. With Ty's assistance, Marry Ressler and Vivian Lehman located isolated copies of Northeast Texas newspapers, dug up stray election returns, and found caches of oral interviews.

Archivists and research professionals also provided important help. Jim Conrad of the James Gilliam Gee Library at Texas A&M–Commerce located more oral interviews and pointed me toward other primary source material. Daisy Harvill of the Aikin Regional Archives at Paris Junior College also helped track down local records. Rebecca Sharpless used her familiarity with the Texas Collection at Baylor University to aid in the search for privately published memoirs of Northeast Texans. Jenkins Garrett, an archivist at heart, generously opened up his postcard collection to me, and over numerous lunches demonstrated his friendship and interest in my work. George Ward of the Texas State Historical Association also hunted photographs and listened patiently to my stories. Ralph Elder of the Center for American History at the University of Texas at Austin and David Chapman of the Cushing Memorial Library at Texas A&M also unearthed photographs and other archival material.

Colleagues at Texas A&M and elsewhere improved the presentation of the information and ideas that grew from this archival material and the early assistance of so many. Julia Blackwelder and Brian Linn read the manuscript and offered thought-provoking comments. Carl Moneyhon and Alwyn Barr both read the manuscript in a more finished state and provided exceptionally useful criticism.

Bob Calvert displayed unflagging interest in this project and read the manuscript with care. During our weekly discussions of points large and small, he recommended new books to read, weighed the logic of my arguments, and highlighted areas that required further research. Even while ill, Bob maintained his good humor and made the work easier and far more fun.

My family also lightened and enlivened the various tasks that produce a book. My children, Erin and Davis, brought joy and a reminder of a different reality to the years I worked on this book. Madge Luquette used her fine eye for detail to ease the burden of proofreading and indexing. When the situation demanded it, she took charge of her grandchildren, leaving their father to work.

Vickie Buenger did the things that authors usually attribute to their spouses. At crucial times in the preparation of this book she shouldered more than her share of the tasks involved in raising two children and running a household. She listened without once screaming, "I am sick of Northeast Texas." More than that she used the skills and the insights developed when we wrote a book together to improve every paragraph of this work. Whatever grace or clarity the prose may have owes much to her. She also provided technical expertise when I encountered various computer problems, and she improved the appearance of the charts and graphs. I lovingly dedicate this book to her—not only because she pointed out that I had dedicated books to everyone but her, but because she has been such a major contributor in bringing this project to completion.

SEEING THE WHOLE BY SPOTTING A PART

O ld-timers give a standard piece of advice on spotting deer in the West Texas chaparral. Look first for an ear or a leg. Light, shadows, and brush trick the eyes into missing the whole, but they seldom hide every part. Historians too understand that a bewildering array of contradictory details, incomplete evidence, or thick layers of interpretation, like light, shadows, and brush, trick observers of the past. They seek out an appropriate part to illuminate the whole. Such is the purpose of this political, economic, social, and cultural history of Northeast Texas, a region that offers much to carry forward in looking at all of Texas and the South.

Based on the experiences of Northeast Texans, historians have underestimated the level, type, and consequence of change between 1887 and 1930. State boundaries influenced this change as the region and almost certainly the rest of Texas diverged from the pattern of neighboring southern states. Significant change did not simply await the external forces let loose by the New Deal and World War II. Instead, a more competitive political arena, an economy with more opportunities and incentives for innovation and growth, and a more fluid society and culture allowed Texans to initiate change before 1930. Those changes and the conditions that produced them prepared Texans to take better advantage of the opportunities presented by the New Deal and World War II. Yet southern characteristics, developed over the previous century, remained obvious.[1]

From the 1820s until near the close of the nineteenth century, Texas, and especially Northeast Texas, grew steadily more like such classic southern states as Tennessee, North Carolina, Georgia, Alabama, and Mississippi. The chance for economic advancement—the viability of slavery and plantation agriculture—drew a steady stream of southerners to

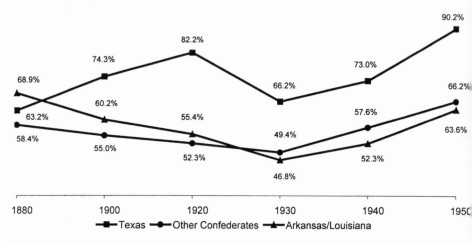

FIGURE 0.1

Changes in per capita income, 1880–1950
(as a percentage of U.S. per capita income).

Source: Maurice Levin, *Income in the Various States, Its Sources and Distribution, 1919,*
1920, 1921 (New York: National Bureau of Economic Research, 1925); Charles F.
Schwartz and Robert E. Graham, Jr., *Personal Income by States since 1929,* supplement to
Survey of Current Business (Washington: Department of Commerce, 1956); Richard
Easterlin, "Interregional Differences in Per Capita Income, Population, and Total Income,
1840–1950," in National Bureau of Economic Research, *Trends in the American Economy*
in the Nineteenth Century (Princeton: Princeton University Press, 1960).

antebellum Texas. As the prospects for cotton improved, new Texans
came increasingly from the Lower South states. In 1861 Texas joined the
original Confederacy of these Lower South states. Significantly, Texas se-
ceded before Arkansas, North Carolina, Tennessee, and Virginia, suggesting it was far from being a border state. The Civil War experience drew
Texans even more tightly into the southern orbit. Texans shared the memory of defeat and the reality of postwar poverty. Less intensively developed, however, Texas continued to draw southerners, white and black, to
its productive and relatively inexpensive soil. By the early 1890s Confederate mythology, a cotton-based economy, a common culture based on
evangelical Protestantism, racial violence, and ties of friendship and kinship linked Texans more firmly then ever to the South. Texans' key role in
the development of southern Populism demonstrated the oneness of Texas
and the rest of the South.[2]

Still, divergence between Texas and the rest of the South began in the
midst of the Populist furor, as suggested by Figure 0.1.[3] Before 1901,
meaning before substantial economic growth in West Texas and before

the discovery of significant amounts of oil in the state, Texans' per capita income diverged from that of the ten other Confederate states. Even more interestingly, it diverged from its neighbors Arkansas and Louisiana. The dip in 1930, however, suggested that Texans' income remained tied to cotton prices, as did income in other southern states.[4]

After 1930, economic development in Texas moved the state rapidly toward convergence with the rest of the United States, but numbers tell only part of this ambiguous story. Bruce Schulman, in his study of the impact of federal policy on the South after 1938, observed that during World War II, "Texas leaders exploited their state's advantages in ways that North Carolina's did not." Texans, led by Jesse H. Jones and other key members of government, obtained more than their share of federal benefits during the New Deal and World War II. Texas farmers, for example, received substantially more benefits per capita from 1933 to 1939 than did farmers in any other southern state.[5] Yet Texans' avid pursuit of those benefits, regardless of how it might upset their traditional society, truly marked them as different from most other southerners. Nothing demonstrated this difference in attitudes and aspirations more profoundly than the key role that Texan Lyndon Johnson played in the Civil Rights Movement. By the 1930s, when Johnson first began his rise to prominence, Texans' past had better prepared them to maximize new opportunities and put aside old prejudices.[6]

Statistical similarity and other similarities with the South before 1887 and greater dissimilarity after 1930 suggest that the years in between hold the key to the emergence of modern Texas. Here lies one part of the whole—answers to why Texas began changing and what prepared Texans to pursue even greater change. Here lies the beginning point of examining how the rest of the South did and did not resemble Texas. Yet too many conflicting details, too few complete sets of evidence, and a confining historiography make writing coherently about the whole of Texas in these years exceptionally difficult.

Geographers call Texas a transitional area and avidly analyze the five or more distinct zones of vegetation, soil, and terrain. The presence of distinctive and long-lasting German, Czech, and Mexican folk islands added to the variety of the cultural landscape. A long border with another country, Mexico, further complicated the Texas past. Still, blacks and whites from the South composed the largest population groups until recent times, and nothing in the climate or terrain of the eastern two-thirds of the state slowed the spread of southern-style agriculture. Even the western third of the state, despite its arid climate, long displayed many southern characteristics, especially regarding religion and race.[7] Yet explaining what was southern and not southern offers such a challenge that some historians of the South have simply ignored Texas, leaving its history for the indiscriminate use of historians of the West.[8]

While the diversity of Texas and its unique location cause mental overload, the paucity of published works on anything but politics in the post-Reconstruction period presents another series of problems. Few secondary sources exist on which to build a broad-gauged study of Texas, and such a book would require mining primary sources from each of the state's many regions.[9]

In part this lack of work on areas besides politics comes from historians' preconceptions. Much of the literature on the South and Texas treats the period from 1887 to 1930 as politically discrete but as economically and socially an extension of the late nineteenth century. Populism, Progressivism, and the legal development of Jim Crow get much attention. Economic growth, when noted, seems minimal and within pre-existing parameters. While some historians acknowledge social and cultural change, many view it as a frozen era. As Edward L. Ayers puts it in *The Promise of the New South*, "The same processes worked throughout the region after 1906 as before." Saying over and over that nothing changed, that the same basic processes continued until the New Deal, keeps us from looking for evidence to the contrary.[10]

Such preconceptions require testing, and the diversity of Texas together with the lack of work on anything but politics argue for a test done in a tightly focused area with the greatest possible similarity to the rest of the South. Among the diverse regions that made up Texas, none were more like the rest of the South than the First Congressional District in the state's northeast corner. South and west of the Red River lay Bowie, Camp, Cass, Delta, Franklin, Hopkins, Lamar, Marion, Morris, Red River, and Titus counties, the focal points of this study.[11] Like most rivers, the Red united as much as it divided the people in its valley, and Northeast Texans shared much with their neighbors in Oklahoma, Arkansas, and Louisiana. This makes the area an ideal spot for close examination, a place to expand analysis of Texas and the South.[12]

A quick survey of the land and people in the eleven counties shows just how representative they were of the Red River area and of the South in 1887. The eastern counties—Bowie, Camp, Cass, Marion, and Morris—mirrored neighboring counties and parishes in Arkansas and Louisiana. Pine forests and acidic, sandy soil predominated in the uplands but gave way to rich, easily cultivated alluvial soil and extensive stands of oak, hickory, walnut, and cypress along the Red and Sulphur rivers and their smaller tributaries. Farmers and merchants could reach the head of navi-

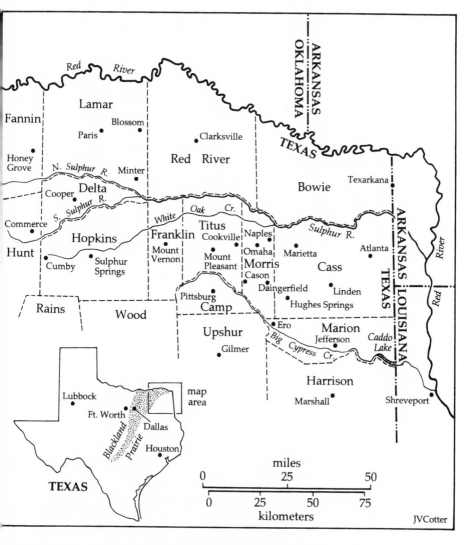

FIGURE 0.2

Northeast Texas. Map by John V. Cotter.

gation on the Red River, and this allowed the development of antebellum slavery and cotton plantations. Large-scale cotton plantations, often utilizing black tenants, continued to dominate the economy after the Civil War as the area filled up with transplanted southerners. In the 1880s, the lumber and railroad industries increased in importance and brought limited manufacturing to the eastern counties, but cotton long dominated the local economy.[13]

Not surprisingly, blacks made up a large percentage of the total population. In 1890 blacks in Marion and Camp counties constituted more than half the population. Despite a slight decline in the percentage of blacks in their total population, as late as 1930 Bowie, Camp, Cass, Marion, and Morris counties combined had about the same percentage black as Louisiana, roughly 37 percent.[14]

The western counties resembled their neighbors in Southeast Oklahoma and North Texas. As you moved westward in Red River and Titus counties, gently rolling prairies with scattered islands of post oaks gradually replaced swampy river bottoms and forested uplands. Pines virtually disappeared. Present, however, were the same rich soils near the rivers and creeks and the easily cultivated sandy soils away from the rivers. In Lamar, Delta, Hopkins, and Franklin counties, plentiful rain fell on prairie soils, and native grasses dominated the landscape into the twentieth century. Post oak mottes and the densely wooded margins along rivers and creeks gave variety to the landscape. Clarksville, in Red River County, served as an early center of trade and commerce, but limited transportation slowed the full development of the antebellum plantation system in the western counties. Even so, the rich calcareous "black waxy" prairies, sandy loam gray lands, and alluvial bottomlands attracted a surprising number of prewar settlers.[15]

As transportation improved after the war, cotton replaced hay, corn, and small grains in the western counties. By 1890 the productivity of the soil made the area a mecca for southern farmers and firmly established it as a center of the cotton industry. Financing and insuring cotton, producing cottonseed oil, and manufacturing gins and other equipment needed in the cotton trade made the region more than just a land of farms.[16]

Despite the boom in cotton, blacks never numbered more than a third of the population of any western county. In 1890 Red River County's blacks made up about 31 percent of the population, while in Delta they made up only 8 percent. As in other areas in or near the Texas Blackland Prairie, converting more acreage into cotton production attracted many more whites than blacks.[17] By 1930 blacks in Lamar and Red River formed only about 22 percent of the population, similar to the percentage in Arkansas. In Franklin, Delta, and Hopkins counties, the percentage black dropped to near 7 percent, about the same as in Oklahoma. Titus fell in between with about 15 percent black.[18]

As Table 0.1 shows, the district grew substantially whiter after 1880. Yet, the percentage black for the district in 1930 remained greater than the

TABLE O.I

First District Population by Race

District Population	1880	1890	1900	1910	1920	1930
Total	126,339	170,001	220,322	239,341	271,472	255,552
White	85,671	118,769	159,071	174,192	204,215	190,451
% total	67.8	69.9	72.2	72.8	75.2	74.5
% change		38.6	33.9	9.5	17.2	−6.7
Black	40,555	51,149	61,231	65,143	67,251	64,505
% total	32.1	30.1	27.8	27.2	24.8	25.2
% change		26.1	19.7	6.4	3.2	−4.1

Source: U.S., *Census: 1880–1930, Population.*

percentage black in Texas or in Oklahoma, Arkansas, Texas, and Louisiana combined.[19]

Other demographic characteristics of the region also echoed those of the cotton-growing South. Northeast Texas lacked the large urban centers that powered the economic development of Texas as a whole but by 1890 boasted two flourishing small cities.[20] Paris, in Lamar County, and Texarkana, in Bowie County, served trade areas that crossed state and county boundaries and had many more manufacturing plants than other towns in the district. This helped Paris reach a population of about 8,000 and Texarkana about 6,000 (Arkansas and Texas) in 1890. Texarkana's factories milled lumber and manufactured furniture and other wood products. Railroad machine shops added metal-working capacity to the industrial mix. The city's boundary crossed over into Arkansas, and roughly 45 percent of its citizens lived in that state. This border status made Texarkana an attractive place for the regional headquarters of several railroad and timber companies. In Paris, flour milling, cottonseed processing, and the production of food products combined with banking, wholesale distribution, and the cotton trade to create a healthy urban economy. As in Texarkana, several railroads met in Paris, making it a leading shipping point. Yet in 1930, the population of Texarkana, by then the larger of the two, still numbered fewer than 30,000.[21]

Their commercial and industrial base gave Paris and Texarkana a slightly different demographic profile from the rest of the region. Nevertheless, in Bowie County, from 1890 to 1930 fewer than 2 percent of the population fit the census category foreign-born white, and that together with the absence of Lutherans and the small number of Catholics sig-

FIGURE 0.3

Broad Street in Texarkana in about 1900. Texarkana grew rapidly after 1890 as
railroads and lumber companies consolidated their operations within its boundaries.
Located astride the border between Arkansas and Texas, the city
soon boasted such modern amenities as electric streetcars.
Photograph courtesy of Jenkins Garrett Texas Postcard Collection, University of Texas
at Arlington, Special Collections.

naled that few German, Czech, Cajun, and Mexican Texans lived there
year round. Even Bowie, the most ethnically diverse county in the region,
fell within typical southern demographic parameters.[22]

Clearly, the Red River did not divide the geography and society of adjacent areas of Texas, Oklahoma, Arkansas, and Louisiana. Nor did the Red
totally divide the economy. As in the rest of the South, tenancy increased
after 1890 and erratic cotton prices dogged farmers, but the citizens of
the Red River Valley suffered fewer economic calamities than southerners to the east. In the 1920s the valley escaped the alternating ravages of a
flooded Mississippi River and severe droughts. Greater productivity partially insulated some farmers from boll weevil damage and wild swings
in cotton prices. Larger towns flourished. Better economic conditions on
the plains of West Texas and in nearby cities like Dallas and Fort Worth
offered a way out.[23] The relative economic health of the region, the nearness of significant opportunities to get ahead, and the presence of islands

of prosperity separated the valley from what Jack Temple Kirby called "retrograde cotton counties of the South."[24]

In Northeast Texas, in particular, more than luck and location separated residents from the most devastated areas of the South. The region, so much like the rest of the South in 1887, arrived at a different end point in 1930 because business trends, law, public policy, aspirations—all shaped by politics and culture—gave the region a bit more prosperity. Being Texan offered subtle economic advantages that eluded other southerners and that allowed higher incomes and different reactions to federal policy. Just as the focus of this study narrows to one time period and one region of Texas, it narrows repeatedly to one underlying question—a question that opens the way to answers to many others. In Northeast Texas did being part of Texas matter?

Answers about the importance of state boundaries traditionally fall in three categories: politics, economics, and culture. V. O. Key posited that Texas's particular racial characteristics made its politics slightly different from the politics of the rest of the South. The concentration of blacks in a minority of Texas counties offered the promise of moving beyond the use of race to gain office and allowed the existence of two competing factions within the Democratic party. While often acting in typical southern fashion, Texans stood the best chance of varying from the norm. Conversely, Gavin Wright argued that eastern Texas had the same closed labor market as the rest of the South and that this limited the economy. For him, and for most economic historians, state boundaries meant far less than the boundaries of a traditional cotton-growing culture. Yet many have argued that another type of culture set the state apart. After observing the state, John Steinbeck wrote that Texas "is a mystique closely approximating a region" and "its unity lies in the mind." Myth made Texas. Northeast Texans' experiences between 1887 and 1930 challenge and qualify all three standard interpretations.[25]

Not two, but three or more roughly equal political factions existed throughout the period from 1887 to 1930. This phenomenon prevented one faction from ever gaining the upper hand without compromise and conciliation and limited conservatives' influence. Among the other southern states, Texas as a whole perhaps most resembled North Carolina. Certainly that comparison struck Schulman when he examined the behavior of their politicians in the 1930s and 1940s. During an earlier time, a coalition of Populists and Republicans controlled North Carolina's government. In the mid-1890s this coalition had more real political power than Texas Populists ever achieved. Using race baiting, fraud, intimidation, and appeals to the Confederate past, North Carolina conservatives soon regained control, and they remained in control into the post–World War II period. In contrast to North Carolina, from 1887 to 1930 conservatives never consistently controlled politics in Northeast Texas or in the state at large.[26]

This dynamic political landscape allowed legal changes that aided the growth of an economy that began to accelerate in the mid-1890s, and economic growth soon joined the distinctive political structure in providing a foundation for change. Instead of being an isolated backwater, Northeast Texas was connected to, and affected by, the even more dynamic centers of economic change in Texas and, through them, to others elsewhere in the United States. These new centers of prosperity offered markets for alternatives to cotton, magnets for surplus labor, and dissemination points for the latest business methods. Nothing in the political system hampered this process. All of this led to a restructured economy and society by the late 1920s. Of course, elements of this restructuring, particularly the increase in the number of sharecroppers, magnified the painful impact of the Great Depression and New Deal policy. The patterns of growth that emerged by 1930, however, also sped recovery. Northeast Texans found themselves better able to do something about what Gilbert Fite called "the unfavorable balance between land and people" that mired southern agricultural areas in poverty.[27]

Culture eventually joined politics and economics in creating an environment that allowed innovation and change, but Steinbeck and others mistakenly assumed that Texans always considered themselves exceptional. Instead, until about 1910 Northeast Texans thought and acted more southern than Texan. Like citizens of the rest of the former Confederate states, they built monuments to the Lost Cause and fervently worshiped the memory of Confederate heroes. Between 1910 and the early 1920s that tendency reversed as Northeast Texans became more Texan than southern. Over the course of the 1920s an attachment to local history and folk culture further obscured a sense of being southern. As these transformations progressed, Texans more freely acted as Americans instead of southerners. Northeast Texans, in particular, increasingly accepted middle-class movements that took women outside the home and family and relied more on the state and federal governments. They optimistically reached for an American future, instead of rigidly defending a Confederate past.[28]

In Northeast Texas, cultural fluidity, economic growth and innovation, and a more open political system operated interactively. Each factor not only influenced the others, the region changed because of its connections to the rest of the state. While Key missed the trifactional nature of Texas politics, he accurately insisted on the importance of the relationship of the parts of a southern state to the political whole. Multifactionalism, for example, benefited from the strength of ethnic communities and from the rapid growth of several large cities with a diverse economy in other parts of Texas. This distinguished Northeast Texas from Georgia, where intense factionalism also made state politics a bit more open and competitive than the norm.[29]

In like fashion, connections between the parts of the state and connections between economics, politics, and culture explained why Texans better exploited the advantages offered by the federal government in the 1930s and 1940s. Gavin Wright pointed out that southern politicians did not use their power to bring federal largess to their region for fear of pushing up regional wages. Yet Wright Patman, who for forty-seven years served the First District in the House of Representatives, consistently led the fight to push up the minimum wage and to expand the availability of credit for the common man. In this fight he took advantage of a tightly knit Texas congressional delegation, a group determined to bring industry and capital to Texas.[30]

From 1928 on, Patman enjoyed unusual popularity in his district, never facing a runoff election. To a large extent, the region's political, economic, and cultural history explained Patman's success. As Key noted and North Carolina demonstrated, the faction representing the less prosperous proved the most unstable, but in Northeast Texas it survived to combine with factions in the middle of the ideological spectrum and elect Patman and others like him. Continuity of leadership and a more institutionalized structure made the less prosperous a reliable voting bloc. Likewise an economy that brought greater competition to small-town shopkeepers gave them incentive to support a congressman who championed anti-chain-store legislation. Finally Patman fit the culture of his time and place. He never used Confederate rhetoric and avoided race baiting in politics. Instead he projected an active pioneer image that stressed a Texan's ability to get the job done.[31]

Differences in race relations in their home districts did not fully explain Patman's and other Texans' variation from a more typical southern pattern. Certainly the gruesome history of lynching in Northeast Texas testified that race counted as much there as anywhere else in the South. After 1887 the pace of lynching quickened in the region and matched the barbarity of anything found in Georgia or Mississippi. Intense local criticism of lynching in the early 1920s, however, drastically reduced the practice. Lynching became un-American, an unacceptable cultural trait with the added liability of being bad for business. Like slavery, postwar poverty, and other southern characteristics, Texans soon wrote lynching out of their state's history and achieved "reconciliation of progress and tradition" by remembering a nonsouthern past.[32]

What mattered though was not simply that Northeast Texans changed their history, but that they enjoyed an extended period without a fixed history. As late as 1920, devotion to Texas history remained embryonic, still moving toward the point where, as one Northeast Texan declared: "In my native state patriotism flourished as does the prickly pear: evergreen and everywhere, however poor the soil, and just as thorny. The cactus may be made edible for the Texas cattle by singeing it with a flamethrower, but not even one of those things could smooth a Texan when, rubbed the wrong way, his patriotism bristles."[33] Like the multifactional political system and the more dynamic economy, a less fixed sense of the past fostered acceptance of new ideas and new attitudes. Whereas other southern states boasted "few supports for innovation," being in transition from the old Confederate myth to the new Texas myth allowed greater flexibility and acceptance of innovation. That as much as anything explained why Texas diverged from the rest of the South after 1930.[34]

By 1930 being modern meant achieving material prosperity through more efficient use of new technology and new methods of business organization. Modernity required a readiness to embrace the federal government's help in remaking the region. Modern Texans rejected the most violent forms of racism, abandoned the innovation-numbing Confederate culture, and accepted an expanded role for women. Being modern meant not just having changed, but readying for further change.

As the chapters that follow outline, these transformations rose from the foundation of a more open political system and a changing economy. They developed within the context of the move from a multiparty to a one-party system and sprang from the interconnection between politics, law, and culture. An erratic economy after 1914 and the broad impact of World War I induced further change. In the 1920s, demographic trends underscored the need to accept modernity, while the political system, despite the impact of the Ku Klux Klan, continued to favor moderate candidates backed by a broad coalition. During the late 1920s, operating within this distinctive political system and reacting to a new culture, Northeast Texans abandoned most aspects of their traditional society. Some may argue that at that point the region and the state ceased to be southern. For good reasons Northeast Texans would never have agreed.

PART ONE

FOUNDATIONS

ONE

THE FLUID AND THE CONSTANT

*Persistent Factionalism, Lynching,
and Reform, 1887–1896*

On Saturday, August 6, 1887, when all knew that the referendum on statewide prohibition lost by 90,000 votes, antiprohibitionists in Camp County staged a derisive march. Wearing blue streamers, they paraded through the streets of Pittsburg for more than four hours. Led by a band, marchers "made considerable show." A man in blue mounted on a horse trimmed in blue and a man in white mounted on a mule trimmed in white brought up the rear. According to the local editor, "The latter represented Prohibition and manifested an unmistakable aversion to following the crowd and, as part of the program, at every angle of the streets he would dart away in another direction, but the man in blue brought him back with a horse whip representing we suppose the True Blue party lash." In response, prohibitionists hung white streamers out their windows as the demonstration passed.[1]

Six years later a more gruesome spectacle unfolded in Lamar County. At 1:00 P.M., Wednesday, February 1, 1893, a Texas and Pacific train with a special coach rolled into Paris from Texarkana. Enraged white citizens surrounded the coach bearing Henry Smith, a black accused of sexually assaulting and murdering Myrtle Vance, a three-year-old white girl. Pressured by law enforcement officers and told to expect to die no matter what, Smith had admitted assaulting the girl and speculated that she died when he pressed his hand over her mouth to keep her quiet. Claiming he was drunk and did not know what he was doing, he pleaded to be shot. His coerced confession failed to win him a quick death. Instead, Smith learned he was to be burned alive. More than 15,000 people watched Smith's elaborate torture and slow burning. After his ashes cooled onlookers scrambled for bits of clothing, fragments of bone, and other mementos.[2]

These two events captured the fluid and the constant in Northeast Texas from 1887 to 1896. Social and economic reform movements stirred intense passions, raising interest and participation in politics to a much higher level. The "party lash" failed Democrats, and the post-Reconstruction political order collapsed, ushering in a period of continual fluctuation in partisan alignments. For a decade Northeast Texans combined and recombined in a kaleidoscope of political alliances.[3]

Meanwhile the increased frequency and awful ferocity of lynchings after 1887 signaled that racism had hit a new plateau. Lynching and reform wrapped together. In 1887 prohibitionists warned that blacks who refused to listen to the logic of their cause would become "still more contemptible and still more akin to the brute." Brutes, black beasts that threatened white homes and families—in white minds those words and phrases justified the torch and rope, election fraud, and assassination. Little wonder that long before the erection of legal barriers to black voting, the influence of the black voting bloc waned.[4]

Incidents just as brutal as Henry Smith's lynching occurred across the South. In that sense Paris could have been in Georgia or Mississippi, and lynching served as the most visible reminder that in the early 1890s Texas remained closely tied to the Southeast. Factional politics also characterized Georgia and North Carolina, but in those states conservatives, taking advantage of race baiting, a more limited franchise, and a less diverse economy and population, proved far stronger than in Texas. While the power of the black voting bloc diminished, opponents of both conservatives and middle-class reformers proved remarkably resilient in Northeast Texas. Multifactionalism and unstable parties, which in a broad sense characterized Texas politics as early as the 1850s, continued to the close of the century. In this continued political fluidity lay the opening wedge of change. Intensely competitive factional politics and emotion-filled reform principles broke ground for the movement of Northeast Texas toward a modern South by improving access to power and allowing innovation.[5]

PRINCIPLES, PRAGMATISM, AND PERSONALITY

Factional politics operated both within and outside the dominant Texas Democratic party. Ironically, the party remains largely unstudied, as scholars pay more attention to its rivals than to the presumed unchanging monolith.[6] Such presumptions need adjustment. Between 1887 and 1896, Democrats won most elections, but party loyalty mattered less than the persistence of three or more distinctive factions that moved in and out

4

of different parties. These factions identified not so much with party as with others who shared their class, race, self-interest, and ideology. Flamboyant and occasionally charismatic leaders added a glue that kept factions together even within a larger party organization. Since no single faction constituted a majority, successful candidates forged a shifting series of coalitions and positioned themselves on issues in ways that attracted enough support from two or more factions to ensure victory.

During the 1887 campaign for statewide prohibition, F. A. Lockhart, county judge of Camp County, purchased the *Pittsburg Gazette,* giving us a window to view this world of shifting coalitions and careful outreach to opposing factions. After announcing he was "decidedly Democratic" because the party was "best calculated to administer good government and protect and prosper the people's interest," Lockhart insisted: "We are free to accredit others with equal sincerity who entertain adverse political opinions, and we have not a word to say that would wound the feelings of an honest man, nor would we willingly those of any man. It is principle we propose to advocate or condemn and not men or classes of men."[7]

As an officeholder and newspaperman, Lockhart could ill afford alienating subscribers or voters, especially since, as he said, Camp's Democrats "persist in some sort of wrangle," and he won the office of county judge by only eleven votes. The existence of competitive factions in the Democratic party and the strength of rival political organizations induced office seekers to court all voters—including blacks.[8]

Still, Lockhart's words represented more than good public relations and political expediency—they testified to the importance of reform movements. He quickly assured his readers: "We are for prohibition. We could not be otherwise in view of the financial and moral wreck the whiskey traffic has wrought and the countless thousands of bleeding, broken hearts that owe their anguish to its agency." A reform mentality led Lockhart to proclaim: "for the sake of humanity change the law and be happy, prosperous people."[9]

Fired by such principles, voters coalesced into long-lasting factions. Pragmatism often kept those factions within the Democratic or Republican parties, because Democrats won statewide elections and Republicans usually held power at the national level. In 1887, however, there were no offices to gain. Thus, the bitter prohibition election not only hardened or created political divisions, it allows the observance of factions in the absence of office seeking.[10]

Northeast Texans fell roughly into five groups that year: conservatives, social reformers, economic reformers, insurgents, and black Republicans. Conservatives and insurgents both opposed prohibition. In a typically southern pattern, prosperous white landowners and merchants often led conservatives who were supported by blacks and whites tied to them by kinship, long association, economic dependency, or shared worldview. Equally southern countryfolk engaged in a traditional combination of farming, herding, and hunting, valued the local community, and resented outside interference. In contrast to conservatives, insurgents were poorer, more isolated, less intimately involved in a market economy, and often opposed the Democrats. The term *insurgent* best describes them because theirs was a vote against outside control, against conformity to party discipline, and for the preservation of their traditional way of life. While the coalition of conservatives and insurgents barely survived the year, in 1887 antiprohibition linked the economic extremes, tying together believers in traditional ways and advocates of as little government intervention in business and society as possible.[11]

Reformers, who later voted as one faction, split on prohibition. Led by editors, merchants, bankers, ministers, and lawyers, one reform subgroup, centered in the region's towns, stressed social order and Protestant morality. The other emphasized equity and economic growth and, while claiming some urban support, drew more votes from landowning, market-oriented farmers. Some leaders, such as Ebenezer Lafayette Dohoney of Paris and Charles DeMorse of Clarksville, bridged both factions, but economic reformers generally opposed statewide prohibition. James S. Hogg, the state's attorney general and champion of state regulation of business, argued that statewide prohibition overly restricted personal choice, diverted attention from economic reform, and disrupted the Democratic party. As Hogg understood, zealous reformers easily bolted his party. Yet in seeking reform, both subgroups expanded participation in politics and stretched the political process beyond its post-Reconstruction boundaries.[12]

While a few blacks voted for Democrats or third-party candidates, until 1887 they usually supported Republican candidates—on the local level, black Republican candidates. Norris Wright Cuney, a skillful black politician, controlled the state party and fended off repeated white efforts to exclude blacks from leadership positions. His organizational ability, connections to the national party, and personality galvanized the black voting bloc. Black Republicans joined Germans, Czechs, and Mexicans in other regions of the state in voting solidly against prohibition and against the cultural conformity urged by middle-class, white, evangelical Protestants. Their votes along with those of conservatives and insurgents doomed the efforts of Dohoney, DeMorse, Lockhart, and other ardent pros.[13]

Despite losing, Dohoney in particular offered valuable insight into the nuances of Texas factionalism. With close ties to economic reformers, social reformers, and insurgents, he carried some from each group into the cause of prohibition and paved the way for their coming together in future campaigns. While demonstrating the fluidity and mutability of factions, Dohoney's career also demonstrated the limits of that mutability. Factions seldom vanished once part of a coalition, and not all members of factions trailed leaders from one cause and campaign to another.

Born in Kentucky and holding a law degree from the University of Louisville, Dohoney moved to Paris in 1859. While still in his twenties, he stumped Lamar County in opposition to secession, a movement led by local Democrats. His efforts bore fruit, and the county voted against secession in the February 23, 1861, referendum. Dohoney followed other Texas unionists into the Confederate army because, as he pointed out, they "could not afford to abandon their homes and families" to avoid military service. After two years and rising to the rank of captain in the Ninth Texas Cavalry, Dohoney returned to Paris, where he helped organize the shipment of supplies eastward. At war's end Dohoney served as a district attorney, and in 1869 running as a moderate, Dohoney defeated four other candidates for a place in the Texas Senate. He served two terms. As a delegate to the Constitutional Convention of 1875, Dohoney authored a local-option clause that first brought prohibition into the political arena. Among the other issues he supported were railroad regulation, homestead laws, banning the carrying of firearms in public, free public schools, and woman suffrage. Tiring of Democratic disregard for the farmer, Dohoney joined the Greenbackers in 1877 and published the *Greenback Advocate*. In 1882 he paid the price of opposing the Democrats when he ran unsuccessfully as the Greenback candidate for Congress.[14]

In 1881 and 1882 Dohoney combined his interest in women's rights and prohibition by inviting Frances E. Willard, national president of the Woman's Christian Temperance Union (WCTU), to speak in Paris. Local women quickly organized the first WCTU chapter in Texas, and his wife, Mary Johnson Dohoney, became a prominent member. At his urging, the Texas Greenbackers took up the prohibition cause and attacked the Democrats vigorously for failing to submit the question of statewide prohibition to a popular vote. With the Greenbackers fading from the political scene, in 1886 Dohoney ran for governor on the Prohibition party ticket and again pushed for a statewide referendum. When the Democratically controlled legislature reluctantly authorized the referendum on statewide prohibition in 1887, Dohoney toured the state speaking on its behalf.[15]

Leaders like Dohoney, as well as their followers, entered the 1887 campaign with a history of animosity for Democrats, and they emerged with even more reasons to remain distinctive. Into the twentieth century, participants remembered 1887 as a time "when friendships were severed and family ties subjected to the keenest trial." These broken friendships, however, occurred in all camps—Democrats, Republicans, third parties, and new voters. Dohoney could not carry all the old insurgent Greenbackers into the cause of prohibition. Indeed insurgents who had never voted before came out to vote against prohibition. Conservative Democrats split with reform Democrats. Reformers who had never voted before came out to vote for prohibition. White Republicans and a few urban black Republicans often divided from the majority of black Republicans over prohibition. Prohibition initiated a process of creative destruction continued by Populism, a process that eventually restructured Texas politics.[16]

Camp County revealed how prohibition began the process of creative destruction in 1887. Prohibitionists carried Precinct 1, the incorporated area of Pittsburg, and Precinct 5, on the outskirts of Pittsburg, by a two to one ratio. They also narrowly carried Precinct 2, which included the village of Leesburg. Stressing that prohibition promised a more orderly society and a better work force, prohibitionists brought some economic reformers in the Pittsburg area and in Leesburg into their camp. Members of the WCTU, "who were present with their smiles and words of encouragement," stressed the morality of prohibition. They also provided more practical reasons for voting for the cause—"The ladies provided free lunch and reasoned with the voters in such a way as to win many votes for Prohibition." The women wore white streamers, the color of prohibition and purity. Such efforts produced the lopsided vote in Pittsburg and carried the county for prohibition.[17]

Despite the blandishments of the ladies or perhaps because of the active role of women, white conservatives still opposed prohibition. Those worried about Democratic unity resented being forced to vote on prohibition, and in retaliation the blue-clad wets marched through Pittsburg two days after the August 4, 1887, election.

While the noise against prohibition came from prominent white "true gentlemen," the victory of the antiprohibitionists in rural precincts suggested that most votes against it came from white and black countryfolk. Precincts 3 and 4 included the plantation area of the county. Blacks outnumbered whites, and despite the presence of several large-scale white landowners, Republicans won most elections through the 1890s. Precinct 3 also contained many small-scale white farmers and tenants who lived isolated from the centers of trade and commerce and who later supported a variety of Populist candidates.[18]

This link between antiprohibition, black Republicans, and rural Populism also surfaced in Hopkins and Lamar counties, where sixteen of the twenty-eight precincts that voted against prohibition voted for the Populist candidate for governor in 1894. In Lamar, an additional three precincts with strong black Republican organizations also voted against prohibition. Black Republicans and white insurgents delivered the votes to defeat prohibition.[19]

As Table 1.1 demonstrates, counties in which blacks made up a very high percentage of the population or in which those living in a town of more than 1,000 made up a very low percentage of the population typically opposed prohibition by a large margin. In counties where these factors were less pronounced or offset each other, voters usually cast their ballots narrowly one way or the other. Counties where rural insurgent voters later gave Populist candidates such as Thomas L. Nugent significant support also tended to oppose prohibition.[20]

Only Delta County varied significantly from this pattern. While the county contained few blacks, Cooper, the county seat, remained small and sluggish. Reflecting the disparity between town and country, in the 1890s Populists carried the county by the widest margins in the district. Yet in 1887 prohibition also carried, perhaps because of the influence of Dohoney or some other persuasive personality. Moreover, Delta's rich prairie soil stimulated a more market-oriented economy, meaning that Populism drew more on the cry for economic reform instead of the tradition of insurgency. With fewer isolated pockets of self-sufficient agriculture, prohibition's middle-class message made headway.[21]

In 1887 belief in principle—prohibition or personal liberty—mattered. Long-standing voting blocs, particularly blacks and white rural insurgents, mattered. The influence of colorful and well-known personalities such as Dohoney and Hogg also mattered. All combined to turn out a record high vote of over 28,000 districtwide. Beyond the extraordinary turnout, as historian Alwyn Barr made clear, the 1887 prohibition campaign loosened "the party ties of thousands," and once loosened, "these could more easily be broken when other issues arose."[22]

In the short run the high turnout of 1887, and the politicizing of new voters it signified, proved more important than the diminished party loyalty of long-time voters. The next year Governor Lawrence Sullivan Ross stood for re-election against Marion Martin, a prominent prohibitionist and proponent of railroad regulation. Although Ross sought compro-

TABLE 1.1

Social and Electoral Characteristics, 1887–1892

County/District	County/District Population Data			1887 Election: Prohibition		1892 Election: Governor			
	Total Pop.	% Black	% Town 1,000+	% For	Total Vote	For Hogg	For Clark	For Nugent	Total Vote
BOWIE	20,267	37%	14%	54%	2,879	39%	26%	35%	3,668
CAMP	6,624	50%	18%	58%	1,172	31%	46%	23%	1,307
CASS	22,554	38%	7%	45%	3,640	45%	10%	45%	3,930
DELTA	9,117	8%	0%	53%	1,462	32%	12%	56%	1,946
FRANKLIN	6,481	13%	0%	36%	1,170	66%	4%	30%	1,101
HOPKINS	20,572	14%	15%	45%	3,658	43%	15%	41%	3,918
LAMAR	37,302	25%	22%	49%	6,364	45%	35%	19%	7,213
MARION	10,862	64%	28%	23%	1,726	45%	39%	16%	2,065
MORRIS	6,580	40%	0%	41%	1,037	45%	11%	44%	1,243
RED RIVER	21,452	31%	7%	48%	3,937	46%	26%	28%	4,223
TITUS	8,190	22%	0%	44%	1,345	41%	15%	43%	1,611
DISTRICT	170,001	30%	13%	46%	28,390	43.5%	23.5%	32.5%	32,225

Source: Election Return 1887, 1892, Secretary of State; U.S., Census: 1890, Population, pt. 1, 328–341, 782–785.

mise between feuding factions, his campaign manager, George Clark, led the antiprohibitionists in 1887 and served as an attorney for the largest railroad corporations in the state. Despite Clark's conservative influence, leaders of the Farmers' Alliance, from which the Populist party grew, generally supported Ross because they still hoped to work within the Democratic party or they opposed prohibition. In contrast, if rural insurgents new to the political process continued voting, they generally supported Martin, who ran on the Independent Fusion ticket. Labor groups, reeling from the impact of the railroad strikes of 1886, strenuously campaigned for Martin. Cuney, trying to strengthen the chances of black Republican candidates who might benefit from labor votes, joined the fusion effort.[23]

Third parties grew slightly and the black voting bloc remained intact in the eastern counties. In Bowie, Camp, Cass, Marion, and Morris counties, where Greenbackers and Republicans traditionally won over 40 percent of the vote, turnout surpassed the record highs of 1887, and Martin polled more votes than previous Democratic opponents. Martin won Camp by a larger margin than any past foe of the Democrats because he attracted new voters who supported economic reform but opposed prohibition and ardent prohibitionists. For both groups, prohibition and economic reform mattered more than party and the last election. Meanwhile Ross drew about as many votes as in 1886.[24]

In contrast, Democrats in the district's western counties polled more votes than usual, and their opponents stayed home or were counted out. In Lamar and Red River, in particular, white insurgent opponents of prohibition in 1887 stayed home, while fraud diminished the black vote. Perhaps white insurgents remained at home because of reluctance to choose between a prohibitionist and a Democratic party whose platform moved closer to the Greenback position by stressing the abolition of national banks, an increase in the money supply, and limited state regulation of corporations. Galvanized neither by the candidates nor the issues, white insurgents reverted to the habit of not voting.[25] Meanwhile, likely supporters of a black Republican-backed candidate either voluntarily did not vote for governor or were victims of fraud and intimidation. In Paris, where blacks made up 34 percent of the population, the Republican candidate for president received over 600 votes, but Martin only 64.[26]

Late-nineteenth-century Texas voters often used two ballot boxes: one for federal and one for state and local offices. Northeast Texas lacked cities over 10,000 until after 1900, and so by Texas law all voters came with two ballots, or in some cases two bundles of tickets, for each race; one ballot or bundle contained the candidates of their party for federal offices and one their candidates for state and local offices. Perhaps blacks refused to support Martin because of his close identification with prohibition and withheld their ballots in state and local elections. More likely, systematic tampering with the black vote in state and local races, begun in nearby Harrison County as early as 1884, had trickled into Red River and Lamar by 1888. If white prohibitionists—angered by black opposition to prohibition and aware that Martin had little chance to win statewide—supported the Democrats and fraudulently removed black votes from the state and local ballot box as a step toward winning local-option elections, then prohibition as much as populism stimulated the removal of blacks from the electoral process.[27]

Jim Hogg's presence on the ticket, running for re-election as attorney general in 1888, further strengthened the Democrats. A former resident of Wood County, adjacent to Hopkins, Franklin, and Camp, in the early 1880s Hogg served as a district attorney and then practiced law in Tyler. He took cases throughout Northeast Texas and earned a reputation as a thrilling courtroom orator. Along the way he formed political alliances with Cyclone Davis, former Democratic county judge of Franklin County, and John L. Sheppard, the district attorney for Camp and six other counties. In 1888 and again in 1890 Davis, the future Populist leader, and Sheppard, a future Democratic congressman, toured the region speaking for Hogg.[28]

Arguing for new state laws regulating railroads, Hogg ran for governor in 1890, and a constitutional amendment allowing the legislature to delegate its regulatory power to a railroad commission shared prominence on the ballot. His foes called him "communistic," but his campaign managers fended off the charge by portraying Hogg as "the people's choice." Meanwhile the tall, heavy-set attorney general used his powerful voice and sense of humor to good effect and easily secured the nomination.[29]

In a race where turnout slipped from the high levels of 1887 and 1888, Hogg won statewide by almost 200,000 votes, the largest margin of victory for any governor in nineteenth-century Texas. Webster Flanagan, the Republican candidate, garnered only halfhearted support from blacks, allowing Hogg, who opposed statewide prohibition and had a record of fair play with their race, to win some black votes. (Again, fraud might account for the shift, but the election was never close enough to warrant the risk of using illegal methods.) Moderate prohibitionists meanwhile had little reason to abandon fellow reformers and support an ineffective Prohibition candidate. Labor and farmer groups enthusiastically supported Hogg because he favored a railroad commission, and old friends like John Sheppard of Pittsburg again aided his campaign.[30]

Across the district, labor groups swung back into the Democratic fold, and the Farmers' Alliance, which had long pushed for a railroad commission, vigorously supported Hogg. Lacking a strong opponent, the Democrats won by impressive margins. Their vote total in each county typically declined from 1888, but the opposition vote declined even more. Flanagan carried only Marion County, and in Camp, Cass, and Morris, several traditionally Republican precincts voted for Hogg.[31]

A reduced Democratic vote, despite the return of labor and prohibitionists, pointed to trouble. Conservatives disliked Hogg and the commission idea, and some sat out the election. Some members of the Farmers' Alliance also criticized the commission as too weak and resented Hogg's failure to address other methods of easing farm problems. In Hopkins, for example, the commission did worst in precincts that would support either the conservative candidate or the Populist candidate in 1892. Attacked from the ideological left and right, the railroad commission amendment passed but drew 80,000 fewer votes statewide than Hogg.[32]

After the 1890 election, Hogg Democrats in the Texas legislature crafted a commission that set rates, required information from railroad companies, called witnesses, and punished corporate misdeeds. Although the Texas Railroad Commission, headed by John H. Reagan—former congressman, senator, and Confederate postmaster—steered a moderate course, state regulation angered most railroad companies and their supporters in Texas. They challenged the commission in the courts and funneled money to Hogg's political opponents.[33]

Like prohibition, railroad regulation divided Democrats, combined former opponents into new political alliances, and attracted new voters. Deteriorating economic conditions gave debate greater urgency, and in 1892 Democrats split into three parties divided by their cures for the economic doldrums and stances on government's role in the economy. New factional coalitions emerged, and the black Republican faction lost cohesion. Yet conservatives, insurgents, social reformers, economic reformers, and black Republicans remained discernable groups operating within the three parties.

George Clark, the leader of the conservative faction, energetically sought the Democratic nomination for governor in 1892. Clark, who stressed "personal liberty" in 1887, expanded liberty's definition to include corporate liberty from state regulation. Clark's campaign slogan, "Turn Texas Loose," summarized his main argument that the state suffered from too many legal restrictions. Laws that limited business caused the economic downturn, but capital to boost the economy out of recession would come to Texas if onerous government regulation ceased and the money supply remained stable and predictable. Endorsements from most of the state's big city daily newspapers built support for Clark's nomination, but his effort fell short. After a tumultuous convention, Clark refused to acknowledge Hogg's nomination and ran in the general election.[34]

Again acting to buttress down-ballot candidates and fend off attempts by lily-whites to end black domination of the party, black Republicans fused with the Clark campaign. Clark sounded like a spokesman for the national Republican party, and indeed national Republican officials encouraged Cuney's support of Clark. In stressing freedom from government regulation and combining conservative and black voters, Clark replayed some themes and strategies of the 1887 prohibition fight, but he failed to attract the insurgent and economic reform vote that helped bring victory to antiprohibitionists.[35]

Between 1887 and 1892 the Farmers' Alliance served as an umbrella organization for economic reformers and insurgents. As the economy worsened, however, anxiety increased among less-efficient and smaller-scale farmers who typically backed inflation of the money supply through the free coinage of silver, a subtreasury plan whereby the government offered support of farm prices, and a more active railroad commission. Drought in the central portion of the state exacerbated the plight of farmers, as did a downward price spiral for cotton. More than half of the state's Alliance members gave up on the Democrats and provided the nucleus for the new Populist party.[36]

Leadership of the new party came from both old Greenbackers like E. L. Dohoney and Democratic stalwarts like Cyclone Davis. Dohoney, dipping into his own pocket to support the venture, published a Populist newspaper, the *Texas Tribune*, and helped write the party's local and state platforms. By making support for local-option laws part of the platform, Dohoney pulled some social reformers as well as economic reformers into the party. Unlike Dohoney, Davis remained loyal to the Democrats until Grover Cleveland, the Democratic candidate for president, opposed free silver or, as Hogg claimed, until Davis believed the third party offered a better chance of holding office again. Davis quickly achieved national stature within the new party, serving on both the executive committee and the platform committee of the founding convention in Cincinnati in 1892. While Dohoney and Davis differed in their political background, they shared support for prohibition and devotion to Protestant denominations that stressed the need to restore contemporary religion to the purity of the early Christian church. Dohoney and Davis gave Populism the aura of a moral crusade and a sense that the path to the future lay in restoring the best of the past.[37]

After an aggressive organizational effort in 1891 and early 1892, the Populists nominated former Democrat and Hogg supporter Thomas L. Nugent of Fort Worth for governor. Nugent, a skilled attorney and judge, shared Dohoney's deeply felt religious views and his commitment to social activism. Marion Martin ran for lieutenant governor on the Populist ticket, solidifying the support of ardent prohibitionists for Nugent. Populists also nominated congressional candidates, including Pat B. Clark in Northeast Texas.[38]

Not all members of the Alliance and certainly not all social and economic reformers joined the Populists. Alliance members who favored free silver and the existing railroad commission but viewed government's role in the economy with caution, or whose status and place in the community tied them to the Democrats, remained Hogg supporters. Like members of the Grange, which also supported Hogg, these farmers typically enjoyed reasonable prosperity and had a long history of voting Democratic. Accustomed to leadership roles in their counties, even if they supported the subtreasury, class influenced their continued allegiance to the Democrats. W. A. Shaw, their leading editorial spokesman, described them as "the conservative and thinking element among the farmers."[39]

Hogg ran a classic three-way campaign by pragmatically positioning himself in the middle on most issues and slicing off votes from each opponent. Claiming to be the advocate of farmers and businessmen, Hogg returned to office with 43.8 percent to Clark's 30.6 percent and Nugent's 24.9 percent of the statewide vote. The minor candidates received less than 1 percent of the vote.[40]

In Northeast Texas, Hogg ran at the same pace that he ran statewide. Nugent finished well ahead of Clark, and the minor candidates received very few votes. Comparing the races for Congress and president, where Republicans fielded candidates, with the contest for governor suggests why the district varied from the state. Committed conservatives willing to abandon the Democratic party made up only, at most, 10 percent of the electorate, and Clark failed to attract all black voters. County figures, as Table 1.1 shows, varied considerably, but the trend suggested by Table 1.2 usually held—the limited number of conservatives and a divided black vote cost Clark any chance to match Hogg or Nugent.[41]

Camp, where F. A. Lockhart led a revolt against Hogg, varied from this general trend, but every other county in which blacks made up over 35 percent of the population gave Clark far fewer votes than Republicans typically won. Indeed, since new voters overwhelmingly supported Nugent, Hogg owed his razor-thin lead in these counties to black voters. In the biggest surprise of the election, Hogg even carried Marion County.

TABLE 1.2
Northeast Texas Elections Returns for 1892

Election Type	Democrat	Conservative/ Republican	Populist
Governor	13,982 (43.5%)	7,567 (23.5%)	10,460 (32.5%)
Congress	16,521 (53%)	4,381 (14%)	10,399 (33%)
President	15,069 (48%)	6,244 (20%)	9,698 (31%)

Source: Election Returns, 1892: Secretary of State.

Because of its large black population and disciplined party organization, every Republican-backed gubernatorial candidate since E. J. Davis in 1869 had carried Marion. As late as 1890 Hogg's Republican challenger received over 60 percent of Marion's vote. Yet in an election where, as in other counties, turnout hit record highs, Hogg finished on top.[42]

Clearly, blacks abandoned the Republican organization and voted for Hogg in Marion and the other eastern counties except Camp. In fact, in a few traditionally Republican strongholds in Cass County, Clark received zero votes and a few black voters apparently supported Nugent. Fraud and intimidation perhaps played a role, but conservatives' wealth, influence, and control of most major daily newspapers gave them every opportunity to investigate fraud after the fact and to prevent it beforehand. Taking advantage of this balance of power between white factions, to a greater degree than in years to come, black voters in 1892 acted on their own.[43]

Blacks faced a difficult choice in 1892. Clark toured the state touting his Confederate credentials and appealing directly for the vote of veterans of the Civil War and the redemption of Texas from Republican control in the 1870s. His economic policies favored the rich and powerful, positions few blacks could claim. Nugent and Martin, on the other hand, ardently supported prohibition. Meanwhile, Senator Richard Coke, who had won the governor's election in 1873 and "redeemed" Texas, came home from Washington to campaign for Hogg. Angered by Clark's refusal to support the regular party nominee, Coke called for the defeat of the "Three C's— Clark, Cuney, and the Coons." Hogg, however, argued that he treated blacks as equals before the law and actively sought black votes to compensate for defections to the Populists. He pointed to his record of protecting blacks from mob action so often that one editor accused Hogg of "pandering to the negroes." Blacks responded by voting for Hogg, and what he stood for, instead of Coke's Democratic party.[44]

Besides fair play for blacks and whites, Hogg stood for balancing the power of major corporations with limited governmental activism, a balancing he deemed essential to the preservation and promotion of local democracy and economic prosperity. In a more moderate fashion Hogg struck the same note as Dohoney and Davis—restoring past purity and moving toward a better future required an active government and the acceptance of innovation. Those innovations included gathering whites and blacks into one political party.[45]

Ward Taylor, an ardent and acerbic champion of local Democrats, embodied this mix of principles and pragmatism. In 1865 Taylor founded the *Jefferson Jimplecute*—"Jimplecute" being an acronym for Join Industry, Manufacturing, Planting, Labor, Energy, Capital (in) Unity Together Everlasting. Taylor used more than pen and press to joust with political rivals. In 1876 a rival editor, stung by Taylor's barbed words, came at him with a bois d'arc club and a whip. After his attacker struck him with the whip, Taylor pulled out a pistol and shot his assailant through the heart, killing him instantly. Taylor took equal aim at the railroad companies he accused of controlling politics in Texas and stunting the economic development of Jefferson. Although it once dominated regional commerce, by 1890 Jefferson had lost trade and population to Texarkana and Marshall. Local leaders blamed railroads for their town's decline and bitterly resented the power of out-of-state companies, especially Jay Gould's Texas and Pacific. They hoped railroad regulation would both boost the local economy and clean up politics. In 1890 Taylor commented that if Texans allowed railroad interests to block Hogg's nomination as governor, "free government may as well be put down as a farce and the masses of the people be branded as idiots and fools."[46]

In 1892 the hated railroad companies seemed poised to pull down Governor Hogg. Good government and economic growth demanded black votes. Playing up Hogg's fairness and the pocketbook motivation for voting Democratic, Marion County Democrats mounted an extensive and successful campaign for black votes. Moreover, Hogg's ideology and image, and a few choice barbs about the association of Cuney and Clark, kept in the Democratic column whites who doubted the wisdom of close ties to black voters.[47]

Black votes, not surprisingly given their smaller numbers, proved less decisive and perhaps less sought after by Democrats in western counties. In Lamar, Clark received most black votes but still lost. Lamar saw a huge upsurge in rural voters, with most new voters supporting Nugent. Despite the work of local Populists like James W. Biard and Dohoney, Hogg's campaign managers in the county still won a plurality by targeting more-prosperous farmers in precincts with a tradition of voting Democratic. The campaigners claimed Populists would raise taxes and cause inflation, worsening farm woes instead of curing them. In a county with exceptionally productive land and a leading commercial center, the argument worked.[48]

Factors beyond soil type, the percentage of black voters, or the size and character of the county seats influenced the results in other western counties of Northeast Texas. On the surface Delta, with soils as fertile as Lamar's, few blacks, and no town over 1,000 in population, looked like an ideal spot for Hogg Democrats. Franklin shared these characteristics except that soils were generally less fertile, making it seemingly an ideal spot for Nugent. Yet Populists in Delta and Democrats in Franklin enjoyed the advantages of efficient organizations, good leadership, and a vigorous local press. Party strength gave Nugent in Delta and Hogg in Franklin something rare in 1892—a majority instead of a plurality of the vote.[49]

Party strength ultimately rested on an intense voter commitment nurtured by a religious style and the belief that the other side went beyond the rules of normal politics. In the western counties both religion and competition created openings for women in politics as well as factional cohesion. In Hopkins County, Mary M. Clardy, an assistant state lecturer and member of the Populist party's platform committee, called for a day of prayer to support her party and worked diligently to prove that Populists did God's work. Another woman, Ellen Lawson Dabbs, a local physician and suffragist, helped lay the groundwork for Populism in Sulphur Springs before she moved to Fort Worth in 1891. Combining prayer and politics legitimized women Populist leaders, especially in an area in which Dohoney and the WCTU exerted leadership. Besides, as in the case of white Democrats seeking black votes in Marion County, the times demanded innovation. Hostility between Democrats and Populists ran high in Hopkins long before the election of 1892. In September 1891, a Populist editor wounded his Democratic rival before being shot and killed in a gun battle in Sulphur Springs.[50]

This intense campaign gave Populists a history to remember, a memory of the revival-like atmosphere and the guns and bullets of the Democrats. That memory, combined with continuity of leadership and the hard times of the 1890s, not only turned out an increasingly large number of voters in the elections of 1894 and 1896, it kept white insurgents a distinct faction long after pragmatism brought them back to the Democratic party.

In contrast, the division of the black vote in 1892 marked the first step toward the end of black political influence. Within five years, in another effort to clean up politics and boost the chances of reform, Jefferson's white leaders had violently forced blacks out of local politics. By then, white violence against blacks was routine.

LYNCHING

Henry Smith, the alleged murderer of young Myrtle Vance in 1893, was born in Little Rock, Arkansas. The twenty-seven-year-old arrived in Paris five years before the murder occurred. On at least two occasions Henry Vance, Myrtle's father and a local policeman, arrested Smith for being drunk and disorderly. Once, Vance clubbed Smith, who in turn stabbed the officer. Many speculated that when Smith saw Myrtle playing alone near sundown on Thursday, January 26, 1893, he seized an opportunity for revenge. Several citizens of Paris saw Smith carrying a white child, but all assumed he worked for the child's family and was returning her from play. The next day Smith worked his way toward Southwest Arkansas where his mother lived, but word reached Paris of Smith's location. On January 31, County Attorney B. B. Sturgeon and a small group of deputies captured Smith near Hope, Arkansas. After bringing him to Texarkana, Sturgeon turned Smith over to a special posse of seventy-five Paris citizens. Once in Paris, the posse passed Smith on to a well-organized band cautioned by local official J. C. Hodges that "they had set aside the law of the statute, and in the execution of their decree should preserve that orderly, quiet and decorous attitude due themselves and the occasion."[51]

Lashing Smith to a box attached to a flatbed wagon, the vigilantes drove their captive through the streets and around the town square of Paris. Then they proceeded to an open field near the Texas and Pacific depot where a platform with a stake protruding through the middle awaited. Charcoal braziers filled with white-hot coals and sizzling hot irons glowed beneath the tall platform. The crowd, tightly packed for over a hundred yards in all directions, watched as posse members pulled a shivering Smith from the wagon. A cold drizzling rain fell as they tied Smith to the stake. His captors ripped his coat and shirt to pieces and tossed them down where the crowd eagerly grabbed each scrap.

Onlookers, whose number exceeded the total population of Paris, gathered for what a reporter for the *Dallas Morning News* called "the most horrible death ever inflicted on a human being." Henry Vance and his fifteen-year-old son carried hot irons up on the platform. Two of Myrtle Vance's uncles joined in torturing Smith. They began slowly rolling the irons across the bottom of Smith's feet and then up the inside of his legs.

FIGURE I.I

Lynching of Henry Smith in 1893. Whites tied Henry Smith to a stake before torturing him with hot irons and eventually burning him to death.
Notice the word justice *cut into the crosspiece below Smith.*
Photograph courtesy of Prints and Photographs Collection, Center for American History, University of Texas at Austin. CN 08222.

A reporter for the *Atlanta (Texas) Express* wrote that when "the iron was pressed to the most tender part of his body he broke silence for the first time and a prolonged scream of agony rent the air."[52]

After methodically burning almost every square inch of flesh, Henry Vance plunged hot irons into Smith's eyes. Then Vance forced irons down his throat. Steam bellowed from Smith's mouth. After two hours of torture Smith pleaded for death. Only then did the mob's leaders pour coal oil on the still living Smith and set him on fire. The crowd heard him groan and thought him dead, but the fire burnt through his bonds and Smith jumped from the scaffold. Bystanders tied a rope to him and hoisted him over the flame until nothing remained but bones and ashes—prizes eagerly sought by souvenir hunters.[53]

On the day after Smith's death, Governor Hogg called for the arrest of those responsible for the lynching. On February 6, 1893, in a message to the Texas legislature he declared: "The public murder at Paris is a disgrace to this state. Its atrocity, inhumanity and sickening effect upon the people at large can not be obscured by reference to the savage act of the culprit himself in brutally taking the life of an innocent child." Neither local authorities nor the legislature agreed. No one faced prosecution for the burning of Smith, and the legislature refused to enact an antilynching law. (Four years later, after an equally grotesque lynching, the legislature finally passed an antilynching law, but the data in Table 1.3 suggest that the law, as enforced, only reduced the rate of lynchings to roughly the 1890 level.) [54]

A sampling of regional opinion by the *Dallas Morning News* revealed that many believed the act "barbarous" but insisted "it set a good example." The public nature of the lynching, the macabre parade beforehand, and the grotesque torture signaled that whites feared black crime whether real or imagined and would go to any length to maintain white supremacy. Nor were comparisons to chilling gladiatorial spectacles or the public executions of Christians in Rome entirely off base. The elaborate nature of the arrangements far in advance of Smith's capture and the collecting of souvenirs indicated that the event had moved beyond punishment to some type of public ritual or sport. The participation of local elites, including J. C. Hodges and B. B. Sturgeon who both later ran for the U.S. Congress, legitimized the lynching. [55]

Henry Smith's lynching matched some common southern patterns. In Texas and in other regions of the South, lynching grew more elaborate and more common after the mid-1880s. One estimate places the number of confirmed lynchings in twelve southern states between 1882 and 1930 at 3,220 blacks and 723 whites. Almost 500, most from 1885 to 1922, occurred in Texas. [56]

Some scholars have suggested that the insecurity of southern white males about their own gender roles and sexuality caused an upturn in

TABLE 1.3

Number of Texans Lynched, by Race and Ethnicity

Race/ Ethnicity	1880s	1890s	1900s	1910s	1920s	1930s
Anglo	79	20	2	3	4	0
Black	64	114	80	55	42	11
Mexican	12	4	2	29	1	0

Source: Daniel T. Williams, *Amid the Gathering Multitude: The Story of Lynching in America: A Classified Listing* (Unpublished: Tuskegee University, 1968).

lynching in the late 1880s. This theory gained credence from the particularly savage treatment of black males like Smith accused of sexual assault on white females. As an outsider with a reputation as a troublemaker and a drunk, he was an inviting scapegoat, a target for repressed rage in a world in which males lacked the aura of Confederate veterans and struggled to bring prosperity to their families. While Smith had a wife in Paris, he lacked extended family in Lamar County or established relations with white elites and the black middle class. No one defended him or pled for mercy.[57]

In fact, more-prosperous and better-established blacks distanced themselves from Smith. After investigators found Smith's hat by Myrtle Vance's body, Gilbert Owens and Noby Robinson, members of the black middle class in Paris, assisted in his capture and return. Robinson, who knew Smith, identified him when the posse caught him in Arkansas. Other members of the black middle class asked to have a hand in Smith's execution. Unlike rural areas, Paris had a well-established and reasonably affluent black middle class. As late as 1885 Creed Taylor, a barber, and Chris Johnson, who had a small freight-hauling business, served on the Paris city council. Johnson also served on the school board. Besides numerous black Baptist churches, the town boasted an African Methodist Episcopal church, a black Methodist Church, and a black Cumberland Presbyterian church. In the 1880s, however, black newcomers attracted by the rapid growth of agriculture and industry swelled the ranks of Paris's black working class by almost 2,000. Like newcomers of all races, they had fewer attachments to local leaders and to churches and other institutions. These new arrivals perhaps frightened both the black and the white middle class.[58]

Rapid population growth, particularly a rapidly growing black population, seemed a constant contributor to lynching across the South. Yet the change was not simply in the number or character of blacks—the number and character of whites who saw these black newcomers also changed by 1890. After a decade in which the black population increased by 187 percent, blacks for the first time made up roughly one-third of the total population of Paris, according to most studies a trigger point for southern lynchings. Meanwhile improved transportation, as the size of the crowd at Smith's lynching testified, allowed whites from a large area to easily and quickly travel to Paris, where they encountered black newcomers unrestrained by ties to white landlords. This confluence of rapid black population growth and enhanced movement of whites to and from Paris potentially triggered the upturn in lynching. After a relatively peaceful history of race relations, in 1892 whites lynched four blacks in Paris, three of

FIGURE 1.2

Middle-class black family in Paris. The booming economy of Paris allowed some blacks to achieve modest levels of prosperity, as reflected in this family portrait.
Photograph courtesy of Larry D. Hunt, Hunter-Bryant Museum, Paris, Texas.

them on September 6 for "rioting" and another on September 23 for rape. Lynching offered a new tool for creating order and maintaining white supremacy.[59]

By this line of reasoning, prosperity and mobility, not hard times and party politics, made Paris a lynching site. While other parts of Northeast Texas suffered economic hardship in the early 1890s, banking, the cotton trade, and cottonseed oil refining insulated Paris from the worst shocks of depressed cotton prices. In part because of the town's size and healthy economy, conservatives played a strong political role in Paris, and Populists never threatened the hegemony of the Democrats. White elites had reason to protect black voters instead of using violence to block their participation in politics. If anything, lynching "rioters" in September 1892 on the eve of the election probably encouraged blacks to vote for Clark as a demonstration of their reliability. Just as Paris lacked economic desperation, it lacked the partisan alignments often associated with white violence toward blacks. Other factors better explained lynching's increased frequency and ferocity.[60]

FIGURE I.3

Cumberland Presbyterian Church, Paris. Among the many substantial church buildings in Paris, this Cumberland Presbyterian Church was for a time the home church of E. L. Dohoney. Women in the Cumberland Presbyterian denomination often took an active and highly visible role in the life of the church, and the organization was closely associated with the Woman's Christian Temperance Union. Photograph courtesy of Jenkins Garrett Texas Postcard Collection, University of Texas at Arlington, Special Collections.

That ferocity, in particular, contrasted with the image of Paris, a city that in the 1890s sparkled as the regional center of urban reform, wealth, and high culture. Its citizens tried to live up to the town's name. Many, like Dohoney, were deeply religious, and fine churches graced every part of town. How could an act not seen "since the latter days of the Roman Empire" happen in Paris? [61]

While several reasons might explain Henry Smith's barbaric death, the history of Paris suggested a link between religion, prohibition, and lynching. Lynchings happened fairly commonly in Texas during and after the Civil War, but most were simple and direct. A mob shot or hanged their victims, who were as often white as black. One source lists ten lynchings for 1882, seven whites and only three blacks. Brutality, ritual, frequency, and focus on blacks increased in the years around the 1887 prohibition referendum. In 1885 thirty lynchings occurred in Texas, and eighteen of the victims were black, including Benjamin Little, lynched for "slander" in Mount Pleasant. After peaking in the mid-1890s, lynching remained a frequent occurrence into the 1920s, and as demonstrated in Table 1.3, blacks constituted an increasingly large percentage of the victims.[62]

At the same time as Smith's death, demands for sobriety, order, and good government peppered political debate in all parts of Northeast Texas. Contrasting younger, newly arrived blacks with long-time citizens, whites decried the breakdown in black behavior. Newspaper editors made a point of printing elaborate obituaries of "old time negroes" and contrasted them with the shiftless, disrespectful next generation. Whites such as Pittsburg native Joe Aldredge praised an individual "faithful Negro" but also quickly condemned those who no longer knew their place. The "radical racism," described by historian Joel Williamson, that depicted this new generation untutored by slavery as the foes of civilization swept the region.[63]

Black opposition to prohibition solidified whites' conception of blacks as foes of social improvement, and this explained in Texas, at least, why the belief that blacks were "rapidly 'retrogressing' toward their natural state of bestiality" took hold when it did. If politics motivated lynching, local-option elections provided the most heat. When Clark, the leading antiprohibitionist in the state, received a large black vote in 1892, the message hit home that prohibition could never win in Paris as long as conservatives controlled black votes. Two years later, in the wake of the Smith lynching, the black vote in Paris took a suspicious slide downward before rebounding when conservatives sought allies to derail a growing movement to make Paris dry. For reformers, lynching, manipulation of the black vote, and prohibition not only controlled blacks, they secured an idealized home life in which Protestant morality flourished. In words that echoed the argument for prohibition, the editor of the *Paris News* hoped Smith's cruel death would "throw one more safeguard around the sanctity of our homes."[64]

Paris lacked a Rebecca Latimer Felton of Georgia who so neatly combined dedication to the Methodist Church, aggressive advocacy of prohibition, repeated calls for the vote for women, and militant racism. Yet the birthplace of the WCTU in Texas did have E. L. Dohoney, who combined prohibition, Protestant activism, woman suffrage, and a more restrained opposition to "social equality." Dohoney's religion and study of phrenology convinced him of the innate inferiority of blacks and the need to keep them separate, but he never condoned brutality. Instead, a more indirect link existed between religion and lynching.[65]

With Dohoney and others, religion acted as a catalyst that stirred them to action and gave them a sense of moral authority. Even Jake Hodges, a political opponent of Dohoney, noted in his speech to the Paris vigilantes that their actions were moral if not strictly legal. Tellingly, neither the southern white Baptist nor Methodist organizations took a strong stand against lynching until after 1930. In fact, the presence of a high percentage of southern Baptists and Methodists, the backbone of the prohibition movement, was as closely correlated with high lynching rates as any other measurable factor. In his 1929 work *Rope and Faggot: A Biography of Judge Lynch,* Walter White argued that "the evangelical Christian denominations have done much toward creation of the particular fanaticism which finds an outlet in lynching." Lynchings had multiple and often idiosyncratic causes, but their new form and increased number owed much to the intolerance and insistence on conformity that accompanied social reforms derived from evangelical Protestant values. Instead of simply defending a traditional patriarchal society, lynching reformed and improved society by radical means. In Paris, where God powered prohibition, the ritualistic sacrifice of a "black fiend" cleansed society.[66]

While politics alone did not initiate lynching, a changing political scene soon stepped up the pace of white violence toward blacks. Governor Hogg, lynching's most prominent opponent, retired from politics in 1894, and Populists challenged Democrats and Republicans for the black vote in Northeast Texas by stressing economic issues. They also mobilized still more rural voters who had previously skipped elections, as well as voters new to the area. Hogg's departure removed the middle way for social and economic reformers, who now faced a choice of aligning with conservatives or aligning with insurgents. Unless motivated by deep-seated antipathy, conservatives and reformers temporarily buried the issue of prohibition and formed a coalition within the Democratic party. Meanwhile white Republicans, perhaps frightened by Populism or mindful of the diminished votes available to their party, also aligned with the Democrats on the local level. When conservatives aligned with reformers and whites left the Republican party, black participation in politics lost its defenders among the local white elite.[67]

RACE AND FACTIONAL POLITICS

Elections in 1894 again featured five factions moving among three or more parties. Nugent once more topped the Populist state ticket and gained the most from the fluid factional alignment. Statewide, Charles A. Culberson, a Democrat who like Hogg moved up from attorney general to governor, won 47 percent of the vote to Nugent's 35 percent. In a race with a record high turnout of almost 500,000 voters, William K. Makemson, the Republican, came in a distant third with 12 percent. A prominent lawyer and political centrist who opposed secession but served in the Confederate army, Makemson did his best to hold his party together, but years of fusion with other parties and the appeal of the Populists made his task difficult. J. M. Dunn, of the Prohibition party, and John B. Schmitz, the lily-white Republican, received the remaining votes.[68]

In Northeast Texas, Schmitz and Dunn received almost no votes, while Makemson and Culberson ran behind their statewide trends. Nugent, on the other hand, narrowly lost the region to Culberson, a native of Jefferson and the son of the district's congressman. Nugent closed on the Democrats by taking away reform votes and black votes that had gone to Hogg and by attracting new voters in rural areas. In fact, in a fair election Nugent probably would have finished ahead of Culberson in Northeast Texas, but in 1894 Democrats used fraud and intimidation of black voters to keep control of local and state government. They also did their best to mend the rift between conservatives and reformers.[69]

Nugent did particularly well in the region's western counties. He won a majority in Titus and Delta and a plurality in Hopkins and Red River. In Sulphur Springs, Nugent did surprisingly well in both white and black precincts, suggesting that Culberson was too conservative for some economic reformers and that the Populist prescription for curing economic ills attracted black voters when they were able to vote free of fraud and intimidation. Even in Franklin and Lamar, Nugent gained votes over his 1892 total and finished better than any past opponent of the Democrats. Nugent might have finished substantially better in Lamar except for the decline in the black vote in Paris. Culberson carried Paris—unlike Sulphur Springs—by a lopsided margin. This margin more than offset Nugent's victory in rural precincts.[70]

In eastern counties Democrats successfully mended the rift between Hogg and Clark Democrats and more openly employed fraud and intimidation of black voters. After Populists in Morris, Bowie, and Cass effectively mobilized the black vote, local Democrats tried to intimidate black political leaders and probably tampered with the vote in some precincts. Small levels of fraud, including the switching of votes from the Populist to the Republican or Prohibitionist column to mask irregularities, reduced the Populist vote and raised the Democratic victory margin.[71]

Camp and Marion offered the best evidence of fraud. Despite Hogg's strenuous campaign for the black vote, Clark still received almost 40 percent of the vote in Marion in 1892. Blacks had fewer reasons to vote for Culberson than for Hogg, yet in 1894 Makemson garnered only 30 percent of the vote. In Camp, a cohesive black faction brought Clark victory, but cohesion had vanished by 1894. As in Marion, Culberson led and Nugent finished third. Roscoe Martin noted in his 1933 study of Populism in Texas that "expert counting of the ballots" by election judges appointed by Democratic officeholders almost certainly accounted for this outcome in these traditional strongholds of black Republicanism.[72]

Apparently the need to manipulate the black vote and the threat of Populism induced a rapprochement between conservatives and reformers. While not an out-and-out conservative, Culberson proved far more acceptable than Hogg to Clark supporters, but the new coalition rested on more than a change in candidates. In Camp County, E. A. King, a wealthy planter, banker, merchant, and mayor of Pittsburg, ended the feud between Hogg and Clark supporters by arguing that necessity demanded "harmony."[73]

Despite the bitter campaign of 1892 and lingering commitment to prohibition, other county leaders successfully emulated King's tactics. A momentary lull in local-option elections undoubtedly helped explain this turn of events and may have been the price reformers paid for the new factional alignment. Reconciliation proceeded more smoothly and prohibition disappeared more completely in eastern counties, but even in Lamar prohibition controversy abated between 1892 and 1898. Why was peace with the conservatives important enough for social reformers to suspend their quest for prohibition? Not all did, of course. A few continued to vote for prohibition candidates for governor, and more remained Populists. In 1894 Dohoney ran a strong race as the Populist candidate for chief justice of the Texas Court of Criminal Appeals. While touring the region and the state speaking for his party, he reminded his listeners of the Populist commitment to local option at the very least.[74]

Still the increased size of the Democratic vote in the region's towns indicated that social reformers and conservatives voted for the same candidate. Pragmatism, class, and race probably best explained this change. Just as reformers stopped pressing for new local-option elections, conservatives stopped trying to roll back local option where it already existed. During this truce, social reformers easily joined conservatives in decrying the patterns of speech, style of religion, occasional drinking binge, or some other supposed mark of rural insurgents—a group Progressives soon labeled "Mossbacks."[75]

Economic reformers remained potentially more sympathetic to insurgents, but such seemingly mundane issues as fence and stock laws and the conversion of more and more land into cotton fields drove a wedge between the two groups. Those who owned small holdings often depended upon access to public land or to their neighbors' uncultivated woodlands. Their stock roamed this land while they hunted it in search of game. Fence laws and the clearing of more land for cotton limited these practices. Between 1890 and 1910 every Northeast Texas county, often precinct by precinct, voted on fence and stock laws. For those interested in keeping the neighbors' cows out of your corn, their hogs off the streets, their horses and mules out of your yard, and their hunting dogs out of your garden—which often translated into economic reformers, fence and stock laws made sense. Moreover, improving the quality of livestock, a constant call from agricultural reformers, required fencing. Likewise, when landowners demanded that cotton be planted from fence line to fence line, there was little space left for their tenants' livestock or for hunting. For poorer rural folk, all this translated into a lower standard of living. When the poor grew poorer, such goals of economic reformers as raising taxes to improve transportation and education drew little support from insurgents. At that point economic reformers also derisively labeled isolated rural folk as Mossbacks.[76]

Race completed the split between reformers and insurgents. Fraud-filled competition for the black vote led to calls for reform—the elimination of black political influence. This neatly fit with prohibitionists' suspicions of black voters and meant that reformers more than any other faction led the way to segregation.

Another election besides the contest for governor spurred on Democratic efforts to put the feuding Hogg and Clark factions back together and added to the calls for the elimination of the black voter. The 1894 contest for the U.S. House in what was then called the Fourth District proved one of the closest, hardest fought, and most fraud-filled elections in the history of Northeast Texas. In a race that featured much debate on the money supply and other fine points of economic policy, Cyclone Davis, the Populist, narrowly lost to incumbent David B. Culberson, a Democrat and father of Charles Culberson.[77]

Davis was born in South Carolina in 1854, but his family moved to Franklin County in 1857. After serving as county judge from 1878 to 1882, he joined the Farmers' Alliance and by 1890 lived in Sulphur Springs, where he practiced law and published the *Alliance Vindicator*. He gained fame, however, as a public speaker. He possessed a loud, penetrating voice and an amazing vocabulary that matched his colorful name, and few Populist speakers in the country overshadowed him. Sprinkling quotes from the Bible and Thomas Jefferson into long alliterative passages, he captivated audiences and swept away his opponents. For Davis, the Bible and Jefferson offered the best route to the restoration of the church and state to its true nature, and better than anyone else, he used these tools to evoke the innate longing in his audience to improve the present by bringing forward the best of the past. The force of his rhetoric earned him the nickname Cyclone, but Davis was more than a windy speaker. In 1892, after helping draft the national party platform, he ran for state attorney general on the Populist ticket.[78]

David Culberson contrasted sharply with Davis. Born in Georgia in 1830, he moved to Upshur County, Texas, in 1856 and served in the state legislature as a Whig. Like other Whigs, he vocally opposed secession in 1860–1861. He moved to Jefferson in 1861 but spent the first two years of the Civil War in the Confederate army, where he served as colonel of the Eighteenth Texas Infantry. After 1863 he worked in the state government, and with the war's conclusion returned to Jefferson, where he became a prominent attorney. Culberson first won election to the House as a Democrat in 1874 and served continuously until March 1897. His association with the ex-Confederates that "redeemed" Texas from the Republicans in 1873–1874 made Culberson a devoted Democratic partisan, and he bitterly attacked the Populists for dividing the white man's party. Befitting his Whiggish antecedents, however, he long backed federal support of railroad construction, and this kept the Clark faction in his camp. Nonetheless, he gained the votes of some reform Democrats by advocating prohibition, railroad regulation, and antitrust legislation. Culberson repeatedly argued for the coinage of silver and a general expansion of the money supply. In 1893 he broke with his party's leader, President Grover Cleveland, and opposed the repeal of the Sherman Silver Purchase Act. Yet, throughout the 1894 campaign, he defended the national Democratic party on the money supply issue. Aware of his opponent's ability and his own age, he refused to meet Davis in joint debate and relied heavily on other Democratic orators.[79]

Culberson never intended to run for re-election in 1894. He announced his retirement and watched the tumult of three Democratic candidates vying to replace him. That year many voters got their first experience with party primaries, as about half the counties held primaries to select their favorite for Congress. The rest selected their choice for party nominee through the traditional convention method.[80]

County conventions and primaries were held on different days in June and July of 1894, allowing the three candidates to focus on the counties one at a time. John W. Cranford of Hopkins County ardently defended the Democratic party and attacked the subtreasury plan and other

"Populist fallacies." Winning several close primaries, he gained the backing of twenty-three delegates. John Sheppard tried to reach out to moderate Populists and draw them back into his party. Only sixteen delegates backed Sheppard. Jake Hodges of Paris joined Cranford in attacking the Populists and politely criticizing the Cleveland administration for failing to inflate the money supply. His arguments and strong local organization won him the fourteen delegates from his home county.[81]

Instructed by their county convention or primary, delegates to the District Convention met on July 31, 1894, in Texarkana. Since the convention required that the nominee receive two-thirds of the vote, the winner needed 35$\frac{1}{3}$ votes, but intense factionalism deadlocked the convention. Despite repeated ballots, not a single delegate changed his vote for the Democratic nominee for the Fourth Congressional District. Frustrated Democrats adjourned and agreed to reconvene in Paris after the state Democratic Convention. Meeting on August 30, delegates took several hundred more ballots with no change. Finally, all three candidates withdrew and the convention nominated Culberson.[82]

F. A. Lockhart blamed the deadlock on "the folly of 'first, last and all the time' instructions." The political system needed fixing. The mix of primaries and conventions held on different days confused voters and allowed manipulation by clever politicians. Requiring delegates to continue voting for their county's choice, even after his chance of nomination ended, invited a divisive convention. For Lockhart a uniform primary "regulated by law" provided the answer. Voters should select all party candidates for all offices at one time in fair and open elections.[83]

Deadlock also derived from regional prejudice and, even more so, from persistent factionalism. Sheppard—born in Morris County, living in Camp County, and planning a move to Bowie County—received the support of eastern counties. Hodges got the vote of his home county, Lamar. Cranford secured the vote of the western counties other than Lamar. This voting reflected more than a fondness for the local boy. The schism between Hogg supporters and Clark supporters did not heal easily, and both Hodges and Cranford had closer ties to the Clark faction than did Sheppard. In the eastern counties, Populists and Democrats were still in the process of dividing, while in the west partisan animosity boiled high. Cranford, from a county where Populists won many elections, attacked the Populists vigorously, while Sheppard called them back to his party. Party veterans probably realized that divided support for the three candidates meant that any of them would lose to Cyclone Davis. Democrats needed a candidate who could draw some votes from the Populists without alienating conservative and reform Democrats. Party leaders may have orchestrated the deadlock and planned to turn to "Old Dave" Culberson all along.[84]

Davis certainly was a formidable candidate. His frequent campaigns for the Democrats in the 1880s and work as an organizer for the Farmers' Alliance had built a reliable base of support in Delta, Hopkins, and Franklin counties. Most voters in the rest of the district recognized his name and remembered his words. In effect, Davis entered the contest with almost all the white insurgent vote already secured. To that he added a percentage of the reform Democrats in his home base in the southwest corner of the district. Only Culberson appealed to enough conservatives and reformers in every county to ensure victory. Culberson also stood the best chance of picking up some black votes because of his ties to Marion's Democratic party.[85]

Republicans and Populists in the Fourth District, unlike those in other Texas congressional contests in 1894, never formally fused. Yet Republicans tarried in finding a candidate and never mounted a serious campaign. Informal fusion occurred in some counties, giving Davis a chance to pick up black votes but opening the door for Democratic tricks. Among blacks, loyalty to their local Republican organizations often overrode Democratic inducements, but the same level of loyalty to the Populists never existed among blacks, who with good reason viewed men like Cyclone Davis as just as racist as the Democrats. Nonetheless, John B. Rayner, a leading black Populist speaker, made a campaign swing through Lamar, Red River, and Morris. He correctly predicted that blacks in Morris would vote for the Populist candidates and would resist all Democratic efforts to buy their vote. Davis lost to Culberson in Morris by a vote of 652 to 691. The Republican candidate received only 14 votes. While Davis charged Democratic election judges with padding their vote and leaving out a few Populist votes, Davis's vote exceeded the Populist tally in both the 1892 and 1894 gubernatorial elections. That required black votes.[86]

Marion County offered a different story. Here Davis received 775 votes, a figure that surpassed the vote for the Populist candidate for governor. The Republican candidate got only 84 votes, but Culberson received 1,208. Such a high figure for a Democrat and low figure for a Republican suggested that Democrats bought or illegally altered the black vote in Marion.[87]

Both sides also used legitimate means to influence white and black voters. Culberson harped on "the wild theories of the Populists," and Davis stressed the impact of Democratic monetary policy on the price of cotton.[88] While Culberson defended Cleveland, Davis argued that tight money and Cleveland's reluctance to move away from a strictly gold-backed system of exchange caused the economic depression that began in 1893. Democrats urged patience and ridiculed dissidents who stepped beyond the bounds of political propriety. When Jacob S. Coxey led a protest march on Washington, Lockhart drolly pointed out: "The Coxey craze rid Texas of quite a number of tramps. There is always something to be thankful for." Given time, Culberson supporters insisted, Democrats could expand the money supply and keep it sound. Besides, they doubted the existence of a direct link between tight money and poor prices for cotton. Democrats committed to economic reform, many blacks, and white insurgents disagreed. Davis repeatedly denounced Culberson for aiding the creditor at the expense of the debtor, and the unpopularity of Cleveland's monetary policy in a district suffering from depressed cotton prices forced Culberson to call more aggressively for expanding the supply of silver money.[89]

Meanwhile Democrats continued attacking Populists as radicals with "visionary theories." They claimed the Populists' tax policy would deprive landowners of their property and reward the lazy over the industrious. Populists, they argued, advocated woman suffrage and more political rights for blacks, and they pointed to Mary Clardy in Hopkins County and other prominent women Populists in Texas and Kansas as proof that "wild-cat schemes" would upend social order. Besides, Populists would drive down land values and slow the return of economic prosperity. In this way, they retained the vote of reform Democrats with enough property to worry about socialism, and they drew conservatives to their camp.[90]

Despite progress in building a winning coalition, hard feelings from the Hogg-Clark split and the flawed nomination process left Democrats worried. They feared ardent supporters of Sheppard, Cranford, and Hodges might sit the election out or, worse yet, vote for Davis. In the end, Culberson's campaign managers turned to reminding voters of their debt to the party and implored: "Do not vote against your party because the nominee does not suit you. A vote for the nominee is a vote for the party, and the success of the party must always be considered above personal objections."[91]

The official election results returned Culberson to Congress by about 1,300 votes. Davis carried Delta, Hopkins, Titus, and probably also Cass County. Local Democratic officials threw out several white Populist boxes in Cass, thereby securing the county for Culberson by 78 votes. Since even without those Populist boxes Nugent won Cass by 500 votes, Democrats probably risked a trip to federal court by altering the vote in federal election boxes. Other tallies looked equally suspicious. Total votes for governor in Bowie and Lamar counties exceeded the total for the House race by 500. Comparing the two races suggested the organized suppression of the black vote in the federal election in Paris and Texarkana.[92]

Davis charged that Democrats voted "dead negroes, dogs, mules and horses" against him, and that party bosses bribed large numbers of blacks. Years later when Roscoe Martin interviewed about twenty politicians from both parties involved in the campaign, all agreed that bribery and fraud aided Culberson. Martin pointed out one way this worked—in Camp more than 120 percent of potential black voters actually voted. Precinct returns for Camp further indicated that Culberson received virtually all the black vote that switched from supporting the Republican in the governor's race to another party's candidate in the House race.[93]

F. A. Lockhart dismissed Davis's complaints with the wry comment, "The Populists charge that the Democrats spent a large amount of money to defeat them. They should not complain if such is the case. They have been demanding more money in circulation and if Democrats aid in carrying out one of their demands they should approve rather than complain."[94]

Culberson, of course, denied Davis's charges, and while Davis contested the results, the vote of 15,873 for Culberson and 14,515 for Davis held. Culberson returned for one more term in Congress. Davis went on to a long career in insurgent politics that took him back to the Democratic party and to the U.S. House as an at-large member from Texas in 1914.[95]

County elections indicated that the strong showing for Davis resulted from more than his powerful rhetoric. In the mid-1890s Populists gained control of the county governments in Titus, Delta, and Morris. In response, the Democratic-controlled state legislature, alleging Populist incompetence, transferred the judicial functions of county governments in Delta and Morris to the district courts. Later in the decade after Democrats regained local control, the state legislature restored judicial responsibilities to these counties. Democratic dominance on the state level made it difficult for county-level parties to survive. Yet intervention in local politics highlighted the strength of Populist organizations and increased the endurance of political factions in many Northeast Texas counties by giving them one more score to settle. Even if they rejoined the party, they retained a skepticism for things Democratic that set them apart.[96]

Fraud and the use of state power to defeat Populism not only left a deep-seated animosity toward Democrats, it affected white attitudes toward blacks. Blacks demonstrated in 1892 and later that in fair elections, like whites, they responded to appeals to their interests—economic advancement, legal rights, and protection from violence. Yet white Populists like Cyclone Davis conveniently blamed the victims of fraud and intimidation instead of the perpetrators. In old age Cyclone Davis defended segregation and still called on "the vengeance of an outraged God" to sweep away his enemies—white and black.[97]

Despite the presence of fraud, two overarching points came clear in 1894. First, victory still required combining two factions, a process that produced middle-of-the-road candidates. Second, one of the goals for this new coalition of reformers and conservatives was the manipulation of the black vote, and this furthered the disintegration of the black voting bloc.[98]

Even though blacks no longer voted as a bloc, they still could determine state and local elections. This gave white Democrats even greater incentive and opportunity to buy or steal black votes in 1896. White Populists in Northeast Texas had the same incentive and opportunity and actively pursued fusion with local Republicans. Especially in the eastern, more heavily black counties, Populists voted for the Republican candidate for president. Republicans voted for Populist candidates for state and local office. This trade gave William McKinley the nineteenth-century record for the highest number of votes for a Republican presidential candidate in the district and the state.[99]

Some Populists voted for William Jennings Bryan on the Populist ticket, or McKinley would have garnered even more votes. That year the national Populist party selected Bryan, the Democratic nominee and advocate of free silver, as their presidential nominee. Texas Populist leaders refused to accept fusion with the Democrats, but some rank-and-file members voted for Bryan on the Populist ticket. This prevented McKinley from carrying Bowie and Cass and raised Bryan's margin of victory in the other counties. In the eleven counties, as a Democrat Bryan tallied 43 percent and as a Populist 11 percent of the vote, and that gave him 54 percent of the total. McKinley garnered over 42 percent, while the Gold Democrat and Prohibition party candidates received very few votes. This voting pattern signaled the renewed multifactionalism of the Democrats. The roughly six thousand Populist voters for Bryan had begun drifting back to the Democratic party. Others, like Cyclone Davis who campaigned for Bryan in 1900, would soon join.[100] Meanwhile, Gold Democrats, typically conservative backers of Clark in 1892, usually swallowed their principles and voted for Bryan.[101]

Aided by corrupt election practices, Democrats also swept the state races in 1896. Some moderate, white Populists, however, probably swung back into the Democratic party in support of Governor Culberson. Jerome Kearby, the Populist, opposed the incumbent in a tightly contested race in the district and statewide. Statewide, Culberson won with 55 per-

TABLE I.4
Pinpointing Fraud in 1896

Area	1896 Votes for Pres.			1896 Votes for Governor		Dem. Votes for Gov. Compared to Votes for Pres.
	Dem.	Repub.	Pop.	Dem.	Pop.	
DISTRICT	18,782	12,482	6,015	20,237	17,714	+1,455
Vote* 38,018						
% Voters 82.4%						
EAST	5,700	6,404	1,559	7,367	6,499	+1,667
Vote* 13,869						
% Voters 85.3%						
WEST	13,082	5,929	4,434	12,870	11,215	−212
Vote* 24,149						
% Voters 80.8%						

Source: Election Returns, 1896: Secretary of State; U.S., *Census: 1890, Population*, vol. 1, 782-782; U.S., *Census: 1900, Population*, vol. 2, 203-206.
  * Total vote for governor, including minor candidates.

cent of the vote, while Kearby received slightly over 44 percent. In the district, Culberson received 53 percent, while Kearby attracted 47 percent of the vote.[102]

Comparing the vote for Culberson with the vote for Bryan indicated just how the Democrats achieved victory in Northeast Texas. As shown in Table 1.4, in the district the Democratic candidate for governor received 1,400 more votes than the Democratic candidate for president. Moreover, the total vote for governor exceeded the total vote for president by 600. In previous elections each party's tally for governor and president nearly matched, and when more than two candidates ran for office the total vote for that race went up. In addition, Populists had far more reason to vote for Bryan than for Culberson. Thus, the Democratic vote for governor and president should have been nearly equal, and the total vote for president should have been higher than the total vote for governor. Election judges appointed by Democratic officeholders probably added fraudulent votes to Culberson's total and in a few cases subtracted votes for Kearby.[103]

Most of the discrepancies in voting came in the five eastern counties with the heaviest black population. In tiny Marion alone the Democratic candidate for governor received 556 more votes than the Democratic candidate for president. In much larger Cass, Culberson picked up 514 more votes than Bryan, almost all of them from heavily black precincts. Given what happened in 1894, fraud accounted for the difference.[104]

In comparison, in heavily white precincts in Delta, Hopkins, and Franklin, Kearby's vote matched or exceeded the combined Republican and Populist vote in the presidential election. It also surpassed the Populist vote for governor in 1894. This pattern failed to hold in Sulphur Springs, the one area in the three counties with a significant black population. Voting patterns suggested the use of fraud, but some urban white Populists also may have moved back into the Democratic party.[105]

One simple indication of fraud comes from comparing the projected number of males over twenty-one with the total number of votes for governor. As Table 1.4 shows, over 80 percent of the district's potential voters actually voted or had ballots cast for them. In the heavily black eastern counties of Camp, Cass, Marion, Morris, and Titus the figure was much higher, and only in Bowie did the percentage of voters who cast ballots fall below the district average. In the western counties instead of adding votes, some subtracting of votes probably occurred. In Lamar, where the lowest percentage of potential voters cast ballots, the vote in Paris surpassed that of 1894, but the vote turned dramatically down in precincts that voted for the Populists in 1892 and 1894. (This indicated these voters were white.) Lamar was also one of only two counties where the vote for president exceeded the vote for governor. Again the decrease came outside of Paris. Some Populist supporters of Bryan may have found both Culberson and Kearby unacceptable. Yet the county's steady increase in rural population suggested the suppression or alteration of the Populist vote. In 1896 fraud seemed concentrated in the heavily black precincts of the eastern counties and in the rural white Populist precincts of Lamar and a few other western counties.[106]

Fraud affected politics in numerous ways. Obviously, it cost Cyclone Davis, who lost a second bid for a House seat in 1896, a chance to hold office. Its linkage with black voters in the minds of whites accelerated demands to remove blacks from the political process by whatever means necessary. The perilous status of blacks, evident in the aftermath of the 1887 prohibition referendum, grew more perilous after 1896. Fraud led to growing demands to clean up politics, to reform the political process by eliminating the black vote and enacting a uniform primary system. Like prohibition and lynching, these new laws were intended to clean up society, and violence accompanied their arrival. Segregation in all forms, the denying of the close relationship between black and white, became, as one scholar recently put it, part of being "a modern American." [107]

When 1896 ended, a higher level of violence and brutality marked the relationship of blacks and whites. New ideas dominated politics: prohibition equaled progress, an active government aided economic development, and clean government enabled the triumph of reform. These ideas and the issues surrounding them remained potent through 1930, and the high level of racial brutality and violence lasted almost that long. Racism and reform soon combined to end the three-party system that characterized post-Reconstruction Texas politics and to destroy the importance of the black voter. Yet the multifactional nature of Northeast Texas politics remained, and the drive to exclude blacks from politics failed to permanently ensconce conservatives in power as it often did elsewhere in the South.[108] Instead the three and sometimes four remaining factions, all drawing strength from allies across Texas, operated within the Democratic party, allowing a more open and competitive political system, a system that assisted economic development.

TWO

COMPETITION, INNOVATION, AND A CHANGING ECONOMY, 1897–1914

After 1896 the political factions of Northeast Texas operated within a rapidly changing economic environment. Each complemented the other. The more-open political system made starting new businesses easier, and their proprietors became a powerful political group that usually supported reform. A new economic base for society, however, sprang from more than politics alone or, for that matter, from more than the impact of new technology and new business methods on a distinctive culture. Leaving aside for the moment these other potential causes of change, this chapter focuses on the opportunities and incentives to change created by a more fluid business climate.

Cotton remained the key to prosperity, and traditional labor-intensive methods persisted in some phases of production and among some farm operators. Yet by 1914 new methods of growing and marketing cotton pointed to the future. Nascent trends in retailing further altered the marketing of cotton and changed how the region's citizens purchased what they needed or wanted. Even earlier, improved connections to broader markets for labor, capital, and goods allowed the emergence of new businesses and forced the restructuring of old businesses.[1]

NEW AND RESTRUCTURED BUSINESSES

Economic activity quickened in Northeast Texas after 1896, and by 1900 increased prosperity seemed possible. For once possibilities turned into realities, and by early 1914 the region enjoyed sustained, though uneven, economic growth. Greater demand for cotton products worldwide, accompanied by a slight rise and improved stability in cotton prices, partially explained rising prosperity. In that sense the region remained dependent upon events that happened far from its borders.[2] Yet even before cotton prices edged upward, railroads, lumber companies, and banks transformed the economy from within the region.

As in the rest of the South after Reconstruction, railroads quickly linked Northeast Texas to the outside world. In the 1870s alone, workers laid roughly 500 new miles of track within the region. Before 1890, however, investors often lacked sufficient capital to ensure long-term success. Two lines in particular suffered from limited capital. To save money, developers built the East Line and Red River Railroad, from Jefferson to Sherman, and the Texas and St. Louis, from Texarkana to Tyler, with a narrow gauge. This made connections to other lines difficult and the ride notoriously bumpy, and it meant that efficient transportation awaited consolidation into larger, better capitalized, standard-gauge lines.[3]

In effect, railroad construction and operation altered the region in two stages, with each stage exerting a different influence. Initial construction allowed rapid population growth, the development of towns and small cities, and the extension of cotton cultivation. Construction ceased as the nation's economy slowed in the late 1880s. After the mid-1890s, trunk lines consolidated into larger and more-efficient enterprises, and new short lines appeared. This second stage provided new jobs outside of agriculture, promoted limited industrialization, more efficiently and extensively connected the region to the outside world, and allowed small cities to take away business and population from the surrounding towns and villages. These second-stage changes also proved critical to the growth of the lumber industry, banking, and retailing.[4]

By the start of World War I, five major lines ran through Northeast Texas, and standard-gauge lines connected the region to two additional national systems. Of the early roads, only the Texas and Pacific (T&P) began with the 56.5-inch standard gauge. By 1876, 200 miles of T&P track circled through the region, sparking population growth, establishing Paris and Texarkana as dominant cities, and allowing expanded cotton cultivation. With resources stretched thin, in the early 1880s the T&P fell into receivership, but it soon forged a close working relationship with the Missouri Pacific. Jay Gould controlled both lines, and by the mid-1890s, they formed a large, well-integrated national system.[5]

Precursors of two other major lines also experienced long years of legal and financial turmoil before emerging as part of well-financed, standard-gauge trunk lines. In 1891 the St. Louis and Southwestern Railway acquired the Texas and St. Louis. After barely surviving the early 1890s, the line usually called the Cotton Belt consolidated its holdings and improved

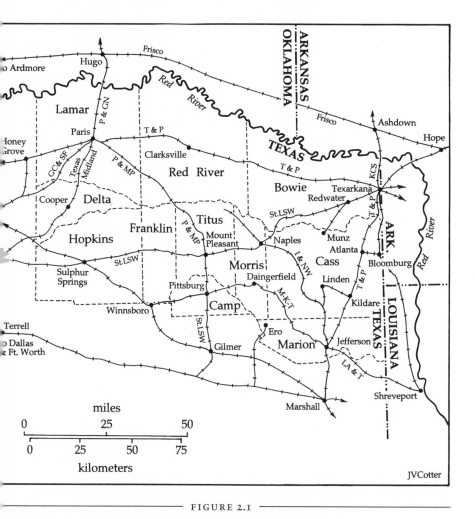

FIGURE 2.1

Railroads in Northeast Texas in 1914. Map by John V. Cotter.

its track, engines, and cars. It soon owned over 1500 miles of track with 150 of those miles in Northeast Texas. Meanwhile the East Line had consolidated with the Missouri, Kansas & Texas. Generally called the Katy, by 1900 the M-K-T system operated almost 1,200 miles of track in Texas with about 120 miles in Northeast Texas.[6]

Earlier, in 1887, the Gulf, Colorado and Santa Fe (GC&SF) built into Paris as part of its agreement to join the Atchison, Topeka and Santa Fe system. Like the Cotton Belt, the Katy, and the T&P, construction on the

GC&SF began in the 1870s. After surviving financial difficulties and up-grading their lines, all four entered the twentieth century as part of stable major systems connected to the rest of the country.[7]

Another type of railroad brought the fifth trunk line into the region. In 1885 the Texarkana and Fort Smith Railway (T&FS) built a ten-mile line north from Texarkana to the Red River. It hauled timber and connected Texarkana to the Kansas City, Pittsburgh and Gulf Railway (KCP&G). The KCP&G purchased the T&FS in 1892 and after 1900 evolved into the Kansas City Southern (KCS), an 800-mile line from Kansas City to Port Arthur, Texas. About 35 miles of the system ran along the eastern border of Northeast Texas.[8]

Like Texarkana, Paris benefited from the construction of short lines. Buoyed by the arrival in Paris of the GC&SF in 1887, local investors dur-ing the next year completed the Paris and Great Northern Railroad, a line running seventeen miles north across the Red River where it inter-sected with the track of the St. Louis and San Francisco Railroad Com-pany. A worsening economy slowed the construction of short lines after that, but in 1897 the Texas Midland reached Paris, linking the city with the Southern Pacific system. By 1900, then, Texarkana and Paris anchored a regional railroad system dominated by the KCS, the T&P, the Cotton Belt, the Katy, the GC&SF, the Frisco, and the SP. Together, they pro-vided excellent connections between every county in Northeast Texas and Kansas City, St. Louis, Memphis, Shreveport, Dallas, Fort Worth, and Houston.[9]

Construction of independent short lines that hauled timber, freight, and passengers to and from trunk lines furthered the transformation of an isolated backwater into a well-connected part of a national and interna-tional economy. Between 1896 and 1914, local investors, lured by incen-tives provided by competing trunk lines, built eight multipurpose lines. Trunk lines often attracted business from rivals by dividing their freight charges for lumber and lumber products with the short lines where those shipments originated. Major companies thus avoided building their own spur lines while guaranteeing a steady volume of business. Until the Inter-state Commerce Commission and the Supreme Court restricted this prac-tice in 1913, local investors scrambled to build lines that both helped their towns and enjoyed a reliable source of revenue.[10]

This boom in locally funded construction not only boosted trade in the region, it provided jobs for area residents. Enthusiastic Northeast Texas boosters claimed in 1902: "Texas has never seen the day when there was more activity in railroad building than is now going on within its bound-aries. No better sign of growth and prosperity is in evidence."[11]

Railroads, however, affected the region unevenly and in the long term both made and unmade cities and towns. Completion of the Paris & Mount Pleasant (P&MP) in 1913 helped make Mount Pleasant a railway center that soon contained the machine shops of the Cotton Belt. For Paris the P&MP culminated a long tradition of local railroad promotion and connected the city to the Cotton Belt. After 1913 five major systems running on their own track or on that of closely allied smaller lines crossed in Paris. These excellent connections to the national railroad grid allowed Paris to become the regional center for the cotton trade and cottonseed oil milling and refining. Wholesale distribution of goods further ensured that Paris remained the leading city of a multicounty region on both sides of the Red River. Gradually Paris took trade and population away from neighboring towns.[12]

Texarkana also gained from completion of the railroad grid. In 1902 the Cotton Belt moved its general offices and hospital to that border city. The T&P and the KCS yards and repair shops already boosted the local economy. Over the next decade excellent transportation and the metal working and machine tool capacity that went with these shops gave Texarkana the best chance to industrialize. By 1914 almost 1,000 Texarkanans worked in manufacturing.[13]

Jefferson followed a different path. Thanks to its water connections to the Red River, before 1880 Jefferson boasted the largest population in the region. Railroads, however, proved more reliable than shallow waterways, and Jefferson lost commerce to nearby cities. As the twentieth century dawned, like so many other community promoters, Jefferson's leading citizens pinned their hopes on railroads and lumber. The Jefferson and Northwestern Railroad, chartered in 1899, began construction the next year on a narrow-gauge lumber line. The company converted to a standard gauge in 1908 and initiated a new building program in 1912. Once completed in 1913, the Jefferson and Northwestern moved freight and passengers to still-isolated sections of the region and provided inexpensive transportation for harvested timber. Unfortunately, Jefferson never recovered the level of prosperity it once enjoyed. Instead, the "push and enterprise" that went with early development as a railroad center meant Texarkana continued siphoning off trade, commerce, and industry.[14]

Much of this push and enterprise focused on the lumber industry. In fact, distinctions between the two industries often blurred, since lumbermen bankrolled the majority of short lines constructed between the mid-1890s and World War I. Members of Clark and Boice Lumber Company owned the Jefferson and Northwestern. Sullivan-Stanford Lumber Company built a tram railroad westward from Naples to the heavily timbered region between the Sulphur River and White Oak Creek. Black Bayou Railroad Company built a short line near the Louisiana border to haul cypress and pine to mills in Queen City and Atlanta in Cass County. Redwater in Bowie County had a mill and a line that ran south into timbered lowlands along the Sulphur. Substantial stands of cypress and yellow pine covered Morris, Marion, Cass, and Bowie counties. Camp, Titus, Franklin, and Red River counties benefited from large stands of pine and hardwoods. Hardwoods in the river and creek bottoms gave variety to the prairie landscape of Hopkins, Delta, and Lamar counties. Short lines carried the timber from lumber camps to mills in the villages and towns of these counties. Trunk lines then carried shingles, doors, sashes, and other lumber products to markets across the country. Railroads even provided a market for the timber industry because they used locally produced ties in their construction and maintenance.[15]

Texarkana, astride the border between Texas and Arkansas, became the regional yellow-pine center, as well as headquarters of the closely related railroad industries. Since railroads arrived in Texarkana earlier than in other parts of Northeast Texas, loggers cut most timber in the immediate vicinity of the town before 1900. Regional lumber companies, however, kept their main offices in Texarkana until after World War I. In 1904 a local journalist estimated that twenty-five large mills operated within thirty miles of Texarkana, and companies or families headquartered in the city owned them all. These mills produced approximately 1,000 carloads of lumber products per month. This meant Texarkana offered far more jobs than any nearby town.[16]

Few lumber or railroad jobs, only managerial positions and those requiring high skill levels, commanded high wages, but workers in all phases of these industries earned slightly higher wages than agricultural day laborers. This disparity between lumber and railroad jobs and agricultural labor helped keep Texas wages higher than the wages of any other southern state. Blacks, who made up roughly half of the total labor force and dominated the unskilled jobs, switched from agricultural jobs to lumber or railroad work when agricultural wages dropped. After learning the trade in the lowest paying jobs, blacks often moved up into slightly higher paying jobs and seldom switched back to agriculture. As early as 1904, wages for section hands, flatheads, choppers, and buckers throughout Northeast Texas pushed up the local wage rate and increased demand for labor.[17]

Much has been made of the isolation of the southern labor market, but in Northeast Texas development of an extensive transportation grid and acquisition of limited skills in the railroad and lumber industries broke down barriers to labor mobility. Other parts of Texas enjoyed even higher wages, greater demand for labor, and more-significant levels of industrialization. Led by lumber and railroads, numerous industries throughout Texas added workers, machines, and more-efficient methods of production. According to the *Census of Manufactures, 1914:* "During the decade 1904 to 1914 the value of manufactures in Texas increased at a much greater rate than that for the United States as a whole." Texas still trailed far behind the industrial centers of the country, but it was finally catching up. As it caught up, demand for semi-skilled workers in construction and other occupations grew in Fort Worth, Dallas, and other urban areas, attracting workers from nearby Northeast Texas. Unskilled agricultural workers seldom left, but those who gained limited skills in the lumber and railroad industries easily departed, creating a more fluid labor market.[18]

The years between 1904 and 1909 saw unusually strong growth in the number of Texas nonagricultural wage earners as their total increased by more than 40 percent. Lumber and railroad payrolls increased sharply, in raw terms and as a proportion of the work force. Like cotton planters, mill owners and railroad managers preferred paying low wages, but steady demand for their products and services encouraged them to hire more workers and raise wages above those paid in agriculture.[19]

Demand for workers also brought other benefits to workers. William H. Knox, who operated a mill for several years near Texarkana, earned a reputation for direct action and sturdy defense of his employees. According to an often told tale, he once shot and killed a white man for abusing one of his black employees. He was never prosecuted. While Knox's legend may loom larger than his life, after 1900 violence against "good, peaceable hard-working negroes" usually called forth loud protests from white progressives and city builders. Perhaps such direct action and protests came from a sense of right and wrong, but surely they also came from the knowledge that black workers and the industries in which they toiled contributed significantly to the mill owner's profit margin and the region's prosperity. They also realized that blacks with even limited skills in industrial occupations could and did leave.[20]

Competition for labor in the lumber industry did more than offer blacks and whites a way out of the lowest rungs on the agricultural ladder. When the price of lumber rose, logging companies seldom found enough labor to rapidly increase production. From the end of harvest to the start of spring soil preparation, farmers took advantage of this labor shortage by using their teams to cut logs on contract and haul them to the mills. Farmers also held a variety of other seasonal jobs, and some even operated small mills, called "peckerwood mills." Lumber camps also provided good markets for truck crops, chickens, eggs, and dairy products. John Marvin Leonard and his brother Obadiah Paul Leonard, who later operated Fort Worth's largest department store, began their business career by selling potatoes to lumbermen. In the decade before 1914, they planted potatoes as early as possible on their family's Cass County farm. After a winter diet of salt pork, cornmeal, and a few canned vegetables, fresh potatoes commanded a premium price in the lumber camps.[21]

From the mid-1890s to World War I, then, lumber and railroads provided low-skill jobs for those who cut the trees and built and maintained the rail lines. They added higher skill jobs for those who processed the lumber and maintained the cars and engines. These industries trained the unskilled, increasing their standard of living and adding to their mobility. In Texarkana and Mount Pleasant, lumber and railroads also added a managerial layer of employment lacking before 1900. In many cases lumber complemented agriculture and added to farm income. Most old-growth forests played out by 1914, but some higher skilled jobs and the managerial jobs remained.[22]

The expansion of lumber and railroads also brought incentives for innovation. Contrary to accepted portraits of the South, lumber and railroad companies combined their efforts with the state and federal government to create "a strong indigenous technological community."[23] Forerunners of this community appeared as early as the 1890s when the state funded several agricultural experiment stations. In the years around 1900 the state funded Farmer's Institutes and Congresses, and both of these educational initiatives depended on close ties to the University of Texas and the Texas Agricultural & Mechanical College. At the same time, farmer's short courses sponsored by A&M furthered the work of agricultural education. In 1903 Seaman Knapp, originator of the concept of a demonstration farm, opened the first such farm in the South outside Terrell, Texas. This farm, near the southwest corner of the eleven-county Northeast Texas region, proved a great success, and Knapp became a hero of biblical proportions. Use of his "Ten Commandments of Agriculture" to combat boll weevils and improve farm productivity won increasing acceptance in Texas.[24]

Among the reasons for this success were railroad agricultural agents who between 1900 and 1914 carried the gospel of diversified farming, scientific cultivation, and careful attention to boll weevils throughout Northeast Texas. Agents of the major rail companies gave advice on fertilizer, farming techniques, and crop diversification. Railroads also offered free passes for those wanting to attend short courses or other educational programs at College Station or Austin. At about the same time, lumber

companies began experimental farms as part of an effort to better uti-
lize cutover timber lands. These businesses, of course, sought increases in
railroad tonnage or value of company land. While many farmers probably ignored the call to farm more scientifically, others did not. Continual
large-scale experimentation with sweet potatoes, peaches, strawberries,
and other fruit and vegetable crops indicated at least limited success at
crop diversification. Use of Texas-developed, improved cottonseed and increased mechanization added further evidence of success. Railroads and
lumber companies helped develop Texas-based centers for experimentation, and they helped disseminate the results of that experimentation to
farmers.[25]

Another factor closely intertwined with agricultural experimentation
increased Northeast Texans' ability and willingness to accept new ideas—
capitalists followed their capital to Texas. William Knox did not manage his timber holdings from Wisconsin. Instead, he moved to Texarkana
and later to Hemphill. In that sense, the Texas economy became slightly
less colonial than that of many parts of the South, because energetic new
entrepreneurs identified with the region and worked to make its future
and their own prospects brighter. In so doing they introduced into the region an alternative power bloc that challenged the leadership of planters
and merchants who had little interest in innovation.[26]

In Northeast Texas, Edward H. R. Green proved the most interest-
ing and important of these capitalists that followed their capital. In 1892
Green moved to Texas to manage his family's Texas-Midland Railroad.
He played a key role in expanding and upgrading that road between
Terrell and Paris. Green evidently fell in love with Texas and at six feet
four inches and in excess of 250 pounds fit the description of a typical
Texan. He cut a large and colorful figure, dressing in a grand style, stump-
ing around on an artificial leg, and enjoying the company of prostitutes
despite the reproving glances of Terrell's upright citizens. He became a
power in the Republican party and a supporter of Texas's black-and-tan
faction led by William M. McDonald, one of the state's most important
black politicians and businessmen. He also built up the local economy of
the Terrell area by investing in numerous businesses and establishing an
experimental farm that worked closely with Seaman Knapp to combat the
damage done to cotton by boll weevils. Once the agricultural experts developed methods for dealing with the boll weevil, according to a friend,
Green "sent men all along the T.M.'s right of way to show farmers what
to do." Examples of colonial exploitation of the Texas economy abound,
and certainly Texans protested the colonial nature of their economy between 1890 and 1920. Yet just as often, men like Green, whose fortune at

his death in 1936 exceeded $40 million, used their money and their political influence to open up the region to new ways of doing business and new ways of thinking.[27]

Green also served as a director and officer of several local banks, and banking joined railroads and lumber companies as interconnected businesses that both caused and profited from rapid change and more-prosperous times. Between the late 1890s and World War I, the number of banks and the amount of capital lent by these banks expanded greatly. Outsiders like Edward Green who brought their millions with them did not transform the region alone. Local capital, accumulated in a rapidly growing banking system, also nourished economic growth.[28]

During most of the nineteenth century, government-regulated banks contributed little to economic growth. In fact, from 1845 to 1869 and from 1876 to 1904, the Texas Constitution banned state-chartered banks. The original ban grew out of the sad experience of many southerners with failed state banks and a general antimonopoly sentiment. Private bankers, who financed the cotton trade, filled the need for banks before 1865. After the Civil War, the national banking system expanded into Texas, but these banks flourished best in larger towns and cities. During the brief life of the Constitution of 1869, the state chartered some banks, but few lasted beyond the reimposition of the ban on state banks in the Texas Constitution of 1876. In rural Northeast Texas, private bankers like R. A. "Lon" Morris of Pittsburg still dominated the banking industry in the first years of the twentieth century.[29]

Yet starting about 1900 the number of national banks increased substantially. Lumber companies and railroad companies needed banks to handle their payrolls and had greater confidence in national banks. Banks also profited from the upsurge in cotton prices and the increased volume of cotton shipped out of Northeast Texas. Handling this increased amount of business, however, usually required pooling the capital of several investors in a national bank instead of relying on one family's capital as most private banks did. Consequently, a few private banks converted to national banks, but new institutions dominated the list of new charters. The editor of the *Pittsburg Gazette* pointed out in May 1904 that since the start of the new century 221 new national banks had opened for business in Texas. Despite the continued strength of Lon Morris's Camp County Bank, later that year a new national bank opened in Pittsburg. The number of national banks surged in Texas, including Northeast Texas, even before the creation of a state banking system in 1905.[30]

Not only did new banks open, assets and lending increased in existing banks. Pittsburg offered a good case study because of the presence of a large private bank and the availability of published statements of condition. First National Bank, started by E. A. King as a private bank, became a national bank in 1893. From January 1900 to December 1911, the assets of First National doubled, going from $145,800 to $303,500. Loan volume more than doubled. Short-term lending to cotton firms boosted the loan volume of all Texas banks in the fall, but even in the winter loans at First National always exceeded deposits subject to checks. By post-1933 standards First National was a very aggressive bank. It had to be.[31]

Just as competition for labor boosted opportunities for the working class, competition for bank customers forced expanded lending. This became even truer after 1905, when the creation of a state banking system stimulated the chartering of many new banks that lent on easier terms than most national banks.[32]

By the end of 1905 the formation of Guaranty State Bank brought the number of banks in Pittsburg, a town of fewer than 2,000 citizens, to four. In order of size they were: Camp County, First National, Pittsburg National, and Guaranty State. The Camp County Bank did a silk-stocking business, catering to wealthy citizens and to local businesses like Tapp Dry Goods or Patterson-Miller Lumber Company. Lon Morris's bank did not offer regular saving or checking accounts and was subject to almost no federal or state regulation. Until 1904 this meant that First National served a broad market underneath the Camp County Bank. After 1904, however, two more banks competed for that business. Since gaining deposits usually required lending to new customers, aggressive lending provided the easiest avenue to growth. Besides, banks did not have as many investment options as they would in later years. Lending to local customers brought the greatest profit and in times of even slight economic growth was relatively safe. Increased competition and the desire to maximize profits drove a steady expansion of lending and lowered interest rates. Despite the promotional nature of such claims, in 1912 a local editor declared with some truth, "Jefferson has three strong banks with plenty of money to advance the farmer, charging only a small rate of interest."[33]

While competing with each other, bankers also recognized that bank failures or the loss of public confidence in banks hurt every bank's business. In October and November 1907 a panic convulsed the world's money centers. Currency shortages occurred throughout the country as customers withdrew their funds. After all, uninsured deposits and the threat of bank failures made customers understandably uneasy. Bankers shared this uneasiness because no bank could turn a profit and keep enough currency on hand to repay all depositors. Besides, since deposit and loan arrangements linked banks in distant places, a run on one threatened many. Working through their local clearinghouse, the four Pittsburg banks issued $30,000 in certificates backed by their good name—enough to pay off edgy depositors and keep currency in circulation. Local businesses honored these certificates, and the panic soon passed in Pittsburg and in other places that followed this cooperative tack.[34]

Lending quickly surpassed pre-1907 levels as an increasing number of banks made affordable credit available to a narrow but growing segment of the population. Camp County's ratio of one bank for every 2,500 people did not differ markedly from that of the rest of Northeast Texas. Even small villages such as Omaha and Cason in Morris County and Cookville in Titus County boasted banks. A partial list of banks as of June 1910 showed that the eleven-county region, with a population of 240,000, had at least seventy-eight banks. Bowie County led the way with fifteen banks, most of them in Texarkana. Total deposits for the county whose 1910 population was 35,000 were $4.6 million. This large figure reflected the contribution of lumber and railroad to banking, but it also reflected new Texas banking laws.[35]

While the lumber and railroad industries brought opportunities to adjacent areas of Oklahoma, Arkansas, and Louisiana, the economic stimulation from banking was much more closely confined within the borders of Texas and Oklahoma, which had almost identical banking laws. The creation of a state banking system in 1905 and the augmenting of the system with deposit guaranty in 1910 fostered unique economic opportunities. As a result, the number of Texas banks grew rapidly.[36]

Most of these banks flourished before World War I. The total resources of the State Bank of Omaha, for example, climbed from $67,000 in September 1908 to $90,000 by May 1912. Although Omaha had fewer than 500 citizens, stable currency values and general prosperity convinced the officers and directors of the bank to increase loans from 32 percent of resources in September 1908 to 77 percent of resources in May 1912.[37]

As the number of banks and the volume of loans increased, bankers became the preeminent town builders, the connecting link between varied business interests. They led the attempts to find a way to prevent boll weevil damage and to gain for their towns the most economic advantage from cotton. In Pittsburg, bankers financed the expansion of the sweet potato industry and the related container industry. In Jefferson, they underwrote a new cottonseed oil mill.[38]

Complaints about a credit shortage still surfaced, as did charges that bankers extracted usurious interest rates from farmers and forced them to plant cotton. Willard Peteet, who in 1915 surveyed farmers, bankers, and merchants to discover "what Texas farmers pay for credit," found much truth in these charges. Interest rates at banks sometimes ranged far above the 10 percent maximum set by law. Many farmers still seemed unused to competition between lenders and failed to shop around for the cheapest credit and the most reasonable terms. Peteet and others who studied the credit situation in Texas between 1912 and 1915 indicated, however, that an important transition was underway. Where competitive bank lending and cash-only merchants both flourished, the cost of credit for farm owners and better-off white tenants was "on the decrease" and often sank below 10 percent. Credit remained closely linked to retailing.[39]

CASH ONLY AND CATALOGS

By 1915 cash-only stores and other types of retailing that featured low prices and high volume were driving the old fashioned furnishing merchant out of business. The arrival of these new stores signaled not only a significant change in retailing, but also a basic change in the structure of society. Historian Thomas D. Clark argued more than fifty years ago that more than any other institution furnishing merchants "embodied . . . the intimate story of the New South." Most commentators since have agreed, but they have missed the supplanting of this institution by cash-only stores, early-day discount stores, chain stores, catalog sales, banks, and cotton companies in some regions of the South in the World War I era. When the furnishing-merchant system waned, all connected to it also faded, and local society grew less closed economically, politically, and socially.[40]

Furnishing merchants usually combined the roles of landlord, storekeeper, cotton dealer, and lender. E. A. King demonstrated the power and influence these southerners wielded. In the 1880s King began selling dry goods and groceries in Pittsburg. Like most furnishing merchants, he conducted much of his business on credit and maintained a two-price system—a higher price for credit purchases and a lower price for cash purchases. He also lent scarce capital to some customers and operated until 1893 as a private banker. King gradually acquired land by foreclosing on those who could not pay. Buying and selling cotton through his store allowed the steady purchase of more land. The price of cotton mattered less to him than the spread between what he paid for the cotton and what he sold it for. Crop lien laws forced farmers to sell their cotton to him if they owed him money for their "furnish," a term used to describe the clothing, supplies, and simple luxuries that a family needed to get through until harvest time. This gave King and other furnishing merchants some control over the spread, and they made a bit of profit even in the worst of times. In fact, poor times offered opportunity. When the price of land and cotton plunged, King could afford to buy even more land. He became Camp's largest landowner, a reality reflected by his social and political standing. King served as Pittsburg's first mayor when the town incorporated in 1891. A year later he ended the feud between the Hogg and Clark Democrats. Later he served as state senator from Camp and Upshur counties. King sold his store before 1900 but retained other investments in Pittsburg. Into old age he remained on the Democratic County Executive Committee and hosted a Fourth of July barbecue at his farm that featured speeches by local candidates for office. King stood atop Camp County's economic, political, and social ladder.[41]

Through the conclusion of World War I, merchants in other communities filled the same roles as King. Most merchants, however, ceased operating as private bankers because they could not efficiently manage the diverse functions of lending, farming, and retailing. After King nationalized his banking operations in 1893, a professional staff took over most duties. It made good managerial sense for King and others to concentrate on agriculture or agriculture and retailing. Publicly chartered banks had the advantage of lower interest rates, a higher volume of business, and more-efficient management. When the number of banks increased, they drove furnishing merchants out of the banking business. As an advertisement for City National Bank in Sulphur Springs pointed out in 1911: "WE ARE MAKING FARMERS' LOANS. If you need money to furnish yourself or your tenants this year, or to make a trade, or to make some improvements, or to buy more work stock, come to see us. We have the money, if you need funds, why shouldn't we get together?"[42]

Merchants retained broad roles in the local economy, owning large parcels of land and serving as directors of local banks, but most stopped lending as individuals except in special circumstances. It would take a careful study based on internal bank records to say just how much these directors still controlled lending. In general, until the 1960s, Texas banks depended upon their directors to approve large loans, and bank officers handled smaller loans on their own. In addition, directors often passed on credit information to the officers. If a director believed someone a poor credit risk or simply did not like them, that person probably would not get a loan. An expanded number of banks and heightened competition for customers, however, gave borrowers alternative sources of credit.[43]

What the expansion of banking began, cash-only stores, high-volume, low-price stores that offered credit, and catalog sales furthered because they undermined the dependent relationship of customer to merchant. As an Ellis County banker commented in 1915, "Bank loans and cash stores are putting credit merchants out of business."[44]

New retailing methods first developed outside of Texas. By the 1880s most major department stores in the North and West did a cash-only business, relying on rapid turnover and a low fixed price to compete with rivals. (Turnover and price complemented each other. If a merchant sold and restocked a spool of thread ten times in a year because of its low price that merchant made more profit than another who only sold the spool of thread once or twice in a year, even if he charged a higher price.) In the 1890s department stores introduced charge accounts and installment credit but limited this service to their very best customers. Credit, in this case, demonstrated status, not dependency. In the meantime variety and dry-goods chain stores such as F. W. Woolworth, S. H. Kress, and J. C. Penney began selling for cash only. They targeted middle-income and low-income shoppers and cut their operating costs in every possible manner, including eliminating the considerable cost of billing and collecting credit accounts. Like early department stores, they relied upon high volume and low prices. They also used special purchases and direct purchases from factories to lower the cost of goods. Chain stores' low operating costs allowed smaller markups of the wholesale price than department stores and forced most department stores to increasingly rely upon the upper tier of customers.[45]

Changes in the distribution of goods accompanied and facilitated these emerging retailing trends. Before 1900 traveling sales agents sold goods to most small-town and crossroads merchants. These jobbers specialized in unbranded products and mixed assortments of goods. They and the companies they worked for served as middlemen between the manufacturer and the seller. Manufacturers soon began advertising their products and handling their own distribution. Large urban department stores such as Monnig Dry Goods Co. of Fort Worth and Sanger Bros. of Dallas also expanded their wholesale operations and sold their own brands. Direct sales from manufacturers and the increased efficiency of sales by large wholesalers cut the price of goods. Advertising branded products increased customer demand for those products. Chain stores like J. C. Penney and catalog stores like Sears, Roebuck and Company and Montgomery Ward and Company took the process one step further by advertising their own private label brands and contracting for the manufacture of products. By 1914 these new trends in retailing and distribution reached even the most remote corner of Northeast Texas.[46]

Sears led the way in the penetration of the Northeast Texas market. In the 1890s the company emerged as the dominant competitor in the mail-order business, and Texans numbered among its best customers. The distance between Chicago and Texas prompted Richard Sears to open his first branch mail-order plant in Dallas in 1906. In 1908 Sears issued a Texas catalog and advertised that it shipped from Dallas. By 1911 the almost 1,400-page Texas catalog rivaled the size of the catalog used in the rest of the country. Trying to catch up with its larger rival, in that year Montgomery Ward opened a distribution plant in Fort Worth. This positioned both mail-order companies to take full advantage of the expanded parcel-post service.[47]

Rural free delivery of first-, second-, and third-class mail started in the 1890s. This allowed Sears and Wards to distribute their catalogs cheaply and customers to place orders. Private express companies still handled most package deliveries, and local merchants relied upon high express charges to keep them competitive with the mail-order houses. As the editor of the *Cass County Sun* remarked in 1908, "The storekeeper and the express companies are turning up heaven and earth to keep down the movement for a parcel post system." In 1912, Congress authorized package delivery, and parcel post joined the mail system in January 1913. Although initially wary of its impact, Sears and Wards profited enormously from parcel post, and their business expanded rapidly through World War I.[48]

Measuring the exact impact of mail-order houses and parcel post on local retailers is difficult, but the increased volume of complaints from local editors signaled the advent of new business conditions. The appearance of Sears' Texas catalog in 1908 must especially have troubled small-town merchants, for that year editor after editor urged readers to shop at home. In one self-serving comment, the editor of the *Cooper Review* proclaimed "local merchants must advertise to compete with mail order houses." Creation of the parcel-post system also caused a ripple of comment. In 1913 the editors of the *Jefferson Jimplecute* urged subscribers to be loyal to Jefferson and "not to send away for anything you can get here." For these editors, mail-order houses were among the biggest enemies of small towns.[49]

Northeast Texans realized, however, that local merchants were partially to blame for the phenomenal success of mail order and other new forms of retailing. After urging retailers to "keep alive, awake, and up to date" and to "keep your prices low," one critic listed the dozen or so problems with local retailing. He closed his article entitled "How to Hold Home Trade" with a call to "establish a cash business." After all, "mail order houses have no credit system."[50]

Seaman Knapp led the way in pointing out the problems with local retailing methods. In 1909 he wrote, "For many years it has been the custom of the Southern farmers to make their crop upon the 'advance system' and while this has been regarded as an economic error on the side of the farmer, by many merchants it has been thought that it was a very profitable way of buying cotton." Knapp happily reported that many farmers were moving away from the advance method and reliance upon furnishing merchants. He insisted, "I have been watching this phase of country life in the South for many years and have come to the conclusion that the 'advance system' is just as great a mistake on the part of the merchant as it is on the part of the farmer." He then argued that traditional methods hurt merchants because the risk of nonpayment forced them to raise prices, which lowered the volume of their business. (Observers in the mid-1910s estimated that Texas merchants collected only 60 percent of their credit accounts.) Furnishing merchants also carried farmers for years without full repayment because their choice was to take the farm or fund the farmer. With the arrival of the boll weevil, farming with tenants required closer supervision than a busy merchant could provide. In that sense, productivity of the farmer and the merchant improved with a cash-only system. "I should not speak so positively, only I have observed for a quarter of a century that where the Southern merchants have changed from an 'advance system' to a cash system, they have prospered very much more than in former years and the number of failures is immensely less." [51]

Merchants in Northeast Texas heard this advice from Knapp and other critics of retailing practices, and some observed developing retailing trends when they went on buying trips to Chicago, Kansas City, St. Louis, and New York. Jobbers and factory representatives also brought news of changes in retailing in other parts of the country. In some cases these emissaries not only brought word of new trends, they refused to advance merchants credit unless they converted to a cash-only business. About 1908, and almost certainly in response to the increased competition from Sears and the pressure of their suppliers, local merchants began experimenting with new retailing techniques. Among the earliest high-volume, low-price stores in Northeast Texas were Cooper Bros. of Cooper, R. N. Traylor of Daingerfield, Anthony & Luedeck of Pittsburg, and J. J. Segal of Jefferson and Atlanta. Perkins Bros., a regional dry-goods chain based in Paris, also began emphasizing low prices. All advertised heavily in several newspapers, stressing low prices and a large selection of branded merchandise. Special purchases offered at exceptionally low prices drew in customers. Some of these stores still had cotton-buying departments and still did a credit business. They stood apart from traditional stores on volume, price, advertising, structure, and competitiveness. [52]

Cooper Bros., for example, outgrew its traditional organization where fabric lay next to flour and bacon beside plows. Abandoning this random organization because customers could not locate merchandise conveniently, it operated in two adjacent downtown buildings: one housed groceries and the other dry goods. It also stressed that customers could return merchandise if dissatisfied, a policy long used by big city department stores to sway wary customers to buy more. Greater efficiency and greater sales volume let the store cut prices even further. Cooper Bros.'s transformation and the appearance of other price-oriented stores balanced the power between merchant and customer. Merchants still controlled available stock and set prices. Yet customers, as the owners of Cooper Bros. realized in 1909, "go where they get the most for their money." Moving toward a cash-only system such as that used by J. C. Penney or S. H. Kress, which opened stores in the region during World War I, was not just good business. Cash only rapidly became essential for survival, because customers not only ordered from mail-order companies, they shopped for bargains in nearby towns.[53]

Eventually merchants agreed on the multiple virtues of cash only. Traditional merchants persisted into the 1920s and fought back against competitors with increased advertising. Yet the cost and complexity of a two-price system and the losses from uncollected debt capped the volume of business traditional merchants could handle and limited their ability to lower prices. Some, like John Hughes & Co. of Atlanta, emphasized that they still purchased or traded furs, eggs, butter, and milk with farmers, and insisted it offered "the very lowest cash prices." Yet when traditional merchants lowered cash prices, they typically raised credit prices to fully cover the cost of offering credit. This only increased the risk of default. The risks and expense of traditional business practices and the increasing number of competitors gradually forced change. As J. T. Webster said when he switched his store to a cash-only basis, "Let us all pay cash and be prosperous."[54]

Hints of just how prosperous the new emphasis on cash purchases made consumers came in Peteet's 1915 survey in which one cash customer commented that he "got half as much again as the credit customers" for every dollar spent. Peteet did a detailed study of prices in Rains County on the southwest border of Hopkins County. According to his figures, a market basket of ten goods that included such basics as bacon, sugar, and flour cost 28 percent more on credit than for cash. High-grade flour, for example, cost $2.63 a bag on credit compared with $2 a bag for cash. The trick was having enough cash to avoid paying on credit or having access to cheaper bank credit.[55]

Cash only and the availability of bank credit also meant that farmers had more opportunities to seek the best outlet for the sale of their cotton. They could hold it off the market and store it in the Farmer's Union warehouse. They could sell direct to large out-of-the-region cotton firms. They also could sell to the local merchant who offered the best price, instead of the one that held a lien on their crop. In 1912, for example, the merchants of Jefferson and Linden engaged in a protracted bidding war for cotton that pushed the local price above that offered on the New Orleans spot market. For these merchants, the cotton selling season was like Christmas. Farm families had money to spend and pent-up demand. Merchants realized that farm families would spend in the town where they sold their cotton. In that sense for merchants that both purchased cotton and sold goods, keeping the price they paid for cotton low was less important than drawing in trade. Competition for customers meant that even the most traditional merchants in Northeast Texas contributed to a system that maintained higher cotton prices and lower retail prices for those who paid cash.[56]

Like most economic changes in the region, lower retail prices waited on the confluence of external and internal forces. Between 1905 and 1914 bank credit increased, low-price stores penetrated the regional market, and rising farm incomes allowed better-off tenants and most farm owners to free themselves from relying on expensive store credit. Spur lines that connected to trunk lines moved shoppers between larger towns and rural areas. Gravel roads increasingly supplemented railroads as every county in the region began an ambitious road-building program. Limited prosperity and these transportation improvements allowed consumers to move from one store to the next.

Again, like most economic changes, this one did not benefit all or benefit evenly. When a new railroad reached Linden in Cass County in 1911 the local editor looked forward to no longer being a "back number." Ironically, Linden's retail community suffered from progress. Consumers could make choices, and they chose the lower prices in the better-managed, higher-volume stores in increasingly accessible nearby towns.[57]

Poorer whites and blacks also missed out on the new freedoms and opportunities offered by bank credit and cash purchases. In April 1916 the *Jefferson Jimplecute* carried a remarkable letter from "Cross Cut a renter." After 1900 agricultural reformers repeatedly advocated reducing the cotton crop to raise its price. Following one more such call, Cross Cut pointed out: "Mr. W. D. B. is arguing cut out the cotton one half or all and at the same time says 'Sam, you and the rest of the negroes on the place plant over half of your crop in cotton. You can have your peas and peanuts in your corn patch provided you give me half and that is the way the cradle is rocking today.' " He then went on to make an essential point. "We have got to see something in the future that will take the place of cotton—go to the bank or merchant to get money or supplies—the first thing they ask you is 'How much cotton have you planted?' Don't ask anything about peas or peanuts. Renters, like I am, have to plant cotton to get provisions." The system blocked attempts to supplement their diet or improve their income by raising alternatives to cotton.[58]

Blacks and poorer whites also found that bank credit evaporated when they needed it most. In the Sulphur Springs area in 1914 when cotton prices plunged, nervous bankers seized farmers' stock and pressured them for immediate payment instead of waiting for the price to rise. Race mattered as much as class. One black landowner lamented that despite his being a well-established and respected farmer, the bank "broke me up." At about the same time, a Pittsburg black complained that every time his white employers thought their black workers were getting ahead, they would "lay them off for two or three days." [59] For poor whites and blacks to take full advantage of the benefits of modern retailing and to move out of dependency required basic changes in the cotton economy. Unfortunately the changes that occurred usually benefited others.

A CHANGING COTTON CULTURE

In Northeast Texas, planting, cultivating, harvesting and marketing cotton ordered the daily lives of farmers and the townsfolk whose sustenance depended directly or indirectly on the crop. While cotton alone did not initiate economic change, the creation of new businesses, especially banks and cottonseed oil mills, and the emergence of new retailing methods were linked closely to the evolution of the cotton industry. Agriculture remained inefficient at the start of World War I, but that should not obscure the impact of a transforming industry.

After 1870 as the transportation network improved and immigration from the older southern states increased, the amount of cotton planted in Northeast Texas rose. The economic troubles of the late 1880s and early 1890s pushed thousands of farmers from the older regions of the South to more-fertile, less-expensive farmland in Northeast Texas. After 1900 cotton acreage went up and down according to the price, the weather, and the boll weevil, but in general climbed steeply upward. Acreage in potatoes, sweet potatoes, and peaches also increased, but not at the same rate as cotton. As in the rest of Texas, through 1930 cotton increasingly dominated agriculture.[60]

More cotton in Texas and elsewhere in the South did not automatically translate into lower prices at the gin. Earlier, from about 1870 to 1900, dramatic increases in southern cotton production brought depressed prices. Although tempered by occasional upward flurries, lower cotton prices and a higher cost of production dragged down the postwar southern economy. As the 1890s closed, however, American demand for cotton increased. New mills opened; old mills expanded. As noted in the U.S. Department of Agriculture's *Yearbook, 1900*, "such was the activity that many mills, North and South, were obliged to run day and night." That year, the high on the New Orleans spot market passed ten cents a pound for the first time in many years. While cotton's price fell back in 1901 and 1902, in early 1903 it increased sharply and stayed at a generally profitable level until August 1914. In the eleven crop years from August 1, 1903, to July 31, 1914, the average annual price dropped below ten cents on the New Orleans and Galveston markets in only two years.[61]

Increased use of cottonseed products also added to regional prosperity. Until 1890 most cottonseed went to waste or was composted with manure and used as fertilizer. After 1890 cottonseed mills and oil refineries provided a common sight and special aroma to the cotton-growing areas of the state. Raw cottonseed yielded oil, meal, hulls, and short cotton fibers called linters. Writers for the *Texas Almanac* estimated that by 1904 these products added $20 million to the state's economy. Not surprisingly, given the weight of the seed and the expense of transportation, the blackland counties of the state, the leading producers of cotton, also led in the production of cottonseed products. By 1914 the $42 million in cottonseed products manufactured in Texas equaled 20 percent of the total manufactured in the United States, and their value surpassed that of lumber. Lumber remained dominant in the eastern counties of Northeast Texas, but cottonseed processing replaced the rapidly declining lumber industry in counties near or in the blacklands—Lamar, Red River, Franklin, Hopkins, and Delta.[62]

Cottonseed meal proved especially useful in fattening up grass-fed cattle, and in the early years of the industry, carloads of Texas cattle spent the winter at local mills before shipment to northern markets. After the founding of Fort Worth's first packing house in 1902, that city's stockyards devoured the cottonseed meal of nearby counties like Lamar. Paris quickly became one of the centers of the cottonseed industry and in 1904 had one of the state's seventeen refineries as well as two mills. Vegetable shortening, margarine, and salad oil all used refined cottonseed oil, and this refinery marked the first step in the emergence of Paris as a food-processing center. By World War I cottonseed had become such a vital source of food oil that the federal government banned its traditional mixing with manure for compost. Increasingly, the larger oil mills located near the gins. If the demand for seed rose, area gins paid higher prices for cotton in seed than other buyers. Thus, demand for seed helped smooth out the bumpy path of cotton prices.[63]

Even in the generally good years preceding World War I, the bumpy path of cotton prices needed all the smoothing available. High prices in 1903–1904 and 1907–1908 led to large crops and plunging prices in the following years. Prices also changed dramatically from month to month and even day to day. For farmers and merchants it mattered more than ever when you bought and sold cotton.[64]

New participants in the cotton trade proved better able to survive price swings. At about the same time furnishing merchants faced more-aggressive competition for the sale of their goods, they also faced an emerging power in the cotton industry—mammoth American cotton firms like Anderson, Clayton & Co. of Houston, Neil P. Anderson of Fort Worth, and Geo. H. McFadden & Bro. of Philadelphia.[65]

Large cotton-buying firms began to emerge in the 1880s and originally worked closely with local furnishing merchants. Sometimes the merchants became their agents, buying cotton on their account. In other cases merchants purchased cotton and sold it every few days to a cotton company buyer. Merchants who purchased cotton on a large scale also formed long-term relationships with traditional factors and wholesale grocers like Wm. D. Cleveland & Sons. This Houston-based wholesaler supplied groceries to merchants and sold their cotton on consignment.[66]

After 1900 cotton firms grew much larger and proved far better at making a profit from the cotton trade than the local merchants. The biggest firms cut handling costs, improved efficiency, and increasingly depended on the skillful use of the cotton-futures market. The futures market allowed firms to transfer all or part of the risk of price fluctuations by hedging. A hedge that transferred all risk required adopting equal and opposite positions in the futures and spot markets. Since the largest cotton firms had the best access to information on the demand from cotton mills and consumers, they usually accepted some risk for the chance to profit not only from the sale of cotton but also from futures contracts. All the major firms formed close ties to the largest banks in their headquarter cities and to major British, French, and German cotton mills upon whom they also depended for financing. Over time, however, the very largest

American companies built up independent sources of credit and dominated the world's cotton trade.[67]

Gradually dry-goods merchants and grocers moved out of the business of buying cotton on their own account, and agents for the big cotton firms replaced them. Merchants concentrated on the increasingly competitive retail side of their business and abandoned cotton buying to those who could do it more cheaply and efficiently. During a transition period from about 1900 to 1920 no one system of marketing cotton predominated.

In Paris, the largest Northeast Texas cotton market and place where merchants faced the most competition from cash-only stores, street buyers purchased ginned cotton on the public square. After farmers hauled their baled cotton to town, buyers cut a small sample and offered a price set by the major firms. In plentiful years buyers colluded to reduce competition, refusing to place a rival bid until farmers rejected the offer made by the initial buyer. Merchants and bankers had no such arrangement. Instead, as they moved out of the cotton buying business, they worked for better prices for their customers. One observer remarked in 1917 that "the store credit system has almost disappeared" in the Paris area. By that time, if not earlier, the intricate connections between cotton growers, merchants, bankers, and cotton buyers had evolved beyond the well-known parameters of the nineteenth century.[68]

Support by merchants and bankers for cooperative marketing schemes indicated just how much the cotton business had changed. In the 1890s furnishing merchants generally opposed the various cooperative buying and selling schemes of the Farmers' Alliance. Between 1904 and 1908 the Farmers' Union, in some ways a direct descendent of the Alliance, tried a cooperative marketing plan in Pittsburg. After the price collapse of 1904, the Union, assisted by local merchants and bankers, constructed a warehouse and issued receipts for stored and insured cotton. Farmers borrowed against these receipts and held their cotton until it reached a higher price. Union members hoped to cut out middlemen and sell directly to cotton companies or mills. They also hoped to control the price of cotton by regulating its flow into the market. Instead of dumping all their cotton on the market in the fall, they sold at other times of the year when the demand rose. Wild price swings associated with the Panic of 1907 and a big crop the next year put the Pittsburg warehouse scheme under.[69]

Elsewhere remnants of both the factor system and the furnishing-merchant system survived. Traditional factors like Wm. D. Cleveland still advertised in local newspapers and handled local cotton on consignment. More often, growers sold their cotton to local merchants or planters who then resold the cotton to mills or large firms. These large firms placed a

FIGURE 2.2

Farmers' Union Warehouse in Pittsburg. This photograph of the Union Warehouse in Pittsburg was taken in 1908, after local merchants constructed a new warehouse and cotton yard for the Farmers' Union. Other agricultural marketing groups, especially the Camp County Truck Growers Association, also used the new warehouse and yard.

Photograph courtesy of Jenkins Garrett Texas Postcard Collection, University of Texas at Arlington, Special Collections.

limit on the price their buyers could pay for cotton. In addition, some local merchants and large planters who owned gins still purchased cotton and held it on speculation.[70]

These local buyers, however, often could not adequately gauge the path of the cotton spot market in New Orleans and were even less aware of the intricacies of the futures market that drove changes in spot markets. In the winter of 1904–1905, for example, cotton prices dropped from eleven cents per pound to six cents per pound in a matter of days. Merchants and planters holding cotton in anticipation of the price going above eleven cents, as it had the previous two years, lost money.[71]

In contrast, major firms reached the point where they and not the largest mills influenced and profited from swings in cotton prices. As N. T. Blackwell explained to readers of the *Omaha Breeze*, "the autumn of 1910 and 1911 were the first years in all the history of cotton that the producer got a good price for cotton, when he had cotton to sell." Blackwell meant that when farmers rushed their cotton to market in the fall, mills lowered the price they would pay for cotton. Local dealers, connected to market centers by the telegraph, quickly lowered their price. Skillful use of futures contracts to transfer some of the risk of price changes allowed large cotton firms to pay a higher price than the mills and hold the cotton for later sale. They, in effect, achieved what the Farmers' Union sought earlier. Blackwell noted, "An enterprising Texas firm in December, 1909, did this very thing, paying from 14 to 15 cents per pound for spot cotton, hedged by future sales, and thereby helped to maintain good prices for farmers' spot cotton." [72]

Lacking the ability to lower risk by skillfully buying and selling futures and without the economies of scale, access to information, and marketing advantages of larger firms, those who purchased cotton on their own account usually paid less for it or took a loss. Farm operators who could not obtain credit elsewhere and owed merchants and planters for their furnish accepted the lower price furnishing merchants paid for cotton. These merchants, however, bore the cost of credit and found themselves increasingly limited to doing business with the poor. Better-off farmers went where they could get better prices for their cotton and for the goods they wanted to purchase. [73]

Efficient production helped separate the poor from the better-off farmers, and efforts to improve efficiency began about the same time as the spread of cash-only stores and expanded bank credit. Cheaper and more readily available credit helped farmers achieve greater efficiency. Still better cotton prices and the need for improved managerial techniques to combat the boll weevil lay at the heart of this upsurge in efficiency.

Newspaper editors agreed that the years between 1903 and 1914 were the most prosperous in memory. In 1908 the editor of the *Paris Advocate* insisted: "Prosperity is returning to the South, and the Texas farmer begins to feel that he is lord of all he surveys." In August 1914 the editor of the *Sulphur Springs Gazette* summed up the causes of this new prosperity: "Of late years the agitation of the soil has been remunerative, and farming is not the unprofitable drudgery it was years ago. The improved machinery for cultivation, the diversified products—the large acreage now managed by a smaller force and the scientific and systematic methods employed all have contributed to our prosperous conditions." [74]

Farmers sought, as W. C. Williams put it, to make farming "more of a business than a drudgery." While horses and mules still powered most implements, farmers took advantage of profits from cotton to buy improved machines that eased the back-breaking labor of years past. The value of farm implements in constant dollars in the eleven-county region increased 50 percent from 1900 to 1910 and 70 percent from 1910 to 1920. (Farm operators increased by less than 8 percent in each decade.) Much of the expansion for the 1910s probably came during the boom years of 1915 to 1920, but the upward trend for 1900 to 1910 and the comments of local farmers and editors indicated that the process began before the war. In any case, the rate of increase for the 1910s more than doubled that of Texas and signaled a significant departure in agricultural methods.[75]

Machinery allowed farmers to cultivate the same amount of land with "a smaller force" and "scientific and systematic methods." Farmers mechanized planting and cultivation, in particular, by replacing one-mule, walk-behind implements with two-mule riding planters and cultivators. A few farmers even tried four-mule machines that handled two rows at once.[76]

Until after World War II, however, the absence of a reliable mechanical cotton harvester limited mechanization, and even the best farmers in Northeast Texas remained less efficient than farmers outside the South. Yet their particular labor market allowed them to become more efficient than most cotton growers in other southern states. Since farmers required enough hands to pick the crop and to hoe the crop once the plants were too large to machine cultivate, in many areas of the South they continued to use the most labor intensive methods of cotton planting and cultivation because these methods occupied their workers through an entire season. It paid not to mechanize. In Texas, including Northeast Texas, the increased availability of Mexican migrant labor after 1910 and the seasonal labor of urban blacks removed this impediment to mechanization. Blacks worked in Paris most of the year, but in the late spring and fall entire families moved out to the cotton fields. Mexican Americans used Texarkana as a base to move through a multistate region. Whites also earned extra money chopping and picking cotton.[77]

This use of seasonal labor allowed a nexus of land, labor, and urban development that varied from a southern pattern. In his 1924 publication C. O. Brannen compared the Texas growing region to other southern cotton belts and commented, "In Texas, where the acreage per tenant is higher than in other regions, the larger part of extra labor is obtained from towns and cities." In other words seasonal labor contributed to a more favorable ratio of land to labor in all parts of Texas, a ratio that permitted greater efficiency and profitability for tenants and farm owners in Northeast Texas. In addition, industrialization and urban growth did not threaten local planters' reliance upon cheap year-round labor. Instead manufacturing and agriculture worked together, with labor moving from one to the other according to the season.[78]

The rise of a technological community complemented this different

Clarksville, Texas.
Home of Long
Staple Cotton.

FIGURE 2.3

*Clarksville long staple cotton. Spurred on by the need to find varieties that helped
limit boll weevil damage or, as in this case, commanded a higher price, area
growers in the years immediately before World War I
experimented with numerous new types of cotton.*
Photograph courtesy of Jenkins Garrett Texas Postcard Collection, University of Texas
at Arlington, Special Collections.

nexus of land, labor, and urban development. Between 1904 and 1920 research cooperatively funded by private individuals, businesses, the state,
and the federal government resulted in the introduction of the Lone Star
strain and several other varieties of cotton. News of these varieties and of
other ways to improve yields and cut costs spread quickly. The Farmers'
Union, county boards of trade, and county extension agents all preached
the gospel of better seed selection, more machinery, and more-efficient
use of labor. County and regional fairs, demonstration shows, and educational programs taught the benefits of new technology and new methods. Most regional newspapers and the numerous agricultural journals
published in Texas joined in the chorus. In 1912 the editor of the *Cumby
Rustler* summed up the plea of many when he wrote: "Brain as well as
muscle must be used on the farm. Now when a scientific method doubles
the yield on a piece of ground, it is too late to sneer at book farming."[79]
    Scientific methods, particularly those advocated for limiting boll wee-
vil damage, made cotton farming far more complicated than before. By
1908 agricultural scientists recommended the following steps for combat-

ing weevils. Burn immature bolls or feed them to cattle. Cut all stalks and plow them under to decompose. Keep the edge of the fields clean. Substitute early-maturing varieties for traditional varieties. Give the fields increased care and cultivation. Knock weevils from the plants at the proper time. Collect all fallen squares and burn them.[80]

Following these steps required more than new technology and new varieties of cotton. It required a new relationship between management and labor. Since farm owners' land often lay in contiguous blocks, weevils that infested one tenant's land could easily move to the land farmed by the owner or other tenants. Lack of effort to lessen weevil and boll worm damage in one unit of a farm potentially lowered yield for the entire farm. Inevitably this encouraged owners to increase control over those who farmed their land.[81]

Southern tenancy, however, restricted owners' control over certain types of tenants. Just as farm ownership differed in scale and style of operation, tenantry varied. Those who paid a cash fee for using land stood at the apex of tenantry and furnished their own labor, seeds, draft animals, and equipment. Next came share tenants who paid owners a percentage of the crop. The owners' share depended upon how much of the required labor, seed, draft animals, and equipment a tenant contributed and on the fertility of the land, but commonly landowners received one-fourth of the cotton and one-third of all other crops. In some cases farmers combined the share and cash-rent systems. They rented land for cotton on the share system and land for other crops for cash. After the arrival of the boll weevil, the risks of growing cotton became too great for most tenants to rent for cash, but the potential rewards remained high enough for a landowner to rent on shares. Around 1910 the improved price of cotton and rising land values encouraged some landowners in the blacklands to require payment of a bonus by the renter. Occasionally, more-prosperous share tenants paid the bonus and turned around and sub-rented to share-croppers, adding another complication to tenantry.[82]

While those at the top of the tenant system experienced considerable variety in their legal arrangements with landowners, the condition of southern sharecroppers seldom varied. Croppers possessed little capital and offered nothing but their labor and that of their family. They commonly farmed for half the crop, and in Texas were often referred to as "half hands." As that term implies, even in Texas where the law provided limited protection for tenants, croppers worked as employees not independent proprietors.[83]

William Humphrey, a novelist who grew up in Red River County, left a vivid remembrance of his sharecropping grandfather. Every year or two his grandfather moved from one farm to the next, all within a few miles of the village of Lone Star. "To the end, going blind with cataracts and feeling his way with his feet in the furrows, my grandfather clung to his dream of gathering a good enough crop for a couple of years in succession to make a down payment on a place of his own and 'work for himself.' Instead, the gathering of his crop and its sale, the one time of the year when he held cash money in his hand, often left him in debt to the owner of the crossroads store for what he had advanced them to keep alive on." In the 1930s Humphrey's grandfather still used a one-horse or one-mule walk-behind plow and never farmed more than twenty to thirty acres of cotton. The houses his grandparents lived in often had mud floors and single-board walls covered on the inside with pages from mail-order catalogs. The windows lacked screens, and in the summer clouds of malaria-carrying mosquitoes filled the house.[84]

Clearly little, including the dependency on the owner of the crossroads store, had improved for whites like Humphrey's grandfather or for blacks in similar circumstances. Yet others achieved the dream of landownership, or at least improved prosperity. Between 1905 and 1910 O. J. T. Leonard, the father of Marvin Leonard, moved from tenant to owner when he purchased a hundred-acre farm near Linden. Lloyd Shockley's family in Morris County completed the same process when they purchased their farm about 1920 after years of struggle with debt. Both the Shockleys and the Leonards concentrated on truck crops, not cotton, and they worked part time in the lumber industry. A USDA study of Ellis County, Texas, indicated, however, that even renters who grew cotton could make money once they put together a bit of capital. In 1914 tenants in this Blackland Prairie county with at least $500 in capital made a higher income than farm owners with many times that amount of capital. An in-depth study of six blackland counties done a few years later indicated that share tenants still made the highest return for their investment.[85]

One local case indicated that what was true of Ellis County was also true of similar areas of Northeast Texas. In May 1911 the *Paris Morning News* published an article on W. L. Dodd, who farmed more than seven hundred acres on shares. On this land near the Red River on the border of Fannin and Lamar counties, Dodd planted both cotton and corn, using the best equipment available and the most modern managerial techniques. "After giving the landlord the usual third and fourth he cleared ten thousand dollars as his share above expenses." Clearly Dodd controlled all aspects of his farm operation and had the capital, machinery, and knowledge to succeed.[86]

This possibility of success as a tenant raises the question of why the

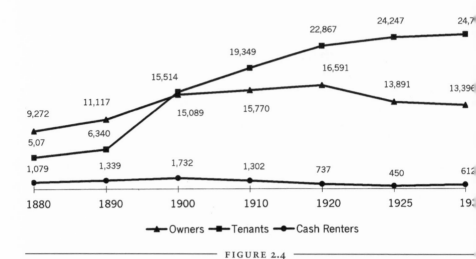

FIGURE 2.4

Owners, tenants, and renters, Northeast Texas, 1880–1930.
Source: U.S., *Census: 1880, Agriculture,* 88–93; U.S., *Census: 1890, Agriculture,* I, 182–189;
U.S., *Census: 1900, Agriculture,* vol. 5, pt. 1, 124–131; U.S., *Census: 1910, Agriculture,*
vol. 7, 655–675; U.S., *Census: 1920, Agriculture,* vol. 6, pt. 1, 664–686;
U.S., *Census of Agriculture: 1925,* pt. 2, 1240–1263;
U.S., *Census: 1930, Agriculture,* vol. 2, pt. 2, 1382–1401.

number of sharecroppers, the poorest type of tenant, rose so dramatically
in Northeast Texas. Perhaps because it was more recently settled or because blacks made up a smaller part of the population, croppers always
formed a smaller percentage of all farm operators in Texas than in southern states to the east. Less time had passed to overpopulate the cheaper
and more fertile soils of Texas. Racism and habits left over from the plantation did not tie blacks as securely to the lowest rung of agricultural
production. (Law, culture, and custom also probably discouraged white
sharecropping in Texas, but those are topics for a later chapter.)[87]

Despite the region's proximity to the rest of the South, farm owners
outnumbered tenants and renters in Northeast Texas until near the close
of the nineteenth century, but in the 1890s, as Figure 2.4 demonstrates,
the number of tenants rose sharply. The census did not separate croppers from share tenants until 1920, but in the 1890s the overwhelming
majority were probably still share tenants. The number of farm owners
leveled off between 1900 and 1920 but declined sharply between 1920 and
1925. Meanwhile, the number of tenants, especially croppers, soared.[88]

Hope as well as despair drove these changes in tenantry. G. L. Vaughan spoke for many other southern migrants when he explained why his family came to Texas in 1908: "The smooth land that was easy to cultivate, and higher wages for work, and the charm that the word *Texas* had in most places won us over." Farmers expected better prospects in Texas even if they remained tenants, and deteriorating conditions in the older regions of the South repeatedly caused an increase in the number of Texas tenants. Other changes in tenantry, however, came not because of optimism but because of land consolidation, sharp rises in land values, and the need for better management.[89]

To some extent landowners favored sharecropping because custom and economic dependency made croppers the easiest group of tenants to control. As the landowners' level of capital contributed to the farming operation increased, so did their level of day-to-day involvement. Cash renters and large-scale tenants such as W. L. Dodd operated like farm owners. Even tenants who farmed modest acreage on shares exerted considerable control over planting, cultivation, and harvesting. In most cases the landowner visited the property only a few times a year and offered almost no direct supervision. Croppers, however, were little different from hired laborers, except that they worked as a family unit. Owners usually lived nearby and closely supervised the crucial planting, cultivating, and harvesting functions. Owners gained further control if they provided their croppers' furnish.[90]

Postbellum tenancy evolved as it did because white and black tenants wanted as much freedom as possible from landowners' direct supervision. Tenantry offered more status and dignity than gang labor. Landlords accepted this process because labor and capital were scarce, but over time the reasons owners accepted the original bargain disappeared from Northeast Texas.[91]

By 1914 few larger-scale landowners lacked sufficient capital to begin an economic transformation. More-favorable prices after 1900 meant they often made enough from their farm operations to finance new machines and new methods of labor from earnings, but access to credit in the expanding state or national banking systems also improved. Better prices and more banks complemented each other. Rising cotton prices increased the value of farmland and cotton in storage, thus augmenting farmers' collateral. Simultaneously, state banks pioneered the use of real estate as collateral and offered more-generous terms on cotton in storage. Use of such collateral encouraged lending by lowering its cost and risks, and for larger-scale farmers at least, debt became a tool for building prosperity. A Mount Pleasant editor spoke for the whole region when he reported in

February 1908, "As a rule the people of Titus County are in better financial condition now than they have been at this time of year for a long time." [92]

Freed from the old incentives to maintain tenant farming in its traditional form, encouraged by the need to control boll weevils, and prodded by Seaman Knapp and other agricultural reformers, landowners and large-scale farmers began a managerial revolution before World War I. In December 1911 describing what he called "a landlord with vision," the editor of the *Pittsburg Gazette* reported, "E. A. King who operates the largest farm in Camp County or perhaps in Northeast Texas, offered prizes this year to his tenants for the best acre of cotton and corn." King demonstrated repeatedly that he knew the right time to make the right move. By 1911 he heard the call of agricultural experts and realized that dealing with the boll weevil and using new methods to gain greater productivity required new incentives and controls. Others followed where he led.[93]

Offering monetary incentives, however, probably yielded fewer benefits for landowners than moving away from farming for thirds and fourths toward the use of half hands. Owners could force croppers to adopt new methods to combat boll weevils or induce them to work more efficiently and maintain the quality of the crop and fertility and productivity of the soil. What owner would pay for fertilizer or other soil improvements only to have a share tenant fail to profit from those improvements?[94]

Used in combination with seasonal labor, croppers also proved inexpensive and relatively reliable. Although they moved about a good deal, croppers could be more stable and usually were more available than hired labor. Too, sharing the proceeds of the crop gave croppers incentive for efficiency. Besides, when cotton prices were good, labor preferred a sharecropping agreement to straight wages.[95]

Finally, landowners usually controlled the harvested crop raised by croppers and arranged its sale. Cottonseed's increased value made control of the crop all the more attractive, especially if the landowner owned a gin or cottonseed mill and benefited from a steady stream of raw material passing through that gin and mill. Thus, changes in cotton marketing, the drive for productivity, and the need to lessen risk encouraged landowners to change from share tenants to croppers.[96]

Because census takers did not record croppers as a separate category from share tenants before 1920, it is difficult to gauge the exact growth in numbers of croppers. Tenants certainly believed landowners, merchants, and cotton firms pushed them down the agricultural ladder. As a result, in Texas and Oklahoma, membership in tenant organizations grew rapidly in the 1910s. The socialist party also gained a large following, and politicians such as James E. "Pa" Ferguson won elections by appealing for the votes of white share tenants and croppers.[97]

Northeast Texans joined in this protest, and that indicated a growing chasm between the bottom and middle of the social and economic order. Studies done at the time and more-recent statistically based studies indicate that in terms of wealth the population broke into roughly three groups. Instead of wealth being concentrated among the very rich, between 1890 and 1914 wealth tended to spread out among the top third of the population. By 1914 members of this group enjoyed greater wealth and a greater share of the overall wealth of the region than in 1890. Those in the middle third were in roughly the same spot or only slightly better off in 1914 than in 1890. Their standard of living improved, but their share of total wealth typically held steady. The bottom third's percentage of total wealth declined and in all likelihood so did their standard of living.[98]

Economic change left not only uneven wealth distribution and uneven standards of living, it left uneven ability to take advantage of economic opportunities. As America moved toward active participation in World War I, tenant farmers with some capital (analysts at the time suggested $500 to $1,000) enjoyed remarkable opportunities for prosperity. Those with less capital sank further down. They were, as one observer noted, "without hope."[99] Rising wages and a more fluid labor market, however, offered increased opportunities for skilled and semiskilled labor. Landowners, business owners, and an expanded professional class also prospered and soon found new opportunities for increased wealth.

Haves and have-nots peopled Northeast Texas, but the haves extended beyond a few elite property owners. In 1914 a broad middle and upper-middle class enjoyed reasonable prosperity, looked forward to new economic opportunities, and exerted considerable political muscle. Instead of being tossed about by government policy or the inexorable transforming power of machines and technology, they influenced policy, encouraged technology, and used machines for their own purposes. They were agents of their own fate.[100]

PART TWO

TRANSFORMATIONS

THREE

A NEW POLITICAL ORDER,
1897–1912

Before 1897, parties mutated with every election, divisive issues alienated neighbors, and fraud and murder became political staples. Out of this chaos emerged a new political order that featured the elimination of the black voter, reduction of the poor white vote, and the winnowing of five effective political factions to three or occasionally four. In this new environment one party, the Democrats, became overwhelmingly dominant.

Nevertheless, as the years between 1906 and 1912 demonstrated, Democrats still divided into pre-1897 factions: conservatives, bifurcated reformers, and insurgents. Instead of displaying mindless loyalty to party, members of these factions listened to the issues, voted according to their principles, furthered their own interests, and followed trusted leaders. Despite the poll tax and the whites-only Democratic primary, the appeal of these leaders and the issues they epitomized could raise turnout of white voters to levels near that of the mid-1890s. By 1912 the competitive, multi-factional nature of the Democratic primary encouraged white political participation and fostered innovation and compromise.

Viewed as a whole, the years from 1897 to 1912 witnessed both a subtraction from, and an addition to, the previous political order. Blacks and the poorest whites lost the most. The white middle class gained the most. These political changes influenced the social, cultural, and economic changes discussed in other chapters. For one thing, it meant that, unlike elites in some other sections of the South, the conservative elite could not easily control any aspect of life in Northeast Texas. Yet as was true of most of the South, turn-of-the-century changes in the political system diminished the opportunity of poor whites and blacks to control their lives. Understanding these broader themes, however, requires first understanding why some Northeast Texans believed their region could "raise nothing but bad politics," and how they acted on this belief.[1]

RACE, LOCAL PRIMARIES, AND THE POLL TAX, 1897–1902

Five years before passage of the poll tax cut heavily into the number of black voters, local primaries eroded black participation in politics and split the Populist party along factional lines. These local primaries varied from county to county and predated the statewide whites-only Democratic primary by almost a decade, but like the statewide primary they helped Democrats retain or regain control of county politics. Along with fraud and violence, local primaries undercut Populist attempts to combine in one party blacks dissatisfied with the economic policy of the major parties, white economic reformers, and white rural insurgents concerned with achieving economic justice and preserving an independent way of life.

Drawing upon examples in other parts of Texas and the South, whites targeted blacks for electoral "reform." Whites claimed that blacks allowed their votes to be bought and sold, and that unscrupulous politicians instead of honest citizens benefited from this system. This justification of racial bias ignored the many examples of white ballot-box stuffing, fraud, and intimidation of black voters. In a classic example of blaming the victim instead of the real criminal, whites moved to eliminate the black vote by any means possible.[2]

This move against black voters came when it was difficult for them to defend themselves. The Supreme Court case *Plessy v. Ferguson* (1896) signaled the reality that the federal government would no longer take any steps to effectively protect black civil rights. Meanwhile between 1887 and 1897, blacks split their votes between many different political camps — conservatives, Populists, Hogg Democrats, and Republicans. Disputes between lily-whites and black and tans further weakened the Texas Republican party, the statewide organization that stood the best chance of deflecting assaults on black voters. Norris Wright Cuney faced increasing opposition from other black leaders and from the lily-whites, and these disputes undermined his efforts to have the national Republican party protect black suffrage. When he died in 1898, his already disintegrating party lost the figure best able to restore black unity on the state level and gain a hearing on the national level.[3]

While the timing of this exclusion of the black voter owed much to efforts to defeat Populism, national indifference to black civil rights, and the division of black voters into competing voting blocs, the style and intensity of this "reform" movement derived from lynching and prohibition. By 1897 lynching had evolved into a type of auto-da-fé, a ritualistic burning of black heretics to cleanse society. Prohibition contributed to the semireligious nature of lynching and gave whites a practical reason to murder blacks and exclude them from the political process. As long as blacks resisted white middle-class rules of morality by voting against prohibition, sweeping Northeast Texas clean of the influence of alcohol seemed impossible. In white minds the exclusion of black voters joined prohibition and lynching as necessary tools in restoring and promoting a Christian family life. Given the religious inspired conviction of this white movement, without federal intervention blacks stood little chance of retaining the right to vote in meaningful elections. Yet they did not go quietly into political oblivion, and when given the opportunity by factional divisions between white conservatives and reformers, blacks voiced their resistance to white supremacy by voting against prohibition.[4]

Poorer rural whites who opposed prohibition and voted with the insurgent cause also lost their chance to vote for candidates other than Democrats. Yet, when competition between factions of the Democratic party heated up, poorer whites—if they could pay the poll tax—voted and exerted more political influence than blacks.[5]

Marion County, scene of the most blatant corruption in 1896, also offered the most brutal example of the imposition of the new political order and what it meant to blacks and poor whites. In 1897 local white elites assassinated two black leaders after they ignored warnings to stay out of politics. The following year the white elite of Jefferson organized the White Citizens' primary with the hope that they could remove blacks from the political process and put the more-sordid tricks of maintaining political power behind them.[6]

The White Citizens' primary in Marion County was an elimination election intended to end the effective political participation of the county's black majority. William Clark, who chaired the initial meeting of the White Citizens, insisted that Marion County be "lifted from the low plain to which she has fallen morally, by reason of the unholy, immoral, disgusting and degrading influences and conditions that face and surround every campaign that has been conducted within her borders for the last ten or fifteen years." Clark went on to claim that unless political offices went to the right type of candidate, Jefferson and Marion County "will never bear the marks of prosperity."[7] In theory the Citizens' primary, like prohibition, would uplift morals and bring greater prosperity by allowing local government to function better.[8]

Open to white Republicans and Populists as well as white Democrats, the Citizens' primary narrowed the field of candidates for local office to one. That candidate ran unopposed in the county Democratic primary, which nominated candidates for local offices after 1898. In most local races the nominee also wound up without opposition in the November general election. The Citizens' primary and the Democratic primary both excluded blacks, and whites used force to block any attempt by local blacks to meet and select an opposing candidate for the general election. By offering local white Republicans offices under the new system, the White Citizens in effect bought off those who might have protested their own exclusion from a chance to win offices as Republican candidates. As a result, when blacks voted in the general elections, they had only one choice for local offices, the nominee of the White Citizens' primary.[9]

Some whites as well as blacks lost political power because of the White Citizens' primary, an institution that continued to operate into the 1940s. As George T. Todd, a local lawyer and Populist candidate for the Texas Court of Criminal Appeals in 1900, reminded readers of the *Jefferson Jimplecute:* "Where a citizens' non party county ticket has been agreed on, as had been done in Marion County, the 'powers that be' have arrogated the right to style such ticket 'Democratic' and only print it on the Democratic ticket. Republican, Prohibitionist, and Populist voters will have to write names or not vote for county officers, or be forced to vote the Democratic ticket which is also fastened on top of the bunch of tickets." In other words voting for local officials on the Democratic ticket encouraged voting for all Democrats. The system made it difficult and, for some, probably meaningless to vote for the Republican or third party candidates for national or statewide office. Marion's voter turnout in the 1898 general election declined from the 1896 level by 1,200 votes, roughly 60 percent. Through 1930, voter turnout in the Democratic primary and general election in Marion remained quite low, since more than in any other Northeast Texas county, the selection of candidates remained in the hands of what the local newspaper described as "our best white men."[10]

Without black votes, conservatives, insurgents, and Republicans had no chance of controlling Marion County. Instead, the White Citizens' primary left the self-described "respectable citizens" centered in the town of Jefferson in control of county politics. These citizens—the lawyers, judges, editors, prosperous farmers, and merchants of the community— matched a profile typical of early-twentieth-century white progressives. Rural white voters, on the other hand, now unable to make a difference

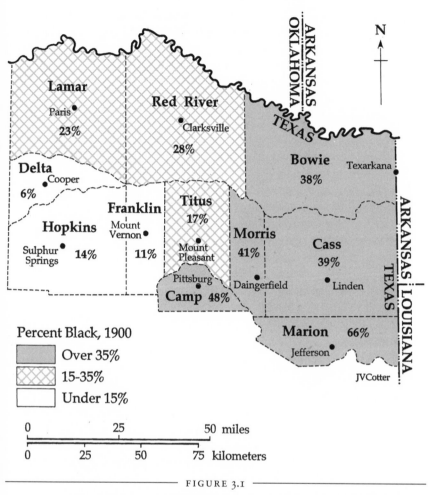

FIGURE 3.1

Blacks as percentage of total population in 1900. May by John V. Cotter.

in local elections simply stopped voting in the Democratic primary and the November general election.[11]

As Figure 3.1 demonstrates, all other Northeast Texas counties had a white majority by 1900 and stronger Democratic organizations than Marion County. They did not need to impose a White Citizens' primary, but most counties used a party primary system to "clean up" politics and reduce the vote and influence of blacks and dissident whites.

By 1898 all eleven counties in the region held Democratic primaries with each county's party organization, sometimes acting on the advice of the state party apparatus, determining who could vote. This often provoked controversy. In 1894 during Camp's first primary, the county Democratic executive committee banned those who did not vote Democratic in the last general election. Many Democrats argued that this alienated conservatives, Republicans, and Populists and handicapped local Democratic candidates who could never carry a general election without support from members of these groups. As F. A. Lockhart, once again a candidate for county judge, put it, Democrats "will be dependent on voters for election who are excluded from the primaries." Lockhart wanted future action—a promise to support the party nominee in the general election—not past behavior to determine who voted in the Democratic primary.[12]

Controversy over who could vote in the Democratic primary resurfaced in 1898. Eventually the Democratic executive committee, headed by E. A. King, moved toward Lockhart's position, but they also specifically excluded blacks. They required that each voter pledge: "I am a white Democrat and agree to vote for the nominee of the Democratic party." White Populists and Gold Democrats could return to the Democratic fold, but blacks lost any chance to influence party nominees. Two years later the county Democratic executive committee required that all voters in the primary swear: "I am a white Democrat. I voted for Sayers for governor at the last general election. I will support the nominees of this primary." This test oath eliminated white Populists and Republicans who had not voted for the Democratic candidate for governor in 1898 and blacks. In 1902 the county executive committee returned to the test oath used in 1898.[13]

Alternating requirements to vote in the Democratic primary may have served as a carrot and stick to attract Populists back to the Democrats. They could either help select the local candidate with the best chance of victory or be edged out of the political process. Easing voting requirements for whites also followed presidential elections. Perhaps Democratic leaders realized that Populists and white Republicans were more likely to vote for their party in presidential election years. Variations in the test oath also reflected the ongoing division between supporters of J. S. Hogg and George Clark. In 1894 an oath requiring primary voters to have voted for the previous Democratic candidate for governor limited the influence of conservatives in the local primary. The tables turned after 1898 when most conservatives again voted Democratic. Reform Democrats then wanted white Populists back in the party because they needed them to win elections and pass legislation, including the poll tax amendment of 1902.[14]

Ironically, local manipulation of the test oath and other aspects of the county primary alienated and gave coherence to the insurgent group but also pointed the way to a rapprochement between white insurgents and reformers within the Democratic party. Once that occurred, party primaries differed from the nonparty primary of Marion County in that they better allowed competition between groups of voters divided by class, partisan history, and adherence to particular leaders.

Congressional elections offered good examples of how the evolving process both gave Populists a cause to remember and a pragmatic reason to rejoin the Democratic party. Comparing presidential, gubernatorial, and congressional elections in 1896 suggested that about 5 percent of the electorate moved or was moved into the Democratic column from 1894. This gave Democratic congressional candidates a safe margin as long as a Republican candidate also ran. Of course, the results also suggested the ongoing possibility of fraud. In 1894 Cyclone Davis lost to Dave Culberson by about 1,000 votes. In 1896 Davis lost to John Cranford by 6,000 votes. A Republican candidate drew about 3,000 votes, almost all of them from Red River, Lamar, and Bowie counties. The surprising strength of the Republicans in counties with traditionally weak Republican organizations suggested that Democrats had hit upon the obvious. As long as a plurality of the vote instead of a majority determined the winner, in black minority counties Democrats gained offices by diverting the black vote from Populists to a third candidate. Democratic leaders could either alter the ballots or encourage a more vigorous campaign by local Republicans. These tactics offered less risk than blatantly adding to the Democratic vote tally because they gave national Republican leaders little reason to intervene in a process that yielded more Republican votes. While Populists long remembered such tricks, when they realized that Democrats could make a three-party system work to their advantage, there was much less reason to cling to the Populist party.[15]

Cranford was too ill to campaign for re-election, and John Sheppard secured the Democratic nomination for Congress in 1898. After J. L. Whittle of Sulphur Springs won the Populist nomination to oppose Sheppard, the editor of the *Texarkanian* wryly commented: "Yes, we can whittle his vote down to a scientific standpoint at the right time and have our Sheppard put him in the populist fold to keep the democratic wolves from getting him." Sheppard won the election by 7,000 votes, and turnout declined to its lowest level since 1890. Precinct-level vote totals for the Democrats roughly matched the vote totals for Bryan on the Democratic ticket in 1896, indicating that hard-core Democrats turned out. White Populists—especially in rural areas—stopped voting. Perhaps rural

FIGURE 3.2

*James H. "Cyclone" Davis, shown here as he looked in the mid-1890s. Davis
engaged in a long-running campaign for a seat in the U.S. Congress. After losing as
a Populist in 1894 and in 1896, he won an at-large seat as a Democrat in 1912.
He ran again in 1922 and helped Wright Patman win election in 1928.*
Photograph courtesy of Prints and Photographs Collection, Center for American History,
University of Texas at Austin. CN 03435.

voters, realizing that Democrats would indeed whittle down their vote by any means necessary, boycotted the election.[16]

When Sheppard ran for re-election in 1900, he faced both a Populist and a Republican challenger. Due to the presidential election and a three-way race for governor, voter turnout went back up—especially in black Republican precincts. Clearly, competitive elections featuring viable candidates influenced turnout as much as the written or unwritten rules of the game.[17]

Democratic reliance upon fraud in competitive elections numbered high on the list of those unwritten rules—even as late as 1900. In Marion local election judges almost certainly added 800 or more votes to the county total for Joseph D. Sayers, explaining why the incumbent governor outdrew every other Democrat in the region. In Camp fraud apparently aided Sheppard's quest for another term in Congress, because while President McKinley carried the county by 19 votes, Sheppard won by 146 and outpolled all other Democrats. Sheppard lived in Pittsburg for many years, which may explain his larger vote total in Camp. Nonetheless, voters still typically voted along party lines. Democrats controlled the vote-counting process in Pittsburg, and as in past cases of fraud, the increase in the Democratic vote and decrease in Populist and Republican vote came almost entirely from the two Pittsburg boxes. Despite blasts at campaign fraud by F. A. Lockhart and his son R. B. "Burt" Lockhart, who had joined his father in the management of the local newspaper, election officials in Pittsburg probably added a few votes to the Democratic column and subtracted some from the Populists and Republicans to give the Democrats a more substantial victory in the race for Congress.[18]

Given repeated defeats, local primaries, and blatant fraud, drawing any votes in 1900 demonstrated remarkable loyalty to Populism and Republicanism and a determination to keep voting no matter what. As Figure 3.3 indicates, the total vote in 1900 remained about the same as in 1892. Because the population kept growing—there were about 10,000 more males twenty-one and older in 1900 than in 1890—a smaller percentage of eligible voters turned out. Yet the dismally low voter turnout that characterized most general elections in twentieth-century Texas still lay ahead. One reason was that in a few counties Republicans and Populists still won local offices. In Camp they controlled one of five voting precincts, and Democrats consistently won only the two large Pittsburg precincts. This meant at least one Republican, often evidently drawing Populist votes, served on the County Commissioners Court through 1906. As late as 1898 C. T. Phillips, a white Populist, represented Camp and Upshur counties in the

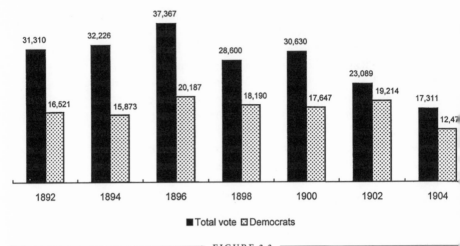

FIGURE 3.3

Turnout for congressional elections, First District, 1892–1904.
Source: Election Returns: 1892–1904: Secretary of State.

Texas House of Representatives. As a Hopkins County Populist office-holder told party activists during the lead-up to the 1900 election, you "have some life in you yet."[19]

Such life evaporated after the election of 1900. Remaining Populists realized that turnout would never return to the levels of 1896, and that if it ever came close, Democrats would simply steal the election. Since they could never win as an independent party, even deeply committed Populists like James W. Biard of Lamar County moved toward accepting a merger with socialists. Others, usually better-off Populists who loosely fit into the category of economic reformer, returned to the Democratic party. As one local newspaper put it, "Texas is hopelessly Democratic." Such a message proved difficult to swallow, and some white Populists temporarily abandoned politics. Yet they did not leave for good, and they did not forget and forgive Democrats. As the editor of the *Hopkins County Echo* explained in 1902, even when former Populists returned to the Democratic party, they came "with a club, instead of lowly and contrite of hearts."[20]

For Democrats, especially reformers still loosely clustered under Jim Hogg's leadership, the election of 1900 carried a different message. Conservatives, after their crushing defeat by Hogg in 1892, slowly rebuilt their influence within the Democratic party. Governor Charles Culberson depended upon conservative voters for survival in his campaign against the Populists, and his replacement, Joseph Sayers, moved further toward the conservative position. Sayers did not fall completely in the conservative camp, but the trend toward conservatism disturbed reformers. Looking around for political allies, they turned to moderate Populists who in 1892 had supported Hogg or had only reluctantly left the Democratic party. Hogg even took a more active interest in politics after 1900 and helped lure back Populists. For these reformers the crucial stumbling block remained the black vote. They knew full well that conservatives could attract black voters and that blacks remained opposed to prohibition.[21]

Black voters faced the hardest lesson of all. In the 1890s they moved from party to party seeking greater influence and supporting issues that mattered to them. They suffered fraud, intimidation, and assassination. After 1897 they also suffered exclusion from politics in Marion County, the center of black political influence in the region. Politics promised many risks and few rewards. Little wonder that leading black politicians like John B. Rayner refused to campaign in Northeast Texas in 1900 and largely withdrew from politics. The ordinary black voter, faced with the threat of violence, abandoned by white Populists, white Republicans, and conservatives, and left without a viable statewide organization, followed Rayner's exodus from an active political life.[22]

In 1902 the congressional election reflected the lessons of 1900. Voter turnout in Northeast Texas sank below the level of 1888, but Morris Sheppard, the Democratic candidate, polled 2,000 more votes than his deceased father did in 1900. Republican and Populist organizations collapsed, with Sheppard carrying every county in the district. Sheppard even won in Delta, a county carried by Populist candidates for Congress in every election since 1892. When James Biard and the few remaining committed Populists in Lamar and Delta counties could not persuade speakers to tour the district and could not field a full slate of candidates, they considered completely disbanding the party.[23]

Precisely gauging the movement of voters from party to party and in and out of the electoral process remains difficult. As Figure 3.3 indicates, turnout fell in 1898 and in subsequent elections from the high levels of 1894 and 1896. The Democratic vote also declined from 1896, but through 1902 remained far above the 1894 total. In fact, in 1902 the Democratic total almost matched that of 1896. This constancy in the Democratic vote perhaps reflected the influence of new voters in the region's growing towns and cities. Yet fraud, which peaked in the 1896 elections, elevated that year's Democratic vote. White Populists returned to their former party or the Democratic total in the general election would have declined further. Some blacks also voted Democratic in 1894 and 1896, but after the arrival of the white primary in every county in 1898, blacks had no reason to vote for Democrats in general elections. Again the relative stability of Democratic totals in 1902 suggested that some white former Populists moved back into the Democratic column to fill the slots vacated by black voters.[24]

While we cannot know for sure, those with modest wealth and a moderate interest in social reform probably first returned to the Democratic party. They likely leaned toward prohibition and had enough property and status to need to influence local elections. Once blacks could not vote in meaningful elections or when conservatives allied with black voters, such white Populists had little choice but to re-create the coalition that elected Hogg in 1890 and rejoin fellow reformers. Besides, improving economic conditions after 1897 made economic reform seem less urgent, and by 1902 only a small ideological distance separated these Populist reformers from Hogg Democrats on most issues, though partisan scars still rankled. When a new man untouched by past wars, like Morris Sheppard, appeared on the scene, they gave him their votes, while in many cases splitting their ticket by refusing to vote for a more conservative Democratic candidate for governor. Morris Sheppard's prominent and articulate support of prohibition made this all the easier. Prohibitionists, such as E. L. Dohoney or Cyclone Davis, could join reform Democrats and influence candidates and legislation, or they could fume on the sidelines.[25]

This movement of some white Populists back to the Democratic party, the diminished ability or willingness of blacks to vote, and the collapse of the Populist coalition came at a critical time. In the 1902 general election Texas voters approved a poll tax that more than any other feature of the new order limited the political participation of poor whites and blacks. Historians traditionally argued that the poll tax, which equaled a significant percentage of the yearly earnings of the poor of both races, only confirmed what was obvious in 1900. Black voting was waning and poor whites had little chance of exercising real political power outside the Democratic party.[26]

Rejecting the concept of the poll tax as simply underscoring what already existed, one historian argued that long-time proponents of the poll tax remained convinced that blacks and poor whites still posed enough of a threat to justify limiting the suffrage. Opponents of the poll tax, often centered in the Populist party or portions of the Democratic party that leaned toward Populism, such as the Grange, previously had blocked the poll tax as an undemocratic restriction on voting. Taking advantage of the post-1900 political doldrums, however, advocates of the poll tax pushed the amendment through the state legislature and secured its passage among the electorate. Political opportunism, not a systematic "reform program" or a "frantic racist upsurge," explained passage of the poll tax.[27]

Instead of resulting from political doldrums, another historian argued, the poll tax's passage was intimately connected to the movement of white Populists back into the Democratic party. A reinvigorated group of Hogg supporters in the Democratic party realized that they needed Populist votes and reached out to them by making the vote ostensibly fairer by having the poll tax serve as a form of voter registration. Populists still resentful of the alleged role blacks played in their defeat and wary of the possible continued manipulation of the black vote, applauded a tax set at a high enough rate to discourage black voters.[28]

Focusing on Northeast Texas suggests each argument has some merit. Voting by blacks and poor whites declined after 1896, but in 1900 remained high enough in several counties to pose a potential threat. Thus, incentive and opportunity existed for passage of the poll tax. Yet clearly Reform Democrats and Populists who had already returned to the Democratic party provided the muscle that gained passage of the poll tax. Cyclone Davis, for example, blamed blacks for past defeats. Not surprisingly, he, like other former Populists and most Reform Democrats, supported excluding them from politics.[29]

Yet focusing on Northeast Texas also adds to understanding of the passage of the poll tax by highlighting the importance of the strength of each faction within a county, local demographic characteristics, the significant level of fraud and intimidation, and the energizing force of reform issues such as prohibition. This does not belittle the impact of race and class prejudice, which remained constant or even increased above the level of the mid-1890s. Rather, the percentage of blacks in the local population, fraud, prohibition, and changes in factional alignments influenced expressions of prejudice and acted together to secure passage of the poll tax. While perhaps not a foregone conclusion by 1900, implementing the poll tax was part of the same process that created county Democratic primaries, deprived blacks of the right to vote in meaningful elections, undercut the power of all opposition groups, and built up the power of the Democratic party.

In particular, the gradual return of all reformers to the Democratic party allowed economic and social reformers to again act as one faction that sought change on a broad front. This reunited group abandoned the tacit agreement not to agitate for prohibition that cemented the mid-1890s alliance between Hogg Democrats and conservatives. Pointedly, antiprohibition organizations, usually funded and led by conservatives, understood the new political environment and opposed the poll tax.

Meanwhile, blacks and the rural white insurgent wing of the Populist party joined the antiprohibitionist organizations in stoutly opposing the poll tax and prohibition.[30]

Prohibition then, provided another piece of common ground between Reform Democrats and dry Populists, and it underscored the class- and race-based arguments for considering the poll tax a necessary reform. In prohibitionists' minds, blacks and poor whites demonstrated their ignorance or bestiality by voting against prohibition, and that supposed ignorance and bestiality justified removing them from the electoral process. For Cyclone Davis, who long supported prohibition and who blamed blacks for his repeated defeats, both prohibition and suffrage restriction provided ample reason to reunite with Hogg Democrats.[31]

The poll tax amendment's specific design reflected its link to prohibition and other so-called reforms. Cities and counties could support local schools by tacking on an extra tax on top of the state levy, and paying that tax was required for all local elections, including local-option elections. Thus, by serving as a form of voter registration, the poll tax made fraud in local-option elections more difficult. It also reduced the black and the rural poor white vote by putting a price tag on voting and requiring that all eligible voters come to the county seat to pay the tax in the month of January. The expense and the difficulty in paying the tax hit hardest at the groups most likely to oppose prohibition, and not surprisingly leading prohibitionists like Pat M. Neff led the charge for the poll tax in the state legislature. Pragmatism as well as ideology probably motivated men like Neff who realized that prohibition united the state's reformers far more than the desire to restrict the black vote. For Reform Democrats in areas of Texas with few blacks, the potential benefit to prohibition gave them reason to support what many had long opposed—a restriction on suffrage. In the minds of reformers, whether committed Democrats or former Populists, the poll tax achieved progressive ends—better schools, clean elections, and prohibition.[32]

Yet, in high-turnout elections such as those from 1887 to 1896, reformers never gained more than 45 percent of the vote. Reformers even when reunited could not win without help from another faction or without reducing the turnout of the opposing side. In 1902 all the other factions stood against them on the poll tax. Conservatives understood that the poll tax made rounding up black and poor white votes against prohibition more difficult. Blacks and white insurgents realized that the poll tax meant disenfranchisement for many of their number and a drastic loss of power for their factions. While discouraged and disillusioned with politics, where any form of Republican or Populist organization remained, they turned out to vote. In these circumstances, instead of simply relying on the apathy and disorganization of their opponents, reformers used widespread fraud and intimidation to secure passage of the poll tax.[33]

Linkages between fraud, prohibition, and factional alignments came clear in Lamar County. After a decade of not voting on prohibition, Lamar's citizens voted on countywide prohibition in August 1902, three months before the vote on the poll tax. Prohibition lost by a count of 4,046 for and 4,562 against, and the total vote exceeded 1896 by 500, making it the largest vote recorded in the county to that time. That led to charges that conservatives imported black voters from across county lines and justified the poll tax in the minds of prohibitionists. Beyond demonstrating the link between prohibition and the poll tax, the vote pointed to the reality that factionalism persisted and reformers could not win high-turnout elections. Blacks still influenced the outcome of elections, particularly when white conservatives sought their vote as they did in all prohibition elections. Rural insurgents also still opposed prohibition, and they still voted. Low turnout in November 1902 did not necessarily reflect simply a loss of interest in politics. Tellingly, only 4,000 people voted in the November general election and almost 80 percent favored the poll tax. Apathy alone could not have caused such a decline in turnout in three months. We cannot label blacks and poor whites disinterested when almost certainly they were cheated and intimidated by those who zealously pursued a wide-ranging reform agenda centered on prohibition.[34]

Two years after passage of the poll tax in an election that saw only 5,000 people cast ballots—3,000 fewer than in August 1902—drys finally won in Lamar County. After decades of limited headway, between 1904 and 1911 the entire district went dry through local option.[35]

Lamar's neighbor, Delta County, served notice, however, that support for prohibition did not automatically translate into support for the poll tax and incentive for fraud. Instead, demographic and factional characteristics determined the election's outcome. Delta's voters narrowly supported prohibition in 1887 and overwhelmingly opposed the poll tax in 1902. Significantly, turnout remained high in Delta, a county with few blacks and one of the strongest Populist organizations in the state. Supporters of the poll tax could not easily demonize blacks in an almost all-white county, nor could they easily suppress or alter the white rural vote where Populist's had won most elections through 1898.[36]

Pittsburg demonstrated what happened when the opposite conditions prevailed—a significant black population and weak Republican or Populist organizations. In 1900 blacks still made up over 45 percent of Camp County's population. Despite this, after 1892 neither Populists nor Republicans exhibited much strength in Pittsburg, but they did control one or two rural voting boxes. Reflecting the dominance of Reform Democrats, in June 1902, F. A. Lockhart complained: "It doesn't seem to be generally known—at least no one ever mentions it—that the people of the State of Texas will vote on a very important constitutional amendment next November. The amendment provides that each voter be required to show his poll tax receipt before being allowed to vote and the proposition is worthy of considerable notice and should be properly discussed." By 1902 organized opposition to the Reform Democratic position no longer existed in Pittsburg, and the poll tax won by a huge margin in an election with relatively low turnout. Lockhart, however, missed what was going on in the rural precincts. Here voter turnout remained high and the poll tax lost.[37]

Districtwide, turnout declined more than 30 percent from 1900 to 1902, and it dropped the most in counties where Hogg received over 45 percent of the vote in 1892, suggesting that the relative strength of the various political factions offered the most consistent clue to the success of the poll tax. Next to Marion, where Hogg Democrats probably once again suppressed or altered the black vote, turnout declined the most in Franklin County. In Franklin, an almost all-white county, Populists never achieved much success, and Democrats' paternalistic reforms and lack of scruples about how they maintained control of the elections both angered and alienated white insurgents. Unlike more-moderate Populists who supported prohibition and came back to the Democratic party rather than abandon hope of influencing politics, insurgents in counties completely dominated by Reform Democrats were either counted out or sat out an election they knew they could not win.[38]

Just how factional alignments influenced Populist voting patterns came a bit clearer in Morris County. Populists carried Omaha, a white-dominated precinct, in every election between 1892 and 1898, and Republicans only got votes for president in 1896. Significantly, the total vote in 1902 almost matched the total vote in 1894, and by a slim margin the poll tax lost. Former Populists in Omaha, some of whom had moved back into the Democratic party as early as 1898, retained a chance to control one of the seats on the County Commissioners' Court, but they needed every vote they could muster. They had less reason to be alienated from the political process and more reason to vote against a poll tax that would cut into their voter pool among poorer whites. Besides, in Omaha long-standing opposition to prohibition bound the insurgent faction together and provided another strong reason to oppose the poll tax. Elsewhere in Morris

County, Hogg Democrats or Republicans typically won elections before 1902. In these precincts turnout plummeted and the poll tax won by an impressive margin. Fraud, not apathy or alienation, probably most often explained declining turnout in areas dominated by Reform Democrats or in which whites believed they needed to suppress the black vote.[39]

In fact, in a sense, apathy hardly applied to the poll tax election. Those who voted in the November 1902 general election displayed unusual interest in the poll tax amendment. Often voters in a general election ignored the constitutional amendments because they lacked understanding or interest, but no such signs of apathy surfaced in this case. In most of the district's eleven counties, vote totals in the poll tax election closely matched those of the contested races for Congress and for governor. Marion was one of only two counties where the poll tax vote lagged far behind the congressional and gubernatorial races. Here the decline came almost entirely from Republican voters, and as already suggested, fraud probably explained the anomaly. If blacks bothered to vote in the general election, it seems unlikely that the political process alienated them to the point of not caring about the poll tax. In Red River, the other county where far fewer voters participated in the poll tax election than the congressional and gubernatorial elections, the decline came from Democratic voters. Reform Democrats, again in charge of counting the ballots, may have thrown away votes from white former Populists who opposed the poll tax.[40]

Repeatedly, fraud intertwined with a county or precinct's racial characteristics, factional history, and attitude toward prohibition to explain the outcome of the poll tax election. Statewide, the poll tax passed by about the same two-to-one margin as in Northeast Texas, hinting that these factors played a role elsewhere. Reform Democrats and even a few Populists proclaimed the many advantages of the poll tax and expressed great hope for the dawn of a new political era. A new political era indeed emerged, although blacks and poor whites whose rights and opportunities eroded with their lost ability to vote did not agree about its bright promise.[41]

On the surface Northeast Texas just after the turn of the century resembled North Carolina, where Populists briefly gained control of state government only to lose out to conservatives, or Mississippi, where racial demagoguery became a political staple.[42] Yet the emergence between 1903 and 1907 of an all-white Democratic primary held on the same day and in the same way throughout the state allowed a return to elections characterized by three or more viable candidates. In this environment, conservatives stood little chance of winning, and especially when social and economic reformers split and charismatic leaders captured their attention, white insurgents returned to politics.

PRIMARIES AND PARTIES, 1903–1907

Passage of the poll tax did not end attempts to purify the political process. Many agreed with Burt Lockhart, who besides assuming an increasingly important role with his family's newspaper served as the secretary of the Camp County Democratic executive committee. In 1904 he commented: "The kind of politics that some counties keep on tap would sicken a skunk. It is a pity that decent people have to be brought in contact with it." [43]

In 1903 these "decent people," many of whom probably condoned fraud the year before, pressured the state legislature into establishing a uniform statewide primary system to replace nominating candidates by conventions or by county primaries held on varying days. This uniform primary system grew from earlier experiments with county primaries where its backers had observed that clever politicians achieved the aura of invincibility by winning a few early primaries and then maneuvered their opponents out of the contest before voters made a choice. The original law allowed a primary for any party that drew over 10,000 votes in the previous general election. After much debate, framers of the law left defining voter eligibility to the county executive committee of the party holding the primary. The state Democratic executive committee quickly recommended that only "white Democrats" be allowed to participate and defined white as "all races except negroes." In Northeast Texas this meant a continuation of the practice of excluding all black voters from the Democratic primary and another round of debate about excluding voters who did not vote for the party in the last general election. Thus, like the poll tax, the uniform primary "cleaned up" politics by excluding black voters from meaningful political participation, but unlike the poll tax or some of the more-exclusionary county primaries, uniform primary laws never openly discriminated against poor whites. The state Democratic executive committee underscored this lack of a ban on poor whites when it failed to recommend that primary voters be required to have voted for a Democrat in the previous election. [44]

Called the Terrell Election Law after its chief sponsor, Alexander W. Terrell, the 1903 law ended the most blatant forms of election fraud. While clearly a racist and from the patrician class, Terrell supported Jim Hogg in the 1890s and, as a member of the Texas House of Representatives, authored the enabling legislation for the Texas Railroad Commission. When he returned to the Texas House in 1903, he still identified with the Hogg wing of the Democratic party. Like other Hogg Democrats, Terrell had no pragmatic reason to exclude white voters not already excluded by the poll tax. Instead, he reached out to former Populists by meeting a cherished Populist demand for a secret ballot in all parts of the state. His law stipulated the sole use of official white ballots handed to each voter by election officials and outlawed prepared ballots distributed to voters in advance. The law defined election precincts and required election judges to oversee a fair balloting and counting process. For the first time, violators of election laws faced large fines and imprisonment.[45]

Initially, the more-complicated and more-regulated system provoked criticism. The editors of the *Pittsburg Gazette* captured the feelings of many in the spring of 1904 when they reported that the "Terrell election law is all right in a few respects and all wrong in a great many. It is suffering from too much legislative attention." The law seemed too detailed and likely to reduce voter participation. After the initial primary, the editors of the *Gazette* were a bit more sanguine and reported: "The election was very quietly conducted, and the new manner of holding elections was favorably commented upon by hundreds of voters, many of whom had been strong opposers of the new law. With the new law revised and simplified and discrepancies eliminated it will be all right." Not everyone reacted as charitably. After looking over the statewide turnout in that year's general election, the editor of the *Jefferson Jimplecute* labeled the Terrell law a "vote killer." The irony of such criticism in a county where whites literally killed black voters evidently escaped the editor.[46]

Greater familiarity with the new procedures and extensive revisions in 1905, however, quieted opposition, eased the difficulty in voting, and further opened the doors to former Populists to participate in the Democratic primary. The 1905 revisions of the Terrell law still simply allowed a primary for any party that drew over 10,000 votes in the previous general election but made a primary mandatory for any party that drew over 100,000 votes. The new law also clarified voting procedures, and these clarifications discouraged overzealous election judges from turning away white voters in the Democratic primary. Most important, while requiring a poll tax receipt for voting in a primary, the revised law did not require payment of all past poll taxes. This enabled poor whites to vote when their economic conditions improved slightly or when the candidates and issues motivated them to vote. Besides clarifying procedures in ways that favored reformers, the second Terrell law fixed the date for the primary as the fourth Saturday in July, the optimum time for participation by farmers. By then the grain harvest had ended, and the cotton crop required little attention.[47]

During the 1907 legislative session, reformers continued what they began in 1905. The legislature banned corporations from contributing to the victory or defeat of candidates, attempted to restrict the participation of antiprohibition organizations, and enacted a uniform test oath for participants. The first new provision fit nicely with other reforms aimed at limiting and regulating the role of large corporations in Texas. The second demonstrated the power of prohibitionists, while the third further strengthened the Democratic party. For Democrats the test oath read, "I am a Democrat and pledge myself to support the nominee of this primary." Those who supported making future, not past, behavior the test of a true Democrat won a permanent victory, and one more hurdle went down for ex-Populists who wished to rejoin the Democratic party. This encouraged voting in the Democratic primary, but it also discouraged support of any rival political party in the general election. Post-1903 changes in the election laws reflected continued close ties to other reform movements, ensured that more white males could vote, and made the Democratic primary the key election.[48]

Members of the state legislature from Northeast Texas expressed some initial skepticism about election reform but by 1907 generally backed the new laws. From 1903 to 1907 the eleven-county region comprised all or part of four Texas Senate districts and ten Texas House of Representatives districts. In 1903 one senator and two members of the House opposed the Terrell law, and five members of the House did not vote on final passage of the bill. In 1905 only one of the fourteen Northeast Texas legislators returned to the legislature. This time two senators and only one member of the House voted against the revised election law. An almost unanimous group of Northeast Texans supported the 1907 modifications. No clear pattern emerged except that senators and representatives from Lamar, a county with a large urban area and a strong Democratic organization, voted for all the new laws, and after the almost complete turnover in officeholding between 1903 and 1905, support for electoral reform increased.[49]

In some ways, the new primary laws and the poll tax only accelerated the trends evident in 1900. Reform Democrats eviscerated their rivals and in the process undermined the importance of the general election. After 1903, participation in the general election plummeted, but, as more former Populists returned to the party, the total vote in the Democratic primary moved above the figure received by Democrats in the general elections of the mid-1890s. As the Democratic party grew and opposition parties vanished, however, a new trend emerged. The Democratic party became even more multifactional than in the early 1890s.

In 1904, the first year in which the poll tax and the uniform primary system both influenced voting, Morris Sheppard received over 23,000 votes in the First Congressional District's Democratic primary. That figure exceeded the total for the 1902 poll tax election and exceeded the eleven-county total received by any Democratic candidate in a general election between 1888 and 1902. Fraud seems unlikely in an election in which Sheppard ran unopposed. Instead, the continued return of white former Populists and Sheppard's reform image boosted the total vote in the Democratic primary. Since blacks voted in the 1902 general election, more whites actually voted in the 1904 primary than in 1902, indicating that Sheppard proved an ideal leader who drew economic and social reformers together regardless of their partisan history. As evidence of his appeal, the Lockhart family and Cyclone Davis lined up behind him. Lackluster candidates for president and the clear realization that the winners of all state and local contests had been determined in the primary contributed to a sharp decline in participation in that year's general election. Yet that decline did not signal the abandonment of politics or even a shrinking of the white electorate below 1902 levels. In fact, turnout in the primary held steady at about 23,000 through 1910.[50]

Turnout also benefited from the decline in the real value of the tax. In 1903, when the poll tax first went into effect, it cost voters in state and county elections $1.75. Many towns added on a $1.00 city poll tax. Since voting in any election required payment of the entire tax, it cost town dwellers $2.75 to vote. At a time when many Texans earned less than $100 per year, this represented a significant amount. Judging from precinct-level returns, this tax, as probably intended, hit urban blacks hardest. In contrast, rural voters, including the large group of small-scale white farmers, paid only $1.75. Between 1902 and 1912, all types of income rose faster than inflation, and the value of money fell about 11 percent. Although $1.75 remained a significant sum for many, it came within the reach of more farmers. Because they were not required to pay past poll taxes, voters who had skipped previous elections could more easily afford to vote by 1912.[51]

Despite the limitations on voting by blacks and poor whites, by 1912 the relative inexpensiveness of the poll tax and the features of the election laws that encouraged white participation gave Texas among the least stringent suffrage laws in the early-twentieth-century South. The demands of a multifactional Democratic party in which reformers needed white Populists to defeat conservatives made it so.[52]

TURNOUT, FACTIONALISM, AND THE
DYNAMICS OF CHANGE, 1906–1912

In 1906 four viable candidates sought the gubernatorial nomination in the Democratic primary. The eventual nominee, Thomas M. Campbell, claimed the mantle of Jim Hogg, who died in 1905 shortly after formally endorsing Campbell. While a supporter of prohibition, like Hogg, Campbell downplayed that issue and stressed the need for economic reform. Oscar B. Colquitt, who founded the *Pittsburg Gazette,* also claimed a close identification with Hogg, but he forthrightly opposed statewide prohibition. In contrast, Micajah M. Brooks strongly supported statewide prohibition. Charles K. Bell, whose position on prohibition remained unclear and who was the most closely aligned with conservatives, rounded out the field. Statewide and in Northeast Texas, Campbell led the field and Bell finished last. Yet both statewide and in the district, Campbell failed to gain a majority because Brooks and Colquitt ran strong campaigns. Since state law did not yet require a runoff primary, the state convention nominated Campbell when supporters of Brooks and Colquitt switched to the leading reform candidate.[53]

Surprisingly, Colquitt did worse in Northeast Texas, where he lived for several years, than in the state at large. That suggested that factional strength, prohibition, and Hogg's endorsement played a significant role in this election. It also suggested that insurgents who should have been drawn to Colquitt's blend of antiprohibition and economic reform did not vote in the numbers they once did and would do again by 1912.[54]

Campbell, on the other hand, gained a plurality through the same type of coalition building and positioning between rival candidates that characterized Hogg's campaigns in the 1890s. Campbell began the campaign with a strong base of support among Hogg Democrats and then sought the vote of former Populists. Realizing he could not afford to alienate economic reformers who leaned toward prohibition or insurgents who leaned against it, Campbell allowed the extremes on the issue to go to Brooks and Colquitt but held the middle by labeling prohibition a nonissue. His coalition lacked blacks who voted for Hogg in 1892, but by stressing his economic liberalism, Campbell reached out to white insurgents and economic reformers with a Populist past. Cyclone Davis even described Campbell as "the nearest approach to old-time Populism that is now before the country." Unfortunately, he almost scuttled Campbell's attempts to walk a middle path by also touting Campbell's long-time advocacy of prohibition, but the power of Hogg's name and a few timely endorsements by antiprohibitionists overcame Davis's well-meaning but ill-conceived attempts to help.[55]

Given the many changes in the political structure, not surprisingly, 1906 did not follow the exact scenario of 1892. Campbell did best in the two counties with the highest concentration of blacks—Marion and Camp. These counties cast a significant vote for Clark in 1892, but this time Bell, the most conservative candidate, received almost no votes. The elimination of the black voter left the Hogg Democrats in almost complete control of these counties, and they delivered for Campbell. Campbell also did much better than Hogg had done in Delta and other Populist strongholds. Results in Hopkins indicated another change from 1892. Colquitt, Campbell, and Brooks each received about one-third of the vote. Prohibition dominated the campaign here, and the intense emotions aroused by that issue made it difficult for Campbell to walk a middle ground. Cyclone Davis's attempts to tie Campbell to prohibition probably grew from this reality in his home county, but as Campbell recognized, Davis's actions only drove the antiprohibitionists into the arms of Colquitt.[56]

By 1906 then, the political system differed from 1892 in several important ways. Blacks lost all ability to influence the selection of officeholders. Conservatives, because they could not form alliances with black voters, exercised far less power. Conservatives also lost power because of the increasing importance of prohibition. In the 1890s it remained possible to oppose prohibition in all forms and still win office. In 1906 even Colquitt repeatedly stressed his support of local option. Meanwhile, Bell suffered from his ambiguity on prohibition and his clear alliance with leading conservative antiprohibitionists. Perhaps of most importance, voters with a Populist past were led to work closely with Hogg Democrats, partly as the result of greater prosperity and partly because of the memory of what it had cost them to break from the Democrats.[57]

Close cooperation between former Populists and Hogg Democrats continued after the election when Campbell and one of the most reform-minded legislatures in the history of the state focused on business regulation, the insurance industry, prisons, and expansion of the state bureaucracy. Campbell proved highly popular and easily won re-election in 1908. Despite limited opposition, turnout in the 1908 primary still roughly equaled that of 1904 and 1906. In Delta County, where several tightly contested local elections heightened interest, the editor of the *Cooper Re-*

view characterized the returns as "a very heavy vote for the county." A larger, more multifactional Democratic party now controlled one of the last strongholds of Populism.[58]

This new Democratic party proved more dynamic than static. Factional alignments shifted within the party just as they shifted between parties in the 1890s, and competition between factions led to a constant search for new voters. As long as no single faction could control the party primary by itself, the system encouraged criticism and innovation— it contributed to the dynamics of change.

Criticism from within the new system usually came from former Populists. In the 1890s Populists controlled Linden and, as in most areas with a significant black population, voters favored the poll tax. By June 1908 the local editor regretted that decision: "We did think that the law requiring one to have a poll tax receipt before one could vote was a good thing, but maybe we were mistaken." He went on to comment on the sharp drop in voting in the general election and the link between liberty and voting. For John Banger, "One's liberties are wrapped up in one's ballot. It is the only means he has of protecting his liberty." Banger even seemed willing to accept an increase in black voting. That sentiment came too late, but the more-moderate stance on race of some Hogg Democrats and former Populists, and their importance in the dominant political coalition, may have discouraged racial demagoguery in Texas.[59]

Race always played a role in Texas politics, just as it did in every other southern state. Defense of white supremacy justified in the minds of conservatives and Reform Democrats the bloody and fraudulent campaign they waged against the Populists in the 1890s. For reformers, good government and prohibition justified the exclusion of black voters through the poll tax and the white primary. Lynchings and assassinations of blacks by whites in the 1890s sometimes had a political motivation. Yet Texas, Northeast Texas included, produced no race baiters of the stripe of Ben Tillman of South Carolina or Theodore Bilbo of Mississippi.[60]

Instead, many Northeast Texans seemed to share the opinion of W. C. Williams, the editor of the *Omaha Breeze*. In a paternalistic way Williams deplored the wholesale application of lynch law. Occasionally "an indolent, thieving negro or a vagrant" might deserve "a good, sound drubbing." Still, the entire race should not suffer for the sins of the few, and the established legal system should usually determine guilt or innocence. This did not mean blacks could forget their place. He recounted with glee: "The other day, in Kansas City, an insolent or uninformed negro man saluted a Texas raised lady restaurant keeper, 'Howdy, honey!' But he didn't get to finish his sentence before she was pumping lead at him."[61]

Whites feared that as the older generation died, so died the black work ethic and proper deference. In 1904 the equally paternalistic editors of the *Pittsburg Gazette* captured white fears of a new generation: "An old-time negro died at Pottsboro a few days ago and he was so well thought of that the citizens bought a nice casket, had his body embalmed and furnished a hearse to convey his remains to the cemetery. There are still some before-the-war negroes in the land and as a rule they are highly respected by the white people, but a large number of the sort that is growing up now hang around the street and do nothing but shoot craps, drink mean whiskey and make themselves generally obnoxious." These racist images helped convince reformers of the necessity of excluding blacks from politics and controlling their behavior through prohibition and vagrancy laws.[62]

Again John Banger disagreed. In 1909 he insisted election laws did little to defend white supremacy: "It is useless to bring in that old gag, 'Negro domination.' Negroes as a general rule, don't want to dominate, and they know if they tried it the horrors of the sixties would return upon them." As he saw it, politicians simply used race to maintain their power. He summed up by saying: "The primaries, manipulated as they are by artful, selfish and corrupt politicians are the final straw that destroys individual interest and not only clogs the wheels of progress, but insures political regression."[63]

Former Populists like Banger voted for the poll tax in 1902 but that did not mean they gave up on the idea that blacks deserved some limited role in politics and a chance at a happier, more-prosperous life. The continuity in positions of influence of people like Banger suggests why Texas had no Bilbo even in a region with a high percentage of blacks and numerous lynchings. Because progressives needed the insurgent vote, even on matters of race, as one historian observed, the continued Populist presence in Texas forced Democrats "to move to the left." At a minimum reformers and insurgents agreed that the worst forms of race baiting and lynching were evil and must be ended.[64]

This post-1906 political system even provided limited opportunities for black agency or, at least, opportunities for blacks to express dissatisfaction. In 1911 conservatives sought out the vote of blacks in the statewide prohibition referendum, and thanks to these efforts, in Marion County about twice as many voters turned out as in any election since 1900. Prohibition lost in Marion, and it almost lost in the other counties with a large black minority population. Instead of regarding this vote as an example of conservatives buying black votes, as prohibitionists charged, it seems more likely that blacks seized the opportunity to protest a system that largely excluded them. Even so, the new system had done its work. Across Northeast Texas, in 1911 fewer voters turned out than in the 1900 general election or even in the 1887 statewide prohibition referendum, and turnout declined most sharply in counties and precincts with a significant black population.[65]

While the excitement of the 1911 prohibition referendum failed to restore turnout to pre-1902 levels, the election brought whites as well as blacks back into the political process. Once back in, whites continued voting. It seemed a repeat of the post-1887 years when newly energized white insurgents also continued participating in politics. Yet after 1911, white insurgents remained in the Democratic party. They stayed because primaries and the poll tax made creation of a rival party difficult, but they also stayed because they found common ground with economic reformers. John Banger's dislike for the primary system did not stop him from agreeing with the progressive editors of the *Paris News* who argued in 1904 "that the professional politician has done Texas more harm than the boll weevil." Conservatives, who held to the traditional view of limited government, controlled many professional politicians such as Senator Joseph W. Bailey. Reformers understood that without compromise and cooperation, these conservatives and their politicians would retain a disproportionate share of political power. Thus to achieve economic reform, insurgents, better-off Populists like Cyclone Davis, and Hogg Democrats struck a moderate note on race and eased voting requirements for whites. Besides, the more whites that voted, the more likely their candidates would win.[66]

Compromise remained necessary because social reformers, economic reformers, and insurgents each retained some factional cohesion. Familiar leadership and old animosities toward Democrats, in part, kept the insurgent bloc from assimilating fully into the reform faction. As late as November 1909, John Banger expressed a high level of skepticism for the two established political parties. He argued, "Yes—we have two parties, divided principally on geographical lines, and it would take one with a powerful magnifying glass to find any real difference between them, except on some impractical side issues and they know it."[67]

Attitudes, ideas, even animosities, seldom last long without an organization to focus and maintain them. In the critical time between the passage of the poll tax and the 1911 prohibition referendum, the Farmers' Union, or as it was more formally known the Farmers' Educational and Cooperative Union, provided this institutional base in Northeast Texas. Founded in 1902 in Rains County, the Farmers' Union soon spread into neighboring Hopkins and from there into every county in the First District. Newt Gresham, a newspaper editor and organizer of the Union, tried to keep politics out of his organization and used as his model the Texas Farmers' Alliance in the days before the emergence of the Populist party. Gresham hoped to resurrect the educational and cooperative functions of the Alliance without the partisanship. In keeping with this goal, initial members included Democrats, Populists, Socialists, and independents. Gresham, however, soon lost his leadership position, and the Union quickly took a role in politics in Texas and in Oklahoma. It helped elect Campbell in 1906, and it also did best in counties like Rains and Hopkins that had a strong Populist tradition. One reason for the rapid growth was that old Populist newspapers like the *Cumby Rustler* (Hopkins County) swiftly picked up the cause of the Farmers' Union. Membership passed 100,000 in 1905, and by 1906 it dwarfed the combined membership of the state's labor unions and commercial clubs.[68]

In many ways the Farmers' Union stood between labor unions and commercial clubs, the forerunners of the modern Chamber of Commerce. Leadership on the local level remained in the hands of landowning farmers. They took the educational role of the Union very seriously, publishing in local newspapers detailed columns on the latest agricultural methods and equipment and promoting local farmers' institutes and short courses on progressive farming. These landowning farmers also promoted the marketing of cotton by building Union Warehouses for the storage of cotton at rail centers. As discussed in the previous chapter, these warehouses appealed to town builders because they encouraged farmers to do business where they kept their cotton and offered a convenient place to store fruit and vegetables bound for urban markets. Thus, the warehouses aided the constant calls for crop diversification that came from newspaper editors, commercial clubs, and boards of trade. Local bankers and cotton merchants also backed the educational programs that made farming more productive and prosperous. More cotton and other crops, raised more efficiently, put more money into circulation locally.[69]

When farmers used the Union Warehouses to help them keep cotton off the market, however, it sometimes put them at odds with merchants whose profit came from moving the crop. Co-operative ventures into building telephone companies also brought farmers into competition with businessmen. Advocacy of tax policies that shifted the burden from farmers to corporations and business again placed them at odds with some Reform Democrats. The Farmers' Union also pushed for the enactment of many traditional Populist proposals. The Union supported limited government ownership of public utilities and increased government control over railroads. Small postal savings banks and free rural mail delivery were other favored government initiatives.[70]

Despite the potential for argument between groups like the Farmers' Union and reform-minded businessmen, these groups usually managed to cooperate. Even newspapers like the *Pittsburg Gazette* generally applauded the aims of the Union and tried to help in their marketing efforts. All sides also remained committed to working within the Democratic party. J. C. Morton, a one-time Populist, edited the *Cumby Rustler* from its founding in 1892 through World War I. In 1912 he remarked, "Gradually but surely the old Populist platform is being torn up and the planks used in the construction of new structures." Those new structures were part of the Democratic party platform.[71]

It also helped that the Farmers' Union never appeared as radical as the Farmers' Alliance or the Populist party. Tenant farmers and sharecroppers never played a leadership role in the organization. Owners and managers, not labor, controlled the Farmers' Union and played the leading role in politics. Still, Union members had a distinctive, close-knit culture that separated them from the primarily town-dwelling reformers. They favored candidates who "had a way of stirring up things and raising sand when others wanted to enjoy a siesta and smoke a cigar in peace."[72]

Thus factions remained divided from each other, but they also remained within the Democratic party. That left them free to combine in a variety of ways. In 1912, for example, Oscar Colquitt, having succeeded Campbell as governor, stood for re-election. His long association with Jim Hogg, support for governmental attempts to stabilize cotton prices, successful advocacy of prison reform, and emphasis on education gave him some standing among both social and economic reformers. His continued opposition to statewide prohibition appealed to insurgents drawn back into the political process by the previous year's referendum. Despite his association with Hogg, conservative antiprohibitionists had little choice but to back Colquitt because his opponent, William F. Ramsey, stridently supported prohibition and based his entire campaign on that one issue. Even white Republicans apparently backed Colquitt in 1912 because they preferred him to Ramsey and knew their own party could not mount a serious challenge to any Democratic nominee.[73]

Despite backing statewide prohibition in 1911, in 1912 voters in the eleven-county district gave Colquitt a narrow victory in the Democratic primary. While not a brilliant orator, as most considered Morris Sheppard, Colquitt projected an energy and combativeness that rural voters admired. When Ramsey's supporters attempted to play the race card and charged that Colquitt won elections by offering concessions to blacks, he bluntly countered by pointing out that blacks did not vote in the Democratic primary. Anything that he did to aid black citizens, such as ending the most abusive forms of prison discipline, he did because it was the right thing to do and not to influence black voters. That direct, pugnacious style and his opposition to forcing all to conform to prohibition drew the largest turnout in rural precincts since the start of uniform primaries.[74]

By the conclusion of the 1912 primary, both the limitations and the possibilities of the new political order emerged. Blacks wielded far less political influence than in 1897, but poorer whites probably exercised more influence because of their ability to tilt primaries to one competing faction or the other. Reformers, especially advocates of moderate economic reform and less-controversial social reforms such as improving public education, stood the best chance of holding office. Conservatives continued to blunt all attempts to achieve statewide prohibition and, in the process, offered blacks a brief moment of political influence. The passion of prohibition and attachment to popular leaders like Colquitt or Campbell could still increase voter turnout despite the primary and poll tax. Instead of fostering a completely closed and inflexible system, the new, larger, and more multifactional Democratic party by 1912 discouraged the most virulent forms of racism, encouraged voting by white males, and in a few years would encourage the voting of white females. Even before 1912 the system allowed the legal and cultural changes needed to promote prosperity.

FOUR

"OLD IDEAS" AND "IMPROVED CONDITIONS"

Law, Custom, and Memory, 1902–1914

Between passage of the poll tax amendment in 1902 and the start of war in Europe in 1914, an improving economy convinced some Northeast Texans that for the first time in decades "the people here can be independent." Whenever that independence seemed threatened, Reform Democrats changed the law in hopes of maintaining prosperity. Other changes in the law raised hopes that not only would prosperity continue but that the people would "grow in intelligence and true citizenship."[1] Progress on all fronts seemed possible. In essence, the political system allowed the passage of new laws, and economic growth and a reform mentality made those laws appear necessary.

Yet not all agreed on these new laws, and by 1911 a growing percentage of Northeast Texans contested the changes in their customary ways of life. Isolated, rural, white Northeast Texans who often voted with the insurgent faction rejected prohibition, found the new reliance on higher education alien, and failed to profit from state banks and other new institutions. Their political counterattack slowed some reforms, but these critics agreed with reformers on the importance of an active government. This agreement allowed insurgent critics of the new order both to work with reformers and to accept limited change.

One significant roadblock barred this path toward governmental activism. Like other southerners, Northeast Texans eulogized the Confederate experience, and judging from monument building and attention to history books, fascination with the Confederacy peaked between 1902 and 1914. A society in transition and uncertain of its future clung tightly to its past, but it also began to turn that past loose. Talk of states' rights or limited government, concepts firmly grounded in memories of why the South fought, continued, and those concepts still gave coherence and meaning to the conservative faction. Yet calls for support based on memories of a southern past gradually lost their force. As the editor of the *Omaha Breeze* observed in 1912, "Old ideas are rapidly passing out and giving place to improved conditions." An improving economy and a competitive political system provided a fertile environment for change, but evolving memory, contested customs, and transforming laws formed a symbiotic relationship with that environment. They grew from and contributed to change.[2]

TRANSFORMING LAWS, 1902–1911

The unsaid instead of the said highlighted the striking legal changes of the new century. In the 1880s and 1890s conservatives loudly opposed attempts to reform the banking system. Skepticism greeted advocates of improved education for farmers and school children. Antiprohibitionists bitterly and stridently raged against prohibition. Between 1902 and 1911 banking laws changed greatly, but with little comment. State laws afforded more educational opportunities for farmers and school children, as education quietly helped separate the haves from the have-nots. Prohibition campaigns lost some of their acidity as local option passed in all eleven counties. Banking, education, and prohibition offer good examples of how challenges to prosperity and propriety transformed a society governed by a multicornered political system in which the poorest whites and blacks did not vote.

In the late 1880s Texans used two types of banks: private banks and banks chartered under federal banking laws. In Northeast Texas private bankers like Lon Morris of Pittsburg held the top spots in the banking hierarchy, and outside of the major railroad towns relatively few national banks existed. At that point, despite long-standing opposition, discussion began about creating a state banking system with lower initial capitalization requirements than those for national banks. Private bankers condemned both the national system and the idea of a state system, arguing that free enterprise unfettered by government regulation best served the industry and the public. By 1890 Populists, on the other hand, insisted that greater prosperity required easier access to capital. They demanded government-controlled banks for the common folk. In 1892, responding to the challenge of the Populists, the Democrat's state platform included a call for a constitutional amendment allowing state-chartered banks. (The need for a constitutional amendment reflected both the restrictive nature of the Texas Constitution and the depth of traditional animosity to government-chartered banks.) In a classic example of staking out the middle ground, Hogg Democrats envisioned a system of privately owned but government-regulated banks that required lower initial capitalization, encouraged small savings accounts, and lent more freely than national banks. Despite winning office, these Democrats failed to place a banking amendment before the public. Perhaps the influence of private bankers remained too strong within the state legislature, or the call for more banks was a sham intended to diminish the Populist vote.[3]

Calls for the creation of state-chartered banking resurfaced in the Democratic platform of 1902, a year in which Hogg Democrats again gained control of the legislature. This time a coalition of reformers and former Populists made good on their promise, and in 1903 William Hodges, a Democratic state representative from Lamar County, introduced the measure authorizing a constitutional amendment allowing state banking. In the next year's general election, the voters of the state passed the banking amendment. The legislature then fashioned banking regulations, and in 1905 the state began chartering banks.[4]

Within Northeast Texas, skepticism about a state banking system persisted through 1900. Paeans to free enterprise issued from private bankers afraid of the increased competition state banks would bring to the industry. The shell of old political rhetoric also made banking reform a potentially contentious issue, with state banking sounding to some like another crazy Populist scheme that elevated the role of government.[5]

Banking issues, however, soon lost their heat as proponents argued that a state banking system would counter the impact of the money trust. Because state banks required lower initial capitalization and offered loans secured by collateral banned in the national banking system, they promised local control of, and greater access to, capital. Helped by an increased indifference to banking issues, a lackluster series of political contests, and the creation of the new primary system that made general elections largely meaningless, advocates of bank reform faced little formal opposition. In November 1904 the banking amendment carried in six of the eleven counties in Northeast Texas but drew less than half the vote of the 1902 poll tax amendment.[6]

The banking amendment did best in Bowie, Camp, Lamar, and Titus counties. These counties contained the fastest-growing cities in the region —Texarkana, Pittsburg, Paris, and Mount Pleasant. Each city boasted a well-organized and energetic businessmen's association that pushed their cities to the front in railroad and highway construction, educational reform, and the attraction of new industries. In Pittsburg, for example, both white and black businessmen operated active associations by 1904. Members of civic improvement associations and business associations promoted the new and decried the old. In all four places, conservatives and insurgents, those most likely to attack state banking, had little chance of mobilizing opposition.[7]

Instead, the only voices raised insisted that state banking represented another chance to expand the local economy and another chance for leading citizens to enrich themselves in the process. As the editors of the *Pittsburg Gazette* phrased it, "Money matters would be easier and a new era of development would begin in Texas." Despite the presence of Lon Morris, the largest private banker in the region, almost 90 percent of Camp's citizens who voted agreed with their local editors and supported state banking. In Bowie, Lamar, and Titus over 60 percent favored the amendment. In comparison, a margin of less than 5 percent separated victory or defeat in most of the other seven counties.[8]

Opponents of state banking in these seven other counties more often than not mistrusted an active government. This mistrust of government came from two directions—from those whose memories of the Civil War and Reconstruction made them resent any increase in the power of government and from former Populists who viewed a government controlled by Democrats as the tool of selfish interest groups. The banking amendment failed in Cass County in part because of the vocal opposition of John M. Fletcher, the editor of the *Atlanta Citizens Journal*. Fletcher, a Civil War veteran and head of the local veterans' association, seldom missed an opportunity to praise the old Confederacy and Confederate veterans. Fletcher emerged as a Democratic leader during Reconstruction and had edited the *Citizen's Journal* since 1879. For this conservative Democrat, state banks not only seemed like a Populist scheme, state systems of any kind threatened local control and white supremacy.[9]

Former Populists also viewed bank reform warily. The bank amendment lost by a slender margin in Delta and Hopkins counties, two centers of Populism and the Farmers' Union. It won by equally slender margins in Morris and Titus counties, two other centers of the Farmers' Union and Populism. Low voter turnout makes speculation on Populist support for banking reform difficult, but a split in Populist ranks may explain the vote in these counties. The interests of large and medium-sized landowners varied from those of small-scale owners and tenants. That division always existed, but issues like banking exacerbated it. Larger-scale owners, both as borrowers and investors, stood to gain the most from a state system. Increasingly. these larger-scale owners moved into the Democratic party—the party that sponsored the bank amendment. Small-scale owners and tenants, if they voted that year, opposed the amendment and remained outside the Democratic party.[10]

Once begun, however, the state banking system drew ex-Populists and reform-minded Democrats into advocating an even larger role for government in banking. After the Panic of 1907, demand increased for a state law requiring the insuring of deposits held by state banks. Traditionalists argued that competition and the integrity of individual bankers best insured deposits. Bank failures in 1907, however, fueled demand for a deposit guaranty law to protect depositors and prevent the undermining of solvent banks by depositors' hysterical demands for their money during every banking crisis. Thus in 1910 when the legislature passed such a law, free enterprise took a back seat to the need for a stable bank in even the smallest community. At a time when Northeast Texans increasingly realized you could not "successfully do business without a bank," government regulation and insuring of deposits not only promised safety and security, it promised the availability of banks.[11]

This steady expansion of the role of government in banking demonstrated two important points. Rejecting old ideas about banking not only brought obvious benefits, it inevitably meant accepting a more active government, a government that would "encourage the flow of cheap money into Texas."[12]

After 1913 both the state and federal governments took halting steps to further expand credit alternatives for Texas farmers and to decrease their dependency on merchants and country bankers. That year the state legislature created a rural credit-union system, but it had little impact on Northeast Texas. For the largest farmers, the establishment in 1917 of the Federal Farm Loan Bank in Houston also provided credit. By 1924 this institution had lent $107 million to 37,000 Texas farmers. S. A. Lindsey, treasurer of the Land Bank, estimated that tenants received only 10 to 18 percent of these loans. Given the number of tenants in Northeast Texas alone and the likelihood that these loans went to better-off tenants with the least risk of default, it was probably too little to do much good for those already without access to credit. Still, such actions demonstrated greater reliance upon all levels of government.[13]

Changes in public education and agricultural education joined banking in increasing reliance upon government and requiring rejection of customary practices rooted in ideology and past political wars. Change required moving beyond a distrust of the world of the mind and an insistence that "No amount of education, science or philosophy will take the place of practical common sense."[14]

Significant efforts to organize public schools first began in Texas during Reconstruction. In their attempt to regain power and discredit Republicans, Democrats labeled the school system a waste of tax money and decried the educational opportunities provided for blacks. Once back in power, Democrats dismantled this first state controlled and regulated system. In 1883–1884, however, the legislature took halting steps back toward centralized control of elementary education and allowed local tax money to again flow to schools. Over the next twenty years, state and local efforts improved elementary education, but as late as 1907 M. G. Bates, the Cass County School superintendent, argued, "We did last year just half as much good toward the education of our children as our school facilities made it our reasonable duty to do." Most schools remained one-teacher, ungraded institutions with a five-month term.[15]

After 1907 changes in state law forced a steady move away from a decentralized, community-based system toward a more centralized and bureaucratically managed system of public education. All the counties in Northeast Texas soon had county school superintendents who oversaw the various districts in rural areas, but despite this effort the gap between rural schools and town schools increased.[16]

Incorporated towns increasingly set up independent school districts outside of the county system. Usually the desire to better fund schools and create a larger pool to draw students for a local high school motivated the push for independent school districts. Even if they desired to raise taxes, citizens in rural districts, often referred to as common schools, faced far stricter legal limits on setting the property tax rate than did citizens in independent districts. Despite this handicap, dedicated educators sometimes carried bright students forward to the secondary level, but overburdened teachers in ungraded schools seldom provided a full range of high school subjects. More advanced education could come only from a larger, better-funded independent school district, and according to state law such districts could be set up only in incorporated towns. As the need for a high school education became more obvious, leaders in these towns acted. In Linden, for example, community builders called an "Educational Mass Meeting" in 1908 to create an independent school district, and they soon constructed a high school. Such high schools quickly became the mark of a progressive town, and reformers consistently linked education to economic growth, improved morality, and the promise of a brighter future. By 1911 it became a standard refrain to argue: "Now it can easily be seen that with an education, good judgement and industry, we may without difficulty rise above the common level, and with the opportunities now afforded in Texas, there is very little excuse for our growing generation to falter."[17]

Among "the opportunities now afforded" were those provided by the rural high school law of 1911. As late as 1910 there were only fifteen incorporated towns in Northeast Texas, and that meant at most only fifteen independent school districts. In an age when poor roads and reliance upon horses and mules for transportation limited the size of school districts, vast areas did without a high school or a graded school of any type.[18]

In drafting this 1911 law, the legislature attempted to provide an equal opportunity for a quality education for rural children. The law established county boards of education and encouraged them to form rural high schools by providing some state financial aid and creating a mechanism for the consolidation of rural school districts. Once consolidated, these districts theoretically could offer elementary, intermediate, and high school classes. Calling it "an effort to give the children a better chance than their parents have had in the world," civic leaders in Cumby, in rural Hopkins County, led the charge to consolidate schools within a four-mile radius of their village. As part of their plan, they proposed transporting children over an improved highway system. Reforms fit neatly together— a better economic future for the children and the village required good roads and good schools.[19]

Cumby proved an exception. It was large enough and prosperous enough to provide a sound tax base and to encourage thoughts of an even more prosperous future. Its population also was almost entirely white. Citizens did not bear the expense of operating two school systems—one for blacks and one for whites. Nor did school reformers have to overcome the opposition of whites who did not want to spend tax money on black education. Places with a larger black population and poorer prospects remained largely unchanged by the new law. As late as 1920 one former Northeast Texas student remembered that "the average country child was fortunate to have the opportunity to go through the sixth grade."[20]

Pin Hook, in Lamar County, was one such place. There one teacher tried to inspire students of varied ages in an environment that discouraged learning. His efforts to raise local standards only brought complaints from parents, who quickly convinced the school trustees not to retain him for the next year. William Owens once read voraciously, but after attending that school, he recalled, "I had books in my hands and wanted to read them, but I could not." In an effort to be like his peers he accepted their contempt for education.[21]

Schools like Pin Hook's survived because the state never equalized funding and because of local opposition to consolidation. Consolidation threatened local control and promised higher taxes for farm owners. Equal funding might have taken money from the independent districts and given it to the rural districts. Instead, what almost inevitably happened was increased centralized control and the growth of a state-level educational bureaucracy. In 1914 the Texas legislature passed a compulsory attendance law, and in 1918 a constitutional amendment mandated free textbooks. During the 1920s centralized control over teacher accreditation and the selection of textbooks increased. As with banking, when met by adversity, educational reformers turned to the state. In so doing they increased acceptance of the role of government in day-to-day life. They also contributed to widening the gap between town and countryside. A dual society emerged—one of good schools and a prosperous economy in the towns and one of poverty and limited educational opportunities in the countryside.[22]

Actually the dual society did not split neatly between town and country. Prosperous farmers who adopted modern agricultural methods joined townsfolk in enjoying the benefits of modern life. Change never came easily or completely. Some caught up in tenantry and debt could not afford to change or were not allowed to change. For others, reliance upon tradition proved the biggest stumbling block. As the reform-minded editor of the *Cooper Review* explained in 1909: "If some old mossbacks had their way, we would still be living in the day of the ox cart and the bear hunter. They see only disaster and bankruptcy in every new innovation and invention, and their dismal croakings are sure to greet the advent of any improvement over the old order of things. They live entirely in the past and are sorely vexed at the rapid advance of progress and civilization." Once again, economic necessity encouraged, and the political system allowed, changes in the law that helped overcome farmers' ingrained skepticism.[23]

For cotton farmers the process of change accelerated about 1900, and insects and disease played a key role in this "revolution in cotton growing." Cotton root rot, a soil-borne disease affecting thousands of plant species, preoccupied researchers at the Texas Agricultural Experiment Station. Created by the state legislature in response to the Hatch Act passed by the U.S. Congress in 1887, the Experiment Station began operation in 1888 as part of the Agricultural & Mechanical College of Texas. Scientists at the station initiated research on root rot that year, and over the next decade discovered that nothing cured it. Yet they established that clean cultivation of cotton fields in the fall, letting land lay fallow, and rotating cotton and grain helped. Success in controlling root rot required changing long-standing practices, giving more careful attention to the land, and turning to the state. It required education—the ability to read and think and the transmission of information. Agricultural bulletins, Farmers' Congresses, demonstration farms, and the development of an agricultural extension service soon drastically altered farming and divided better-educated, larger-scale owners from others who worked the land.[24]

What began with attempts to understand cotton root rot accelerated after the arrival of the boll weevil. In 1904 the ll weevil, which entered Texas from Mexico in 1892, reached the Red River. Weevils, especially following a mild winter and a warm wet spring, could cause severe damage and drastically reduce cotton yields. If the Texas farmer was "lord of all he surveys," he was a lord under siege. Almost immediately, agricultural reformers circulated information on how farmers in other sections successfully combated weevils. Unlike years past, the first decade of the new century saw farmers more ready to heed the call to adopt new methods. The potential disaster for farmers and townsfolk loomed too large to continue doing things the old way. Besides, Seaman Knapp's demonstration farm showed skeptical farmers that improved methods could lessen weevil damage. According to Burt Lockhart: "The advent of the boll weevil and other pests destructive to cotton has brought about a change in farming methods. Careless, slipshod methods, which were never profitable except by chance, will be less so. The man whose crops are profitable will be wide awake to the most approved methods and avail himself of every available means to hedge against the boll weevil and other cotton pests."[25]

Again larger-scale landowners probably differed from less wealthy and more poorly educated farmers in their reaction to the boll weevil. Tenants and small-scale owners had less time, less money, and less incentive to learn and put into practice the new methods of farming. Older farmers in particular, victims of habit and poverty, clung to traditional methods.[26]

Larger-scale owners also enjoyed closer connections with merchants and cotton dealers in the towns, and this too encouraged innovation. Working through the Farmers' Union, businessmen pushed cotton growers into greater activity and experimentation. In 1907 the merchants of Clarksville offered prizes to local farmers who demonstrated the greatest skill and energy in eradicating the boll weevil. Within two years Red River County farmers were picking up fallen debris from infested cotton plants and using other new techniques without any incentive from local merchants.[27]

Seeing the good done in Red River and acting out of self-interest, merchants in nearby cities sponsored the same contests. As Wren Hart wrote in 1909: "Not for years has there been indications of as much improvement and growth in Cooper as there is at present." The spread of the boll weevil threatened this happy circumstance, and reformers acted to prevent a slowdown in economic growth.[28]

Texas counties also responded to threats to prosperity by expanding the county agent system. County agents appeared in some Texas counties in 1906—before any other state and before federal law encouraged creation of an extension service. In 1911 the Texas legislature passed, and Governor Colquitt signed, laws allowing each county to fund an extension agent and a demonstration farm. Three years later the Smith-Lever Act formalized on the federal level a system already in place in Texas. Agricultural education had moved beyond the Farmers' Union, farm journals, and farmers' short courses taught in College Station and Austin. By 1914 a Marion County farmer declared:

> Our agricultural schools are everywhere. We have seen new theories taught and actually put into successful use. We have seen the "scientific farmer" once scoffed at and ridiculed—we have seen him prove to be the practical farmer; we have seen him double his production per acre, improve his products, plant and harvest new and unheard crops with success. Much attention has been given to the farmer and his crops, and rightfully so, for on his success or failure depends, in the last analysis, the prosperity of the commonwealth. A great work has been and is being accomplished, and the results speak for themselves. Truly the farmer is being taught amply in the science of production.[29]

This Marion County farmer went on to call for government research into the marketing of alternatives to cotton and the distribution of that information to farmers. Even in Marion, where maintaining white supremacy still preoccupied reformers, a larger source of knowledge emerged. Government-sponsored research instead of tradition lit the way to the future. This required better legislation and better government programs. Authority and power lay outside the family, the village, the town, even the county.

Prohibition reinforced the basic principle taught by public and agricultural education: extending the reach of government extended progress. Soon after passage of the poll tax altered the political system, every county in Northeast Texas, through the passage of local-option laws, prohibited the sale of alcohol. The thirsty could still satisfy that thirst through the mail, from agents of railroad companies, at the pharmacy, by home manufacture, or in Marshall, Dallas, or Fort Worth. Portions of Arkansas and Louisiana also still allowed saloons. Not content with limited access to booze, prohibitionists in Northeast Texas began calling for the passage of a statewide ban. In 1911 they had their chance.[30]

While the prohibitionists lost statewide, they carried every county in

Northeast Texas except Marion. In doing so, they overcame the argument that local option allowed greater freedom and individuality while state-wide prohibition required an unnecessary increase in the power of government. No matter how prohibitionists tried to frame the question, their foes, led by Governor Colquitt, pointed to the obvious. Statewide prohibition marked a major transfer of power from the local to the state level. Antiprohibitionists, realizing the strength of the argument, hit repeatedly on the virtues of local option. It preserved the traditional freedoms of an American people; it was Jeffersonian as opposed to Hamiltonian.[31]

In 1887, because of such sentiment and because a very high percentage of eligible voters turned out, prohibition fared badly in Northeast Texas. Only the voters of Bowie, Camp, and Delta counties favored the amendment. Over 77 percent of Marion's voters opposed closing saloons. By 1911, with reformers in firm control of the new political system, few doubted the outcome on the local level, especially since the poll tax reduced the size of the two biggest groups opposed to prohibition—blacks and poor whites. Lack of competition may have dampened the enthusiasm of local pros, but they realized they needed every vote to carry the issue statewide. Yet despite population growth in every county, the eleven-county vote total in 1911 lagged behind the 1887 total. One local commentator predicted this discrepancy and said that "in recent years people have become more careless about voting either way."[32]

Actually, the 1911 vote reversed recent trends. The vote declined from 1887 in only four counties, and even in those counties the 1911 vote surpassed that of the previous Democratic primaries. In Lamar the total vote fell more than 1,200 from 1887 to 1911, and that large figure accounts for most of the decline in the districtwide vote. Except for Paris, almost every voting box in the county held fewer ballots. Boxes carried by the Republicans in the presidential election of 1904 and isolated rural boxes in which more than 60 percent of the voters supported the Populists in 1894 showed the biggest decline. This suggested that two groups did not vote: blacks and white insurgents.[33]

One additional bit of information suggested that whites suppressed the black vote in Paris and that it was more than a case of blacks not paying their poll tax. In the 1909 local-option election the antiprohibitionists carried Paris. In 1911 they lost Paris and the vote declined by 300. Perhaps the strong prohibition vote in the county's villages discouraged the antiprohibitionists, but organized efforts to limit the black vote probably played a role.[34]

The other counties where turnout declined from 1887 to 1911 confirmed Lamar's trends. Cass, Marion, and Red River all had a sizeable

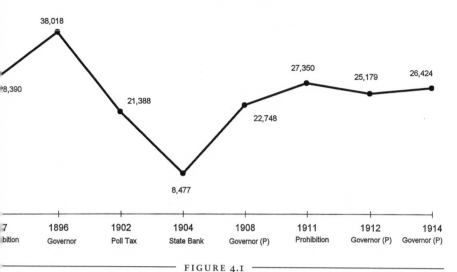

FIGURE 4.1

Voter turnout, 1887–1914.
Source: Election Returns, 1887, 1896, 1902, 1904, 1911: Secretary of State; *Dallas Morning News,* July 30, 1914; Mike Kingston, Sam Attlesey, and Mary G. Crawford, *Texas Almanac's Political History of Texas* (Dallas: *Dallas Morning News,* 1992).

black population, and precinct returns in Cass, in particular, strongly suggest that whites suppressed the black vote or blacks simply had given up trying to vote. Still, in all three counties, and especially in Marion, the vote was dramatically higher than that of recent primaries.[35]

To amplify a point made in the previous chapter, instead of simply reflecting the barriers to voting in the new political system, the 1911 referendum generated renewed interest in politics among blacks and whites. As early as February, newspapers reported that poll tax receipts set a new record and correctly predicted a high turnout—a turnout that exceeded the turnout of every presidential election from 1904 to 1928 and, as Figure 4.1 demonstrates, exceeded the vote in the 1908, 1912, and 1914 Democratic primaries. Black voters—ineligible to vote in the primaries—accounted for some of the larger turnout, but precinct returns indicated that rural whites also voted in greater numbers.[36]

These rural whites often split into two distinct groups—with wealthier white landowners supporting prohibition and poorer whites opposing it. Wren Hart's description of Hopkins County echoed across the region. "The prohibition rally here Monday was the biggest thing Sulphur Springs has had in many a day, and its success far outstripped the expectations of even the most sanguine pros. Prominent citizens from every section of the county began pouring into town early in the morning, and by 10 o'clock a big crowd had assembled at the Court House." Prominent citizens led the prohibition campaign. Isolated rural whites and blacks opposed it.[37]

Burt Lockhart made an interesting comparison of the 1887 and 1911 prohibition campaigns. "Election day passed without any friction or unpleasantness. If any harsh words were used we did not hear them. If either pro or anti gave offense in presenting their side of the question certainly the public was not made aware of it. This was in striking contrast to the election of 1887 when friendships were severed and family ties subjected to the keenest trial. So much for toleration and the signs of the time." It was indeed a sign of the times—a sign that in 1911 class and a desire to be "progressive" accounted in part for the prohibition vote.[38]

Editor after editor spoke of the support of prohibition by the better folk. Whether dwelling in town or the countryside, those aspiring to the upper class supported prohibition or lost status. A type of community censorship took place. In Pittsburg and Leesburg, the Women's Christian Temperance Union and groups from the Baptist and Methodist churches organized parades and fed prohibition supporters. Pure white remained the color of prohibition, and white-clad Sunday school children marched in favor of prohibition on election day. No blue-clad antiprohibitionists challenged their legitimacy as they had in 1887. Outside the towns, Camp County voters still opposed prohibition, but this time they did so quietly and without the aid of local elites.[39]

By 1911 supporting statewide prohibition demonstrated status and promised proper conduct for the masses. Local option had helped, but enforcement remained a problem. Access to liquor continued, as did the opportunity for purveyors of whiskey and beer to corrupt the electoral process. The rest of the state deserved the benefits of a "righteous cause." To achieve this cause, prohibitionists insisted on extending progress by extending the reach of government, and in that sense prohibition merged with other progressive issues.[40]

Antiprohibition, on the other hand, meant opposition to an active government. Mrs. H. A. Benefield, the leader of the Women's Christian Temperance Union in Jefferson, summed up a key difference between prohibitionists and their opponents when she wrote: "When liquor papers announce that in certain sections of this State, the people will not obey a state prohibition law, they not only brand people in such sections as being a lot of criminals, but also that law-breakers are more influential and powerful than the State of Texas. Any man who believes such nonsense is bound also to believe that popular government is a stupendous

FIGURE 4.2

Ladies in white. In this photograph, taken about 1902, New Boston women wore the white garb associated with purity and prohibition. The local Woodmen of the World, a group closely affiliated with Congressman Morris Sheppard and with the prohibition movement, sponsored this parade.
Photograph courtesy of Jenkins Garrett Texas Postcard Collection, University of Texas at Arlington, Special Collections.

failure." Prohibitionists joined fellow reformers in willingly using the full power of the state and optimistically believing that popular government could solve even the most vexing social problems. Thus, the 1911 prohibition campaign not only stimulated a renewed interest in politics, it sharpened the split between advocates and opponents of an active government and heightened the class dimensions of this dispute.[41]

CONTESTED CUSTOMS, 1911–1914

As the prohibition election indicated, rural whites returned to politics to counter threats to their customary way of life. Like fence laws, hunting and fishing laws, and to some extent educational reform and good roads, prohibition limited traditional behavior. These laws applied a standard of conduct determined outside of the rural communities of Northeast Texas—a standard requiring paying taxes, fencing your livestock, hunting and fishing according to a fixed schedule, and staying sober. In some sense this was a class conflict. A middle class of town dwellers and more-prosperous farmers favored prohibition, progressive agriculture, better roads, fencing livestock, consolidating high schools, building a sanitary public water system, and reforming banking. A class of poorer rural whites who often lived in tight-knit rural enclaves either opposed these measures or had no interest in them. This latter group possessed enough power to fight back in the courts, to continue the third-party tradition, and to join winning political coalitions. In another sense, however, a class analysis of the divisions between these groups obscures as much as it reveals. Rural folk won in the courts and at the polls because the ideology of an active government and the pragmatic drive to win competitive elections gave them enough in common with at least some middle-class reformers to make common cause in the legal and political system.[42]

Court action typically involved Texas usury laws. A long-standing ban against usurious interest rates remained seldom used until the years just before World War I when a flurry of legal actions against banks and credit merchants for charging excessive interest threatened to put them out of business. In these years prosperity induced some lenders to raise their rates and that led to protest, but perhaps more importantly the custom of governmental activism took hold. Judges and juries more willingly ruled in favor of those using the usury laws. Lawyers took their cases.

In a survey done in 1915, farmers in the neighboring counties of Van Zandt, Raines, Hunt, and Hopkins recounted why they brought legal action under the usury law. According to one farmer whose farm lay near the border of Rains and Hopkins, in the fall of 1914 the start of war panicked many local bankers. They reacted by tricking farmers into consolidating their loans at higher interest rates. In his case the bank consolidated two loans for about $300, made the loan payable in three weeks, and charged $84 in interest for those three weeks. They then threatened to prosecute him for fraud when he filed suit. Angered as much by the bank officers' lack of respect as by the economic consequences of their actions, the farmer pressed his case and won double damages. Other farmers in the Hopkins County area who "resented the insult" and had suffered economic damage took heart and followed his lead. Interest rates began falling and bankers quickly condemned the worst offenders among their fraternity.[43]

While the local Socialist party avoided any connection with these suits, many who took legal action favored their cause. Texas socialism was an intriguing "might have been," another in a long line of third parties stretching back to the 1850s. With the primary system blocking the rise of third parties and the natural voting base of the Socialists undercut by the poll tax, Socialists received only a scattering of votes. Northeast Texas, however, proved one of their strongest areas, and without the impediments of the new political system the Socialist party probably would have done much better.[44]

Socialism clearly grew from Populism and from the Farmers' Union. As early as 1902 James Biard of Lamar County, who at the time remained an active supporter of the dying Populist party, weighed the feasibility of joining the Socialists. Another old Populist, J. E. Banger, wrote in 1908, "The man who holds honest labor in contempt has not a Christian spirit in his heart." Such a man "seeks to live off the labor of others and is therefore a robber." For Banger, the transformation of labor he saw around him assaulted human dignity, and he admitted leaning toward the Socialists. In 1910 Socialists in Bowie County purchased a local newspaper and turned it over to editor Thomas H. Davis. Davis used the paper to add to the party's membership rolls.[45]

Even with the poll tax and primary system, those membership rolls would have grown larger except for the rise of James E. Ferguson, who strongly backed changes in the state law governing rents and interest rates in the 1914 Democratic gubernatorial primary. Ferguson, known as "Farmer Jim," quickly became the dominant World War I era political personality in Texas, and his nickname indicated his main supporters. As early as 1911, angry farmers in the Blackland Prairie organized a Renters' Union because landowners adopted the practice of requiring from tenants a bonus above the usual one-third of the cotton and one-fourth of the corn. Other landowners charged rent for the houses they normally furnished tenants as part of the rental agreement. Agricultural economist J. T. Sanders wrote in 1922, "The subject of rent and land problems in general became the main issue for the gubernatorial campaign of 1914, and the successful candidate was elected mainly because of his advocacy of an antibonus law."[46]

Most renters, convinced by improving prices and the productivity of the blacklands, grudgingly paid the bonus, but in 1914 owners paid a political price when the Democratic primary hit record highs for voter participation. As Figure 4.1 indicates, in Northeast Texas the total vote for governor in the 1914 Democratic primary nearly equaled the vote in the 1911 prohibition referendum. In part, high turnout derived from several other contested races, yet Ferguson clearly helped push up the vote in rural precincts.[47]

Ferguson, a self-educated banker from Temple, craftily combined opposition to continued public debate of prohibition and a call for equitable

treatment of renters. Opposed by Thomas Ball, one of the state's leading prohibitionists, Ferguson did surprisingly well in Northeast Texas. In
a series of close elections, Ball, who claimed to be a "Hogg Progressive
Democrat," won eight of the eleven counties in the region. Districtwide
only a few hundred votes separated the two candidates. Ferguson's success came despite prohibitionist fervor and the opposition of such leading
newspapers as the *Jefferson Jimplecute* and the *Pittsburg Gazette*.[48]

The *Jimplecute,* the only newspaper in the region edited by a woman,
hit Ferguson particularly hard. M. I. "Miss Birdie" Taylor carried on in
the direct and forceful style of her father, Ward Taylor. Dismayed that the
Farmers' Union, despite its commitment to nonpartisanship, campaigned
actively for Ferguson, she refused to believe that prohibition came second
to economic policy. On the eve of the election, she fervently hoped that
rank-and-file members "are not going to permit their noble organization
to be prostituted with any kind of a sell out to any kind of a political campaign." Ferguson came within seventeen votes of beating Ball in Marion
County. Although disappointed, Taylor confidently predicted that next
time "the progressive Democracy will prevail." What she failed to understand was that Ferguson could not have done as well as he did in Marion,
where turnout remained low in rural areas, without as least some votes
from that "progressive Democracy."[49]

In the other ten counties, high turnout in long-dormant rural precincts
favored Ferguson. Ferguson's strong showing in the district revealed that
Texas Progressivism meant more than prohibition and provided more examples of traditional Texas multifactionalism. Economic reformers still
had some kick. In 1892 they split their vote between Hogg and the Populist candidate for governor. In 1914 they helped elect Jim Ferguson. In the
process they reached out to rural insurgents, long absent from the polls.
Since population growth slowed in the 1910s and blacks could not vote
in the primary, a higher turnout in 1914 than in past primaries meant that
nonvoters of the previous decade paid their poll tax and voted for Ferguson. Clearly, the total vote and particularly the percentage of eligible
voters who voted did not come close to mid-1890s general elections, but
1914 extended the pattern evident with Colquitt's victory in 1912. A trun-
cated and more moderate version of the old Populist coalition of rural
insurgents and economic reformers emerged. Burying prohibition, which
still often separated them, remained essential. Like Hogg in 1892, Campbell in 1906, and Colquitt in 1912, Ferguson achieved this by taking a
murky middle ground. He never claimed to oppose prohibition, although
he long opposed local option in his home county. He just asked for a

break from the noise to focus on the economic plight of landless farmers. Enough voters agreed to elect him.[50]

As governor, Ferguson's actions and those of the legislature elected with him forced the translation of rhetoric into reality. Even the modest changes in the law enacted under Ferguson encouraged the custom of seeking political and legal redress to economic injustice, a custom that grew in Texas while it withered in other southern states. Governmental activism remained a viable option to insurgents who voted for Ferguson, even if that active government brought prohibition. At least in this they found common ground with all reformers. In a passage that also indicated that wounds from the 1892 gubernatorial campaign still stung, one local editor captured this shared attitude: "The cry of 'fewer laws and better laws' should deceive no one. It is but an echo of that infamous shout 'Turn Texas loose,' which set up in the Clark campaign." To do nothing cost votes.[51]

Between 1915 and 1917, during Ferguson's administration, the state legislature enacted not only a law protecting renters, but also statutes aimed at increasing the supply and decreasing the cost of credit. Ferguson and the legislature acted out of a desire to bind voting blocs to their campaigns, not out of a desire for justice. That reality, however, should highlight instead of diminish the point that land reform and affordable credit mattered to enough voters to sway a supreme pragmatist like Ferguson, described as having "no fixed policy positions other than personal advantage." While the appearance of radicalism on farm issues risked losing some of the conservative antiprohibition vote, inaction on land and credit issues risked losing his most ardent supporters. Ferguson cleverly split the difference. In the process he even won over the editor of the *Jimplecute*, who in 1915 declared: "it would be a waste of time, money and much good breath to run anybody against Ferguson next year. He seems to get along well with everybody, does things, carries out his policies without friction and so far seems to stand for an economical business administration."[52]

In the end, perhaps, Ferguson's coalition of conservatives, economic reformers, and insurgents proved too sharply divided along class lines to exist for long. Unlike Colquitt, who always supported higher education, Ferguson allowed his political enemies to portray him as the foe of the University of Texas. While he supported such measures as compulsory education in the public schools, in his first term Ferguson expressed reservations about higher education, especially at the University of Texas, which he regarded as an elitist institution. In his second term when he vetoed almost the entire appropriations bill for the university, the Texas

House voted for impeachment. The charges against Ferguson, including the ten counts upheld by the Senate, had all been made before his re-election in 1916 and had been previously ignored by the voters and members of the legislature. In the end political misjudgment—attacking the University of Texas—not simply malfeasance in office, ended Ferguson's second term. Ferguson resigned one day before the Senate's judgment against him was announced in 1917, but he remained a powerful force in Texas politics despite being barred from holding any further state office.[53]

While agricultural reformers sometimes favored Texas A&M, townsfolk increasingly viewed the University of Texas as "the crown of the Texas system of education." During the 1910s the university expanded its extension role through the University Interscholastic League (UIL). The UIL organized statewide competition in athletics, debating, essay writing, and spelling. Reformers viewed these activities as ways to teach citizenship and improve local high schools. Northeast Texans eagerly advertised the university and proclaimed that it should be the destination of high school graduates. Especially in more-urban areas, attacking the university meant attacking the entire educational system. Once again the class distinctions evident in the 1911 prohibition campaign mattered. Given the close link between education and progress, assailing the university moved Ferguson into the category of rural mossback in the minds of reformers. In 1917 college remained a middle class dream instead of a common aspiration, and attacks on that dream split Ferguson's coalition on class lines. As one critic stated, "In closing the University, which is not only the pride of Texas, but of the whole South, Governor Ferguson closes the door of hope to thousands of boys and girls who have no other way to get a college education."[54]

Although Ferguson could not sustain a coalition of conservatives, economic reformers, and insurgents, his two successful elections demonstrated that the new political system allowed legal changes unseen in other southern states. These Ferguson-era statutes did little for sharecroppers, but contemporary analysts agreed that they materially aided cash renters and better-off share tenants. Tellingly, these groups were far more likely to pay their poll tax and to vote than were croppers. Contemporaries also agreed that Texas stood alone among the cotton states of the South in protecting the landless in even a minimal way. Rent and credit laws and other conditions peculiar to Texas led one student of the plantation South in the early 1920s to repeatedly use the phrase "except in Texas." A multifactional Democratic party, law, and contested customs made the plantation region of Texas—including Northeast Texas—different from the rest of the South. Yet, like the others who analyzed the region, C. O. Brannen still found Texas enough like the rest of the South to include it in his study.[55]

"Except in Texas" revealed the importance of state borders instead of the homogeneity of geographic and economic systems. It also suggested that something in the use of Texas history and culture made a difference. A few months after the 1911 prohibition election, the *Omaha Breeze*'s editor boasted: "The natural ability of Texans to solve all necessary problems when they become thoroughly aroused is well known. Our fathers wrestled with the mighty wilderness and savage man, and conquered them both. Shall we not wrestle with the gigantic problems of industrial life in the twentieth century and solve them." His counterpart at the *Jimplecute* responded, "Why certainly Texas and Texans will continue to develop and spread out until achievement unthought of even now shall have been accomplished in her wonderful borders." There was an increased sense that Texas possessed a different destiny and a different history from the rest of the South.[56]

EVOLVING MEMORY

From the Civil War to about 1910, southern memories remained far more important than any sense of Texas exceptionalism.[57] Occasional mention of special days from the Texas past and commemoration of Texas heroes appeared in the region's newspapers, but in 1904 efforts to save the Alamo ranked far behind building a monument to Stonewall Jackson. In fact, citizens of the region usually disregarded things Texan, even in political stump speeches. Instead, Northeast Texans acted and spoke as southerners. Memories of Texas's past made no difference in politics, suggesting that they made no difference in daily life.[58]

Southern memories, however, appeared constantly. In 1908 when the editor of the *Paris Advocate* looked around him at the quickened pace of the economy, he proclaimed that "prosperity is returning to the South." Mention of Texas followed, but the South came first. In a classic example in 1898, the editors of the *Pittsburg Gazette* quoted with obvious agreement this passage from the *Gilmer Mirror*: "We in the South will leave the defense of the Union to the North hereafter, as she has got all the honors of the late Spanish War, and expect the Southern soldiers to do their dirty work in Cuba and Porto Rico. Our volunteers will stay at home next time." America was still plural—a union of states not a nation. A distinctive and hypersensitive South, which clearly included Texas, resented slights by the North. It remained us versus them, and instead of the Spanish American War promoting nationalism, in Northeast Texas it promoted southernism.[59]

Nothing better embodied the South than Confederate veterans' organizations. These organizations first appeared in Northeast Texas in about 1890, and between 1904 and 1914 their members spearheaded the building of monuments in every county seat in the district. One of the first and most elaborate monuments went up in Paris in 1904. Busts of Jefferson Davis, Robert E. Lee, Stonewall Jackson, and Albert Sidney Johnston faced out from the top of a large square granite base. Builders cut a lone star and laurel wreath design into the sides of the base. From the middle of the busts rose a granite shaft topped by a full-length statue of a Confederate soldier. The statue was made in Italy, but the rest of the monument probably came from Georgia. Monuments in the other counties typically did not match Lamar's $5,000 price tag or elaborate design. Franklin and Cass had simple marble shafts. Red River had a similar, but less detailed, version of Lamar's monument. Veterans in Titus County were among the last to erect a monument. In 1911 a monument similar to that in Red River went up. To pay for the monument, the local chapter of the Daughters of the Confederacy sold pies and box lunches in Mount Pleasant on Saturdays, and the Dudley W. Jones Camp of United Confederate Veterans solicited donations.[60]

Even in the midst of this celebration of the South, subtle signs of Texas influence crept in. The use of the lone star reflected a mixing of Texas and southern symbols. Texans also claimed Albert Sidney Johnston, who participated in the Texas Revolution, as their particular hero. One year after completion of the Paris monument, a memorial by sculptor Elisabet Ney went up at his gravesite in Austin. Ney, who a few years earlier had executed life-sized statues of Stephen F. Austin and Sam Houston, worked outside the influence of southern romanticism, and her artistic renderings of Texas heroes have become standard features of modern Texas nationalism.[61]

Before World War I, however, Johnston's memorial in Austin together with the Confederate monuments scattered through Northeast Texas became "sites for anchoring memories" of the South. Such a strong connection between monuments and everyday life existed that when a tornado damaged the Confederate Memorial in Linden in 1908, it made the front page of the region's newspapers. The city's failure to immediately repair the monument drew criticism even though more-pressing needs lay all around.[62]

Northeast Texans also participated in other rituals that evoked Confederate memories and tied them to the rest of the South. On May 10,

CONFEDERATE MONUMENT, PARIS, TEXAS.

———————— FIGURE 4.3 ————————

*Paris Confederate monument. Like other southerners, Northeast Texans publicly
displayed their attachment to the Lost Cause by building monuments to
the Confederacy in their county seats. This monument in Paris,
completed in 1904, was among the most elaborate.*
Photograph courtesy of Jenkins Garrett Texas Postcard Collection, University of Texas
at Arlington, Special Collections.

FIGURE 4.4

*Linden after the tornado. Identification with Confederate monuments grew so
strong that when a tornado destroyed much of Linden in 1908, Northeast Texans
complained loudly when damage to the local monument did not receive immediate
attention. As this photograph shows, more pressing needs existed.*
Photograph courtesy of Jenkins Garrett Texas Postcard Collection, University of Texas
at Arlington, Special Collections.

1910, they celebrated "Jackson Statue Memorial Day." Local school children each contributed ten cents to a fund to erect a statue of Stonewall Jackson in Richmond, Virginia. Organizers of the campaign expressed optimism that "every school in the Sunny South will do its part." No record exists of solicitations from black school children, but the whites of the region subscribed enthusiastically to the fund.[63]

Funeral rituals and veterans' reunions added to this connection to the South. When a prominent ex-Confederate died, his elaborate, front-page obituary signaled the passing of the most visible reminders of the Civil War. Each local and national reunion of the United Confederate Veterans also took up much space in the newspapers. At these reunions, "only rarely was 'the Star Spangled Banner' played, and when it was, nobody rose. Nor was it sung, for very few even knew the words." Instead the bands played "Dixie," accompanied by rousing rebel yells.[64]

Northeast Texans also supported the widespread efforts in the South to record the valiant efforts and lofty purposes of the Confederacy "accurately." In 1908, in a full-page panegyric to "The Lost Cause," a local editor pronounced the dead beyond help. Instead, the living must ensure "that on the pages of deathless history's brightest galaxy the names of Davis, of Lee, of Jackson, of Johnston and the hosts of those who wore the gray are written there, and those who 'stood in the trenches' are among the first." As with the Paris monument, the common soldier stood above the generals, but all remained part of everyday life.[65]

Efforts to ensure that correct history made it into print continued until the eve of World War I. In July 1914 the *Jimplecute* carried a news item on the creation of the George W. Littlefield Fund at the University of Texas. Pointing out that "writing history the wrong way is a charge that frequently has been made by the Southerner, reconstructed and otherwise, against the bulk of American history authors since the Civil War," the editor praised the efforts of Littlefield, a Confederate veteran, to immortalize "the facts" of southern history.[66]

Yet, as more Confederate veterans died, the attention given to Confederate reunions and Confederate history diminished. In August 1910 the *Omaha Breeze* published an obituary of James Harvey Johnston written by his son. "Squire" Johnston moved to the Omaha area in 1852 from eastern Tennessee. Like others from that region of Tennessee, he opposed secession but fought in the Confederate army. His son closed the obituary: "To his comrades, we will say that he has answered the last roll call and is now resting 'under the shade of the trees,' and soon all who followed that 'tattered banner' will sleep beside him." By World War I, living symbols of a southern and a Confederate past with their flags, parades, conventions, and associations increasingly joined Squire Johnston. A new generation took their place.[67]

More than the passing of a generation initiated the rise of Texas mania. Memories of wartime death and destruction never vanished quite as completely in Texas as they seemed to do in other Southern states.[68] This anecdote from the *Omaha Breeze* captured the realism amidst the romance: "In the last days of the Confederacy, General Longstreet observed a soldier in tattered clothing standing in mud and a beating rain during a halt in the column. The soldier, soliloquizing for the benefit of the bystanders, said: 'I love my country. I could die for my country. "Breathes there a man with soul so dead who to himself has never said, this is my own, my native land!" And if I am ever through with this war—I'll be d——d if I ever fall in love with another country!' " The editor of the *Breeze* went on to comment: "No doubt that is about the way many poor soldiers felt in those times, and most of them have been striving ever since to make this glorious Southland everything but a howling battlefield."[69] Moving beyond a wasteland required leaving behind a saccharine view of the South that idealized slavery and minimized the blood and horror of war. It soon meant emphasizing Texas instead of the Southland. As "old ideas" passed "improved conditions" followed. The concept of progress, both economically and socially—scientific agriculture and prohibition—slowly pushed history and memory in a new direction.[70]

As this intellectual shift occurred, the economy improved and Texans grew more important in national affairs. Perhaps this combination of a hint of realism, the passing of the Confederate generation, an improving economy, and national stature explains why after 1910 Texas increasingly came first while mention of the South came second. The timing of this shift in emphasis, however, suggested that prohibition, which highlighted the usefulness of an active government, also influenced the new function and style of history and myth. Prohibition, like the new memories of Texas, exuded a confidence that the world could be perfected. The best lay ahead. In celebrating a slightly different past from other southerners, Texans committed to a different future—one that more quickly buried the ghosts of Confederate and Reconstruction era prejudices against an active government and one that made them more American and less southern.[71]

None better represented the complexities of this transformation in emphasis from southern to Texan than Morris Sheppard. In 1912 Sheppard, the widely admired thirty-seven-year-old Congressman from the First District, sought and won a seat in the U.S. Senate from Texas. Known as a gifted orator and ardent supporter of prohibition, Sheppard also embraced almost every other progressive-era reform. He worked tirelessly to interest the federal government in constructing a navigable waterway from Northeast Texas to Shreveport, the last easily navigable point on the Red River. In a score of other ways he promoted the economic interest of his constituents by harnessing the power of a more active federal government. Like his father, Sheppard appealed to former Populists as well as reform Democrats. He was an early advocate of federal action to combat the boll weevil, and he earned a reputation for getting things done efficiently in the House of Representatives. Perhaps to reassure conservatives among his constituents, at home he delivered carefully crafted and eloquent lectures on the history and character of the South, paying particular attention to the valor of the Confederate generation.[72]

A crowd in Linden greeted a 1909 speech in which Sheppard emphasized "the unwritten history of the South, secession and the great struggle" with wild enthusiasm. The local reporter for a newspaper that typically rejected calls to keep the South distinct from the North summed up Sheppard's address by saying, "Words are inadequate to describe it, human language is too lame, the mind cannot conceive of it, exaggeration is impossible, as the tired fancy falters in its sublimest heights in an attempt to portray it." Such responses to his speeches helped make Sheppard unbeatable in his district.[73]

Yet Sheppard never let southern romanticism stand in the way of progress, bridging the gap between guarding the past and creating the future. While glorifying the Lost Cause, he scorned attacks on the federal government based on states' rights, the Civil War, and Reconstruction. The image of a silver-tongued champion of the South, a staunch prohibitionist, a believer in the promise of government, and an effective advocate of economic development stood him in good stead in 1912.[74]

Two years later war began in Europe, initiating an even more accelerated period of change. By war's end memories of Texas and of the United States overwhelmed the Lost Cause. Far more than the Spanish American War, the First World War helped Texans think like Americans instead of southerners. Texans joined a common effort for the good of mankind. In Austin, George Littlefield, who did so much to ensure the writing of history from a southern point of view, erected a fountain in memory of the dead and wounded of the Civil War and World War I.[75] In Texarkana, Captain James Thomas Rosborough, another wealthy entrepreneur, organized efforts to erect a similar monument to both the Confederacy and the soldiers of World War I. This veteran of extensive action in the Civil War donated the land and gave or raised the $10,000 needed to erect the monument. The ship bringing the marble statue arrived from Italy in the summer of 1918, "at a time when national patriotism was at a high pitch."[76]

As the war closed, the Fourth of July took on restored luster—a luster bright enough to eclipse some of the memories of the Civil War. In 1920 one explanation of what the Fourth meant compared the Civil War and World War I: "In 1861 this nation, grown to large proportions and unable to reconcile its sectional differences entered upon the greatest civil war of history—father against son, brother against brother, neighbor against neighbor. In 1917 this same country, by then the greatest of earth, crossed the most devastating war the world has ever known. This time it was father and son, brother and brother, neighbor and neighbor—no section, no creed—just an outpouring of that nation." Americans fought "not for conquest or for the love of fighting, but only in defense of right, justice, humanity and our national independence." More than simply a celebration of the past, the Fourth let people rededicate themselves to the future. "We have much to celebrate on Independence day, but with the aid of him who created all peoples and all things we will have more as time goes on. In the spirit which has lived since the days of '76."[77]

The Civil War now appeared through the prism of World War I, and while it never vanished completely from the public mind, the particular way it was remembered changed. For example, raising money for the war effort through the sale of Liberty Bonds called to Birdie Taylor's mind the effort of the rich in the Civil War. "During our Civil War there were men who could see their sons go to be shot, but who would raise all sorts of fuss if a Negro man was taken. It was his valuation that caused the racket. That same class is going to be hard to shake loose from his dollar now." In that sense World War I accelerated the trend to see the Civil War in a more realistic fashion. The war became an event in the American epoch, instead of the apogee of southern nationalism.[78]

Conversely, Texas history assumed increasingly mythic proportions. Mention of March 2, Texas Independence Day, and April 21, the anniversary of Sam Houston's victory over the Mexican army in the Texas Revolution, picked up after 1910, but real notice of those days awaited the end of the war. As with the Fourth of July, celebration of these days now became a time to point to the future as well as the past. A writer for the *Paris Morning News* declared before one such memorial day, "The spirit of Texas lives and the great commonwealth is finally going to achieve its destiny."[79]

While this transformation away from the dead hand of a southern past grew stronger during and just after World War I, the process had already begun before the war. The process depended upon the passage of laws that substituted new sources of authority, new business institutions, and new rules of behavior for traditional ones. While customs remained contested, even the followers of Jim Ferguson accepted local option, governmental activism in the economy, and the value of public education. Eloquent spokesmen for the South like Morris Sheppard argued for social and economic reform, and before long speeches about the glories of the Texas past replaced set pieces on the South.

In August 1914, Hopkins County Democrats provided a benchmark in this transformation and the others discussed in this chapter. Meeting in their annual convention, party leaders offered a set of resolutions supporting the Wilson administration and all its policies. Tariff reform and the Federal Reserve system earned special praise, but a long list of other reforms drew support. A few disgruntled party members offered a substitute set of resolutions. Echoing Jim Ferguson's call to "stop the agitation of the liquor question," they advocated local option but not statewide prohibition and voiced concern for the intolerance of the majority. Their resolutions also opposed woman suffrage and initiative, referendum, and recall. The substitute resolutions met "a thunderous negative." Only two voted in their favor. Then with "a whoop" party delegates passed the entire set of original resolutions. Instituting woman suffrage, extending prohibition, and more-efficient government joined with currency and tariffs as concerns of the day. None talked of tradition or the Confederacy. The talk centered on a brighter future for Texas—a place with a special history and a special destiny. Achieving that destiny soon meant surviving an economy that soared and fell at dizzying rates.[80]

FIVE

AN ECONOMIC
ROLLER COASTER, 1914-1930

While a steady, if limited, upward climb best characterized the economy in the two decades before 1914, the two decades after it resembled a roller coaster. Outbreak of war in Europe brought the collapse of cotton prices, but by 1915 they, along with land prices, raced toward record highs. Prosperity lingered briefly after the war, but all thoughts of the arrival of an age of sustained economic growth ended with the sharp recession of 1920-1921. Cotton prices and the Northeast Texas economy rose and fell through the rest of the decade, but throughout the period improved transportation and changes in business organizations knit the region more tightly together and more completely linked it to the rest of Texas. Unstable prices, improved transportation, and evolving business structures encouraged and allowed substantial outmigration by those in the middle of the economic spectrum.

After 1914 three key factors shaped the economy of the region: volatile cotton prices and yields, rising then falling prices for farmland, and growing connectedness within the region and to other areas of Texas. Taken together these factors encouraged seemingly contradictory trends. In an effort to offset volatile cotton prices and yields with greater efficiency and productivity, sharecropping and mechanization grew at the same time. As farm owners and better-off tenants left the region for better opportunities elsewhere, land holdings consolidated in fewer hands, but because of reliance upon seasonal labor these were not traditional cotton plantations. Cotton acreage increased, but so did diversification away from a cotton-based economy. The handling of cotton and the business of retailing grew larger and more efficient, but this meant that smaller towns and villages lost population to larger trade centers. Rural folk living in a semi-subsistence and cooperative economy, who often looked poor to casual observers, disappeared and were replaced by truly poor sharecroppers knit almost completely into a cotton producing, market-oriented economy. Thus, the economy changed in ways that anticipated or predated changes usually associated with the New Deal or World War II, and it changed in ways that brought the region to a crisis point in 1930. By 1930 prosperity existed alongside poverty. Some were worse off than in 1914, but those able to take advantage of new opportunities and changing circumstances were not.[1]

NEW OPPORTUNITIES, CHANGING CIRCUMSTANCES, AND WORLD WAR I

Near the end of 1917, a usually cautious resident of the region proclaimed, "This is the year that Northeast Texas has made good." Excellent prices and yields for cotton, rising land values, higher wages, new crops, more manufacturing, increased use of machines, and the ripple of an economic boom in the oil industry and in nearby cities all generated optimism and record bank deposits. A big cotton crop and high prices allowed even most tenants to clear a profit that year (see Figure 5.3). Yet this happy circumstance was more than a one-year, wartime bonanza. Making good began almost a decade earlier when the opening up of western Texas created challenges and opportunities for Northeast Texans—challenges and opportunities that demonstrated the influence of volatile prices and yields, land values, and increased connectedness.[2]

Traditionally, southerners moved west when opportunities narrowed. That certainly accounted for the rapid growth of Northeast Texas up to about 1905. By that date, however, west meant moving deeper into Texas and Oklahoma. Rising land values in the region diverted settlers from Northeast Texas, and active promotion by railroad companies attracted them to the region west of Fort Worth. Cheaper western land not only drew settlers from the Southeast, farmers from Northeast Texas sold land whose value seemed to exceed what it could produce and moved west. Despite continued population growth, between 1900 and 1910 the number of white farm owners virtually stopped increasing in Northeast Texas. Soon after 1910, tenants whose numbers kept growing, outnumbered farm owners for the first time. This happened about a decade later there than in the state as a whole.[3]

Newspaper editors, taking note of diminished growth in the number of landowners, actively promoted their counties while deriding western lands. In March 1908 the editor of the *Bonham News* asserted, "A man who can buy improved land in Fannin County at from $18 to $40 per acre and who will then go to uninhabited plains and buy prairie dog towns, cactus hills and rocky canyons at from $10 to $30 an acre needs a guardian." In Clarksville the editor of the local paper graciously allowed, "If West Texas people fail in crops this year they will only have to come to this county to get plenty of cotton picking." Ridicule showed concern. Local business leaders sounded an alarm about the new migration patterns. Local editors who depended upon them for advertising revenue responded by plugging their counties and deriding western Texas and Oklahoma. Despite this derision, through the 1920s whenever plentiful rains fell in West Texas and land values changed in Northeast Texas, people left the region for a "land of bright promise."[4]

Despite the threat of drought, West Texas offered farmers several advantages. Dry summers and cold winters retarded the spread of boll weevils. The flat terrain made the use of machinery feasible and profitable. As one ex-resident of Morris County wrote, "I am breaking the land with a sulky plow which takes three horses to pull it. Don't have to walk any plow out here, and you know that suits me fine."[5]

Economic development in West Texas threatened prosperity in Northeast Texas by ending the upward push on land prices and the demand for goods and services provided by new settlers. The movement of some of the most enterprising local citizens westward threatened to make the region an economic backwater. These fears combined with momentary declines in cotton prices and problems with boll weevils to foster a search for alternatives to cotton. If West Texas claimed the position of the cotton-growing area of the world, Northeast Texas needed a substitute. Besides, the best solution to low cotton prices and low yields due to boll weevils was to plant less cotton.

After the boll weevil arrived and cotton prices declined in 1904–1905, farmers planted Elberta peaches and Irish potatoes in Northeast Texas. Camp County farmers planted over 100,000 peach trees. Prairie counties like Hopkins experienced even more substantial crop diversification as railroad expansion and consolidation made shipping easier and faster. Peaches, potatoes, strawberries, and other truck crops went out by the carload. All these crops yielded more value per acre than cotton and for smaller-scale landowners offered a way to remain on the land. The formation in almost every county of Truck Farmers' Associations also stimulated diversification. Often acting as part of a multicounty group, these associations worked to ensure large enough crops to make shipment to the North feasible. Scientific and systematic agriculture meant not just improved cultivation of cotton, but the growing and marketing of other crops.[6]

While the search for alternatives to cotton proceeded across the South, the rise of new, nearby markets made this search a bit more successful in Northeast Texas. Emerging oil fields on the region's rim added to the demand for fruits and vegetables and created job opportunities for the residents of Northeast Texas. No significant discoveries of oil occurred in the eleven-county region until the 1930s, but oil was found in nearby portions of Louisiana before World War I. Oil production near Caddo Lake began in 1904, and by 1910 the Caddo Lake Field led Louisiana production. In Cass County, which bordered Caddo Parish, acreage in fruits and vegetables rose after the discovery of the Caddo Lake Field. Production of peaches, white and sweet potatoes, and watermelons all increased between 1900 and 1910. In addition, petroleum-related jobs in the Shreveport area probably put a floor on wages in adjacent counties and parishes.[7]

Wartime demand brought the commodity most associated with twentieth-century Texas into still greater prominence. Petroleum's price raced skyward after 1914 and with it climbed the demand for workers to produce, transport, and refine the petroleum of Louisiana, Arkansas, Oklahoma, and Texas. After the discovery of the large Ranger Field in 1917, major fields quickly ringed Northeast Texas. This added to the economic stimulus provided by the Caddo Lake Field.[8]

Pipelines and refineries soon clustered in Fort Worth, the city nearest the Ranger Field. Describing oil's impact a writer for the *Fort Worth Star-Telegram* gushed in December 1918:

> The story of oil—oil in unbelievable quantities—has taken hold and suddenly all the world is informed that Fort Worth, Texas is the leading oil center of the South! Even the school boy now boasts that Fort Worth has more pipe lines radiating out to the rich fields of gas and oil than any other city in this section. The fact is that Fort Worth actually has 60 percent of the oil trunk pipe line mileage of Texas and weekly the report comes that some new refinery is going to be built as soon as material can be had and is going to build its own pipe lines to the fields.[9]

Despite the enthusiasm of its boosters, Fort Worth shared the prosperity derived from oil and related financing, manufacturing, and distribution with other cities of the region. Houston, Dallas, Shreveport, Oklahoma City, and Tulsa joined Fort Worth to surround Northeast Texas with fast-growing cities. Suddenly, Northeast Texans found new economic opportunities next door. Unlike lumber, which also experienced a wartime boom in nearby areas, the importance of urban growth and petroleum endured.[10]

Through the 1920s, petroleum continued to create good-paying jobs, stimulate urban growth, and provide new markets for Northeast Texas farmers. Petroleum's impact reached far beyond production. Creative individuals with backgrounds in water-well drilling, blacksmithing, or in railroad machine shops invented new tools in Texas and manufactured them within the region. The high volume of oil initially produced in Trans-Mississippi fields encouraged the construction of refineries. Once these were in place, it was cheaper to pipe the oil from later discoveries to regional refineries than to build new ones. In addition, oil-tool manufacturing and refining clustered in a few larger cities. The regional management, financing, and insuring of these manufacturing concerns grew around the cities, further accelerating their population growth.[11]

For landowners, the World War I and 1920s oil boom also brought a new and long-lasting source of income. Despite the absence of producing wells in the eleven-county area, the high price of oil and the discovery of major fields on the rim of the region encouraged the leasing of mineral rights from landowners. Because the prolific Caddo Field lay just across the Louisiana border, landowners in Cass and Marion enjoyed the benefits of increased leasing as early as 1917. By 1919 oil speculators and oil companies began drilling exploratory wells in many parts of the two counties. At about the same time landmen, the name typically given to those charged with acquiring leases, purchased leases in every county in the region. Through the 1920s, each new discovery of oil in the Trans-Mississippi South sparked renewed interest in leasing. Lease money, of course, did sharecroppers and tenants little good. Like the federal crop payments to cotton farmers in the 1930s, however, this windfall allowed landowners to purchase equipment they would not have otherwise acquired. Part of the upsurge in the value of farm equipment in Northeast Texas noted in chapter 2, particularly that part that surpassed the statewide average, derived from the surplus capital brought in by leasing mineral rights.[12]

Other new opportunities came with the continued development of Paris and Texarkana as manufacturing centers. In the 1910s, as the timber in adjacent areas played out, Texarkana lost many smaller lumber mills, but other mills became more efficient. Fewer mills and more-efficient mills accounted for the slight decline in workers noted by census takers between 1914 and 1919 but also explained why the value added by manufacturing continued to expand. As manufacturing concerns related to

Paris, Texas. South Main Street after fire of March 21st, 1916.

FIGURE 5.1

Paris after the fire. The fire of 1916 so extensively damaged Paris that local residents divide the history of their town into the period before and after the Great Fire. Thanks to a quick response by insurance companies and a healthy World War I era economy, Paris quickly rebuilt.
Photograph courtesy of Jenkins Garrett Texas Postcard Collection, University of Texas at Arlington, Special Collections.

railroads consolidated their operations in the city, the number of jobs available expanded again, and by 1925 one in three Texarkanians worked in manufacturing.[13]

Paris, meanwhile, benefited from the sharp increase in demand for food oil stimulated by war in Europe. Much of the world's prewar food oil came from France, Italy, and Spain. With supplies cut off, cottonseed oil increased in value. Area mills and refineries even convinced farmers to raise peanuts and added the production of peanut oil to their enterprises. As a result, the number of manufacturing jobs almost doubled in Paris between 1914 and 1919. This occurred despite the disastrous fire of 1916 that destroyed most of the property on the public square and about ninety blocks of the residential area. Citizens of Paris lost almost $11 million worth of property, but rebuilding began almost immediately. Insurance companies hired a private train and brought a special car to Paris, and for months it stood on the Frisco tracks serving as the headquarters for claims agents. Citizens took their insurance money and re-invested in their town, and civic leaders made every effort to make Paris better than ever. By 1918 one newcomer described the primary street as "a smooth polished floor with white houses and trees on either side, with green grass in the yards and beds of petunias in the sun." A place of beauty and wealth, Paris held out far more promise than the surrounding countryside. The end of the war, however, brought the European producers back into the food-oil market, and employment in Paris factories slumped in the early 1920s. The addition of dairy-related industries at mid-decade stabilized the demand for manufacturing workers, and the industrial workforce soon returned to 1919 levels.[14]

To a more limited extent, what happened in Paris and Texarkana also happened in other smaller cities in the region. When William Humphrey's father abandoned the life of a sharecropper to work as a mechanic in Clarksville at the conclusion of the war, he joined many others who found a way out of poverty without leaving their home county.[15]

New industries, more jobs in town, new crops, new sources of capital, and expanded markets in emerging cities on the region's periphery added a dynamic quality to the economy. Yet above all else, cotton still determined prosperity. The brief but sharp economic downturn in the fall of 1914 demonstrated just how central cotton remained. Frightened by the start of war, Europeans shut down their cotton trade, and by October 1914 prices were 33 percent lower than in October 1913. The crisis soon passed, however, and cotton prices escalated significantly during the war. Prosperity washed over the region, but ironically, this prosperity promoted tenantry instead of farm ownership.[16]

As prices climbed so did the amount of land planted to cotton. By 1920 cotton acreage in Northeast Texas exceeded 1910 levels by 50 percent. Some of this increased acreage came from land previously devoted to corn. In 1910 acreage planted in corn roughly equaled cotton. By 1920 farmers planted twice as much cotton as corn, and by 1925 the ratio had grown to three to one. Increased productivity in growing corn and the substitution of cars and trucks for mules and horses allowed some substitution of cotton acreage for corn acreage. Yet farmers also grew less of what they and their animals ate because they found it cheaper to buy corn from even more productive growers in the Midwest. Some criticized this move from corn to cotton as unpatriotic because it limited the nation's food supply, but farmers found it hard to resist the high price of cotton. As a result farmers became more specialized, more market oriented, and more modern.[17]

Except for this switch from corn to cotton, acreage in other crops either held steady or slightly increased in the 1910s. Instead of represent-

TABLE 5.1
Improved Acres per Farm Operator

Location	1900	1910	1920	1925	1930
District	41.6	44.1	46.1	43.9	46.8
Texas	55.6	65.5	71.6	92.3	92.7
Arkansas/Louisiana	39.4	39.8	40.3	37.7	36.5

Source: U.S., Census: 1920, Agriculture, vol. 6, pt. 2, 560, 596, 664–686; U.S., Census of Agriculture, 1925, pt. 2, 914, 982, 1110–1139; U.S., Census of Agriculture, 1935, vol. 1, pt. 2, 670, 696, 742–763.

ing a move away from alternatives to cotton, the new acreage in cotton came from land never before planted to crops. Cutover timberlands and hilly land previously used for pasture became cotton fields during the war. In 1917 Clayton D. Brown, a Dallas real estate promoter, purchased approximately 20,000 acres from Sullivan-Stanford in Morris and Titus counties. He divided the land up into small parcels, selling some and using croppers on others. The high price of cotton and the cheap price of these infertile cutover lands and similar land tempted others to buy land and use croppers. Hands remained available because for most croppers even the price of these inexpensive lands remained beyond their reach.[18]

At the same time, the value of the region's best farmland soared. Owners reacted by either selling or trying to match increases in land values with increases in the return from the land. This meant farming the land more intensively. Because cotton demanded more labor per acre than any grain crop or than stock raising, when landowners switched from corn to cotton or brought new land into production they reduced the total number of acres their tenants farmed. In the eleven counties the number of farms of 100 acres or more decreased by 275, or 4 percent, from 1900 to 1920. The number of farms of 20 to 99 acres increased by 8,449, or 40 percent. (The census treated each tenant holding as a farm, and land ownership probably remained concentrated in the same hands or even in slightly fewer hands.) Moreover, growers utilized a much higher percentage of this land for crops. Measured in terms of improved acres, farm size actually increased marginally in these twenty years. As Table 5.1 indicates, the ratio of improved acres to farm operators was 42 to 1 in 1900 and 46 to 1 in 1920. Total acreage per farm decreased, but more of the available land was under the plow.[19]

These changes clearly reflected an increased use of sharecroppers, greater concentration on cotton, and a move away from semisubsistence agriculture. Decreases in the size of each tenant holding and increases in the amount of improved acres meant that woodlots, unimproved pastures, and similar land disappeared, making a lifestyle that mixed some open-range stock raising with farming virtually impossible. In that sense the plain folk on the fringe of commercial agriculture were worse off, especially croppers. One study done around 1920 found that croppers worked the smallest holdings, while share tenants' farm size nearly equaled that of owners. This suggested that the increase in improved acreage per operator probably came from the increased use of machines by owners and better-off tenants, while croppers with limited access to machines also had limited ability to increase the acreage cultivated per farm worker. Smaller acreage also derived from croppers almost exclusive concentration on cotton, which, even in the best of cases, still demanded much hand labor. For those whose parents could not buy them land or who sought one more chance to rise up the agricultural ladder to the status of landowner, soaring cotton prices made farming even a small acreage in cotton look attractive. At the same time, soaring land values made buying good farmland impossible and kept most of them in the sharecropping class. In that sense the impersonal forces of cotton prices and land values increased the number of croppers.[20]

Yet it is hard to escape the conclusion that landowners' efforts to squeeze all the profit they could out of their increasingly valuable land caused much of the increase in sharecropping and cotton production between 1910 and 1920. Landowners, of course, argued that rising land values forced dividing their holdings into smaller lots to avoid losing potential profit. The antibonus law passed in the Ferguson administration probably also encouraged using croppers. If landowners tried to increase the return from their land by charging share tenants a bonus above the typical thirds and fourths, they faced the risk of prosecution. Rising prices for cottonseed and the ability of many owners to control the seed produced by croppers also boosted use of this form of tenantry. For croppers, the greed of landowners, not impersonal economic forces, seemed to keep them on the bottom rung.[21]

Croppers, however, could not blame inflation on landowners, although like most Northeast Texans the croppers joined in condemning speculators and middlemen. At least until 1920, the general rate of inflation, while quite high, lagged behind the rate of increase of cotton prices and land values. Still, since croppers and share tenants failed to gain from the rising value of land, inflation hurt them worse than owners. After holding relatively steady for a decade, consumer prices increased by over 50 percent from 1916 to 1919. This wartime inflation caused consumers to become increasingly price sensitive and pushed them toward cash-only stores. For croppers still bound to the furnish system, however, the cost of their furnish went up higher than the inflation rate. Thus, while inflation hurt everyone, it hurt the poor the most.[22]

Landowning farmers and large-scale tenants, however, bore the cost of another type of inflation—rapidly rising wages. Labor's cost and scarcity demonstrated just how closely connected the region had become to the rest of the state and to the country as a whole. During the war, the demand for labor was extraordinarily high across the country, nowhere more so than in the large cities and oilfields of Texas, and this pulled whites and blacks of all types from Northeast Texas to better jobs in other parts of Texas. Blacks also left Northeast Texas for Chicago and other cities in the North and West, just as they left the rest of the South. As Burt Lockhart noted with alarm in July 1917, "The negro exodus from the South has been heavy the past year, the total number to leave being estimated at more than 350,000." The army also took its share of young black and white males from the region. As a result of these combined factors, just as farmers begin to mechanize some phases of cotton production and depend on seasonal labor to cultivate and harvest the crop, labor vanished or grew more expensive. Probably because of the rapid growth of Texas cities and the oil industry and the ability of workers to move from place to place and industry to industry, daily wage rates for farm labor rose substantially faster in Texas than in any other southern state. By 1919 farm labor earned about 15 percent more per day than in the rest of the South.[23]

Despite high demand and high wages, Northeast Texas farmers usually secured enough labor. In Red River County landowners imported blacks from Mississippi to work their land and then used the local sheriff to protect them from attack by poorer whites anxious to maintain high demand for labor and high wages. These whites undoubtedly resented the difficulty in rising to the status of landowner even in the best of times. In turn, landowners responded to the high wage rate for farm labor by substituting croppers for day workers, which only increased the anger of whites convinced that the landowning class meant to keep them on the bottom rung. Yet, as long as cotton prices remained high and lack of skills or family responsibilities made leaving difficult, whites and blacks accepted the status of cropper.[24]

At the same time, a new source of cheap seasonal labor emerged. Fortunately for area cotton growers, the high wage era of World War I coincided with chaotic conditions and limited economic opportunity in Mexico following the Mexican Revolution of 1910. Mexican migrant workers flowed steadily northward during the war.[25]

Actually, as early as 1904 Mexican migrant laborers based in Texarkana worked on the railroads and a few farms in Northeast Texas. As a consequence, by 1906 more Catholics worshiped in Bowie than in the other ten counties combined. Yet, for the rest of Northeast Texas, the 1910s marked the first time that significant numbers of Mexicans lived and worked at least part of the year in the region.[26] By 1917 the importance of this labor source aroused worries that fear of the draft would drive Mexicans from Northeast Texas. The editor of the *Honey Grove Signal* asked in June 1918, "Where is the country going to get labor?" His answer was women and foreign citizens. With relief he pointed out that "the doors are already open to Mexicans."[27]

With the end of World War I, interest in Mexican migrant labor dwindled but did not disappear. In most parts of Texas, including the Northeast corner of the state, the use of cheap Mexican labor allowed the expansion of truck farming. These workers also fit neatly into the already established pattern of relying on labor that lived off the farm during cotton picking and hoeing seasons. During World War I, Texas Mexicans established a pattern for the 1920s. Often using the railroads, they moved from bases in cities like Dallas or Texarkana into the cotton fields, vegetable fields, and fruit orchards of Northeast Texas as demand for labor peaked. This seasonal labor system, a key ingredient to success with increased mechanization of cotton and the growing of fruits and vegetables, was in place by 1920.[28]

Use of seasonal and migratory labor was just one way in which changes in the region's cotton economy usually associated with the 1930s or 1940s sprang from World War I. More interesting in many ways was the move in a few counties away from cotton to an even more valuable crop. For sweet potatoes, at least, the war hastened the shift away from cotton. Sweet potatoes, unlike most fruits and vegetables, kept well and were a traditional southern staple. Wartime demand for food lifted their price to levels that made growing sweet potatoes as profitable as growing cotton. In Camp County, the Pittsburg Storage Company opened for business in March 1917 and contracted for 5,000 bushels of potatoes. Peanuts and other highly touted substitutes for cotton quickly faded in importance, but sweet potatoes remained an important crop for decades.[29]

Pointing to "big crops and high prices for everything," close observers of economic life in Northeast Texas agreed things had never been better than during World War I. They wondered, however, if the impact would be temporary. Would the region use this bonanza to escape drudgery and debt? Would sweet potatoes and other specialty crops help permanently diversify the economy? Historians have wondered the same thing, but phrased it differently. Did the war encourage basic structural change in the economy and society? The high prices of cotton did not last. Debt returned to shadow some farmers. The use of Texas Mexican migrant labor, the importance of sweet potatoes, and the opportunities provided by the oil industry lasted. In addition, the 70 percent increase during the 1910s in the real value of farm machines and implements occurred in part because the wartime economy generated enough money for farmers to pay for new machines. Those machines added to the efficiency of their owners long after the war. Machines, their owners, and village merchants, however, left Northeast Texas between 1920 and 1925. That suggests that any structural change in the economy was wrapped up with cotton and land prices, and with the reorganization of the business of cotton marketing.[30]

STRUCTURAL CHANGE IN THE AFTERMATH OF WORLD WAR I

Structural change in the economy meant both a change in scale and a change in type. This notice from December 1919 reflected both: "F. E. Prince has purchased H. M. Robertson's farm property consisting of 360 acres and situated 6 miles northwest of Pittsburg. Consideration $12,000. Mr. Prince's land interest now amounts to 1300 acres, nearly all of which is situated in Camp county. He has purchased a tractor and will use it in cultivating a good deal of his land next year." Across the region, in town and in the country, this pattern repeated itself—farms and businesses grew larger, more efficient, and more mechanized.[31]

As was true of F. E. Prince's farm operations, during and just after the war, major cotton firms grew larger and significantly improved their efficiency. Like farmers who purchased gins, they also became increasingly vertically integrated. Seeking "the economic line of transit," Will Clayton moved the headquarters of Anderson, Clayton from Oklahoma City to Houston in 1916. His company, along with a few others, purchased interests in major European importing firms and began to market their commodity directly to European cotton spinners. This allowed them to gauge future demand for cotton more accurately. Responding to turbulent prices, large cotton firms also cut costs by consolidating the handling of cotton in larger towns, such as Paris and Texarkana. Major companies even moved some facets of cotton processing completely out of the region to the port cities of Houston and New Orleans, and they built or purchased an increasing number of gins and cottonseed-oil mills. These gins linked to mills purchased cotton-in-seed directly from farmers, by-

FIGURE 5.2

Cotton in the square at Paris. This photograph, taken about 1915, shows the vitality of the Paris square during the cotton-selling season. Paris increasingly dominated the cotton trade and retailing in a broad area of Northeast Texas and Southwest Oklahoma.
Photograph courtesy of Jenkins Garrett Texas Postcard Collection, University of Texas at Arlington, Special Collections.

passing the traditional system entirely. By war's end a handful of firms led by Anderson, Clayton and McFadden & Bro. had the capital, access to credit, and facilities to dominate the world's cotton trade.[32]

Merchants who purchased and resold cotton found competition with firms like Anderson, Clayton difficult. J. T. Webster, a Pittsburg merchant, proclaimed in October 1918, "I am only buying my store customers' cotton." Other than that he was out of the cotton business, and he was not alone. As he pointed out, "There are hundreds of cotton firms, many of very large capital that find it impossible to do business under present conditions, and have merely hung up and quit until the war is over." For Webster, retailing generated far more income than buying cotton. Indeed, he purchased cotton only to settle accounts or keep his long-standing customers happy.[33]

Webster went on to highlight a key reason for the growing dominance of large firms: price volatility and unpredictability. World War I initiated an intense boom-bust cycle in cotton prices. Prices rose dramatically from 1914 to 1920, but war news or crop reports caused rapid declines or increases in prices. Accurate information and the ability to offset price fluctuations through the futures market allowed larger firms to profit. One poor price prediction, on the other hand, could bankrupt local cotton dealers. No wonder Webster reduced his exposure by reducing the amount of cotton he purchased. He knew the war would soon end. He remembered the downward plunge in prices in 1914. Despite record-breaking bank deposits, wartime brought unwelcome price volatility—a visitor that refused to leave.[34]

From 1920 to 1930 cotton prices fluctuated more than ever, increasing the necessity of remaking the region's basic industry. In April 1920 the spot market price in New Orleans hit forty-one cents per pound. The price dropped to eleven cents a pound in April 1921. By December 1923 it had climbed to almost thirty-five cents per pound. In October 1926, following a record crop, it was less than thirteen cents per pound. In 1927 the price peaked at twenty-two cents per pound.[35]

Volatile prices put a greater premium on efficient handling of cotton, and during the 1920s cotton firms again grew vertically and horizontally. Anderson, Clayton cut the costs of moving cotton and ensured a steady stream of cotton by experimenting with different types of bales and by centralizing the grading of cotton in Houston and New Orleans. Control of still more gins and oil mills increased their ability to buy cotton directly from growers. By the mid-1920s Anderson, Clayton alone handled over 15 percent of the American crop, and twenty-four firms handled over 60 percent of the crop. Buyers increasingly transacted business with growers at the gins instead of in town, as they moved toward a more seamless flow from field to mill. Cotton from company-owned or private gins streamed to massive storage facilities without stopping for inspection and weighing until it reached New Orleans or Houston. This required greater trust between buyer and seller and closer relationships between the ginners and the firm. Large landowners who owned gins became, in effect, agents of a major company. With less competition and more-accurate knowledge of the market, cotton firms passed price declines on to the farmer more rapidly than ever before. Large firms maintained or even increased the spread between purchase price and selling price, leading to criticism and protest from rural regions like Northeast Texas where farmers charged large companies with manipulating the market for their own profit.[36]

In the mid-1920s Northeast Texas merchants, particularly in the eastern counties where farms were smaller and less productive, still purchased cotton from established customers either to keep their business or to settle outstanding debts. Banks also acquired cotton as part of debt settlements. During the cotton-buying season, banks and merchants usually sold their cotton to the agents of cotton companies at the close of each business day. In Paris, cotton buyers checked the cotton futures market every fifteen minutes and adjusted their price up or down accordingly. In smaller markets, cotton companies gave buyers a daily limit. As with the merchants of Jefferson and Linden in 1912, stiff competition pushed merchants to pay more than the going rate for cotton. They actually took a small loss to attract customers to their stores. Even bankers would engage in what they termed "advertising" and buy cotton for a bit more than the going rate to build up the trade of their community. Since most of the cash for the day-to-day transactions came from short-term lending by banks, they made up for any losses by increasing the volume of their lending. Merchants and bankers, however, had become essentially agents of the major cotton companies, not active participants in the trade. The risk had grown too great to remain in the cotton business, as the president of the Farmers National Bank of Paris found out in 1922 when his speculation in the cotton futures market caused the failure of his bank. Increased awareness of such examples of the consequences of high risk completed the transformation of cotton marketing.[37]

Likewise, the risk of rapidly declining land prices helped transform landholding patterns. During the war, prairie counties like Lamar, Hopkins, Delta, and Franklin experienced particularly sharp increases in land values. From the 1880s on, land values in these counties on the western edge of the region outpaced the rest of Northeast Texas. They contained some of the most productive soils for raising cotton in the South, and their flatter terrain encouraged the use of machinery. Wartime demand for cotton increased their land values at a higher rate than for the rest of Northeast Texas, and by 1920 farmland in these counties, measured in constant dollars, sold for 70 percent more than in 1910. Not surprisingly, plummeting demand for cotton after 1920 caused land values to decline 20 percent from 1920 to 1925. Not every county experienced such a severe price spike, but all saw land values rise then decline between 1910 and 1925. In such an economic climate it made sense for middle-sized owners like H. M. Robertson to sell out and retire or move west where they could purchase lower-priced land. It made equal sense for F. E. Prince to acquire land enough to ride the ups and downs of cotton price swings and to keep his tractor operating full time.[38]

Actually, falling land prices joined high inflation, erratic cotton prices, and devastating boll weevil infestations to make the early 1920s a very

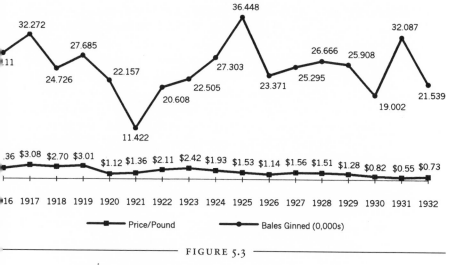

FIGURE 5.3

Cotton prices and bales produced in Northeast Texas, 1916–1932.
(New Orleans spot market prices in 1991 dollars; 10,000 bales.)
Source: *Texas Almanac, 1926, 139–142; Texas Almanac, 1936, 239–241; Yearbook of*
Agriculture, 1934, 466. (Average price for each crop year, August 1 to July 31.)

difficult time for farmers. Figure 5.3, which gives the fluctuation in bales ginned and the average price, indicates some of that difficulty.[39]

In 1919 and early 1920, Northeast Texans grumbled about the rapid rise in the price of everything they purchased, yet, as Figure 5.3 reflects, cotton prices adjusted for inflation stood at record highs. Most farmers remained better off than they had been in decades. At the start of the 1920 crop year that August, the cost of labor and supplies continued to increase but few predicted calamity and most counted on continued high prices for cotton.[40]

In October 1920, just when many Northeast Texas farmers wrapped up harvesting their crop, the price of cotton broke and soon fell to half of the 1916 level. To make matters worse, in 1921 boll weevils decimated the area's cotton crop and yields sank to pre-1900 amounts. Weevils hit hardest in Delta, Franklin, Hopkins, and Lamar counties, where farmers ginned 47 percent less cotton than in 1920. No wonder that from 1920 to 1930 the number of farm owners in these counties declined by more than 25 percent. Farm owners not only sold land before it lost value, they avoided dealing with boll weevils.[41]

Falling cotton yields across the South stimulated a price rise beginning in September 1921. At about the same time, inflationary pressures eased so that it no longer cost more to live than most growers made on their cotton. Land prices, however, continued skidding downward. When the price of cotton broke in 1920, the price of land followed. Unstable yields caused by boll weevil damage further eroded land values. For some, land held a sentimental value and for most landownership conveyed status. Above all, land was an investment whose steadily increasing value made ownership preferable to renting. Not surprisingly, more farmers sold out in western counties where land prices were highest and boll weevil damage greatest, but once land prices dropped, farm owners all along the Red River sold out before the gains of previous years were wiped out. From 1920 to 1925 the eleven-county region lost 18.5 percent of its white and 9.5 percent of its black farm owners.[42]

Having an attractive nearby destination point, a convenient way out of a slumping economy that allowed them to remain cotton farmers, eased the movement of farm owners out of the region. Northeast Texans enjoyed easy access to the booming Texas South Plains, one of the last frontiers of American agriculture. In many cases they also had kin and friends who already lived in the region. In fact, local histories of the South Plains indicate that 25 percent of pre-1920s settlers came from Texas counties north of a line from Dallas to Jefferson. The right stimulus triggered a classic chain migration where those leaving home were comforted and encouraged by the presence of familiar people at their point of destination.[43]

Land prices provided that stimulus to migrate. As Figure 5.4 demonstrates, in the early 1920s land prices in the South Plains began to climb but remained lower than in Northeast Texas. It was a good time to sell depreciating land in Northeast Texas, move west, and buy appreciating land. The family of Thomas C. Wiseman explained in simple terms his decision "following World War I" to move from a county south of the Red River to the South Plains: "Land boomed to higher prices and he decided to look elsewhere for the same quality land but less costly."[44]

Besides, mechanization remained more feasible and the boll weevil far less devastating in western Texas. Mexican migrants provided cheap labor, and farmers began harvesting cotton by raking the fields with a skid or stripper outfitted with close-set prongs. Even if the farmers did not yet use tractors, they used four-mule teams and more efficient implements. Few blacks purchased farms on the South Plains, probably because violence and intimidation kept black pioneers out of the area, or because they lacked the capital to succeed where farms were larger and more mechanized. White farm owners and white share tenants, lacking these impedi-

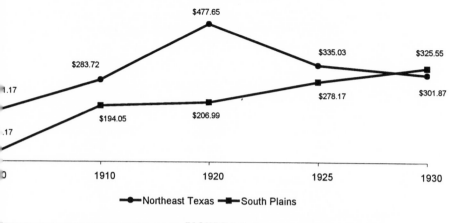

FIGURE 5.4

Farmland's value per acre, 1900–1930 (in 1991 dollars).
Source: U.S., *Census: 1900, Agriculture,* pt. 1, 125–131; U.S., *Census: 1910, Agriculture,*
vol. 7, 655–675; U.S., *Census: 1920, Agriculture,* vol. 6, pt. 2, 664–686;
U.S., *Census of Agriculture: 1925,* pt. 2, 1140–1170; U.S., *Census: 1930, Agriculture,*
vol. 2, pt. 2, 1424–1445.

ments, abandoned Northeast Texas and joined Wiseman in the move to the South Plains.[45]

As farm owners left the region, they took their machines with them. Since the value of farm implements declined far more sharply between 1920 and 1925 than the number of landowners, more-prosperous share tenants, whose greatest assets were implements, probably also left. Thus the swift decline of levels of mechanization below the 1920 benchmark joined the decline in land prices to seemingly confirm the limited and temporary economic impact of the war.[46]

Yet such a straightforward conclusion ignores several key points. The amount of improved acreage in the region dropped more swiftly than the value of machines and implements, meaning the per-acre level of mechanization remained well above 1910 levels. In addition, the war years initiated a shrinkage in the number of farm owners and consolidation of land holdings that continued for decades. To that extent the war left the region's agricultural economy more efficient and potentially more prosperous. It left it what many soon called more modern. Still, because croppers replaced machine-owning tenants, the war also left the agricultural economy and society more sharply divided between the well off and the desperate.[47]

TABLE 5.2
Implements and Machines per Improved Acre (in 1991 dollars)

Location	1900	1910	1920	1925	1930
District	$19.40	$24.72	$36.02	$25.12	$27.29
Texas	$24.82	$29.66	$33.54	$25.61	$32.31

Source: U.S., *Census: 1900–1930, Agriculture.*

EFFICIENCY AND ITS COST

Growth in the number of croppers obscured an important reality—migrants from Northeast Texas left behind an agricultural economy still striving for greater efficiency. Nothing better demonstrated this than the shrinkage in land in production between 1920 and 1925. Just as soil conservation programs later reduced acreage in cotton, owners converted back into woods marginal, cutover lands planted to cotton during the war, and the amount of improved acreage in the region returned to barely above the 1910 level.[48] As indicated above, this meant that although the value of farm implements shrank by 30 percent between 1920 and 1925, those remaining implements tilled and cultivated fewer acres. In fact, the value of farm implements measured in constant dollars was 12 percent higher in 1925 than in 1910. Moderately stable prices and yields after 1925 even encouraged further mechanization. According to the *Paris News*, despite the difficult times of 1926 and 1927, mechanization of Lamar County farms resumed in 1928. As Table 5.2 indicates, the value of machines per improved acre in 1930 approached the war-induced high of 1920.[49]

This increase in mechanization accompanied a slight increase in improved acreage and land planted in cotton between 1925 and 1930. During this five-year span share tenants declined in number in all counties except Bowie, Cass, and Marion. In those three counties, newly drained swampland provided some opportunities for share tenants. Meanwhile farm owners kept declining in number in all eleven counties. The continued growth in croppers did not keep up with the loss of owners and share tenants during the 1920s. As a result of this decrease in farm population and increase in improved acreage, the ratio of land to farm operators improved marginally, and by 1930 operators on average farmed a fractionally higher amount of improved acreage than in 1920. Thanks to the rapid conversion of ranches to large mechanized farms in West Texas, the ratio of improved acres to operators improved dramatically for the state as a whole. Yet the ratio of land to labor also improved, if only slightly, in one of the most typically southern portions of the state (see Table 5.1). Unlike farm size in other southern states, farm size in Texas increased in the 1920s.[50]

This increase in land per farm operator did little to halt the increased use of sharecroppers, common to the entire South. In Northeast Texas, boll weevils and relocation opportunities accelerated this turn to croppers, especially in the western counties, where before 1920 use of croppers had lagged other parts of Northeast Texas. By 1930, the number of croppers in Delta and Hopkins counties stood 30 percent higher than in 1920, and their tenant profile approached the regional norm. Weevils hit these counties hard, and owners surely tried every method to reduce their losses. Turning to more easily managed and closely supervised croppers held out the possibility of reducing weevil damage. Weevils, on the other hand, gave share tenants a good reason to try farming elsewhere. At the same time hired hands, being younger and often unmarried, probably left for the cities or West Texas. Without share tenants and hired hands, landowners turned to croppers, whose families and poverty kept them in the area.[51]

Race further restricted the ability to leave. Almost without fail, the newly arrived croppers in the prairie counties were black, those whose poverty and race prevented them from moving to the South Plains. Blacks left the South after 1915, but the first to leave had work experience outside the cotton patch. Of course, when blacks became desperate enough, they did not let their lack of industrial experience stop them from leaving. Many young, unmarried blacks exercised this option. Fear of the unknown and the need to protect their families kept black croppers from radical changes in location and occupation. They would, however, move several counties away if a better opportunity presented itself in agriculture.[52]

Delta County offered a good example of how black migration played out. The census gives us a tantalizing set of numbers for Delta. Three hundred fewer rural blacks and one hundred fewer urban blacks populated the county in 1930 than in 1920. Black females under age twenty-one declined by 37 percent. Black males under age twenty-one declined by 33 percent. The under-seven population of both races declined by 34 percent. Yet the number of black farm owner and black cropper families increased over the decade. Taken as a whole, the numbers indicate that young unmarried blacks or young married blacks with small children left (or had fewer children). Blacks who lived in small villages and possessed skills and experience useful in manufacturing or construction probably also left for Dallas, Chicago, or some other rapidly growing city. Hired hands—the young—also left. More-established black families, typically sharecroppers, remained or even moved into the county. Perhaps some share tenants slid down the ladder to become croppers. More likely they left, and croppers from other counties or, at least in one recorded case in Red River County, from as far away as Mississippi moved in. Meanwhile, blacks with some capital, either Delta County share tenants or residents of other counties, purchased land as its price declined after 1920.[53]

Delta County cotton acreage increased as well. In fact, total acreage in cultivation increased. Labor could leave while acreage in cultivation expanded because Delta's farmers purchased machinery at one of the highest rates in Northeast Texas. Still, since the mechanization of cotton harvesting and other key phases of production proceeded slowly, the need for seasonal labor swelled as cotton acreage multiplied. Whites could not supply this labor because the white population of the county also declined. Instead, black residents of Dallas and Paris filled seasonal labor needs, reducing the need to keep hands on the payroll year round.[54]

Laws and law enforcement officers propped up these labor arrangements. In May 1922 heavy rains delayed the cultivation of cotton near Paris. The end of the month and the arrival of drier weather found farmers scrambling for hands. Using the threat of prosecution for vagrancy, Paris constable Frank Geron rounded up a hundred blacks and hauled them to nearby farms. Packing as many as eleven blacks in a car, other local law enforcement officers joined in forcing hands to chop cotton. Idle blacks found on the streets of Paris had to contribute to the new economic order or go to jail.[55]

Although Delta and Lamar represented the extreme, every county in the region experienced similar changes in the labor pool. Seasonal labor and croppers replaced hired hands and share tenants. While demographic trends made croppers the most available form of labor, economic reality made them the most desirable. When cotton and land prices fell in the 1920s, landowners pushed harder to convert to cropping. Given the difficulty in mechanizing cotton harvesting and the expense of using fertilizer, using more-efficient labor offered the simplest and least expensive way to improve productivity. Tilling, planting, cultivation, and boll weevil control needed more attention than ever before. Managerial changes begun a decade before in prosperous times became all the more vital. Earl Bryan Schwulst, a close observer of the blackland counties, caught the spirit of this transformation in the 1920s when he insisted that landlords and bankers must exert more control because of "tenants shiftlessness and slipshod methods of tilling the soil." He was particularly concerned about share tenants who had no economic incentive to build up the soil and who lacked the supervision of a landlord. Croppers also still represented the potential for greater profit by increasing the owner's percentage of the crop and offering an opportunity to furnished food and clothing on credit. Despite the risk of erratic cotton prices and tenants who skipped out without settling up at the crossroads store, sharecropping promised owners prosperity in uncertain times.[56]

After 1922 prosperity eluded some cotton farmers, but not all. Except for 1926 and 1929 the rest of the decade saw a decent combination of high yields and acceptable prices. In 1925 almost every county set production records, and the price remained higher than in 1921. The next year yields plummeted and huge crops in other areas of the South sent the price below 1921 levels. In 1927 and 1928 yields and prices rebounded. Even 1929 was a better year than 1921. From 1930 to 1933, however, prices lower than any in the twentieth century stunned cotton farmers and those who depended upon them (see Figure 5.3). The simple survival of cotton farmers in these bleak times, however, suggested that greater use of machines and a higher level of improved acres per farm operator made them more efficient than in 1900.[57]

In the meantime, the continued rapid growth of urban areas in other parts of Texas not only offered markets for alternatives to cotton, it helped maintain the ratio of land to labor. When the land per farm operator shrank to levels that made earning a living difficult, nearby cities provided an alternative for the desperate.

For Northeast Texas, Dallas was the most significant of these rapidly growing cities. Discovery of oil in Mexia and other points directly south of Dallas in the 1910s increased the integration of the city's bankers and businessmen into the petroleum industry. The reach of these bankers and businessmen broadened considerably after the selection of their city as the regional seat of the Federal Reserve in 1913. Banking, petroleum, wheat and cotton processing, and favorable state legislation encouraged the rapid growth of the insurance industry. Woodworking plants and railroad shops added blue-collar jobs. Reflecting this dynamic growth in jobs, in 1920 Dallas passed Houston in population and trailed San Antonio by only a few thousand. By 1930 its population of 260,500 exceeded the population of the eleven-county region.[58]

Those who migrated to Dallas from Northeast Texas had their lives transformed, but even those who remained felt the impact of the rapid emergence of a huge, nearby urban center. Only sixty miles separated the southwestern corner of Hopkins County from Dallas. All the counties enjoyed excellent rail connections to Dallas, and hard-surfaced highways connected the major points of Northeast Texas to the city by the mid-1920s.[59]

For counties bordering Louisiana, Shreveport served the same function as Dallas. Caddo Parish grew from a population of about 83,000 in 1910 to about 125,000 in 1930. On a smaller scale, the concentration of banks, insurance companies, law firms, and oil companies that caused the growth of Dallas also benefited Shreveport. Shreveport, too, had long been the major wholesaling center for Northern Louisiana and played an important role in the cotton and lumber industries.[60]

As Dallas and Shreveport grew, demand for fruits, vegetables, meat, eggs, and dairy products increased, and the value of agricultural land adjacent to the cities also increased. Oil drilling in Caddo Parish also drove up the price of land. When farms turned into suburbs and oil fields, agricultural production moved farther from Dallas County and Caddo Parish.[61] By 1925, as the editors of the *Texas Almanac* noted in their entry on Delta County, "Much attention is paid to the dairying and poultry raising industries and the nearness of the county to large population centers gives it a ready market." [62]

Nearness depended as much upon improved transportation as it did on actual distance. Just as railroads allowed the emergence of the lumber industry at the turn of the century, automobiles and good roads allowed farmers to transport raw milk, eggs, and chickens to processing plants and to move produce directly to urban markets. Again like railroads, the good-roads movement fell into roughly two stages: initial halting efforts to build roads, and later more-successful attempts to knit the region into a seamless transportation web.

Initial efforts began about 1910 when Northeast Texans declared their region "fifty years behind the world in the matter of roads." In most counties talk remained greater than action until the World War I years when areawide good-roads organizations began coordinating multicounty road projects. Local politicians also began calling for increased aid from the state and federal governments, but full participation by the state awaited the mid-1920s. Until then, county governments continued to take the lead in road building, meaning some counties, like Lamar, built a significant road system and others did not. By the mid-1920s, however, most of Northeast Texas had either hard-surface highways or gravel roads. At that point, state aid and the imposition of uniform standards began to take hold. By the early 1930s, an all-weather road system connected most of the region. Anything perishable could then be transported quickly to processing plants.[63]

Good roads particularly helped the dairy industry, and by 1930 Delta,

Hopkins, and Lamar numbered among the major dairy counties in Texas. Milk production in these counties increased by almost one million gallons between 1919 and 1924 and by over one million gallons between 1924 and 1929. By 1930 Hopkins County alone produced almost four million gallons of milk, an increase of more than a million gallons from 1920. Farmers brought their raw milk to town, and Sulphur Springs soon contained a Carnation Milk Factory and a Kraft Cheese Plant. Prairies, after all, were natural grass-growing areas, and the limestone in the soil increased milk production. Such advantages combined with proximity to a large and expanding market made dairying the preferred alternative to cotton.[64]

Vegetable and poultry production also flourished as roads improved, and Camp County in particular became a center of these alternatives to cotton. Pittsburg enjoyed excellent rail and highway connections to Dallas one hundred miles to the west and to Shreveport seventy-five miles to the east. In the surrounding county and adjacent Upshur County, friable soil encouraged production of sweet potatoes and other vegetables. In 1925 tiny Camp County's farmers planted 500 acres in sweet potatoes, more than twice as many as any other county in Northeast Texas. In 1929 cropland planted in sweet potatoes had increased to almost 900 acres, about 2 percent of the total for the state. Chicken production, meanwhile, jumped during World War I, slumped at mid-decade, then rebounded by 1929. Before long, chickens joined sweet potatoes as the mainstays of Camp County farmers. As chicken production grew, so did the production of sorghum and other small grains used as chicken feed.[65]

Despite the size of the sweet potato crop and the increased importance of chickens and other livestock, in 1930 cotton remained Camp's most valuable agricultural product. It brought farmers about $625,000, while sweet potatoes, its nearest rival, brought $315,000. Cotton offered security and familiarity. Unlike corn, it produced a crop even on marginal soils and resisted drought. It generally produced a higher return per acre than wheat or other small grains. In some ways, new technology actually increased reliance on cotton. As cars and trucks replaced mules and horses, the large market for hay and oats dwindled. Hoping to offset erratic prices by increasing yields, landowners also turned to recently developed machines and techniques to convert wetlands into cotton fields, and they used more fertilizer. For most, cotton remained the preferred crop.[66]

Besides, other crops had problems of their own. Potatoes, sweet potatoes, strawberries, peaches, and other vegetables and fruits required intensive hand labor. Perishable crops required a quick harvest and machines offered little help. Fruit and nut crops required a greater initial investment per acre than row crops. Once planted, trees required careful attention but did not produce for several years. Marketing and storing alternate crops posed additional hazards to would-be producers. Farmers put off committing acreage to anything but cotton, corn, and forage crops until processing and shipping facilities for fruits and vegetables existed locally. Yet without sufficient acreage in such crops, establishing processing and storage facilities posed serious risks. Further, railroad agents insisted on full carloads of peaches or other fruits and vegetables before they would ship them long distances. Most fruits and vegetables required quick shipment, and any delays in marketing or inadequate storage could spoil the fragile harvest. Even sweet potatoes demanded proper curing and storage to preserve the quality of the crop.[67]

In testimony to the problems with alternatives to cotton, in 1928 and 1929 Camp's growers had to scramble to ensure the planting of enough acres of black-eyed peas to allow J. B. Henry & Sons to install a thresher and a manager in Pittsburg. Still, growers succeeded, and the close relationship between grower and marketer essential to fruit and vegetable crops ensued. By 1940 sweet potatoes accounted for more than 60 percent of the value of all Camp's crops, and a shipping-basket factory and a vegetable-canning factory were the largest employers in the county.[68]

These difficulties with alternative crops and the slow pace of transition away from cotton buttress the traditional argument that rural Texas, like much of the South, converted to a modern agricultural economy after 1933. This argument ignores both the significant differences in the cotton industry that developed in the previous two decades and the establishment of new agricultural endeavors during the 1920s. Dairying, sweet potatoes, and chickens did not suddenly appear on the agricultural scene after 1933. Instead, all began to grow in importance during World War I and became vital parts of the farm economy by 1930. Moreover, continual attempts to diversify away from cotton signaled that farmers in Northeast Texas willingly took risks and made sudden changes. The mindset necessary for the move away from cotton existed before 1930. So too did transportation and marketing networks; otherwise experimental alternatives to cotton would have failed immediately.

By 1930 signs of modern agriculture abounded. Large farms closely linked to gins were far more common than in 1920. Farmers used more machines per acre, and managers exerted more control over labor. Less-favorable conditions for the hatching of boll weevils after 1921 increased yields, but farm operators also did a better job of combating the weevil. Machines improved planting and cultivation. Fertilizer use increased. Diversification, particularly concentration on chickens, sweet potatoes, and dairy cattle, added to farm income. With fewer owners and share tenants and a slightly improved ratio of land to labor, the structure of farming also changed. By most practical measurements, Northeast Texas farmers had already started down the path that the Great Depression and government bureaucrats would soon force upon all southern cotton growers. In that sense, transformation rather than stasis characterized the region.[69]

Connectedness rather than isolation also characterized the region. What happened in the South Plains and in Dallas and Fort Worth mattered in rural Northeast Texas. Migration to the South Plains allowed farmers who went and farmers who stayed to improve their ratio of land to labor. (This also probably occurred in rural Oklahoma.) In like fashion, Dallas and Fort Worth offered an attractive destination for those who struggled to keep up with a rapidly changing village and small-town economy. Residents of small towns and villages experienced difficulty in the 1920s; yet the degenerating economy did not mire them in lives as desperate as those of sharecroppers. Instead, they joined farm owners and share tenants in leaving the region for brighter prospects elsewhere.[70]

In fact, the depopulation of villages predated the loss of rural and small-town population. Before World War I, changes in the cotton industry favored the larger towns of the region. The merchants and cotton brokers of Texarkana, Paris, Pittsburg, Sulphur Springs, and Jefferson remained competitive with still larger firms in New Orleans, Dallas, Houston, and Shreveport. They used the enhanced transportation network to take away cotton business from villages like Linden. That same transportation network and a rapidly expanding mail-order business allowed local residents to buy what they needed elsewhere. They either shopped at less-expensive, high-volume, cash-only stores in nearby towns, or they ordered from Sears or Montgomery Ward.[71]

Wartime worsened the circumstances of village merchants and tradesmen. J. T. Webster, the Pittsburg merchant who complained about the negative impact of the war on small-scale cotton dealers, confirmed a trend suggested by the available population figures for communities with a population of fewer than 2,500 in 1920. Despite the robust economy, most of these villages lost population in the 1910s, while all eleven counties and all towns over 2,500 gained population. Even the rural population, of which these villages were part, increased over the decade. By 1920 more Northeast Texans lived on isolated farms and more lived in towns over 2,500, but the small villages characteristic of life in the post–Reconstruction South were on the decline.[72]

While it is impossible to say exactly who left, semiskilled and skilled workers involved in the cotton trade and members of the merchant class

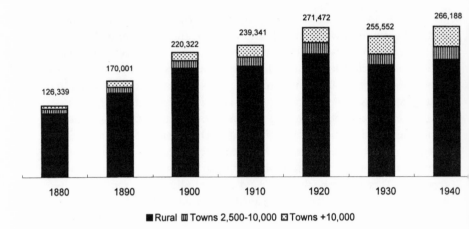

FIGURE 5.5

First District population, 1880–1940.
Source: U.S., Census: 1880–1940, Population.

surely led the exodus. Opportunities were too bright elsewhere for those with drive, talent, and experience to remain in the villages of Northeast Texas.

O. J. T. Leonard and his children offered a good example of the movement of the village merchant class to nearby cities. Leonard farmed and ran a struggling general merchandise store in Linden. During World War I his children Enola, J. Marvin, Obadiah P., and G. Thomas moved first to Dallas and then to Fort Worth. In 1918 the siblings pooled their resources and opened a small general store in downtown Fort Worth. In less than a decade the family turned a $900 initial investment into one of the largest department and grocery stores in Texas. As commentators frequently noted, the war shook the family loose from Linden, and it created new opportunities in Fort Worth.[73]

Not just the middle class left the towns and villages of Northeast Texas. The elite of the prosperous larger towns left for the still grander vistas of nearby cities. Porter Ashburn Bywaters began his business career in Honey Grove in Fannin County. Taking advantage of kinship connections, he and his family moved to Paris in 1908 and founded a wholesale grocery company. The company prospered, and in 1917 he moved his headquarters to Dallas and his family to the exclusive suburb Highland Park. One son, Jerry Bywaters, became a noted Dallas artist, but the other worked in the ever-expanding family business. Interestingly, Paris Wholesale Grocery furnished several key managers for Leonard Brothers. By

1920, while white farmers relocated to the South Plains, townsfolk moved along a well-defined migration chain from Northeast Texas to Dallas and Fort Worth.[74]

After 1920, changes on the farm, in the cotton industry, and in retailing damaged the village economy more than ever before, and that damage extended to towns with a population under 10,000. As Figure 5.5 shows, for the first time towns of between 2,500 and 10,000 lost population from one census to the next. When farm operators and share tenants left the region, merchants lost customers. Even if they did not lose customers, replacing owners and share tenants with croppers reduced the rural sector's income. Reduced income equaled reduced consumer spending. When cotton firms centralized the handling of cotton and linked gins to cottonseed mills, small towns and villages lost jobs and, even more important, lost retail trade. By the late 1920s editors offered exaggerated inducements in a desperate effort to revive the cotton trade in their towns. One editor claimed that if you brought your cotton to his town "you will find courteous, big-hearted buyers on every side to extend you every kindness." Price won out over a big heart, and as roads improved, farmers easily took their cotton to the largest and best-paying markets. Without the cotton trade to lure shoppers to their towns and villages, retailers suffered.[75]

Continuing changes in the retailing industry heightened the difficulty of village and small-town merchants. As roads improved and the use of cars and light trucks increased in the 1920s, shoppers spurned the limited choices and high prices of small-town and village merchants. Merchants and those dependent upon them left for better opportunities elsewhere. In one example, Naples, in Morris County, lost about 5 percent of its population in the 1920s. Ironically, W. R. Watts of the *Naples Monitor* proudly pointed in 1925 to an editorial from the *New York Times* that argued, "since the opening of the century and especially during the last ten years the South has had to be 'reborn' intellectually, agriculturally and transportation wise." The editor offered stark proof of that rebirth in 1929 when he commented that fifteen years ago the horse and buggy were common. Now "there is not a child in our grammar school who can remember ever to have seen a livery stable." A reborn South unfortunately worked to the detriment of Naples, and editor Watts spent the decade urging subscribers to shop at home and avoid "allegiance to a distant metropolis." Shoppers, however, drove to the better-managed, higher-volume, and lower-price stores available in larger towns. They also shopped with the rapidly expanding mail-order retailers whose goods could reach local customers more easily than ever.[76]

In fact, by decade's end, mail-order companies had evolved into low-price, high-volume retailers along the lines of J. C. Penney. In the early 1920s Montgomery Ward experimented with outlet stores in the basements of their mail-order distribution centers. By mid-decade Sears and Montgomery Ward had begun opening stores that combined distribution of catalog items with retail sales. Ward's opened such a store in Paris in 1928, and it quickly became a major competitor for area merchants. Supplied from the giant Fort Worth distribution center, the store offered low prices on a variety of goods and had the advantage of Ward's extensive advertising and good name. Paris merchants probably welcomed the store, because it increased overall customer traffic in the business district. Outside of Paris the new Montgomery Ward store had the opposite effect. Customers from smaller towns and villages, lured by the new store, shifted the retail revenue stream from their local merchants to merchants in larger towns or to chain stores.[77]

Montgomery Ward's success signaled that economic prosperity in this reborn South required size, capital, and managerial skill lacking among small-town and village merchants. This challenging economic scene combined with the previously described new opportunities nearby to cause ten of the eleven counties in the region to lose population. Only Bowie County, led by strong growth in Texarkana, gained population over the decade. (It took both push and pull factors to cause outmigration. During the 1930s when the economy performed even more dismally but there were few attractive places to go, the region gained population.)[78]

Conditions remained difficult in the more than sixty villages of less than 2,500 population in the eleven-county region. Available population figures suggest an important pattern. Every village below 500 lost population between 1920 and 1930. Taken together, the villages listed in the census lost about 8 percent of their population. This rate surpassed that of the rural population as a whole and almost matched that of towns between 2,500 and 10,000.[79]

In these small towns the economy and population spiraled downward, with each problem contributing to further problems. Uncertain cotton prices, for example, put severe pressure on the Texas banking system. If banks and their major borrowers guessed wrong on the price of cotton, they faced disaster. The cotton crisis of 1926 in particular caused borrowers to default on their loans, and overextended and poorly managed banks never recovered. As a result, in Cooper the First National Bank failed in 1927, severely damaging the local economy. Such failures accelerated the decline of small towns whose best bankers moved to cities where the sharp growth in the number and size of banks drove up the salaries of bank employees. This brain drain contributed to the further deterioration of the local economy. From 1920 to 1930 towns between 2,500 and 10,000 lost 8.7 percent of their population. In comparison, towns over 10,000 gained population in the 1920s. Size mattered.[80]

Not even the development of truck crops and dairy farming broke this downward economic spiral in most smaller towns. Despite the interest in truck crops in Delta County, Cooper lost population in the 1920s. In part, Delta's soil and terrain made cotton more profitable than other crops. Any increase in acreage in fruits and vegetable came at the expense of oats and other small grains. Cooper also lay too close to Paris and Sulphur Springs. Hard-surface roads ran from Cooper to the two larger towns, and rails had connected them for decades. Just as the buying and handling of cotton increasingly centered in larger towns, so did the marketing of alternatives crops. Farmers took their milk to Sulphur Springs and truck crops to Paris for processing and shipping.[81]

Even more than Sulphur Springs, Paris benefited from this change. After 1900, business leaders in Paris built a transportation web centering on their city that prevented nearby towns from competing as market centers. Their motto was "modernize—or lose." By the 1920s Lamar stood in the forefront of the good-roads movement, as boosters proclaimed "new roads make Paris the 'mecca' of the region." Before 1930 the local business community laid the groundwork for the eventual location of a large Campbell's Soup plant in their town by making Paris an entrenched collection point for vegetable and meat products.[82]

In smaller towns, if farmers grew alternatives to cotton, dealers processed them in Paris or Texarkana. Crops that needed little processing, such as watermelons and peaches, moved directly to market. As a result, despite the growing importance of the dairy industry, even Sulphur Springs joined Jefferson, Clarksville, and Mount Pleasant in losing population in the 1920s.[83]

Pittsburg proved an interesting exception to this trend of population loss among towns under 10,000 in population, and thanks to the particular needs of the sweet potato industry, it gained population. Blacks in particular moved to Pittsburg as sweet potato acreage expanded in Camp County. They helped harvest sweet potatoes, peaches, and strawberries and prepared them for shipment. In the off-season they worked in the town's basket and crate factories or sawmills. Increasingly, available Mexican migrants probably provided additional labor essential to the expansion of specialty crops. These new patterns of labor kept hands available for the cotton harvest, and therefore evoked little opposition from Camp's cotton growers.[84]

In Cooper, blacks left. Marketing centers developed elsewhere. Seasonal workers lived elsewhere. Whites left as well. In every town between 2,500 and 10,000 except Sulphur Springs, whites left at a higher rate than blacks. White population even declined slightly in Pittsburg in the 1920s. The economy could not sustain population growth, especially when opportunity lay close at hand.[85]

Black and white, rural, village, and town dweller, all faced a new economic world by the late 1920s. W. A. Owens, who left Paris for good as the decade closed, captured this transformation poignantly. In his conclusion to *A Season of Weathering,* he wrote:

> With a kind of desperation I said goodbye to my mother and walked out South Main Street . . . to flag a ride to Dallas. After an hour in the hot sun I watched a car slow to a stop and heard my name called. It was the George Graves family, who had lived in Pin Hook long ago. They had moved to the blackland and had, they told me, done well. They had a house, a car, a living to show for their work. I had nothing. They were friendly and offered to crowd up a little to give me a ride, but I did not take it. They were only going to their farm in Glory, and for me that was off the main road.[86]

Owens's comments suggested important characteristics of the pre-1930 economy. Forget tales of unrelenting woe in which nothing fundamental changed. Some prospered dramatically, others experienced the economic calamity often associated with the rural South of the 1920s. Having a place to go, links to other areas of Texas, contributed to prosperity and presented new opportunities.

From Maryland to Texas, undoubtedly other subregions of the South underwent a similar economic transformation. Citrus in Florida, strawberries in South Louisiana, and rice in Central Arkansas all transformed local economies before 1930. Likewise, pockets of the South showed an even more marked divergence between the rich and the poor than did Northeast Texas. The region differed in its location. Large Texas cities demonstrated a vitality and—thanks to railroads, food processing, and petroleum—a level of manufacturing rare in most areas of the cotton-producing South. These cities provided markets, jobs, and a floor on wages in Northeast Texas. Residents of villages and small towns suffered from hard times, but they had a place to go. Opportunities in the petroleum industry or on the South Plains added to locational advantages. Shifts in cotton prices and land prices caused farm owners and share tenants to leave and enhanced the ratio of improved acres to farm operator and machines to improved acre. Established access to Mexican migratory labor and to day laborers in urban areas furthered this process and distinguished Texas from the rest of the South. Location allowed even a cotton-based economy to modernize and to anticipate the changes more often associated with the New Deal. Yet not all could leave. In at least one way Northeast Texas resembled any cotton-growing region in the South. On the eve of the Great Depression the gulf between the rich and the poor widened.[87]

Yet, rather than thinking of the economy as a prelude to the Great Depression, we should take it on its own merits. The World War I years brought unparalleled prosperity while accelerating such fundamental changes as the drive for industrial-style efficiency in agriculture. The depression of 1920–1921 combined with boll weevil damage to undermine the regional economy. Despite this, and the difficulties in 1926, the rest of the decade was reasonably prosperous. During all this time, farmers became more efficient and diversified. They also became less numerous, and croppers increasingly provided the labor on the land. These croppers missed the opportunities and suffered the woes of the 1920s, leaving them worse off in 1930 than in 1910. Croppers, especially older black croppers with families, remained stuck in poverty. Small-town and village merchants and tradesmen, as well as share tenants and farm owners, were more fortunate. They had a place to go. If Paris or Texarkana held no hope, Dallas or the South Plains offered new opportunities.[88] For share-croppers the Great Depression marked a pivotal event. For others the Depression interrupted a process begun two decades before.

SIX

WORLD WAR I AND
A SHIFTING CULTURE

In the midst of the transformation of Northeast Texas into a place with a growing gulf between the better off and the desperate came World War I. This war gets little credit for the transformation of the modern South. At best, historians describe it as a starting point for the momentous process that truly got underway after the start of the New Deal. At worst, the war was a flash in the pan without lasting consequences.[1]

In Northeast Texas the World War I years neither marked a simple beginning point nor faded without consequences. The economic changes discussed in the previous chapter offered a good example of how this process worked. From early in the century, cotton prices and land values rose while cotton marketing consolidated in larger towns. Wartime conditions accelerated these trends and began others. Jobs in Fort Worth and Dallas or moving to the Texas South Plains grew more attractive. More capital from oil royalty payments, higher land prices, and higher cotton prices enhanced farmers' balance sheets. As a result, the war diminished the hold of "constraints" to outmigration as "information, finance, and job availability" all improved.[2]

Profound social change accompanied economic change. The number of smaller farm owners, skilled labor, and village merchants shrank because of the war and the abrupt and tumultuous end of the economic stimulation it provided. Sharecroppers multiplied. Urban blacks and black farm owners left. Mexican migrant laborers filled their place. As with the economy, observers noticed faint signs of some of these social and demographic trends before 1914, but the war made change obvious and more permanent.

Change also assumed subtle new patterns—patterns associated with a shifting culture rather than simply flowing from economic or demographic changes. The cultural underpinnings of politics that required frequent mention of the glorious South and tacit acceptance of states' rights eroded. After much discussion but limited action before the war, women altered their roles and changed their place in society. Lynching gradually lost some of its quasi-religious features, gained an economic motivation, and eventually came under more-direct attack by whites and blacks than ever before. All indicated the weakening of a culture based on memories of the Lost Cause.

LYNCHING AND SOCIETY

During World War I, Northeast Texas editors went out of their way to paint the North as inhospitable to blacks. In a June 1917 editorial entitled "Black Man Stay South," Burt Lockhart admitted that the occasional "bad nigger" in the South suffered at the hands of a mob. In the North, however, even a "good nigger" was "mobbed, beaten, and run out of town." Given the rapid departure of both white and black labor during the war, such diatribes made economic sense. So did calls for better treatment of blacks, particularly those of the "better sort." Economic reality demanded a step toward racial justice.[3]

Calls for better treatment like renditions of northern horrors probably seemed like mere words to blacks. Especially when actions belied the words. In September 1915 two brothers, Joe and King Richmond, after arguing with the owner of the land they worked, got into a shoot-out with the sheriff of Hopkins County. The brothers killed the sheriff and wounded his deputy. A mob soon formed and went after the two blacks, killing Joe and wounding King. After bringing both into Sulphur Springs, the mob burned King to death and tossed Joe's body on the fire for good measure. A large crowd witnessed the burning, but no one tried to stop the mob. Yet soon thereafter, as Figure 6.1 indicates, lynchings diminished until war's end.[4]

In all, white Northeast Texans lynched forty-six blacks between 1883 and 1923. Mobs lynched three whites before 1900, but none after that date. Unlike other parts of the state, Northeast Texas recorded no Mexicans dying at the hands of a lynch mob in those forty years. Only Camp, a heavily black county, and Franklin, with few blacks, had no recorded lynchings. Paris and Lamar County led the dubious list of lynching sites with thirteen. While Lamar had the largest total population in the region and in most years the largest black population, size alone did not

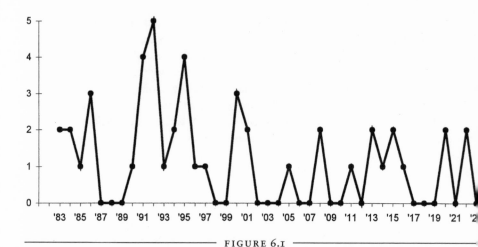

FIGURE 6.1

Lynchings in Northeast Texas, 1883–1923.
Source: Daniel T. Williams, *Amid the Gathering Multitude: The Story of Lynching in America: A Classified Listing* (Unpublished: Tuskegee University, 1968).

explain the preeminence of the county on the lynching list. In comparison, Bowie and Cass counties, with smaller total populations and about the same number of blacks, each had only five lynchings. (Based on the 1920 population, 1 in 1,000 blacks were lynched in Lamar and 1 in 2,300 in Cass and Bowie combined.) Marion, the only majority black county, had three times the black population of Hopkins but the same number of lynchings, reinforcing the conclusion that blacks faced a higher risk of lynching in counties where blacks made up less than 35 percent of the population. (Again based on the 1920 population, 1 in 1,000 blacks were lynched in Marion, while 1 in 425 were lynched in Hopkins.)[5]

Lynchings came in bursts, and during the forty years represented on the graph, three significant lulls in lynching occurred: 1887–1889, 1902–1904, and 1917–1919. Until 1923 and probably beyond, however, the shadow of lynching constantly hung over life in Northeast Texas. Still, the slackening in the number of lynchings during the war seemed less associated with temporary political or economic factors than earlier lulls and more associated with cultural change.[6]

While lynching spiked after 1919, the well-entrenched practice virtually disappeared in the region and in most parts of Texas after 1922. During the war, the intense need for black labor and fear that blacks would move north probably made a difference. In other words, the war drove home the importance of black labor and the importance of maintaining an image that attracted rather than repelled blacks. Yet economic self-interest cannot entirely explain the decline of lynching, which long had a religious or cultural component. The undermining of that facet of lynching during the war goes far toward explaining the disappearance of this unique feature of life in the New South.[7]

One story serves as a signpost of this process—the burning of Herman Arthur and his brother Ervin Arthur on July 6, 1920, in what turned out to be the last recorded lynching in Lamar County. On Friday, July 2, Scott Arthur, Violet Arthur, their daughters, Mary and Eula, and their sons, Herman and Ervin, loaded up their possessions. They lived on the farm of J. H. Hodges, four miles northeast of Paris, and when Hodges and his son William realized that the Arthurs were about to move out, they tried to stop them. By then only Herman and Ervin Arthur remained. Tempers flared, both sides carried arms. Using shotguns, Herman and Ervin Arthur killed J. H. and William Hodges.[8]

Newspaper accounts claimed that the Arthurs owed Hodges money, but the facts in the case remain murky. The Arthurs certainly disputed the claim that they owed a just debt, and family tradition maintains that earlier the Hodges came to the house when only Mary and Eula were home. The Hodges knocked over the kitchen stove when it was full of food and threatened to kill Herman. Faced with violence, the family took the advice of Herman, a World War I veteran, and refused to pay or to stay. According to his nephew, "when the white folks started shooting Uncle Herman showed them what he had learned in the war.[9]

Herman and Ervin Arthur immediately fled to Oklahoma, but the marshal and deputy of Valliant found them on the outskirts of that city. Despite pleas to transfer the two young men to another Texas jail, the Oklahoma officials brought them back to Paris. Once back in Paris, the two blacks admitted they had shot the Hodges, but claimed it was self-defense because the Hodges shot first. After the brothers were locked in the city jail, the district judge mounted the courthouse steps and urged the crowd to go home, promising a speedy trial. As in 1893, a group of local citizens had other plans. Although local leaders told the gathering crowd to let the law work its course, "there was no effort made to disperse" them. Instead, they milled about, listening to "much talk of an inciting character." About 7:30 in the evening of July 6, the crowd-turned-mob used sledge hammers to break down the jail door. Officers asked them to stop but never used force to make them stop. The doors fell quickly, and the mob seized the Arthur brothers and carried them to the fairgrounds on the outskirts of town. Taking only about half an hour, the mob chained the two men to a stake and burned them to death. Afterward mob leaders unchained their victims' charred bodies and dragged what was left of Herman and Ervin Arthur behind an automobile through the black section of Paris. More than 3,000 people witnessed the lynching.[10]

Unlike blacks in 1893, Paris blacks in 1920 barricaded themselves in their houses and got out their guns. Either whites or blacks broke into every hardware store in the city, and it looked for a time as if a full-scale race riot would break out. As the mayor of Paris rode through town trying to prevent a riot, shots rang out. City police stood guard on every corner. Eventually, the white mob dispersed and no blood was shed. For several days 250 well-armed whites patrolled Pine Bluff Street, which separated the white from the black section of town. Organized by Mayor J. M. Crook and composed of the town's leading citizens, this special committee insisted "that no abuse or ill treatment of either race by the other would be tolerated." In a further effort to calm the tension, some local whites helped the remaining members of the Arthur family to migrate to Chicago.[11]

In another sign of changing white attitudes, on July 9, Reverend R. P. Shuler, pastor of the First Methodist Church in Paris, cut short his sermon at a local revival meeting to read a prepared statement. Published the next day on the front page of the *Paris Morning News,* Shuler's statement admitted Ervin and Herman Arthur's guilt and mourned the loss of J. H. and William Hodges. Yet the minister insisted that the mob did much more harm than good. Declaring that "mob law is the menace of our Southland," he made several important points. Condemning the dragging of the bodies through the black section of town, he insisted that the perpetrators deserved "the severest punishment that can be meted out by our courts." Not only did the mob overstep the bounds of decency, it broke the law—"the protection of society and defense of the American home." Finally, Shuler argued that "our community will suffer beyond repair" because the mob's action will earn universal condemnation. In other words, vigilantism hurt the business and image of Paris.[12]

While the alleged crime in 1920 differed from that in 1893, the local response diverged even more markedly. Only 3,000 gathered in 1920 compared to 15,000 in 1893, and the lynching of the Arthurs lacked the elaborate torture of Henry Smith. No local citizens condemned mob action in 1893. Ministers and newspaper editors did so in 1920. Public officials openly cooperated with vigilantes in 1893; they passively resisted in 1920. Blacks helped capture Smith in 1893. They armed themselves in 1920. While Reverend Shuler clearly saw Paris as part of the South, he also insisted its citizens needed to act like the rest of America and abandon the practice of lynching. In 1893 apologists justified the lynching of Henry

Smith by claiming it protected the home. In contrast, Shuler insisted the sanctity of the "American home" demanded an end to mob law.[13]

World War I contributed to the difference between the response of 1920 and that of 1893 and all other pre-1917 lynchings. Paris had its share of black veterans who, like Herman Arthur, would not simply accept white brutality. In 1919 federal investigators reported that the city's black veterans met with fellow blacks to urge them to stand up for the rights due all Americans. Blacks did not leave their homes and riot, but they also did not wait passively to become victims of white violence. In addition, to the extent that the war concerned ideals and required service to America, it underscored the need for right action. It helped make the American way more important than southern white folkways.[14]

Yet wartime conditions also probably laid the groundwork for this lynching. As in the 1890s, the lynching followed sudden growth in the black population. In rural Lamar County, the black population increased 20 percent in the 1910s. The rise in sharecropping, caused in large part by extraordinary wartime prices for land and cotton, accounted for this. For some whites, control of newly arrived, and to them unknown, blacks demanded such vicious and public displays.[15]

Not just growth but rapid change in the size and nature of the black population seemed tied to lynching. Besides those in Lamar, the other Northeast Texas lynchings between 1910 and 1920 all took place in counties that lost black population. Red River had three lynchings, Hopkins two, and Marion one. In all three counties towndwelling blacks took advantage of the demand for semiskilled work elsewhere, and left. Black farmers also left these three counties, as well as Lamar. Black sharecroppers replaced them. Perhaps the swirl in the population, the movement of poorer blacks unknown to whites into an area, caused the increase in lynching during the first years of the war in Europe. In that sense, class as well as race accounted for the upsurge in lynching. The lynching of the Richmond brothers in Hopkins in 1915 and the Arthur brothers in Lamar in 1920 grew out of disputes between landowner and croppers. Lynching was a form of labor control in a scarce labor market where blacks could easily move several counties over and find employment. This increase in economic opportunity caused blacks like the Arthurs to resist what they perceived as unjust treatment. Whites in turn grew increasingly determined not only to maintain the labor pool, but to force blacks to stay in their place.[16]

Widespread instability fed this desire to keep blacks within the traditional order. The immediate postwar years left Northeast Texans wondering if the world had gone "mad." Labor unrest, price gouging, and the movement of blacks out of the South all contributed to a sense of anarchy. Belief that the world might fall apart—that blacks would now openly challenge white authority—contributed to the white mob's use of ritualized brutality toward blacks they did not know.[17]

In contrast, well-known blacks with ties to paternalistic white elites enjoyed some freedom from the threat of lynching. Marion County, for example, had the strictest forms of political segregation in the eleven-county region—a system backed up by more than its share of lynchings. It also had one of the best-established black populations in the state. Sam Fisher, a black share tenant from a highly regarded family, proved that despite strict segregation blacks could play a role in public discourse. In 1916 the local editor published a letter from Fisher that sharply criticized a local white agricultural reformer. Two years later the editor published a lengthy notice of the death of Fisher's mother, praising her as a "good Christian woman." Black churches and schools, the underpinning institutions of the middle class, also received support from local whites. Special events and noteworthy achievements all appeared in local newspapers— indicating not only that editors recognized black achievements but that blacks subscribed. Well-known and right-acting blacks were not the demons that newly arrived black croppers were to the whites of Hopkins and Lamar counties.[18]

Better-off blacks also responded to violence by leaving, a reminder that the scarce labor market and the rapidly changing nature of the black population worked both ways. These factors probably caused white landowners to brutalize croppers in an attempt to maintain control, but they also meant kind words and gentler treatment for those outside that class. As the mention of black activities in local newspapers indicated, the black working class and middle class were too important to the local economy to totally alienate.[19]

By 1920 white civic leaders well knew blacks could leave their towns because, despite the prosperity of the 1910s, four of the five largest towns in the region lost black population over the decade. Even though the total population of both Jefferson and Sulphur Springs increased, each town lost 20 percent of its black population. The pattern repeated in Mount Pleasant and Texarkana, which gained in total population but lost a small percentage of their black population. Only Paris, the largest and fastest growing of the five towns in the 1910s, offered enough economic opportunity to offset potential violence and attract blacks. Its black population grew by almost 500, or 14 percent. Anxious not to lose the black working and middle class, white elites in Paris repudiated lynching and the dragging of victims' bodies through black neighborhoods.[20]

In the aftermath of World War I, then, urban blacks from Northeast Texas not only more militantly resisted lynching and other forms of discrimination, they migrated along an established route from the region. Like whites, they most often moved to nearby Fort Worth or Dallas, but Chicago, Kansas City, and other northern cities also drew blacks from the region during the war. Blacks moved along these migration lines in even greater numbers in the decade that followed, and as the story of the Arthur family illustrated, the urban white merchant class in particular had little choice but to try to preserve their customer base and the local workforce by moving to reduce lynching and other forms of violence.[21]

Not just urban blacks left Northeast Texas. The decline in black farm owners during the early 1920s suggests that even in rural areas blacks higher up the class ladder left. Again, such changes probably did not start in 1920. Instead, like white landowners, blacks took advantage of inflated land prices and began leaving during and just after World War I. Racial violence almost certainly also influenced their decision to leave. Where they went remains unclear because white prejudice and violence probably kept black farm owners from moving to western farmland. Theirs was a more complex calculus than white farm owners, one that balanced economic opportunity with freedom from lynching. White merchants understood this calculus and sought to end lynching. Despite their efforts, blacks with the money, status, skills, education, and expectations of a propertied class left.[22]

Blacks were not the only lynching victims in World War I era Texas. In 1915 alone, twenty-six Mexican Americans died at the hands of lynch mobs. Tellingly, none were lynched during 1917–1919, the years of peak demand for their labor, and none were lynched in Northeast Texas. While labor-hungry Northeast Texas elites rejoiced that their region was "already open to Mexicans" in 1917, just how wide open and how many Mexican Americans entered the door remains imprecise.[23]

Certainly fewer Mexican Texans lived and worked in Northeast Texas than in other parts of the state, but as discussed in the previous chapter, economic opportunity and a calculated appeal for their labor drew them into the region during World War I. Since census takers often made their count in seasons when migrants worked elsewhere, few Mexican Americans appeared as residents of Northeast Texas in 1930, the only year during this period that the census placed Mexicans in a distinct category.[24] That year more Mexican Americans, 133, called Bowie home than any other Northeast Texas county. Texarkana's position as a major railroad terminus made it a natural population center for Mexican migrants even after construction ended. They could move throughout Arkansas,

Louisiana, Oklahoma, and Texas on the railroads in search of work. Red River with 96, Cass with 78, and Lamar with 57 trailed Bowie's Mexican American population.[25]

The 1916 and 1926 *Census of Religious Bodies,* however, suggests a larger seasonal Mexican population before 1930. In 1916 and 1926 about 1,500 Roman Catholics lived in Northeast Texas, with more Catholics in Bowie than any other county. Given that the area never attracted many European Catholic immigrants or Louisiana Cajuns, this number probably included Mexicans mixed with some Anglo Catholics.[26]

In between those measurement points, the racist rhetoric that put Mexicans somewhere between whites and blacks disappeared from the region, making it a more hospitable place for new arrivals. That and the need for labor suggests that the number of Mexicans probably increased after 1916 and then receded to pre-war levels by 1926. By then, racist rhetoric had increased and jobs decreased. After that the number of Mexicans continued declining, as reflected by a 30 percent drop in the number of Catholics from 1926 to 1936.[27]

Despite this swirling population, no lynchings of Mexican Americans ever occurred. Perhaps Northeast Texans of European descent never classified Mexicans as "black" enough to need the discipline of lynching. Perhaps their numbers remained too few for an incident that traditionally provoked lynching to occur. Certainly, the protests of the Mexican government about mistreatment of their countrymen played a role, but so too did economic reality, cooperative actions by Mexican immigrants, and Mexicans' uncertain racial identity in the minds of Anglos. That meant Mexican Americans' presence added one more note of ambiguity to the racial landscape of the World War I era, one more group of non-Anglos that should not be lynched.[28]

Wartime declines in lynching proved temporary. The year 1922 saw sixteen blacks and one Mexican American lynched in Texas. Two blacks were lynched in Northeast Texas. Yet in some ways the war ushered in a change in how the region thought about lynching. The black middle class in particular received kinder words and gentler treatment. Whites used ritualized violence to put black sharecroppers in their place, but they also criticized lynching as un-American and removed some from the list of those eligible to be lynched. In 1912 one commentator voiced the attitude of many whites when he called lynching the act of an "indignant and righteous public." Not much had changed since 1893. In 1919 three white men from Upshur County were charged with lynching, and to ensure justice, officials moved the trials outside the region. Some local whites collected funds for the men's defense, but others condemned lynching. The three received only token sentences, but the act of trying them at all was remarkable.[29] At about the same time, something equally remarkable occurred—the spread of new perceptions about the roles of women and greater acceptance of women active outside the home.

WOMEN'S ROLES

Burt Lockhart offered a detailed analysis of the emerging roles of women. In March 1918 he insisted that he did not know nor had he read about a contemporary woman "who is willing to be a silent partner in the business of a man's life, whether that business be running a kingdom, writing poetry, thinking great thoughts, or running a business." Undoubtedly, Lockhart's wife—who helped run the *Pittsburg Gazette,* took a lead in organizing the Liberty Bond Drive, and led the local Women for Hobby Club during the 1918 gubernatorial primary—influenced his thinking. She served as his example of a "new woman" with equal rights and responsibilities.[30]

As in other cases of social change, new women did not emerge during the war without precedent. In the early 1880s women working within the Woman's Christian Temperance Union or the Cumberland Presbyterian Church took a prominent place in the fight for prohibition.[31] This was especially true in Paris, home of the first WCTU chapter in Texas. Gradually, the role of women in other Protestant denominations expanded, and the long-running prohibition fight led to calls for woman suffrage. As the example of Paris indicated, this was particularly true in the larger towns and among upper- and middle-class women bound together through church or civic organizations. After 1900, women also began holding down jobs typically reserved for men. W. C. Williams, editor of the *Omaha Breeze,* noted in 1908 that "Miss Bell Burdette was elected county treasurer of Red River county by an overwhelming majority, yet she could not vote for herself nor swap votes with her opponent." Commenting on a woman who ran for county clerk in Camp County in 1910, Williams observed: "There is said to be no law against ladies holding office in Texas, which we think is right and it does not seem like there should be any law against ladies voting for men and measures, and for one another." A year earlier, J. E. Banger of the *Cass County Sun* went a step nearer equality. He insisted that when women possessed the strength and knowledge needed for the job they should "engage in masculine occupations as freely as they like." It was not out of character for the region, then, for Hopkins County Democrats to include woman suffrage on their list of proposed reforms in August 1914.[32]

After American entry into World War I, however, women's roles in public affairs increased. So did the defense of their new roles by local editors, especially M. I. Taylor of the *Jefferson Jimplecute*. After her father, Ward Taylor, died in 1894, she and her brother operated the paper together until 1914. For the next twelve years she owned and operated the *Jimplecute* by herself.[33]

Taylor shunned the term reformer but seldom missed a chance to advance the cause of working women. In a 1917 editorial entitled "Women in Trousers" she wrote:

> Sane people of both sexes will welcome the adoption of any garment that will aid them in the performance of their duties and make life less irksome for them. A few senseless prudes will of course be horrified, but the prudes have not made the world, have been of little benefit to it, and they will not end it. Women in trousers are inevitable. It must come. And the sooner we become reconciled to the thought the easier it will be for those upon whom necessity forces the innovation.

Aggressive women from families of high standing had long played a part in public life in Northeast Texas. World War I, however, increased their number and acceptance by a wider slice of the population. As Birdie Taylor explained, women in the business world once provided the exception not the rule. Now because of the war women were "in business to stay." While Taylor received some criticism, the *Jimplecute* drove all competitors out of business, suggesting that her views, although perhaps unorthodox, still fell within the boundaries of accepted opinion.[34]

During the war, women moved into politics as well as business. Although slowed by the need to obtain a two-thirds majority in the state legislature to change the suffrage requirements spelled out in the Texas Constitution, supporters of woman suffrage took a half step toward their goal after a change in the law governing primary elections. Such change required only a simple majority of the legislature and the support of the governor, and by 1918 white women could vote in the Texas Democratic primary, but not in the general election.[35]

In Northeast Texas, they turned out in large numbers to vote for William P. Hobby, who signed into law the bill allowing women to vote in the primary. Hobby moved up from lieutenant governor to governor when Jim Ferguson resigned, and Ferguson, seeking retribution for his impeachment and conviction the year before, opposed Hobby. Ferguson, despite his legal troubles and his opposition to prohibition, retained a dedicated core of supporters in the region and in most areas of Texas.[36]

Ferguson's vote-getting ability as much as ideals and issues caused Hobby and his supporters to give women the right to vote in the primary. Men gave women the vote in the primary because of the Texas political system—not the war, not the long record of women's volunteer civic endeavors, and not even prohibition or some other reform cause common to men and women. Hobby was every bit as much a political opportunist as Ferguson. He realized that in the Democratic primary he needed the votes and would receive the votes of women interested in suffrage and reform. Conservatives, particularly those still caught up in defending and memorializing the Lost Cause and in stopping prohibition, would not vote for Hobby. Rural insurgents, many now share tenants or croppers, and some economic reformers concerned with economic equity also would not vote for Hobby. If they voted for Ferguson, these factions could defeat Hobby. Yet conservative and insurgent women were far less likely to participate in politics than women from the factions most likely to support Hobby—social reformers and moderate economic reformers. Given the political system in Texas, Hobby added to his voting base by helping give women the right to participate in the Democratic primary. Tellingly, he showed much less enthusiasm for helping them change the constitution so they could vote in the general election. Thus, instead of marking some great shift in how Texans thought about the roles of women, voting in the primary marked the continued influence of Texas multifactionalism.[37]

Still, for whatever reason women gained the vote, once they could vote they quickly became a force in local elections, tilting politics even more in favor of the reform factions. One example of the new role of women came in Camp and Upshur counties. There J. Ben Hill, the representative of the two counties in the state legislature, opposed Ferguson's impeachment in 1917 and echoed Farmer Jim's rhetoric in his bid for re-election in the July 1918 Democratic primary. Trying to attract the same farm vote as Ferguson, Hill stressed his opposition to ending the ban on using homesteads as collateral for loans. Underscoring his Texas patriotism, he built on his image as defender of the family farm by insisting:

> The wisdom of the heroes of San Jacinto is supreme with me. They braved the hordes of Santa Anna and the wild Indians in order to set up a home, giving protection to their wives and babies. I saw that their wisdom was supreme and in this age of materialism let us perpetuate their memory by forever hushing the mouths of those who would make our State into a few

large estates and forever remember that the home and protection is the great object of the State.

Hill went on adroitly mixing Texas exceptionalism with devotion to the Lost Cause and defended states' rights and limited government. Evoking the memory of Confederate heroes, he stood against any further centralization of power in the hands of the national government.[38]

Hill's two opponents, W. A. Kennedy and J. D. Lawrence, countered by claiming they were not landgrabbers but progressive businessmen. They lambasted Hill for his support of Ferguson and implied that opposing centralization of power meant opposing the war effort. They also made much of their support for education reform and Hill's unwillingness to move aggressively on that issue. Near the end of the campaign, Hill again sought to array the common folk against the greedy and unscrupulous rich by appealing to "the loyal yeomanry of this district."[39]

Hill reserved his sharpest attacks for Kennedy, repeatedly accusing him of taking advantage of his tenants. This helped Lawrence, who carried four of five rural boxes. Hill carried the other rural box. Interestingly, the box Hill carried voted against prohibition in 1911 and 1887, supported the anti-statewide-prohibition candidate for Congress in 1912, and consistently voted against road and school taxes. It was also the only box in Camp County won by Ferguson and lost by Annie Webb Blanton in 1918. It represented the last bastion in Camp of the yeomanry who backed Populism but opposed prohibition and other infringements on males' individual rights. Despite victory in this precinct, Hill finished third in the race and did not even carry his home county of Upshur.[40]

Hill garnered enough votes, however, to prevent the other two candidates from gaining a majority. By 1918 election laws required a runoff primary between the top two finishers if no candidate obtained a majority in the initial primary, and Lawrence and Kennedy moved on to the second primary, where women and their issues proved decisive. Both candidates lived in Pittsburg, splitting that town's vote, and both boasted strong prohibitionist and anti-Ferguson credentials. Women voters in Upshur County, however, gave solid support to Lawrence. Perhaps they listened to Hill's charge that Kennedy was a landgrabber, but Lawrence's strong support of public education also secured women's votes. He went out of his way to point out that he more than Kennedy stood for modernizing and improving the public school system as well as the state university and college system. Women's votes helped him lead in the initial primary and win the runoff.[41]

While not simply a result of some massive shift of thinking, this local election suggested that giving the vote to women in the primary contributed to a changing place for women in society and altered politics. Candidates who questioned women's right to an active role in politics and opposed their causes lost. Hobby demonstrated a keen awareness of this when he linked his campaign with efforts to elect Annie Webb Blanton as the state superintendent of public instruction. A link with Blanton neatly combined Hobby's campaign with efforts to improve public education, a well-established goal of reform-minded women, and with the right of women to participate in politics.[42]

Hobby needed every vote he could muster. Charging that an elite clique closely aligned with the University of Texas had seized the reins of power in the state, Ferguson orchestrated a well-publicized and effective campaign. He championed old-style democracy and equality, as opposed to Hobby's elitism. Ferguson even turned the tables on his critics by charging that Hobby corruptly manipulated the appointment process to the benefit of his wealthy friends. To discredit charges that he could not legally hold office, Farmer Jim repeatedly insisted that because he resigned before his conviction was announced, he remained eligible to serve as governor, and he charged that Hobby and his friends cooked up his impeachment for their own political advantage. The former governor also championed the cause of organized labor and contrasted his record of support for working men and women to Hobby's friendship with the Texas rich.[43]

Hobby fought back by focusing on Ferguson's alleged corrupt practices while governor, his gutting of the University of Texas, and his disloyalty to President Wilson and the war effort. The owner of the *Beaumont Enterprise* and former chair of the state Democratic executive committee, Hobby enjoyed widespread support among the newspaper editors of Northeast Texas. Although a reluctant prohibitionist with long-standing ties to those more interested in business than social reform, he championed improved education and governmental efficiency. He also understood his fellow journalists' drive to build up their home communities.[44]

In Northeast Texas, education further clarified the distinction between Hobby and Ferguson. Almost every speaker for Hobby toured the region in tandem with a speaker for Blanton, and the local people introducing the touring speakers included women long interested in education and civic improvement. Usually these women, such as Mrs. E. A. King and Mrs. R. B. Lockhart of Pittsburg or Mrs. Robert Singleton of Cooper, represented prominent local families, not radical feminism. They never used their first names in public, but instead conformed to the etiquette of the day by using Mrs. and their husband's first name or initials. None-theless, these active club women led attempts at civic improvement and played highly visible roles in their communities. The images and linkages were clear. Support the rights of women. Support education and civic im-provement. Oppose Ferguson. Support Hobby, prosperity, propriety, and progress. Both Hobby and Blanton carried most Northeast Texas coun-ties, and precinct-level returns suggested that they drew from the same pool of voters.[45]

Ferguson lost in 1918 where he had won in 1916. As elsewhere in the state, the disloyalty issue hurt Ferguson in Northeast Texas, but Fergu-son also went out of his way to oppose woman suffrage, arguing that it violated tradition and would let ignorant black women vote. In addition, Ferguson's attempt to cut the budget of the University of Texas and con-trol its administration tagged him as a foe of education. That gave women further grounds to support Hobby and Blanton. Perhaps education mat-tered more to women for reasons other than filling their traditional roles of nurturing the next generation. As Birdie Taylor pointed out, wartime conditions opened new opportunities for women, but taking advantage of these new opportunities required an education.[46]

Ferguson carried only Titus County, the only county not carried by Blanton. Many railroad union members made their home in Mount Pleas-ant, the county seat, and apparently responded to Ferguson's effort to win the union vote. Titus's leaders may also have resented the new role of women. In 1909 they refused to hold an election for school board when women entered the contest. Such attitudes held down the vote of women and helped Ferguson, who admitted after his defeat that women voted against him 10 to 1.[47]

Women's overwhelming rejection of Ferguson in 1918 suggested that they held an altered place, but not necessarily a totally new position, in society. During the decade before the war, commentators agreed that women powered a host of reforms that fell into the categories of civic improvement or social uplift. From the building of concrete sidewalks in Cooper to upgrading the schools in Jefferson, women prodded and pulled their often recalcitrant menfolk toward more-modern times. Clearly not all women joined in these efforts, as class and race continued to divide reformers able "to vie with men for supremacy in the realm of initia-tive and action" from other Northeast Texas women. Middle- and upper-class white women, however, organized groups like the Ladies Voting Club of Cooper and accepted leadership roles in Liberty Loan drives, charity organizations, prohibition campaigns, and educational reform movements.[48]

Much of the nineteenth-century notion that men and women had separate spheres of activity lingered. Men made money. They built up the local economy. Women nurtured and educated the next generation, providing beauty and culture. While they might have separate interests, increasing numbers of women lost any inhibition about advocating their causes aggressively. As County School Superintendent Alice Emmert told the voters of Marion County, "Shame on the voter who will vote to hurt instead of help the child in the country." In 1917 Birdie Taylor insisted that all citizens retain "an upward vision" that would "keep the fires burning brightly on the social matters." A few years later the Jefferson Woman's Committee urged women to pay their poll tax because, unlike men, "women must look for issues and to moral principles, not to money and to party lines."[49]

As this lingering sense of different roles but similar willingness to act suggested, old ideas and new ways often ran oddly merged. In Clarksville, the home of a pre–World War I female county treasurer, the all-male school board required that female teachers in the 1930s be widows or unmarried, and besides those teachers only one woman, a lawyer, earned her living in one of the male-dominated professions of medicine and law. Except for black domestics and unmarried women school teachers, few women worked outside the home. Before World War I, Clarksville—despite being the home of Eugene Black, who claimed to support education—shut down its Carnegie Library rather than bear the expense of maintaining it. On the other hand, efforts to combat mosquitoes and other menaces to public health dated to early in the century and owed much of their success to Red River County women.[50]

Closing a library never happened in nearby Paris. Here as in Jefferson, the wives of wealthy businessmen combined with professional women to push for a series of reforms. After the devastating fire of 1916 that destroyed 104 blocks of the city, women led the movement to beautify the town, to build parks, to erect monuments, and to build impressive new public buildings—including a museum and library. Women worked with the Paris Board of Trade and experts in city planning to make Paris "one of the most up-to-date small cities in America."[51]

While having women "out among the influences away from home" made some men uncomfortable, World War I confirmed the more-active and public role of women evident before the war. Building on the habit of voluntarism, middle- and upper-class women sold liberty bonds, worked for the Red Cross, and increasingly participated in politics. In the election of 1918 these women used the experience and associations gained from wartime activities to continue their push for a better educational

system. Education reform, as much as prohibition and support for grant-
ing woman suffrage, became the tool candidates used to gain women's
votes.[52]

Not everyone accepted the changing status of women. One year after
losing to Hobby, Ferguson partially evened the score for women's contri-
bution to his loss when he helped defeat a woman-suffrage amendment to
the Texas Constitution. Early in 1919 suffrage leaders expressed the hope
that Texans would vote on this constitutional amendment by itself the
next August, giving them time to mount an extensive campaign unclut-
tered by other issues. Prohibitionists, however, wanted to quickly pass a
state amendment that would make Texas dry for the few months before
the already ratified Eighteenth Amendment to the Constitution dried up
the entire country in January 1920. They pushed Governor Hobby and the
legislature to act quickly on all constitutional amendments. A compliant
legislature approved four constitutional amendments, including prohibition and woman suffrage, and they set the vote for May 24, 1919. To make
matters worse, the legislature linked giving women the right to vote with
taking the vote away from aliens who did not have full citizenship. Before 1919 any male twenty-one years old or older who initiated the process of becoming a citizen could vote, even without full citizenship. While
women could vote in the Democratic primary and hoped to vote on this
amendment and the state prohibition amendment, they were ruled ineligible. Thus those from whom the vote was to be taken could vote, but
those to whom the vote was to be given could not vote. Few aliens lived
in Northeast Texas, but blacks who paid their poll tax and antiprohibitionists probably opposed woman suffrage because they realized it would
strengthen their political opponents. Meanwhile, with the deck stacked
against them, many advocates of suffrage abandoned hope of passing a
state referendum and turned their attention to securing the vote through
an amendment to the national constitution.[53]

In Jefferson, Taylor helped organize a last-minute attempt to secure
passage of the suffrage amendment by publishing a special supplement to
the *Jimplecute* calling on progressive citizens to redeem the Democratic
platform of 1918 and vote for suffrage. Writers in the *Jimplecute* argued
that all supporters of prohibition, clean streets, and better schools should
also vote for equal suffrage because women, once they voted, would provide increased support for these causes. S. P. Brooks, president of Baylor
University, summed up this argument by saying: "It would be a shame for
foreigners who are aliens in thought and sympathy to continue to have
privileges that our Texas women are not allowed to have. For my part I am
unwilling to strike back at our women who have done so much to win the

war. I vote for equal suffrage." Despite such last-minute efforts, woman suffrage lost in Marion County by a vote of 196 against and 184 for. About 100 fewer citizens cast ballots in this election than in the 1914 and 1916 Democratic primaries, indicating that some male Democrats took little interest in the election. (Since some blacks may have voted, determining how many Democrats did not vote is difficult.) Reflecting this apathy among reformers, the other constitutional amendments also lost in the county.[54]

Lacking even the effort of Marion County progressives, suffrage lost by a wider margin in six other counties in the First District. As in Marion County, turnout was low. Suffrage carried only in Bowie, Delta, Lamar, and—adding another detail to its idiosyncratic record—Red River. Voters in Camp and Cass joined those in Marion in defeating all four amendments. One local analyst insisted that aliens and their supporters came out to vote, while proponents of woman suffrage stayed home. If the two concepts of taking the vote from aliens and giving the vote to women had not been linked, perhaps both would have won, but judging from returns in Northeast Texas, a region with few aliens, the linkage of woman suffrage with prohibition hurt the cause of expanding suffrage as much as anything else. Traditional opponents of prohibition turned out to vote wet and voted against woman suffrage as well. Meanwhile, advocates of prohibition stayed home, aware that the national government would make Texas dry the next January. Suffrage leaders also turned their attention elsewhere, hoping that passage and ratification of the Nineteenth Amendment soon would bring women the right to vote.[55]

A month later, in June 1919, the Texas legislature ratified the recently passed Nineteenth Amendment, making Texas the first southern state to vote for the suffrage amendment and the ninth overall. As Birdie Taylor exulted, women seemed on the verge of exerting greater political power than ever before.[56]

Voting registration offered one gauge of whether reality matched the exuberant celebrations of suffrage leaders. In 1920, poll tax receipts from Marion and Camp counties indicated that town women voted far more often than country women. That year, one woman paid the poll tax for every four men in Jefferson. In the rest of Marion County, one woman paid the tax for every twenty men. This occurred despite widespread knowledge before the January 31, 1920, deadline that there would be a hotly contested gubernatorial primary. The high percentage of blacks in the countryside of Marion County and a history of suppressing voter turnout made that county something of a special case. In Camp, however, a still-smaller percentage of eligible women paid the poll tax, and most of them lived in Pittsburg. Heavy rains that January cut off the country-side from Pittsburg and Jefferson. Some suggested women less willingly braved the elements to make the required trip to the courthouse to pay their tax. On the other hand, country folk read newspapers less often and seldom actively supported progressivism. Fewer country women read the calls to register and fewer habitually supported progressive reforms.[57]

Although not to the exaggerated degree of women in Camp and Marion, country women voted less frequently than town women across Northeast Texas. For progressives, however, this proved a blessing. Their voting strength went up, while that of the most isolated parts of the countryside did not. Women voters made towns and town causes increasingly dominant. As Taylor put it, "Women Have Hearts," and they changed party politics and the attention given to issues in the region. Increasingly, Northeast Texas reformers agreed that "a government that is run without the advice of women is a one sided government." [58]

Through the 1920s, women in Paris, Pittsburg, Jefferson, and the other towns of the region heeded Miss Birdie's admonition not to forget social causes. They promoted paved streets and public health. Using the power of the state government, they ensured the purity and safety of the local water supply, and they backed the construction of citywide natural gas, electrical, and sewer systems. Prison reform and creation of state and local parks drew support. Improving public education remained a central issue. Reflecting their new importance to the reform coalition, more Texas women served in the legislature and held more important offices both statewide and on the county level during the 1920s than in any decade until the 1970s.[59]

Outside of politics, women's roles changed in more-basic ways—family size decreased or spacing between births increased.[60] Evidence of this change lies in the census figures that divided the entire population by age groups. For decades the youngest group of Northeast Texas children of all races and ethnicities increased about 15 percent every ten years. From 1910 to 1920 the youngest group grew by only 6 percent. This decline in the growth rate occurred while the growth rate of other under-twenty-one age groups increased and the percentage of adult women in the population reached new highs.[61] Thus, the number of young children grew less rapidly than the number of potential mothers. The ratio of children to women decreased, suggesting that birth rates declined over the decade.[62]

Other possible explanations for this change in age distribution exist, but none better explains the shifting rate of growth of the age groups.[63] The youngest group of children could not leave by themselves, and signifi-

TABLE 6.1
Ratio of Children to Women, Black and White, 1910–1930

Group and Age	1910	Change	1920	Change	1930
All blacks –21	35,864	0.88%	36,179	–9.19%	32,855
Black female 21+	15,132	1.75%	15,396	3.10%	15,874
Black ratio	2.37	–0.85%	2.35	–11.92%	2.01
All whites –21	93,287	14.78%	107,071	–14.54%	91,505
White female 21+	38,722	20.54%	46,677	4.51%	48,784
White ratio	2.41	–4.78%	2.29	–18.23%	1.88

Source: U.S., *Census: 1910, Population,* vol. 3, 806–847; U.S., *Census: 1920, Population,* vol. 3, 991–1012; U. S., *Census: 1930, Population,* vol. 3, pt. 2, 976–989.

cant outmigration of white women of child-bearing age began after 1920. Black women of child-bearing age did leave before 1920, but those who left made up too small a percentage of the female population for their absence alone to explain this change. White migrants from the South, often families with young children, bypassed the region after 1905, but again their numbers alone probably could not explain this change. Life expectancy did not increase, meaning that women beyond child-bearing age did not suddenly become a much larger percentage of the adult female population. Local newspapers and the *Biennial Reports* of the Texas State Department of Health contained no indications of epidemics of childhood diseases. While Northeast Texans died of influenza, the disease struck all age groups, not just the youngest children. In the end, nothing adequately explained the changes in age distribution except a decline in birth rates beginning between about 1910 and 1915.[64]

Limited evidence also hints at some difference between black and white birth rates in this era. The censuses of 1910, 1920, and 1930 did not divide the age groups by race and gender except as under twenty-one and twenty-one and older. This makes any observations about differences in birth rate between blacks and whites tentative. Still, from 1910 to 1920 the numbers of black women twenty-one and older increased at about the same low rate as all blacks under twenty-one. Of course, black outmigration during the war complicated the picture, but in a crude form the children-to-women ratio remained virtually the same. Meanwhile, the number of white women twenty-one and older increased by over 20 percent while the white population under twenty-one increased by 15 percent during the decade. This pattern continued after 1920 when, as Table 6.1 shows, white women twenty-one and older increased at a higher rate than black women twenty-one older, and all whites under twenty-one decreased at a much sharper rate than all blacks under twenty-one.[65]

In addition, during the 1920s, Delta, Franklin, and Hopkins counties, with the fewest blacks as a percentage of the total population in the region, had the sharpest declines in the youngest age groups. Although young white farm couples clearly abandoned western counties like Delta, their departure alone cannot explain this trend. In fact, in Franklin, the over-eighteen population grew but the under-seven and seven-to-thirteen age groups both declined by about 25 percent. All of these trends strongly suggest birth rates probably declined primarily among whites.[66]

Yet by 1930 the two groups neared parity. The ratio of all blacks under twenty-one to black women twenty-one and older declined slightly from 1910 to 1920 and declined at an even greater rate from 1920 to 1930. Again the movement of young black couples out of the region during World War I complicated the picture because many black women who remained in the region may have simply moved beyond their peak child-bearing years by 1930. Still, the process of limiting childbirths or increasing spacing, begun among whites in the 1910s, probably also touched the lives of blacks by 1930.[67]

Class, however, influenced birth rates as much as race. Figures given in the *Census of Agriculture, 1925* indicated a lower ratio of children to women for farm owners than for the entire farm population, which included tenants and hired hands. The ratio for black farm owners was higher than for white owners but was lower than the entire white farm population. Owners of both races comprised a middle, or in some cases an upper, class, and attributes common to those classes—such as greater education, access to information, and income—probably played a role in declining birth rates.[68]

Urban environments also influenced birth rates. Texarkana, in Bowie County, offered superb opportunities for economic advancement after World War I. As a result, Bowie County gained population in the 1920s while the other ten counties lost population. No doubt part of that gain came from young couples. Bowie County had the sharpest rise in the eighteen to twenty and the twenty-one and older population of any county in the area. Even with this gain in young couples, the number of children under seven grew at the slowest rate of any population group from 1910 to 1930, suggesting the urban setting contributed to a decline in birth rates.[69]

Even blacks evidently moved to lower the birth rate in a growing urban environment. As noted, in the ten counties that lost population from 1920 to 1930, a low percentage of blacks correlated closely with a high decline in young children. Only Camp, where blacks made up roughly 40 percent of the population and young children still declined at a rate greater than the regional average, proved an exception. Camp was also the only one of the ten counties where the black urban population grew, suggesting that, like others in an urban setting, newly arrived blacks in Pittsburg moved to limit child bearing.[70]

Efforts to limit family size marked a major departure from past cultural norms. As Birdie Taylor put it, "In every age of the world up to the present, the ultimate object of woman's existence has been marriage and maternity."[71] In the late nineteenth and early twentieth century, large families were the ideal, even if they were at times an economic liability. Birth control methods, although known by 1900, lacked acceptance. Yet, after remaining stable for decades, birth rates declined in the World War I era. While race, class, and urban living affected the extent and timing of the decline in births, by 1930 this process touched everyone.[72]

Just as in the case of women in public life, unspoken doubts if not outspoken debate about family size probably existed before 1914. Some scholars suggest that an increased emphasis on education spread a value system that encouraged a decline in fertility. Northeast Texans, particularly townsfolk and the middle and upper class, diligently upgraded their schools in the decade before World War I, and perhaps their efforts explain why the decline in birth rate began at the same time or even a bit earlier than the start of World War I.[73]

Still, the cotton crisis of 1914, the temporary absence of some young men in the armed forces, the unpredictable nature of the economy, the beginning of outmigration, or some other economic or demographic factor or factors associated with the war seemingly gave the decline in birth rates a permanent character. As Table 6.2 suggests, as late as 1940 birth rates had not returned to pre-1914 levels.[74]

Despite this postwar permanence of declining birth rates, the initial cause of the decline remains difficult to identify. One scholar argued that "a fundamental shift in values" occurred "collectively and without conscious premeditation" before most changes in family size and structure.[75] This raises the possibility of a paradigm shift in values and ideals on the eve of the war, a shift that broadly affected life in the region. W. C. Williams believed this was so in 1912 when he pointed out that "old ideas are rapidly passing." Yet the importance of factional politics in bringing women the right to vote in the primary and the defeat of the 1919 state constitutional amendment giving women the right to vote in the general election warn us that old ideas hung on with tenacity. Without the particular circumstances created by World War I, the spread of a new culture or a new value system may not have extended beyond the white elite for

Pub.by Jno. W. Foscue   West End School Building,
Sulphur Springs, Texas.

—————— FIGURE 6.2 ——————

*Sulphur Springs High School opening. In the years during and just before
World War I, Northeast Texans in the larger towns upgraded their school buildings
and curriculum. The opening of this high school in Sulphur Springs offered
the town's leading citizens a chance to congratulate themselves
on their progressive attitude.*
Photograph courtesy of Jenkins Garrett Texas Postcard Collection, University of Texas
at Arlington, Special Collections.

—————— TABLE 6.2 ——————
Age Distribution in Northeast Texas, 1910–1940

Age	1910	change	1920	change	1930	change	1940
Total	239,341	13.4%	271,472	−5.9%	255,552	4.2%	266,188
–7	47,369	6.0%	50,194	−20.3%	40,026	−8.6%	36,571
7–13	43,901	15.2%	50,589	−14.9%	43,074	−12.0%	37,900
14–15	11,409	17.6%	13,413	−12.3%	11,764	−1.3%	11,608
16–17	11,020	12.2%	12,367	−0.5%	12,306	−7.3%	11,409
18–20	15,378	8.1%	16,622	3.5%	17,200	−5.4%	16,268
21+	110,265	16.4%	128,323	2.2%	131,182	16.2%	152,432

Source: U.S., *Census: 1910, Population,* vol. 3, 806; U.S., *Census: 1920, Population,* vol. 3,
991–1012; U.S., *Census: 1930, Population,* vol. 3, pt. 2, 976–989; U.S., *Census: 1940, Population,* vol. 2, 793–805.

decades. The war quickened and extended the impact of the paradigm shift that allowed a change in birth rates, a greater acceptance of varied roles for women, and more-numerous and vocal challenges to lynching. It helped develop a new culture evident in the politics of the region.[76]

POLITICS AND CULTURE

As the events depicted in this chapter illustrate, culture broadly defined was in flux before World War I, and the war both accelerated prewar trends and carried the region in new directions. Politics, particularly the issues and rhetoric of the campaigns, offer us another way to think about this changing culture, for successful candidates necessarily reflected the ideas and values of their day.

When Morris Sheppard announced for the Senate in 1912, five candidates entered the Democratic primary and began campaigning for his spot as representative of the First Congressional District. Horace W. Vaughan declared his candidacy early. He was born in Marion County in 1867, but his family soon moved to Linden. In 1886 he moved to Texarkana, where he practiced law with his father. Vaughan had a distinguished record as a district attorney and while serving in that office went to great lengths to stop the lynching of blacks accused of crimes. Between 1910 and 1912 he served one term in the Texas Senate representing Bowie, Cass, Morris, and Marion counties.[77]

H. Bascom Thomas of Sulphur Springs announced his candidacy at about the same time as Vaughan. Thomas was about five years younger than Vaughan and, like him, supported prohibition. As a state senator and in other offices, Thomas earned a reputation as a maverick—always ready to challenge the entrenched economic interests that he believed dominated the Democratic party. Despite this, he enjoyed support from the business community of Sulphur Springs, probably because he was one of them, having edited the *Sulphur Springs Gazette* and engaged in several profitable ventures. Thomas had both ardent friends and strident enemies within his state senatorial district of Hopkins, Red River, Titus, Delta, and Franklin counties.[78]

B. B. Sturgeon and Fred Dudley, both of Paris, soon followed Thomas and Vaughan into the race. Sturgeon, who as county attorney played a prominent role in the lynching of Henry Smith in 1893, later won election as state senator from Lamar and Fannin counties, serving in the 31st Legislature with Thomas and in the 32nd with Vaughan. Slightly older than

Vaughan and a less aggressive campaigner, he was a committed member of the Democratic party with a history of opposing the Populists. Also an advocate of prohibition, he had played an important role in the 1887 and 1911 attempts to gain statewide prohibition and in local-option elections in Lamar County. Describing himself as a champion of progressive causes, Sturgeon advocated reforms almost identical to those supported by Thomas and Vaughan.[79]

Fred Dudley, on the other hand, opposed statewide prohibition and expressed reservations about increasing the power of government. He opposed some progressive reforms but supported direct election of senators and a federal income tax. Allying himself with both conservatives and more-radical former Populists, Dudley tried to put back together the white portion of the coalition that voted against prohibition in 1887 and 1911. In a statement aimed at reminding voters that the federal government, if unchecked, could modify or eliminate laws and customs that maintained white supremacy, Dudley promised to defend "the rights of citizens of a sovereign state to settle local affairs."[80]

Eugene Black of Clarksville, another prohibitionist, briefly campaigned but withdrew in April. Perhaps he was afraid that he would so split the prohibitionist vote that Dudley would gain a plurality and thereby a seat in Congress. Besides, other candidates had more political experience and better-organized networks of support.[81]

Each candidate brought some strength to this crowded field. Dudley appealed to ardent antiprohibitionists. Sturgeon appealed to reformers for whom party mattered as much as principle. Vaughan and Thomas tried to bridge the gap between insurgents and economic reformers. Vaughan also enjoyed the advantage of facing no other candidates from the eastern part of the First District. Lacking other compelling issues or long-standing loyalty to an incumbent, voters supported the candidate from their neighborhood. Vaughan, who spent his entire life in Marion, Cass, and Bowie counties, drew solid support in the east.[82]

Yet Vaughan also did well in his foes' backyard, finishing a close second in Red River, Lamar, and Hopkins counties, and leading in the district's eight other counties. In 1912, party rules and state law did not yet require a runoff primary if no candidate received a majority, and that July, Vaughan won the Democratic nomination by a plurality of 1,500 votes over Thomas, his nearest competitor. Dudley finished third and Sturgeon last.[83]

Sturgeon lost votes to Dudley in Lamar County and ran a weak campaign in Vaughan's old Texas Senate district. Frequently, he came across as less progressive than Vaughan and more closely identified with the

older Confederate generation and the more-rabid defenders of white supremacy. His history of vocal opposition to Populism also hurt his chances
to extend beyond the hard-core Democratic party vote of Lamar County.[84]

Fred Dudley and Bascom Thomas ran better across the district than
Sturgeon. Thomas did well enough in Sulphur Springs to carry Hopkins
County. He also did well in Leesburg, the only town of any size in Camp
County other than Pittsburg. Dudley carried two of five precincts in Camp
and ran reasonably well in Marion County, doing best in precincts that
opposed prohibition and road taxes. In other words, he did best where an
activist government threatened the citizens' way of life, and he did best in
those precincts not controlled by the "serious, conscientious" sort who
championed prohibition.[85]

Vaughan, however, nearly matched Thomas among progressives in Sulphur Springs, Paris, and Clarksville, and he easily bested Dudley and
Thomas in rural precincts that supported prohibition in 1911. In the larger
towns of the eastern counties, he finished far ahead of all challengers.
He did this by stressing issues beyond prohibition that allowed him to
build an effective middle-of-the-road coalition. Thomas and Sturgeon
both pointed out that Vaughan had been a drinking man before being
elected to the Senate. They charged him with hypocrisy, of wanting prohibition for the masses but not for himself. Vaughan in turn pointed to
his service on the state committee of the Anti-Saloon League and charged
his opponents with slander, corrupt election practices, and trying to rig
a preprimary vote in the western counties to ensure a solid vote against
him. In Como and Pickton in southwest Hopkins County, his supporters
effectively tarred Thomas as an old-fashioned practitioner of dirty politics. Instead of cleaning up polluted politics, an avowed goal of prohibition, Vaughan charged that his opponents used prohibition to lower
the tenor of the race. In fact, attacks on his prohibition record probably
helped Vaughan in some rural areas because they increased his appeal
among committed antiprohibitionists and reminded old-time Populists of
the dirty tricks of the 1890s. They responded by voting for Vaughan. For
town dwellers, Thomas was a "man that stirs up a row," and that image
helped Vaughan minimize any damage done by attacks on his prohibitionist credentials.[86]

Focusing on honest elections allowed Vaughan to bridge the gap between town dwellers and country folk—between reformers and insurgents. In every speech and advertisement, Vaughan promised a host of
reforms aimed at cleaning up and improving the political process. After
observing the 1912 primary, R. W. Fanning of the *Sulphur Springs Gazette*
commented, "we need more laws governing politics." Vaughan, unlike

Thomas, Sturgeon, and especially Dudley, promised more laws and more government. Like Sheppard, Vaughan often evoked the memory of the Confederacy and was a major supporter of a campaign to fill "the gap in your library and in every southern home and school" with a "true" history of the South. Yet, unlike Sturgeon or Dudley, he did not seem frozen in the past.[87]

Vaughan quickly became a committed supporter of Woodrow Wilson. He took particular interest in the creation of the Federal Reserve and supported the decentralized system of Reserve Banks. Yet, like Wilson, Vaughan doubted the wisdom of nationwide prohibition. Vaughan's letter to his constituents in May 1914 indicated that he feared placing too much power in the hands of the federal government. In other words, he suddenly sounded like Dudley and Sturgeon in 1912. States' rights, the Lost Cause, fears of a return to Reconstruction, all intermingled in Vaughan's defense of rejecting federal action on prohibition. In the July 1914 Democratic primary, he lost his congressional seat to Eugene Black, who supported nationwide prohibition. As the *Sulphur Springs Gazette* commented, this time "Mr. Vaughan's principal strength is in the country."[88]

On the eve of the July primary, Eugene Black and Horace Vaughan met in joint debate in Omaha. Vaughan stressed his service to the district while in the House and his knowledge of conditions facing farmers. Black criticized pork-barrel politics and governmental inefficiency, and he claimed to be a better prohibitionist. The nub of the debate, however, quickly became Black's charge that Vaughan lacked morality. In 1905 the sheriff caught Vaughan playing poker in Bowie County. Forced to admit being convicted of gambling, Vaughan claimed to have given up poker. Black used this incident to buttress his oft-repeated charges that Vaughan was "all over the map" on every moral issue and frequently drank liquor. Black, on the other hand, was "a noble Christian gentleman."[89]

Black preached and practiced civic and private virtue. An active Methodist interested in "the religious and educational uplift of his country," Black exuded the courtliness that came with a well-established family and a university education. Years of operating a thriving law practice and ownership with his brother of a prosperous wholesale grocery and soft-drink bottling company bred familiarity with economic conservatives anxious to safeguard established wealth and social order. To reformers Black demonstrated that diligence and propriety brought prosperity. He promised clean government, efficiency, and virtue. He promised greater federal aid for local businesses and landowning farmers. He promised to extend the reach of the federal government by backing nationwide prohibition. Black never mentioned the South or the Lost Cause. Instead, his was a middle-class American morality.[90]

Of course, Vaughan did his best to counter Black's image, and in a few towns he held onto his vote from 1912. Still, in a very close race, Black reversed the situation of 1912. He did very well in his home area and stayed close enough to Vaughan in the eastern counties to win a slender victory. Because Jim Ferguson's campaign for governor attracted additional voters to the primary, voters more likely to support Vaughan, this was an especially revealing race. Black's local organization came through in a big way, delivering a 1,800 vote margin over Vaughan in Lamar and a 1,200 vote margin in Red River. On the other end of the district, in Cass and Morris counties, rumors spread that Morris Sheppard quietly urged voting against Vaughan because of his failure to endorse nationwide prohibition.[91]

These rumors and heavy spending by Black on advertising and campaign organization created a distinctive image for the challenger, setting him apart from the incumbent. Citizens of Sulphur Springs and several of the larger villages of Hopkins County identified with Black's success and his education. Vaughan, on the other hand, retained the country ways of rural Cass County. He had read law instead of attending a university and it showed. Vaughan carried every small rural box in Hopkins County. When the total vote passed a hundred, however, Black either won the box or did much better than in the smaller boxes. Vaughan's advantage of incumbency and his appeal in the countryside and smaller villages made this a very close election. Vaughan actually carried seven of the eleven counties in the district. Yet by 326 votes out of a total of about 25,000, the image that better fit progressive conceptions of the future won the election.[92]

Vaughan won in 1912 without receiving a majority and lost in 1914 by fewer than 350 votes. Such narrow margins of victory and defeat raise a caution flag when it comes time for sweeping analysis. Yet some signposts on the eve of World War I seemed clear. In 1912 Vaughan won by clearly enunciating the need for more laws to "let progress predominate." He won because he stood for clean elections and civility. He won because he best appealed to reformers and landowning farmers.[93] Two years later Black undermined Vaughan's image as a social reformer and upright citizen. This, together with his ability to draw some support from economic conservatives, offset Vaughan's strength in the countryside where his stand against nationwide prohibition, because it overly enhanced governmental power and threatened individual liberty, helped him with more-isolated rural voters.[94]

Unfortunately for Vaughan, urban dwellers and progressive agriculturalists made up an increasingly high percentage of the total vote. They might enjoy a melodramatic moment while watching the popular play *The Clansman,* but ties to the Confederacy no longer made an extension of federal power an abomination. Despite his impressive reform credentials, Vaughan let Black make this an election between a mossback and a business-minded progressive who supported nationwide prohibition. Progress won over tradition.

Politics remained intensely competitive and closely balanced between multiple factions, but new realities emerged as war began in Europe. Propriety in election practices and personal behavior mattered a great deal more. Despite appeals to Confederate tradition, prohibition demanded an increase in federal power. By 1914 advocates of limited government might influence, but could never control, politics. Instead, their opponents changed congressmen to continue going "forward to better things." [95]

War changed this comfortable world, this sense of the inevitability of progress, and it unleashed new cultural crosscurrents. Yet in the end it also confirmed the role of the federal government and further undercut the hold of traditional southern culture.

Determined to preserve progress on all fronts, Birdie Taylor warned in a June 1917 editorial entitled "Deliver us from Hatred" that American entry into World War I could turn good people hard and cruel, that the foreign born in particular were at risk. She closed by saying, "We are now impelled by one consuming desire, the freedom of humanity in its broadest sense, and the greatest freedom to which we can attain is freedom of heart from rancor and bitterness." What made this all the more astounding was that she knew few Germans or other foreign-born citizens, who for the most part lived far from Northeast Texas.[96]

Two years of war cost Taylor her compassion for those outside her ken. In September 1919 she insisted: "Bolshevism has spread its red wings generally over Europe, and is even invading this country to a dangerous degree. The man who can not respect the American flag and American institutions should be conducted to the border line and kicked across." A month later the situation seemed worse: "The greed of the capitalist and the arbitrariness of labor must be curbed. The agency that will not voluntarily submit to reason must be forced to do so. The government must take action, drastic as the conditions may warrant. The man who considers himself greater than the people must be crushed by the nation. There is no other alternative, if we are to preserve the free country our forefathers builded for us." [97]

A race riot at nearby Longview, railroad disputes in Texarkana, and labor problems in Paris made 1919 a frightening year for the middle-class citizens of Northeast Texas. All of America seemed "tottering on the brink of revolution." Their solution was not simply to turn inward and shore up traditional morality. Instead of retreating into the past of limited government, fear evoked calls to extend the reach of government.[98]

In fact, for most Northeast Texans wartime meant a clear break with the past. As Burt Lockhart wryly put it, "With national prohibition and woman suffrage in sight, the professional politician may be forced to run for office on his merits." Instead of campaigning on old issues or aligning in voting blocs based on those issues, politics could change. The past was dead. (Although in terms of voting blocs far less dead than Lockhart imagined.)[99]

Even for the poor, the experiences of 1917–1919 cultivated a restlessness with old ways. Innocent kissing games turned more serious as young girls and boys abandoned prewar restraints on sexuality. Young men, if not carried into the army, left because the war changed how they thought. As one Northeast Texan observed about his brother who was drafted at war's end but never served: "The war was over and Monroe was restless. My mother and grandmother blamed the draft. It was the draft that got him thinking about leaving home. He was not wanted for the draft, but he wanted to leave home and strike out on his own."[100]

The war changed even those already established in a promising career, such as future congressman Wright Patman. Patman abandoned his profitable law career and volunteered for duty. Disqualified for officer training camp in the army because of a minor heart problem, he won a transfer to the Coast Guard and the rank of lieutenant. After serving in various parts of the country, he returned home in 1919 and resumed his law practice. He brought with him a deepened commitment to public service, especially on behalf of the common soldier and common people he believed responsible for victory, and a deepened belief in the ability of the federal government to work for good.[101]

Even in the most difficult of areas—the politics of race—white Northeast Texans turned to the national government. Through 1922 Texas still trailed only Georgia and Mississippi in the number of recorded lynchings. Hatton Sumner, a powerful member of the House of Representatives from Dallas, led the opposition to new federal legislation aimed at stopping lynching. Yet Sumner's objection to the federal lynching bill based on states' rights no longer drew universal support.[102]

Commenting on federal legislation to curb lynching, the editor of the *Paris Morning News* pointed out the futility of arguing for states' rights. Most rights had already passed to the federal government to achieve some worthy purpose supported by Republicans and Democrats. Besides, "The States—including Texas—have not put down mob law; and while they have statutes of various sorts designed to punish those guilty of it these statues are not enforced." Fear kept Texans from acting against lynching—fear of being "put in the position of condemning mob law because the men responsible always seek to make it appear that those condemning the mob are excusing the crimes." Nonetheless, for social and economic progress to continue, lynching had to end even if it required a more active federal government.[103]

This acceptance of the role of an active federal government marked a cultural as well as a political shift, for it indicated a weakening of the hold of the Lost Cause, a weakening of the desire to maintain a South distinctive from the rest of America. For women, in particular, defense of a distinctive South meant conforming to traditional gender roles, and in that sense when they voted, became more active in the life of their community, or limited the number of their children, they rejected the Confederate past and joined an American future. Perhaps they substituted celebration of Texas folkways and memorial days for worship of the South, but far more than women in any other southern state, Texas women escaped the hold of a memory and a culture used to keep them in their place. While this break with the past owed much to the peculiar nature of Texas politics, like the broader acceptance of the role of the federal government and the criticism of lynching, it could never have arrived so completely and cleanly without the war.[104]

World War I then had a broad and permanent, if not unprecedented and immediate, impact on Northeast Texas. In this cotton-growing region of the South, the war not only accelerated the economic and social trends noted in the previous chapter, it gave new impetus to changes in the culture of the region that slowly simmered beneath the surface before 1914. Observations on matters of the mind, particularly the mind of the many as opposed to the gabby intellectual, remain tentative. Still, something resembling a paradigm shift occurred in Northeast Texas from 1910 to 1920. Looking back, one participant in the process declared, that the war sowed "the seeds of progress."[105]

Yet a cautionary tale remains. In March 1922 nighttime raiders in Cass County dynamited thirteen concrete vats used by the state for the compulsory dipping of cattle to control disease. According to newspaper reports, this was "the second time this has happened—last time the Rangers were sent in and probably will be sent in again."[106] For some Northeast Texans the 1920s brought a sense of loss of power and control that provoked violence.

SEVEN

WOMEN, THE KU KLUX KLAN, AND FACTIONAL IDENTITY, 1920–1927

Despite substantial economic and cultural change, in 1920 political factions in Northeast Texas retained a familiar ideological identity. As in 1887, traditional conservatives spoke of the Confederacy and wanted as little governmental action as possible. Social reformers sought prohibition, infused politics with a religious ardor, and considered education a way of teaching right behavior. Economic reformers turned to the state and federal governments to promote greater prosperity and economic equity. Rural insurgents struck out at attempts to control their behavior and limit their economic opportunities. When given the chance, blacks sought economic opportunity or protested unequal treatment.

Of course, by 1920 these factions operated within a vastly different political structure. The whites-only Democratic primary replaced the general election in determining who held office. Blacks and poor whites faced greater hurdles to voting. Women now voted. Yet within the Democratic party, conservatives, reformers, and insurgents still vied for control and still depended upon coalition building to gain that control.

After 1920 the Ku Klux Klan, in particular, forced hard choices about the role of religion, individual freedom, the status of women and blacks, the rule of law, and the validity of a secret society within the Democratic party. Many whites shared the vague sense of a society gone wrong that lay behind the Klan or enjoyed the pageantry and camaraderie of the organization. Yet, once the Klan itself became a political issue, factional identity and ideology changed in important ways. The old conservative ideology, already undermined by a cultural shift away from intense reliance upon memories of the South, virtually disappeared. New conservatives, preoccupied with social order, took their place. These conservatives still called for government to stay out of the economy, but they also called for government to police the behavior of their fellow citizens more intensively. Economic reformers and social moderates, their ranks swelled by the addition of women voters, held the political middle. By the mid-1920s these Northeast Texans saw lynching, the Klan, and the iron grip of the ghosts of the Confederacy as a threat to progress. Rural insurgents, their place in society much diminished, melded in with organized labor and cooperated more closely than at any point since the early 1890s with economic reformers and moderate social reformers. These changes in factional ideology and identity set the stage for the triumph of a New Deal–style coalition of small-town businessmen, farmers, and labor.

Before this mid-1920s pattern emerged, there came a time of discordant political crosscurrents. Just when candidates who championed states' rights and glorified the Confederacy lost much of their public appeal, the Ku Klux Klan, obviously dependent upon the myths of the Civil War and Reconstruction, grew in influence. This Klan also grew because of fears aroused by anything that hinted of socialism, fears so intense that Northeast Texans called for the use of force to discipline the thinking and actions of their fellow citizens. The Klan, however, soon demonstrated the liabilities of seeking right behavior through force, especially force uncontrolled by law and established political procedure.

SOCIALISTS, CONFEDERATES, AND THE ROLE OF GOVERNMENT

Immediately after the war, fear of socialism, outrage at profiteering, anger over strikes, and alarm over the depopulation of the countryside provoked even the generally optimistic Birdie Taylor to wonder if her country was "on the brink of revolution."[1] Taylor looked around and declared: "Again this paper, deems it a duty to sound a warning to the young men of our towns, villages and farming communities. Stay away from the big city." Soon she feared that food production would suffer for lack of labor in the countryside. Besides, what type of life could crowded cities offer that compared with rural pleasures? Tellingly, her solution was to turn to government. She closed her lament with this plea: "If there be wisdom in the seats of the mighty it is time that it be brought into play." Others joined her in calling for government action and expressing alarm over current conditions.[2]

This willingness to use government marked a subtle evolution in the political ideology of Northeast Texas. Conservatives once feared government, especially the federal government, and they couched their actions in terms of defending the Confederate past. If society seemed out of control, as it had in the 1890s, the local elites and the middle class handled the situation at the local level or, if need be, at the state level. Those days were gone and with them vanished a limited degree of political tolerance, at least tolerance for whites.

Even before 1920, members of the Board of Trade in Paris and newspaper editors in larger towns grumbled about communism and socialism. Despite this grumbling, Socialists ran for office in Northeast Texas from early in the century until American entry into World War I. They never threatened Democratic hegemony, which probably explained the tolerance of local elites. Yet Socialists provided an alternative to the two traditional parties. Editors accepted them and sometimes even published their opinions. They campaigned within the bounds of normal political activity, and their call for government ownership of key industries seemed only a stronger version of Democratic calls for a more active government. In the 1916 presidential election, Socialists received about 6 percent of the vote in Northeast Texas, running strongest in Morris and Bowie counties. Probably because of support from former Populists, more than 20 percent of Morris County voters backed the Socialist ticket.[3]

Socialists offered members of the old insurgent faction an option to voting for Democrats. When landowning farmers moved into closer cooperation with reform Democrats, tenants and small-scale owners voted for Socialists, or they voted for Jim Ferguson. Indeed, most observers agreed Ferguson's presence on the ballot kept down Socialist vote totals. Not only did the Democratic party remain divided into factions, it commanded a lesser degree of loyalty than usually assigned it. As George Mathena, a fifty-five-year resident of Red River County and former tenant farmer, told an interviewer in 1974, political parties mattered little. He simply voted for the cause and the "deserving" person.[4]

Amid calls to "snuff out treason" and fears that the Bolshevik Revolution would spread from Russia, tolerance for diverse political opinions diminished in 1919 and 1920.[5] It especially fell among the region's elite, who neatly dovetailed such sentiment with traditional calls to reduce government involvement in business. Correctly reading those most like him and moved by the Red Scare of 1919, Eugene Black became much more cautious about such things as government control of the railroads. Socialism by 1920 was not simply bad politics to most white Northeast Texans; as Europe demonstrated, it was immoral and a threat to social order. Most agreed that "Bolsheviki by any other name smell just as bad." Thus the movement against socialism affected ideology in three ways. First, those long disposed against an active role for government in the economy gained new ammunition. Second, others like Black who usually favored a stronger role for government now took a second look at what a government could and should do. Third, despite retreating on government's role in the economy, Black and others who grew more conservative increasingly relied upon the government to police radical behavior.[6]

While consigning socialism, communism, and any organization vaguely like European revolutionaries to the outer reaches of the political universe, middle-class reformers also remembered that during the war government action lifted up the local economy and that government action on prohibition and woman suffrage brought long-sought moral and political reform. Farm and labor groups took an even dimmer view of conservative calls for a retreat from governmental activism. For members of these factions, an active government directed by men of energy with new ideas promised an end to economic instability, the chance for economic equality, and further progress in improving the morals of the age. Simultaneously, the continued cultural shift toward use of American and Texan symbols, images, and memories discussed in previous chapters, lessened the power of the old cult of the Confederacy.

None in Texas spoke for the Confederacy and for states' rights quite like Mississippi-born Joseph Weldon Bailey. After a decade of service in the House, Bailey became a U.S. senator from Texas in 1901. He resigned from the Senate in 1911 amidst charges that he took payments from the Waters Pierce Company, which in violation of Texas antimonopoly law continued to operate in the state although it was a wholly owned subsidiary of Standard Oil. A gifted orator, Bailey often evoked either Jefferson Davis or Thomas Jefferson in his speeches. During his years in office, Republicans usually controlled the House and Senate, and Bailey earned praise from some for his heated and grandiloquent attacks on the opposition. Others found him full of talk with few accomplishments.[7]

After leaving office, Bailey remained active in Texas politics, usually opposing national prohibition and woman suffrage. These causes threw him into an uneasy alliance with Jim Ferguson, and before Ferguson's impeachment, the two dominated the Democratic party. Grown restless outside of the limelight, in 1920 Bailey left his lucrative law practice and ran for governor. It was a campaign between the old Democracy and the new, except one new wrinkle aided Bailey—his repeated criticism of organized labor's insistence on a closed shop. More than any other, Bailey popularized calls for open-shop laws that would prevent unions from demanding that all workers at a particular company join a union.[8]

Pat Neff, one of two major opponents of Bailey in 1920, differed markedly. The speaker of the Texas House when the Terrell Election laws were formulated early in the century, Neff defended the poll tax, segregation, woman suffrage, and national prohibition. In a pointed appeal to Ferguson voters, Neff also championed land reform. He made little mention of organized labor and avoided calls for an open shop. This let him keep the solid support of social reformers and attract many economic reformers and rural insurgents. Neff's neutral stand on labor attracted conservatives with a personal dislike for the controversial Bailey and some labor leaders who admired other parts of his platform.[9]

R. E. Thomason proved the most interesting of the major candidates because he advocated modifying the poll tax system to encourage more whites to vote. This earned him support from organized labor and some farm groups, but Neff and others instantly seized on this to argue that Thomason's proposals opened the doors to increased black participation in politics. Thomason, like Neff, had also served as speaker of the Texas House. In 1919, while speaker, he zealously favored national prohibition and woman suffrage, and led the anti-Ferguson faction in the House. Because of his record as a reformer, champion of organized labor, and anti-Ferguson officeholder Thomason enjoyed strong support in urban areas, including Paris and the much larger cities of Dallas, Houston, and San Antonio.[10]

In some ways the 1920 primary paralleled elections in the early 1890s, with factions combining and recombining in different coalitions. Ferguson's supporters combined with conservatives to bring Bailey a first-place finish in most of the region's counties, and after the vote was tallied, Bailey led Neff by a slim margin in the district and statewide. Neff led in a few Northeast Texas counties and did particularly well in small towns such as Jefferson, where his strong showing allowed him to narrowly lead in Marion County. Thomason failed to lead in any of the eleven counties in the region but trailed Bailey by a narrow margin in Lamar. A fourth candidate, B. F. Looney, also received some votes, especially in Camp, Delta, Hopkins, and Franklin counties. Looney, the most ardent supporter of prohibition in the field, resided in Hunt County, west of Delta and Hopkins. The vote for the former state attorney general also echoed the 1890s when the Prohibition party attracted pockets of support. Looney acted as the spoiler, preventing the two other prohibition candidates from defeating Bailey in Delta, Hopkins, Franklin, and Camp. Looney also helped Bailey finish slightly ahead of Neff statewide.[11]

Unlike pre–World War I election laws, however, the law now required a runoff if no candidate received a majority. In that runoff Bailey added few votes to what he received in the first primary, and Neff carried every county in Northeast Texas except Titus and easily won statewide. Once again, the candidate in the middle, the moderate reformer and advocate of governmental activism, won.[12] In an editorial that emphasized the need to discipline both capital and labor, Birdie Taylor proclaimed the need to "throw out the radicals on both sides." That is exactly what the political system usually did.[13]

Parallels between earlier elections and 1920, however, did not explain everything. Changes in election law clearly favored candidates like Neff. In fact, under the old laws, if all four candidates had remained in the race, Bailey would have been elected. As the issue of the open shop suggested, more than the system had changed. Together with fear of socialism, the open shop soon helped turn social reformers into new conservatives. More importantly, women voters altered the dynamics of elections. While fewer women voted in 1920 than in years to come, those that voted typically lived in towns and favored Neff, Looney, or Thomason. Their impact and the general strength of the reform movement came clear in the runoff primary in August, when their votes helped Neff trounce Bailey by a wider margin in the district than statewide.[14]

Ironically, women had done much to build up the Confederate myth that formed the basis of so many Bailey speeches. Although perhaps now of a different class and a different type, women also helped kill off that myth in politics—especially when it was used to attack an active government and woman suffrage. In their defense of the status quo, opponents of prohibition and woman suffrage dredged up images of the Lost Cause too often for their own political health. Eventually, reformers like E. L. Dohoney labeled Joe Bailey's Lost Cause rhetoric "insane" and an "effrontery" to common sense. As that attitude took hold, one of the major stumbling blocks to a more active federal government disappeared.[15]

More than practical politics undermined the hold of the old Confederacy. For cultural as well as political reasons, after 1920 old-style conservatives had as little chance of winning office as Socialists. This did not mean that Northeast Texans stopped thinking of themselves as southerners, but it did mean that opposing the federal government because it was the southern thing to do no longer carried the same weight. In 1921 the *Jefferson Jimplecute* reprinted an article by K. E. Scott defending the extension service. Critics called the extension service an encroachment on state and individual rights. Scott countered that "every bone and sinew" of his body was southern, but he did not "see the point raised." After all, "one of the fundamental reasons given in the preamble of our constitution for the establishing of our federal government was 'to promote the general welfare.'" Since "we are an agricultural people" the best way for the government to promote the general welfare was through the extension service. It was "our constitution," an American constitution, not a Yankee constitution. In like vein, American precepts for success—science, an active government, and above all education—provided the keys to the future, and elected officials prospered who understood that cultural and pragmatic reality.[16]

Eugene Black's success at the polls certainly reflected this new reality. The image of a noble Christian gentlemen, a proponent of national prohibition and "educational uplift," Black easily won re-election to the U.S. House after his narrow initial victory in 1914. Through 1920 he repeatedly articulated a vision of an increased role for the federal government that extended far beyond prohibition. During these years almost every point on his platform required a more active government. Among other things he called for "the enlargement and extension of our Federal Bureau of Education and a close cooperation by the United States Commissioner of Education and his department with the state education authorities." As Black grew increasingly cautious about the role of government in the economy, this continued emphasis on the role of government in education seemed coercive or irrelevant to portions of the countryside. Before, conservatives and insurgents had found common cause in resisting attempts to control individual behavior. After 1920, however, as education demonstrated, disparate definitions of the proper role of government and varied rewards from the efforts of that government widened the barrier between new conservatives and country folk.[17]

When W. A. Owens began his education in Pin Hook, each local community largely controlled and financed its own schools—resulting in vast differences in the quality of education. Pin Hooks' poor soil and the old-fashioned agricultural methods employed by area farmers led to a favorite local saying, "You can make a better living by accident on the blackland than you can by trying on sandy land."[18] Not surprisingly, the children of poor places like Pin Hook attended poor schools that seldom went beyond the sixth grade. Those who controlled the rural schools were quick to save money by shortening the term or firing the teacher. Children drifted in and out of school, and some never learned the basics of reading and writing. As previously described, in the 1910s the Texas legislature enacted a series of reforms such as mandatory attendance, free text books, and giving county superintendents increased power. Until decades later, however, the legislature refused to provide adequate funding for country schools. Instead in the 1920s, the state tried to force the local schools to upgrade by raising the admittance standards at state-supported colleges and universities. In 1924 when Owens journeyed to Commerce to continue his education, he found himself handicapped by his poor educa-tion and was almost denied an opportunity to attend classes. As the col-lege president told him, "We have to raise the standards, and somebody's going to be hurt. The first ones hurt will be country boys like yourself." [19]

Children in the towns and larger villages had a much better chance at a good education after the state became more active. State reforms and a better economy permitted their parents to increase the funding of local schools and to create consolidated high schools. For these parents, an enhanced education promised economic opportunity for their children and provided effective advertising of the vitality of their communities. With the battle cry "let progress predominate," compulsory attendance and other school reforms gained acceptance because a better education opened up the future to "new ambitions." In that sense, education served as both a cause and consequence of the shift in values and ideas discussed previously, and it helped justify an increasingly active government.[20]

Education, however, divided as much as it united the region. Many educational reformers clearly hoped to improve moral values as well as intellectual abilities by expanding the reach of public schools. For black and white children the school taught conformity to middle-class ways. In addition, country folk suffered from a growing inequality between their schools and those in the towns and larger villages. Educational inequali-ties and forced conformity brought resentment of being left out, left be-hind, and left to do what others demanded. This resentment made any type of political alliance between new conservatives and rural insurgents virtually inconceivable.[21]

Educational inequalities were only one example of a growing diver-gence between townsfolk and country folk and only one example of the forces reshaping politics. Out of an idealized vision of the past, out of fear of a new age, and out of the narrowing definition of right behavior that education both fostered and reflected came the Ku Klux Klan.

THE KU KLUX KLAN AND WOMEN VOTERS

Soon after the 1920 election the Ku Klux Klan spread to every county in Northeast Texas, achieving its greatest strength in the largest towns, Paris and Texarkana. Tellingly, Paris also provided some of the most pointed criticism of the Klan. Like the prohibition election of 1887, the Klan set neighbor against neighbor, forced a rethinking of old ideas about govern-ment, and altered the political system by further restricting the types of political coalitions found in Northeast Texas.[22]

FIGURE 7.1

*Ku Klux Klan, 1920s. This Klan march in Waco in the early 1920s drew large
crowds. Such marches often occurred after dark, and organizers heightened the
sense of drama by skillful use of lighting. Similar marches occurred in Paris and in
other towns in the Blackland Prairie and Northeast Texas.*
Photograph courtesy of Cushing Memorial Library, Texas A&M University.

More than anything else about the 1920s, the Klan defied easy classification, and it continues to do so. It was reactionary and progressive,
for the law and against the law in the same breath. Yet it was more than
an "irrational" fringe group. At its peak in 1921–1924 the Klan included
millions of American men and women from all regions of the country and
all social and economic classes. This second version of the Klan began
in Georgia in 1915 and arrived in Texas in 1920. Klan organizers from
the main office in Georgia took advantage of the Annual Reunion of the
United Confederate Veterans held in Houston in October 1920 and of lingering bitterness and fear from the race riot of 1917. After organizers reminded Houstonians that returning black veterans might again demand
their rights, Sam Houston Klan No. 1 burned its first cross and held an ini-
tiation ceremony on October 8, 1920. Within a year, more than a hundred
other Klan chapters appeared in the state.[23]

While the Klan's secrecy and the absence of detailed records limits our
understanding of it, judging from Northeast Texas the Klan prospered

because of the right environment and the right stimulus. The uneasiness indicated by the rabid fear of Bolshevism, the uncertain economy, and a nostalgia for an idealized past provided a hothouse for the Klan, while attitudes about gender, religion, and race stimulated Northeast Texans to join and to act.[24]

All versions of the Klan thrived on racism, but different circumstances broadened the impact of race on the 1920s Klan beyond the latent belief in white supremacy. As the near riot following the lynching of the Arthur brothers in Paris in 1920 testified, blacks' willingness to defend themselves, as well as efforts to organize resistance to discrimination, increased after World War I. For whites worried about social decay, about the decay of white supremacy compared to olden times, this newfound black assertiveness often demanded a response—joining the KKK. The key here was the widespread and determined nature of black responses to white aggression. A federal investigator reported that in December 1918, with the war barely over, black residents of Kildare in Bowie County gathered at the African Methodist Episcopal Church. After lamenting that the government "forced the Negro to go 3000 miles away to fight for Democracy when they should have been fighting for Democracy at home," the preacher looked forward to the return of well-trained black veterans experienced "in killing white men." He told the audience to "arm themselves with Winchester rifles" and join the veterans in a war for their rights as Americans.[25]

As an incident in Marion County indicated, this was far more than idle talk. On August 8, 1920, McKinley "Buck" Beal wandered by a yard with a pile of tempting watermelons cooling under a shade tree. He inquired of the price from a young white girl of about his own age. The two teenagers, one black and the other white, agreed on a quarter as the price for the melon Buck picked out. He handed her a dollar bill which she stuffed down the front of her dress. After she refused to give him his change, an angry Beal reached for the dollar, tearing her dress in the process. She screamed, and the woman who owned the house rose from her nap and fired a shotgun at Beal. Ashamed of her actions, the girl claimed Beal assaulted her and a white mob came after him.[26]

In the meantime, Beal fled to the home of his father, Alf Beal, a leading citizen of the primarily black community of Kellyville. His family got out their rifles and made preparations for the mob they knew was coming. They rigged up a scarecrow clothed with a blue denim shirt and felt hat, and when the mob arrived they raised and lowered it so quickly that the attackers believed it to be human. As soon as the white mob stood to fire, the Beal family, safely hidden behind stout walls and in holes under outbuildings, riddled them with steel-jacketed shells. When Marion County sheriff Will Terry left with a carload of wounded, he declared he had had enough and was not coming back. The remaining members of the mob asked to talk. When Buck Beal crawled out of his spot under an outbuilding, his brother Manse shot him dead. He later said he did it to spare his family from being victimized by lynching. Shaken by the good marksmanship of the Beals, the mob left and dropped the matter. The next day one of their number died from his wounds, and others remained crippled for life. The white girl who started it all later admitted her foolish actions, and the knowledge that she caused two deaths led to a mental breakdown. She spent much of the rest of her life in the state insane asylum. In an ironic note that demonstrated the close proximity of white and black in Marion County, her name was Lillie Beal.[27]

Across Texas, blacks not only took up arms, they joined the National Association for the Advancement of Colored People. Although founded almost a decade before, the NAACP attracted few members in Texas until the close of the war. By then the national leadership of the NAACP actively recruited in the South, and incidents like the Longview Race Riot of 1919 increased black determination to resist white aggression. As 1919 closed, almost 8,000 Texans belonged to the more than thirty chapters in Texas. Violence and intimidation, often endorsed by elected officials, quickly reduced the number of NAACP branches in Texas. Led by Governor Hobby, the state not only failed to do anything about such atrocities as the Arthur lynching in Paris in 1920, it used its power to crush the NAACP. In such a climate white vigilante groups like the Ku Klux Klan thrived. Their purpose, as W. A. Owens recalled, was to "keep the niggers in their place." [28]

Texarkana, with one of the state's seven surviving NAACP branches in 1921, quickly joined Paris as a center of Klan activity. In February 1922 four masked men shot and killed P. Norman, an alleged bootlegger, while he was in the custody of Deputy Sheriff W. T. Jordan. Jordan was later indicted for murdering his black prisoner, and the district judge launched an investigation of Klan involvement in the case. A few days before his death, Norman and a neighbor ran Jordan off the neighbor's farm, and Norman called the deputy "some hard names." At about the same time, a masked band dumped four whites in the newsroom of a local newspaper and instructed them to report they had been whipped for adultery and other conduct the masked men defined as immoral. While the victims delivered their message, the intruders held all those in the newsroom at gunpoint. That May a mob battered down the door of the Miller County jail on the Arkansas side of Texarkana and seized a black prisoner accused of shooting and killing a deputy. Some wore masks as they tied the rope around his neck to the back of a car. After pulling him behind the car until he strangled, they burned his body.[29]

Events in Texarkana, like those in Paris, suggested a link between black resistance to white supremacy and the growth of the Klan, an often violent Klan. (Those who stress the essentially nonviolent nature of the Klan and suggest that racism was only one of many causes for its growth should take a closer look at Texas.) Yet, as the whipping of the four whites dumped in the Texarkana newsroom demonstrated, Klan violence lashed out beyond the black community to include whites charged with sexual immorality or violation of prohibition laws.[30]

In January 1922 Klansmen wielding a leather strap beat a white Lamar County farmer under indictment for making illegal alcohol until blood flowed and then tarred and feathered him. In March five masked men seized a white farmer in a Paris candy shop. After beating him, they told him to go home to his wife. During 1921 and 1922, few months passed without some report of Klan violence. The majority of the victims were rural whites. They experienced beatings, tarring and feathering, and physical intimidation, but were not maimed, crippled, or killed. Klansmen, usually townsfolk, claimed that they acted to stop violations of prohibition laws or marital infidelity, and, striking a religious note, they enjoined their victims to go and sin no more.[31]

As in the case of late-nineteenth-century lynchings, the Klan's growth and its ferocity owed much to religion. Its rituals and ceremonies drew heavily from the Protestant church. Singing "Onward Christian Soldiers," Klan members paraded down main streets across Texas. They furthered this image of doing the muscular work of God by constant reference to Romans 12:1, which called for those who sought a new life in Christ to "present your bodies as a living sacrifice."[32] Klan organizers insisted they "performed a wonderful work in behalf of the Protestant descendants of the 'Makers of America' in every state in the Union." Klansmen marched into church on Sunday to make donations. Ministers defended the organization. Judging from the description of Klan marchers in Paris on Saturday, February 12, 1922, these were not young, restless lower-class whites with nothing better to do. After the Klan marched through the streets, they returned without their masks, giving the reporter for the *Paris Morning News* every opportunity to examine their faces. All were over thirty, and many were "graybearded." Regional ministers moved among the crowd of onlookers and participants. While no women marched in the parade "a considerable number of ladies" came from the surrounding area to witness the spectacle. All acted with a fervor derived from their religion.[33]

In Fort Worth, fundamentalist minister J. Frank Norris used the Klan and it used him. In Northeast Texas, however, fundamentalism came later to the region and, instead, more-fragmented religious impulses fed the growth of the Klan. These included both efforts to restore Christianity to its original purity and efforts to improve society through such religiously inspired reforms as prohibition. In 1905 the Landmark Baptists, headquartered in Texarkana, established their first General Association. Like the Primitive Baptists, the Churches of Christ, and some Pentecostal or holiness groups, which also grew rapidly in the region, Landmark Baptists sought a return to the landmarks of the church in the first century after the life of Christ. All of these churches reacted against modern trends such as the teaching of evolution, the use of history and critical analysis to study scripture, and the joining of several denominations in ecumenical organizations. Modern women who cut their hair short and engaged in "male" occupations, and men and women who ignored traditional taboos against sex outside of marriage, became particular targets for believers in restoration theology. Yet the Churches of Christ, unlike the closely related Disciples of Christ, never aligned with the Klan or with prohibition movements. Divided from other Protestants by theology, class, and rural character, members either resented being forced to conform or despised the better sort who dominated the Klan. The Disciples, on the other hand, more readily embraced ecumenicalism, an organized mission effort, and broad efforts to improve society. It was at this point — between efforts to restore and efforts to modernize — that the Klan seemed to best flourish. Restoration theology or perhaps some early pangs of fundamentalism also touched the two largest denominations — Baptists and Methodists, and they too provided a hothouse for Klan recruitment. Somewhere between retreating from the world and accepting part of the modern world while trying to improve it lay a point that made Klan membership appealing.[34]

Like the Lost Cause from which it also borrowed, the Klan became a type of civil religion that sought the preservation of old-time values, but again like the Lost Cause, the Klan made living in the world easier by promoting a more uniform set of beliefs. In the nineteenth century, rural people went to town to escape the routines of evangelical Protestant morality. They acted free from the constraints of their rural communities, but prohibition, the Klan, and other self-described reform movements increasingly forced an end to this practice.[35]

This need to enforce a modern, town-based moral code and restore traditional Christianity stimulated concern for shifting gender roles and for the morals of the next generation—both major themes of Klan activity in Northeast Texas. In that sense the Klan concerned women, the supposed teachers of morality and protectors of civilization. Women who agreed that the Klan acted against "proven enemies of society and decency" joined men in supporting the organization. If they conceived of their purpose in life in a traditional manner, perhaps they were even more likely than men to support the Klan. Yet women who resented being pushed into constricted and stereotyped gender roles also opposed the Klan. Thus, Klan insistence upon traditional gender roles gave some women an extra reason to oppose it beyond resentment of its secret nature or abhorrence of its violence, and it gave other women an extra reason to support it.[36]

Jefferson, the scene of the most violent suppression of black voters in the 1890s, offered an interesting window on the relationship between gender and attitudes toward the Klan. This town of about 2,500 people had a relatively large group of second-generation Jewish merchants and bankers who viewed the growth of the Klan with alarm. It also had an entrenched group of middle-class black craftsmen and small business owners. Well-organized, influential, and progressive women added to the mix. Reacting to criticism from these groups, the Klan requested that Birdie Taylor publish a defense of their principles in the *Jimplecute*. She complied with the request on June 14, 1922. Addressed "to the People of Jefferson and Marion County, of whatever creed, race or sex," the Klan's two-column statement of principles was intended to assure Jews, blacks, and women that "contrary to reports circulated by our enemies we are not anti-anything, but strictly pro-American and pro white supremacy." The Klan opposed the "immoral, the undesirable and the law violator," not good citizens of any race, creed, or gender. Yet, as Taylor probably understood, their words cost as much support as it gained. The Klan wanted "tall men, sun crowned who live above the fog" to defend helpless "pure womanhood." Under the veil of defending the law, they warned of going beyond the law. They attacked all that was alien and defended all that fit their definition of Americanism. Women long active in business or public causes who accepted the need to wear trousers in some situations, as well as members of minority groups, found little assurance of the good intentions of the Klan. They formed a very visible core of opposition to the Klan, and as a result in Jefferson there was no rush to join the Klan because it was what the better sort did.[37]

In Paris and other Klan centers, on the other hand, women apparently supported the male-only organization but never formed their own Klan chapters. The female branch of the Klan, called Women of the Ku Klux Klan, appeared in Texas in 1923. It had strong local chapters in the larger cities, particularly Fort Worth and Dallas, but no record exists of official Women of the Klan organizations in Paris, Texarkana, or other points in Northeast Texas. Perhaps the intense feud that broke out in 1924 between backers of Mrs. J. T. Bloodworth of Fort Worth and women loyal to Hiram Evans, the Dallas dentist who led the national Klan organization, stymied development. At any rate, women friends of the Klan in Northeast Texas participated in Klan activities and presumably voted for Klan-endorsed candidates, so politics offered the best clue about the different attitude of women and men toward the Klan.[38]

In 1922 the Klan played a prominent role in most elections, including those for governor, senator, and representative. In so doing, the Klan's activity not only revealed much about the different voting patterns of men and women, it altered the identity and ideology of political factions. That year Cyclone Davis again sought victory in the First District and challenged Eugene Black for his seat in Congress. Although never as clearly identified with the hooded order as Earle Mayfield, the official Klan candidate for senator, Davis coyly angled for Klan support. Actually, except for prohibition and segregation, Davis stood too far outside the middle-class sensibilities increasingly wrapped up in Klan membership to fit neatly within the Klan fold. Still, instead of trying for part of the Klan vote, Black engaged in several well-publicized attacks on the Klan and did his best to focus on the link between Davis and the Klan. This meant the 1922 race for the U.S. House gave voters the choice of a candidate loosely affiliated with the Klan versus a vocal opponent of the Klan.[39]

Yet this was far from a single-issue race. When voters cast their ballots in July 1922, the economy had not recovered fully from its worst downturn since August 1914, and cotton prices remained depressed. The seemingly intractable problem of dealing with boll weevils and a recent onslaught of pink boll worms added to voters' ill temper. That July, most voters could not foresee the improved yields and higher cotton prices of 1922 through 1925, while memories of the best of times remained strong. These circumstances prompted voters to embrace causes and candidates that promised a more active government. Gubernatorial elections often took center stage, but in times of depressed cotton prices and a declining economy, Northeast Texas voters—as they had done for three decades—realized only Congress could help.[40]

Davis, like Jim Ferguson who that year ran against Mayfield for a seat in the Senate, still spoke for those eager for the government to play an active role in the economy. Cyclone remained as alliterative as ever, accusing Black of selling out to "profit puffed plutocrats."[41] Black's support of the Esch-Cummins Transportation Act of 1920 quickly became a key campaign issue and Davis's best example of this sellout. Instead of promoting competition in the railroad industry, this law encouraged some mergers for the sake of efficiency and profitability. It also took away from state railroad commissions any last power to regulate rates and gave that power to the Interstate Commerce Commission. Davis charged that the law favored Wall Street at the expense of main street and violated states' rights. Jim Ferguson and Earle Mayfield picked up these charges in their Senate race, where both candidates used them to their advantage in a crowded field. Since organized labor, particularly railroad workers, generally opposed the bill, such charges aided Davis, Ferguson, and Mayfield in some counties in Northeast Texas. Interestingly, Morris Sheppard, who once held Black's spot as the representative from the First District, opposed Esch-Cummins in the Senate. Sheppard knew his district and his state and, unlike Black, understood the danger of supporting such a bill.[42]

Railroad legislation grew more relevant as the nationwide rail strike of 1922 worsened. Set off by the loss of jobs and wage reductions that accompanied railroad consolidations, the strike virtually halted rail traffic across the country in July 1922. As election day, July 22, approached, trouble broke out in nearby Denison between labor union members and strike breakers brought in by the rail companies. Rail companies quickly hired protection. Violence followed. Conservatives and business progressives called on Governor Pat Neff to invoke the open-port law passed in the Hobby administration. Neff resisted all calls to act before the election, fearing that he would alienate rail workers who regarded the law as antilabor and designed to limit the effectiveness of strikes. Rail workers at Paris, Mount Pleasant, and Texarkana, in particular, closely followed events at Denison. Both the rail strike and the Klan dominated the closing days of the governor's election, with newspapers like the *Paris Morning News* attacking Neff as much for his stand on labor as for his awkward silence on the Klan.[43]

Earlier in the year, State Senator H. L. Darwin of Paris condemned Governor Neff for not doing more to stop the Klan's violent acts and suggested that Neff's inaction warranted opposition in the coming Democratic primary. Darwin's friend Harry Warner, editor of the *Paris Morning News,* responded to the challenge and ran against Neff in the Democratic primary because "he is lacking in moral courage." Such criticism almost forced Neff into a runoff. After straddling the fence on labor issues and the Klan, Neff avoided a runoff by only 50,000 votes and won re-election in the July primary. Neff did even worse in the First District, where Warner's candidacy allowed Fred Rogers, a close ally of Jim Ferguson and Joe Bailey, to lead in several counties.[44]

Meanwhile Cyclone Davis made the most of labor troubles, charging that Black opposed the best interests of the working man and that Esch-Cummins aided capitalists at the expense of labor. As he put it, Black's vote was "a wanton and abject surrender of our country to a bunch of railroad nabobs." He tried to make his appeal modern by attracting women voters and the progressive merchant vote. Again and again, however, he struck notes reminiscent of old-time populism. The rich used their greater access to governmental officials to profit at the expense of the honest, hard-working, plain folk.[45]

Election results in Camp County, where Black won only one small rural precinct, indicated that he lost votes because of his identification with the elite propertied class. Despite the support of influential local editor Burt Lockhart, he even lost the two Pittsburg precincts by a narrow margin. After 1914 Camp's voters consistently supported Black, and he clearly fit the image of the local board of trade. He stood for economic growth, a reasonable level of governmental activism, and opposition to radicalism. As Lockhart put it, "he persisted in addressing his constituents as honest, intelligent human beings." Davis's appeal was more emotional and visceral. He stirred the fires that inspired conversion. He brought a simple message of the way out of the wilderness—vote for him and against the elite. For a small town, Pittsburg had a large industrial workforce. Perhaps these workers identified with Davis's attacks on those who exploited labor and voted for Esch-Cummins.[46]

Given that vote, Black probably was lucky to have the Klan and Davis's long record of insurgency as issues. He could still claim to stand for education, order, prohibition, and an urban ethos. In that sense, men and women who supported the Klan in towns like Paris faced a difficult choice. Black stood for many of the things they believed in, but he spoke against the Klan.

Opponents of the Klan, including women, had an easier choice. During 1922 in Bowie, Cass, and Marion counties, Black's supporters, including his future opponent Wright Patman, used the taint of the Ku Klux Klan to convince progressives to vote against Davis. Unlike the 1914 election, this election resulted in Black's carrying these counties by impressive margins, thanks in large part to women's votes. Black, for example, won in Jefferson but lost the rest of the county. His large margin in Jefferson, however, allowed him to carry Marion County, where he lost every precinct in 1914. New voters, not a change in heart, made the difference in the two elections. Jefferson recorded many more votes in 1922 than in 1914, while the vote in rural precincts remained constant. Since women in Jefferson paid their poll tax while women outside the county seat usually did not and the male population of Jefferson declined in the 1910s, the new voters probably were women.[47]

Other returns indicate voters in Jefferson rejected the Klan instead of simply favoring Black's probusiness record. Not only did Black carry the city by a large margin, Davis's vote total in a two-person race barely exceeded Mayfield's total in a six-candidate race. The Klan divided the town's voters, and most voters spurned the Klan as much as they spurned Davis.[48]

Delta County offered another example of the role of women in 1922. This county traditionally favored the candidate who advocated an active role for the government in the economy and who, like Horace Vaughan in 1914, appealed to rural voters. Davis had always done well in Delta for that reason and because he lived in neighboring Hopkins County. Early in the campaign, Davis seemed almost a sure winner in the county, and he attracted large crowds when he spoke in Cooper. Yet Davis lost the county by 200 votes. That year three women ran for county office, and women turned out to vote in record numbers. Indeed, the vote in the primary equaled or exceeded the turnout for any election since 1887. The Klan, which made several well-publicized attempts to attract new members in Cooper, contributed to turning out this record vote. Evidently, however, they turned out more opponents than supporters. In the Senate primary, the combined vote for Culberson, Ferguson, and Cullen Thomas, each of them vehemently anti-Klan, easily surpassed the combined vote for Mayfield and Robert Lee Henry, another Klansman. Comparing these two races with those of 1914 strongly indicated that the Klan cost Davis the support of new voters—of women. Evidently enough women favored Black or opposed the Klan to defeat Davis.[49]

Lamar County, on the other hand, demonstrated that the Klan brought Davis votes as well as cost him votes. Usually Black carried Lamar, with the largest number of potential voters in the district, by over 2,000 votes. In 1922 he carried Lamar by only 1,500 votes, and the turnout exceeded every election since 1896. While the Klan and labor issues added to Davis's vote and increased the turnout, Black held on to enough of his traditional support to carry the county. Black also polled over 80 percent of the vote in Paris. Davis, however, received only a slightly lower total than Mayfield in each of the city's four wards. Mayfield, in fact, led the five other candidates for the Senate in every ward. Davis, never before this popular in Paris, probably owed his 600 votes in the city to the Klan and to organized labor. Some of those votes in this whites-only primary also surely came from women.[50]

Another factor complicated the race and accounted for the high turn-out in Lamar—Jim Ferguson. Ferguson, Mayfield's chief opponent in the Senate race, always drew voters to the polls. Like Davis, Ferguson enjoyed "a considerable personal following" in the countryside that voted for their champion in campaign after campaign. Again like Davis, the former governor often was identified as a rural mossback by middle-class urban voters, and they went to the polls to ensure his defeat. Not surprisingly, Ferguson led in almost every box outside of Paris but finished fifth in Paris. In any event, the excitement generated by Ferguson, Davis, and the Ku Klux Klan drew a remarkably high turnout in rural Lamar County. For once, rural voters participated at a higher rate than urban voters. That alone went far in explaining why Davis came within 400 votes of defeating Black in the district.[51]

Given the huge rural vote, the sluggish economy, Black's seeming reluctance to have the government play an active role in that economy, and the aid the Klan gave Davis in Lamar, Black was fortunate to have won. The vigorous anti-Klan campaign carried on in Delta County and in the eastern counties of the district proved essential to his victory. If either Cass or Bowie together with Marion or Delta had gone for Davis, it would have sunk Black. Anti-Klan sentiment, especially among women, gave Black a victory.[52]

Victory in 1922 marked a transition in Black's career and in the life of his party. Three basic questions traditionally helped organize and give coherence to factions and coalitions between factions: What was the proper level of government intervention in the economy? What was the proper level of individual freedom? Who should vote and control politics? Contesting for votes in hard times, arguing about the virtue of the Klan, and increasing political participation by women scrambled old political alliances based on answers to these questions and made possible the emergence of new ones. By successfully tagging Black as the friend of those who benefited from a government that did little, Davis laid the groundwork for his eventual defeat, and he moved insurgents, labor, and economic reformers closer together. Davis also undercut Black's appeal to those who favored some measure of government control over individual behavior. Both Davis and Black favored prohibition, the traditional gauge of where a candidate stood on the continuum between control and freedom. By loosely affiliating with the Klan, however, Davis achieved something new—a coalition between advocates of social control and advocates of individual freedom. Black won by retaining the vote of many who saw him as a proper role model or who admired his support for education and other reforms aimed at improving public character. In that sense he kept some advocates of social control and right behavior. He also attracted to a greater degree than ever before the vote of those who favored keeping government out of the economy. Yet by attacking the Klan as undemocratic, as a secretive and baleful influence on the Democratic party, Black also achieved something new. Those concerned with opening up the electoral process aligned with economic conservatives.

Local editors decried the "teaching of class hatred" in the 1922 primaries. Yet, as in 1887, more than sharply defined class lines influenced the 1922 elections. The continued presence of three or more mutating political factions and a passion-filled issue—this time the Klan—brought a huge voter turnout, a turnout aided by the presence of women and diminished by the absence of blacks.[53]

Women's increased voting rate and the emotion-charged issue of the Klan helped make the 1922 Democratic primary the first election in the twentieth century to match or surpass the record high turnouts of the mid-1890s. The 1924 primary drew even more voters to the polls. As in the period from 1887 to 1896, the causes of increased turnout included both economic reform and the drive for social conformity. The Klan, like prohibition before it, supercharged the electoral process, hastening the evolution of new types of conservatives and creating novel but fleeting alliances between political factions. New conservatives soon stood arrayed against an increasingly close partnership between middle-class economic reformers and those estranged from their more-prosperous and proper neighbors.[54]

IDEOLOGY AND POLITICS, 1924–1927

Despite the lackluster Democratic campaign on the national level, in 1924 Texas Democrats held their most interesting and probably most important election since the creation of the primary system. It was certainly the most convoluted, with a staggering total of nine candidates for governor, four of whom drew at least 15 percent of the vote. After an elimination primary with another Klan candidate, Felix D. Robertson ran as the official candidate of the hooded order. Lynch Davidson sought the vote of business progressives and advocates of the open shop. T. Whitfield Davidson most resembled a New Deal liberal. Miriam A. Ferguson ran with the help of her husband, Jim.[55]

Miriam Ferguson's campaign featured the typical anti-elite, anti-intel-lectual, and anti-big-city themes of other Ferguson campaigns. Jim Ferguson also had a long history of opposition or at least neutrality on prohibition and the enforcement of prohibition laws. Miriam's motherly image and the chance to elect a woman to high office convinced some social reformers and suffragists to vote for her despite their reservations about her husband. Still, in her first campaign her identity remained more closely aligned with her husband's than in later years, and she insisted, "I am adopting and approving the platform which Jim has already announced." This meant passionate commitment for and against the Fergusons.[56]

The Klan, too, aroused deep passions for and against. Its strident call for law and order, including rigid enforcement of all prohibition laws, angered and repulsed some voters while attracting others. Its violence, secrecy, and threat to take control of the Democratic party did the same. Ferguson and Whit Davidson repeatedly attacked the Klan, while Lynch Davidson bobbed and weaved trying to attract a few Klan votes, but by the end of the campaign he also denounced Robertson and the Klan.[57]

In part, the Klan assumed the place of the old social reform faction, and Robertson made a point of stressing his stance in favor of prohibition and woman suffrage. Like other Klan candidates, he also emphasized law and order, trying to build on fears of a crumbling society. Two factors, however, blunted his attempts to build a winning coalition of new conservatives and reformers—Klan violence and a growing perception that the Klan fostered political corruption. Through the use of elimination primaries, Klan leaders attempted to concentrate the Klan vote on one candidate, but their plan backfired. All of Robertson's opponents in the first primary accused him of corrupting the political process and of giving a secret organization undue political influence in the selection of officeholders. For others, Klan violence and willingness to go beyond the law made it "an enemy of constituted government." The irony of claiming to promote law and order while drawing support from the Klan did not escape all Northeast Texans. Besides, to some the Klan seemed increasingly like an organization that soured business. In the end, instead of building a winning coalition of several factions, the Klan split existing factions and combined the splinters into one temporary whole.[58]

Miriam Ferguson's candidacy also rearranged factional alliances and altered accepted ideology. On the one hand, because of her husband's record, she spoke for those concerned with personal liberty and for those in the countryside who believed her husband and perhaps themselves the victims of a plot by the rich and well educated. Yet she also appealed to those who distrusted the Klan's role in politics, disliked its violence, and believed that a traditional woman might fit what Texas needed in those tumultuous times. Some reformers and conservatives could find enough in Miriam Ferguson to vote for her, even though they would never have voted for her husband.[59]

Even with so much background noise, the first 1924 Democratic primary offered a useful gauge of the strength of the various factions in the Democratic party. Lynch Davidson's vote statewide came from urban counties, and in the district he did best in Lamar County. Districtwide he ran fourth, barely ahead of the combined total of the minor candidates. Miriam Ferguson, statewide and in the district, ran best in rural areas. While finishing second statewide, she trailed both Whit Davidson and Robertson in the district. Whit Davidson actually carried the most counties in the district and polled over 25 percent of the total vote. A resident of nearby Marshall, he did well in the eastern counties but also ran strong in the old Populist strongholds of Delta and Hopkins. Support from organized labor helped him in Bowie and Titus. Robertson, thanks to a strong showing in Lamar and a first- or second-place finish in every county except Franklin and Morris, led the regional vote. Both in the region and the state he received about 30 percent of the vote and made it into a run-off with Miriam Ferguson.[60]

Given the number of candidates representing every shade of the political spectrum, those who voted for Robertson in the first primary probably were members of the Klan. (A non-Klansman might support Robertson instead of Ferguson in the second primary, but not the first.) Thus, we can assume that roughly 30 percent of the voters belonged to the Klan in 1924. Klan strength did not reach that level everywhere—Lamar certainly had a stronger Klan than Franklin or Morris—but every county had pockets of Klan support.[61]

Without the alternatives provided by the two Davidsons, in the second primary voters faced difficult choices—choices that moved them toward a more enduring coalition and different ideological emphasis. A large part of this emerging coalition and different ideological emphasis derived from the vote of women and the role of the Klan. Voters faced the choice of an anti-Klan, antiprohibition candidate versus a candidate with the clearest possible identification with the Klan. Ferguson and her husband used Robertson's ties to the Klan in campaign speech after campaign speech. In Cooper, for example, Jim Ferguson lambasted the Klan from the top of a cotton bale for over two hours. Despite the heat of a mid-August day, between 5,000 and 6,000 men and women cheered enthusiastically inside the tin cotton shed that barely held the crowd. Ferguson hit repeatedly at the violence and lawlessness of the Klan and stressed its threat to open and democratic politics. As in the late 1890s, the key issue became not social reform or economic reform, but the purity of the political process. For those truly interested in restoring society to its traditional ways, Ferguson painted Robertson as the devil not the savior.[62]

The anti-Klan message hit home. Turnout for the runoff exceeded that of the 1922 primary by 5,000 votes and, even more astoundingly, surpassed the first primary. In fact turnout exceeded any other election between 1887 and 1930. In Lamar County alone the turnout increased by over 1,000 from 1922 to 1924. To the chagrin of the editor of the *Paris Morning News*, Robertson carried the county, but only after an intense and often bitter campaign against the Klan. According to observers, women voted in extraordinarily high numbers in Lamar and around the district. Drawn either by opposition to, or support of, the Klan or by the chance to elect the first female governor, they listened to the speeches alongside men and went to the polls. In doing so they permanently established women as a voting bloc to be reckoned with.[63]

Given a choice between a woman whose husband opposed woman suffrage and a supporter of the Ku Klux Klan, female voters chose the woman. While women in Paris may again have backed the Klan candidate in the runoff, elsewhere the towns, where women voted in almost equal numbers to men, went against Robertson. This brought Ferguson almost 54 percent of the region's vote in the runoff and victory in nine of eleven Northeast Texas counties. Statewide a lopsided vote for Ferguson in counties dominated by Texas Germans and Czechs gave her a slightly higher percentage of the vote, but in general the same tendency held. Robertson won in larger, more-urban counties such as Lamar and Dallas, where the Klan and prohibitionist organizations delivered the votes. In counties dominated by smaller towns, he lost by a significant margin.[64]

Felix Robertson's defeat fixed an outer limit on the appeal of new conservatives. Instead of championing individual and corporate freedom, these conservatives relied upon either group action or government sanctions to limit individual behavior. These new conservatives, and here Lynch Davidson served as a good example, sometimes ran as advocates of business interests and sought to avoid being lumped with the Klan. The Klan, however, took the goal of social conformity to its logical conclusion and demonstrated that campaigns for moral purity ran the risk of undermining individual freedom, the rule of law, and the role of the non-Klan voter in the Democratic primary. This meant that identification with the Klan limited a candidate's chances of building a coalition between conservatives, reformers, and insurgents.

In particular, those who believed themselves largely excluded from the benefits of educational or economic advances and those who resented the enforced morality of the Klan and prohibition, groups like organized labor or isolated rural voters, acted as insurgents had acted since 1887. They voted for their established leaders, for candidates whose record promised some attempt at achieving economic equity, and against those who would force them to conform to someone else's rules of conduct. Despite its appeal to those who sought to keep black Texans in their place, the 1920s Klan never developed a strong following in the countryside because it also sought to keep many rural whites in a place defined by someone else.

Meanwhile in the small towns, reformers either came to see the Klan as bad for business or they too felt left out of the economic and social changes of the 1920s. As the economy grew more centralized and as citizens left the small towns for better economic prospects, government's potential to save and improve their future became more important than prohibition or some other social reform. While small-town leaders might sympathize with those who believed moral decline lay all around them, they could and did make common ground with traditional Ferguson supporters. This was especially true because Miriam Ferguson allayed concerns about a society turned upside down by portraying herself as a very traditional woman.

In that sense women solidified an emerging alliance between groups that some would soon call the New Deal coalition. Women in towns of all sizes and more-educated or wealthier women from the countryside voted in large numbers in 1924. Some of these women voted for Klan candidates, but most did not. Whether they voted differently from their husbands, fathers, and brothers remains difficult to tell. Yet it seems reasonably clear that they did not vote, outside of the largest cities, for Klan candidates. In Camp County, for example, the Klan made a major drive to attract new members in 1924, and Robertson carried Pittsburg by a small margin but lost the county. The vote in the small villages and rural areas of the county surpassed anything since the 1890s, a clear indication that women voted and that they voted for Ferguson. Ferguson, as recently pointed out, positioned herself as a traditional woman whose motherly advice offered a far better cure for the moral instability of the day than Klan violence. She fulfilled a traditional female role of moral arbitrator. Yet she also gained the votes of those anxious to have a woman in office regardless of her political past. Women voters helped bridge the gap between reformers and insurgents by rejecting violence, and they undercut the claim of new conservatives to some type of moral superiority by fulfilling their traditional roles. This allowed a broader spectrum of women and men to vote for Miriam Ferguson than for her husband, and it demonstrated the difficulty conservatives of any type faced in winning elections even before the Great Depression.[65]

In fact, after 1924 not only did Klan influence precipitously decline, candidates and coalitions whose ideology drew close to social and economic conservatism also lost support. At the start of the 1920s, Eugene Black appeared almost unbeatable. His stand on the Esch-Cummins Bill and on farm export legislation, however, clouded the picture of Black as an exponent of active government. Opposition to the Klan and the vote of women brought him victory. When the Klan vanished as an issue, Black became increasingly vulnerable. Both Black's decline and the disappearance of the Klan did not mean Northeast Texans abandoned the hope of improving the moral climate of their region. Indeed, a candidate with credentials as a fighter of vice and corruption without the taint of the Klan stood a good chance of defeating Black. This was particularly true if that candidate also argued in favor of a more active government. A candidate who combined the old insurgent faction with reformers and limited Black to the new conservative vote would win.

Black's vulnerability owed as much to the emergence of a new public conscience as it did to his increased conservatism. After the ambiguity and discord of 1920–1924, Northeast Texans enjoyed a period of relative unanimity on such issues as the limits and promise of government, the need for citizen activism, antilynching, and the inappropriateness of the Klan.

Wright Patman anticipated the essence of this new public conscience in 1921 when, as a member of the Texas House from Cass County, he introduced three bills for consideration by that body. The first strengthened the penalties for two or more people conspiring to injure or intimidate another, especially if the conspirators wore a disguise or mask. His other bills aimed at stopping interracial sex, wife desertion, and nonsupport of children. While the first bill hit directly at the Klan, Patman claimed the other two undermined the need for a Klan. Thus, through legislation, Patman sought the end of a secretive and undemocratic force and the end of the justification of that force. Government, not the mob, best served the community. While Patman's bills failed in 1921, Patman's approach anticipated what became the norm.[66]

Antilynching also indicated willingness to abandon mob action. After 1922 no recorded lynchings occurred in the district until 1942. In Paris and Texarkana much of the opposition to lynching centered in the towns' newly organized Rotary Clubs. Founded just after the turn of the century, the Rotary Club spread to Texas in the World War I years and appealed primarily to the business community. In its ideal form the club stood for "the Golden Rule in business" and "service above self." In Texarkana the club put up a $100 reward for information on the Norman murder, which, ironically, the local chapter of the Ku Klux Klan matched. In both Paris and Texarkana the local Rotary Clubs organized petitions condemning lynching. These clubs, together with groups such as the Chamber of Commerce, served as formal meeting points for business leaders and offered them a chance to discuss ways of improving their communities. Service above self held appeal as a motto, but in reality anything that improved their community also improved their business prospects. Lynching ended—if it truly ended instead of going underground—because it hurt business and a town's public image.[67]

Sporadic cases of lynching continued in other parts of Texas, such as the 1930 lynching in Sherman, two counties west of Paris, where a determined mob undeterred by a Texas Ranger fired the courthouse to seize an African-American male accused of assaulting a white woman. Yet, in general, lynching slowed across the state, while it continued at only a slightly reduced pace and with no public opposition in Mississippi. While the link between improved business conditions and reduced lynching remains nebulous, it seems safe to argue that the type of community action organized through such vehicles as Rotary Clubs replaced the Klan and lynching. That not only slowed lynching in Texas, it contributed to Texans' ability to close the gap with the rest of the country while Mississippians remained the poorest of the poor.[68]

The move against lynching also paralleled Patman's three bills aimed at undercutting the Klan. Removing lynching removed the primary source of black militancy, and without black militancy, justification for the Klan diminished. In Paris after the 1920 lynching of the Arthur brothers, business leaders patrolled the street dividing the white and black sections of town. Throughout the early 1920s the *Paris Morning News,* the traditional voice of the business community, led the fight against the Klan and against lynching. Using variations of the phrase "lawlessness and law cannot coexist," the editors of the *Morning News* linked the Klan and lynching over and over again. Neither had a place in a modern Texas. Ending one required ending the other.[69]

Dan Moody, a candidate for governor in 1926, embodied this new public conscience as well as anyone in Texas. Those outside Texas declared he represented "a new Texas of the public schools, of the universities, of growing industries, of immigration and of a widening future." His major opponent that year, Miriam Ferguson and her husband Jim, on the other hand, stood for "Demagogy and hill-billyism." Opponents charged that the Fergusons again ran state government for personal profit and that leaving them in office embarrassed prosperous and progressive Texans. Actually, a third major candidate ran for governor that year, Lynch Davidson—meaning the July primary once more loosely conformed to the 1892 model. Davidson held the conservative wing, Moody reached out from the center, and Ferguson depended upon insurgent voters. Moody carried every county in Northeast Texas except Marion and Titus in the first primary. Ferguson carried those two and placed second to Moody in the rest. Davidson did best in Lamar and Bowie, the most urban counties.[70]

In Morris County, Ferguson and Moody supporters waged an intense campaign, made more entertaining by the presence in the race of local minister O. F. Zimmerman. Running as "God's partner," Zimmerman spent most of his campaign attacking Moody for being in league with the devil and big business. While he got seventy-one votes in his hometown of Naples, he polled few votes elsewhere. Perhaps his attacks on Moody helped Ferguson, who carried the Omaha precinct and two rural precincts. That fit a pattern with the rest of the region. Ferguson carried rural precincts and those with a Populist tradition. Moody carried the towns like Naples and Daingerfield that hoped to grow into thriving cities. Interestingly, in another twist reminiscent of the 1890s, officials threw out the Omaha precinct because of voting irregularities. Moody then carried the county by two to one in the runoff.[71]

In fact, Moody carried every Northeast Texas county in the runoff with Ferguson and won by an impressive margin statewide. Ecstatic foes of the Fergusons sounded off about the end of an era. Once again they were wrong. Building on a base of rural tenant farmers who believed themselves left out of the prosperity of the modern age and aided by the devastation of the Great Depression, Ma Ferguson won re-election as governor in 1932.[72]

Like Cyclone Davis, the Fergusons seemed a permanent and unalterable political force. Especially in times of intense political or economic instability they rose to the top. This invites the judgment that little changed after 1914. Yet after the mid-1920s a new public conscience emerged—an ideology that more fully rejected the Klan, lynching, social conservatism, and the argument that true southerners rejected an active government. Perhaps the shifting economy left little choice in this evolution, but the new role of women in politics and the revolt against the Klan shoved the process along as well. Exponents of this new virtue firmly believed that "progress will be made once the people are aroused." They further argued that the "spirit of Texas lives and the great commonwealth is finally going to achieve its destiny."[73] Celebration of being Texan and determination to achieve the prosperity due all Americans forced those who grew too conservative to tread an even more difficult political minefield.

PART THREE

MODERNITY

EIGHT

POLITICS AND CULTURE, 1928

In 1928 Eugene Black lost his seat in Congress to Wright Patman, and A. W. Neville began writing his long-running column "Backward Glances" for the *Paris Morning News*.[1] The events were connected. Just as Horace Vaughan and Joe Bailey held on too long to the glorious Confederacy, Black failed to reflect a culture that increasingly stressed the heroic nature of local plain people and the importance of Texas symbols. That caused his defeat as surely as his failure to articulate the economic concerns of the small merchant class or the opposition of a growing coalition between economic reformers, insurgents, and labor. It was not just that Black grew more conservative and more conservative in a way that limited individual freedom and economic opportunity. He no longer evoked his time and his region.

Yes, Black opposed a greater role for the federal government in managing the railroad system, and he seemed reluctant for the government to smooth out the ups and down of cotton prices. His reaction to socialism demonstrated a willingness to use government force to impose right behavior, a willingness that severely limited his appeal to insurgents and labor. As he became a new conservative—one who hesitated when asked to expand the role of government in the economy, but who willingly used government to impose morality—Black drove the other factions closer together. Thus Black like other new conservatives helped create the coalition that defeated him—a group soon called the New Deal coalition. Yet in Northeast Texas the glue that bound that coalition together derived from cultural change as much as ideology and self-interest.

THE CULTURE OF LOCALISM AND RELIGION

Alexander White Neville was born in Virginia in 1864 and moved to Paris with his family in 1879. Called Sandy or Judge Neville by his friends, he began working for the *Paris Morning News* in 1884. He soon left the *Morning News* to run a print shop and, eventually, his own newspaper, the *Paris Advocate*. In 1902 he returned to the *Morning News,* where he remained until his death in 1956. For many years he proudly called himself the oldest working newspaperman in Texas. His first big break as a reporter came in 1893 when his stories of the horrifying lynching of Henry Smith appeared around the country. In that and in his coverage of the 1916 fire in Paris, he displayed a keen eye for detail. It was not as a reporter but as a writer of local history with that same eye for detail that he earned the most prominence. His column "Backward Glances" and his two books *The History of Lamar County* (1937) and *The Red River Valley Then and Now* (1948) remain important sources of local history and folklore. His gritty observations captured the essence of people he described as possessing "refined rusticity." [2]

What launched Neville on his quest to record the everyday life of his region? For that matter, why did two proper ladies who insisted that they be known as Mrs. Arch McKay and Mrs. H. A. Spelling write the history of Marion County? What made William A. Owens and William Humphrey storytellers and collectors of folklore and folk music? Despite all Owens's attempts at replacing his country background with high culture, what drew him back to the shaped notes of his childhood? [3]

Answers to why the region pulled its sons and daughters home lie in a passage from Humphrey's *The Ordways* (1964). He declared that "collections transmitted from father to son of proverbs and prophecies, legends, laws, traditions of the origins and tales of the wandering" connect members of the "tribe." It was this "feeling of identity with the dead which characterizes and explains the Southerner." Ironically, in collecting the legends of their place, Neville and others accelerated the conversion of Northeast Texas from southern to western. [4]

The same year that Neville began his column and Patman won his first election to Congress, Henry Nash Smith wrote in the Dallas-based *Southwest Review* that it was time to "set about adjusting ourselves to the actual conditions of our life." In their own ways Neville, McKay, Spelling, Owens, and Humphrey did just that. As Owens wrote in his first autobiographical volume: "So I am from Pin Hook and Pin Hook is part of me. All of my life has been a flight from it, but now, after many returnings, I see that it has overtaken me at last." The process required adjusting memories to life, but that did not imply more- or less-accurate memories, simply the need for adjustment.[5]

Memory preoccupies more historians than ever before as they seek to understand why their published work stands rejected in favor of the myths and fables of public memory of our past. Texas, Northeast Texas in particular, suggests that history and memory were tools shaped by and shaping politics and economic endeavors.[6] Thus the history, myth, or memory of what it meant to be white influenced the actions of white croppers and tenants in Neil Foley's *White Scourge*. In a similar way, the history, memory, and myth of what it meant to be a Northeast Texan, almost always defined by whites, swayed political behavior. Obviously there were exceptions to this rule. Oral traditions within the African-American community, including memories of slavery and lynching, partially defined what it meant to be a black Northeast Texan. Humphrey, whose Cherokee ancestors powered his caustic appraisals of the region, also differed from many others. Yet the key point remains that a cohesive body of memories and myths influenced how people acted.[7]

Memories and myths changed with time, and vestiges of a Confederate culture, so dominant before World War I, never completely disappeared. Telling southern stories, singing southern songs, and building southern monuments kept the region tied to that Confederate past. Yet that past increasingly existed in equilibrium with being Texan. As Owens, who came of age during this span, put it, "I was an unreconstructed southerner, as well as a Texas chauvinist." [8]

Increasingly, however, being Texan meant being American. It allowed reaching for an American dream unencumbered with memories of slavery, defeat in the Civil War, and Reconstruction. In another ironic twist, historian Eugene C. Barker, who earlier helped convince George Littlefield to fund the study of southern history, in 1925 published his biography of Stephen F. Austin, which prepared the way for the identification of Texas as western, uniquely American, and simply unique. Others joined Barker, such as J. Frank Dobie and Walter Prescott Webb, who in the years after World War I highlighted the indigenous, unique, or at least nonsouthern aspects of Texas culture. Webb wrote about barbwire and windmills, and Dobie about cowboys, cows, and horses. In Northeast Texas, Neville wrote of the full range of humanity in the Red River Valley. His "Backward Glances" covered "life in the raw." [9] These new ways of viewing the past allowed new solutions to present problems.[10]

It seems a bit odd, an intellectual stretch, that modernization depended on backward glances. Yet, they were different backward glances, new backward glances. They stressed the real, the natural, and the practical.

They fit "a utilitarian, hard facts age." They replaced the languid, passive, romanticized images of the cavalier South. Much as Barker's *Austin* did, these other backward glances stressed American notions like the conquest of the frontier by rugged, heroic pioneers "without the blare of trumpets." These writers used history to instill pride and encourage hard work and self-reliance. Backward glances emphasized vignettes that fit a go-ahead, get-ahead world. They reflected a world of winners, not losers. They were part of the world that lauded the "industrial captains of Paris" in the same vein and on the same page as the Texas pioneers.[11]

Concern for the local, however, never merged completely into being Texan. Instead, over the course of the 1920s, concern for the county level and the immediate region squeezed out southerness. By 1928, instead of swinging back and forth between southern and Texan, attachments to the Red River Valley and to Texas defined the poles. While reaching for the American dream by celebrating their Texas heritage, regional residents preserved their own local and particular identity. Perhaps change derived from the passing of the frontier, the leaving of traditional ways behind, a force that continued to stimulate modern Texas writers like John Graves or Larry McMurtry. Yet the rise of localism reflected very particular circumstances unique to the 1920s.[12]

In his work *The War Within: From Victorian to Modernist Thought in the South,* Daniel Joseph Singal observes, "one must not prejudge the relationship between culture and society. The lines of influence can flow either way: in some cases thought may follow upon social change, in other cases it may effectively reshape society, and in still other cases the link may be dialectical." Singal warned that "the connection between culture and society will rarely be simple." The transition from celebration of the Confederacy to celebration of Texas and the Confederacy, and then to Texas and a culture of localism, amply illustrated his argument.[13]

For Northeast Texans the original dialectic gyrated between being southern and being American—between being culturally defensive and economically innovative. Even before the surge of patriotism associated with World War I tipped the scale in favor of Americanism, the region's citizens gradually solved the problem by stressing their Texas heritage. By the 1920s this offered a convenient compromise. Instead of totally assimilating into America, they became Texans: innovative, risk-taking entrepreneurs with accentuated American characteristics. Good sense dictated the replacement of old ideas of limited government with new ideas from the Department of Agriculture or the Texas Agricultural Extension Service. Politicians who missed this cultural change paid the price. Horace Vaughan's loss in 1914 and even more clearly Joe Bailey's loss in 1920 represented the end of the Confederate myth. Other causes contributed to their political defeat, but the sense that they were old-fashioned moss-backs played an essential role in the elections.[14]

After 1920 the widespread American search for the authentic and real contributed to the celebration of local history and culture. Just as "Blind Lemon" Jefferson came out of rural Texas to perform for large crowds of northerners eager to hear authentic Texas blues, Neville told the real story of Northeast Texas. The real story did not focus on big planters and genteel cavaliers, but rather on everyday people struggling to survive and enjoying their simple pleasures.[15]

Yet society also contributed to the rise of localistic culture in a much more direct way. One of the most common complaints about life in Northeast Texas went something along the lines of a 1922 editorial in the *Paris Morning News* entitled, "Why not buy it at home?" After decry-ing the tendency to shop by mail order or journey to nearby urban areas, the editorial writer—perhaps A. W. Neville himself—insisted, "There are very few things which are not to be had in Paris just as good and generally somewhat cheaper than they may be had in Dallas or other of the large cities." Just as Paris swallowed the trade of Cooper, Dallas increasingly swallowed the trade of Paris. That meant not only a loss of business, but status, position, and authority. Though Paris fared far better than smaller towns such as Cooper, Jefferson, and Naples, it ceased to be the mecca its promoters long envisioned. In response, Neville's stories and other cul-tural activities deliberately posed an alternative to Dallas. The big city had glamour and glitter, their home had an authentic folk history.[16]

The story of the frontier past also offered inspiration. Neville closed his *Red River Valley Then and Now,* which was based on his column "Back-ward Glances," with remembrances of George W. Wright, usually consid-ered the founder of Paris. Clearly proud of the "fair country" of the Red River Valley, Wright argued it was worth all the difficulties. Then he asked, "How would you like to go through the half of what I have stated? Yet you complain at your several lots at the present." Using Wright's words Neville reminded his neighbors to "feel thankful" for what they had.[17]

Localism, however, did not simply imply the opposite of being Texan nor simply replace being southern. It contributed to an evolving myth of being Texan and celebrated heroes who fit an American model. Neville had the choice of many compelling personalities to focus on in his *History of Lamar County.* Sam Bell Maxey who served in the U.S. Senate, J. J. Cul-bertson who founded the Southern Cotton Oil Company and who used his wealth to beautify Paris, and William Johnson McDonald who gave the money for the creation of the University of Texas's McDonald Observatory all called Paris home. Yet two others held center stage: E. L. Dohoney and John Simpson Chisum.

Neville, a long-time advocate of prohibition, clearly admired Dohoney's persistent struggle to dry out his state and county. Calling him "the Father of Prohibition in Texas if not in the South," he carefully detailed his forty-year struggle for prohibition. Yet Dohoney also served several other useful functions. As an opponent of secession who served in the Confederate army, he fit better into the Americanization of Texas than unreconstructed Sam Bell Maxey. Dohoney demonstrated independence and dedication to a cause by leaving the Democratic party. An intellectual who wrote on sociology, religion, and the pseudo-science of phrenology, Dohoney established that Paris had the talent and high tone of much larger cities. Dohoney was an American—so American that he titled his autobiography, *An Average American*. Yet he fit the need for local color, for Texas eccentricity.[18]

Chisum, born in 1824 in Tennessee, moved with his parents in 1837 to what was soon to become Lamar County. His father pursued many business opportunities and quickly became one of the largest landowners and richest individuals in the area. In the 1850s Chisum began buying and selling cattle and managing herds for others. As Lamar County filled up with farmers, Chisum moved west in search of cheap grass and seldom returned to the county after the late 1850s. During the Civil War he drove one herd east for the Confederate army, but he avoided service in the war. Instead, he concentrated on making money and fighting Indians. After 1872 he confined his operations to New Mexico and Colorado, but when he died in 1884 his family buried him in Paris next to his parents. Instead of celebrating the Confederacy, paying tribute to Chisum underscored his importance as one of the original Texas cowmen—daring, innovative, and eccentric. He was a cowboy who read books and seldom wore a gun unless he intended to use it. Like George Littlefield, who put western scenes on the doors and the walls of his bank in Austin, Chisum put a western face on Lamar County. By elevating Chisum to the status of local hero, Neville contributed to the transformation of Northeast Texas from southern to western, a process confirmed by naming a high school in Paris, Chisum.[19]

Dohoney and Chisum stood opposite to Jefferson Davis and other southern heroes cherished by Horace Vaughan, Sam Maxey, and Joe Bailey. As reluctant Confederates, Dohoney and Chisum rapidly put the war behind them. Both took risks and advanced new ideas in business or politics. Both read and thought about questions of the day. Both stood out in ways that made them American, not southern. Their eccentricities,

FIGURE 8.1

Paris policemen in "Confederate" hats. This picture of two Paris policemen was taken in 1901, but these uniforms were worn for many years. The hats were modeled after Confederate cavalrymen's hats, with numbers replacing the CSA between the wreaths. Over the years, citizens came to regard the hats as western, not southern.

Photograph courtesy of Larry D. Hunt, Hunter-Bryant Museum, Paris, Texas.

though, still made them Texan. Neville offered them up for emulation, and in so doing moved his people further from the South.

Other towns had similar role models celebrated in newspapers and county histories. In Pittsburg, Lon Morris served as an example of frugality and generosity. He began by operating a one-man private bank, and by his death in 1934 he owned a percentage of numerous banks in Northeast Texas. Always generous to his church, he served as a local Methodist minister. Such generosity did not extend to his children. He lived plainly, spending little money on them or himself. Instead, in the 1920s he gave his entire estate to Lon Morris College in Jacksonville. Among his distinctive traits was the habit of never wearing a hat. While this alone stood out in a time when men always wore hats, he added to his eccentric image by always carrying an umbrella. A successful and extremely hardworking banker unafraid of violating the conventions of fashion or perhaps even unaware of such conventions, Morris was as unsouthern as Dohoney and Chisum.[20]

Morris's gift to a regional college also demonstrated the strength of the culture of localism. He put his fortune into the service of his region. J. J. Culbertson did the same. Local citizens dedicated the Culbertson Fountain in the plaza at Paris in 1927. Designed by architect J. L. Wees, the fountain stood in stark contrast to the Confederate monument down the street. Instead of four Confederate generals, water flowed from the mouths of four lions. The neo-classical structure, like the Littlefield Fountain in Austin, marked a new era in commemorative art. While it easily could have appeared in any city in the country, it was part of the culture of localism in the sense of demonstrating that Paris mattered. Like Dohoney and Chisum, it was both American and a distinctively regional icon that influenced future generations to think beyond the boundaries of the South.[21]

No one got further beyond the boundaries of the South, or for that matter beyond the boundaries of the planet, than William J. McDonald. Like Lon Morris, this Paris banker had big plans for his profits. When he died in February 1926, he left about $1 million to the University of Texas for the construction and equipping of an "observatory for the promotion and study of the science of astronomy." After visiting Harvard, the amateur astronomer evidently decided that his state needed to keep up with the much better endowed universities in the northeast. He wanted Texas to take its place among the regions boasting great universities.[22]

While interesting and appealingly eccentric, just how typical were people like McDonald? Moving beyond the literate and the wealthy always poses challenges, but fortunately religion offers a clue to the extent

FIGURE 8.2

Culbertson Fountain in Paris. German-born J. L. Wees gave the Culbertson Fountain a classic look that distinguished it from the commemorative art of the Lost Cause. Ever since its dedication in 1927, some have considered it ugly, but most view it as a distinctive feature of life in Paris.
Photograph courtesy of Jenkins Garrett Texas Postcard Collection, University of Texas at Arlington, Special Collections.

of cultural change. In the 1920s churches faced some of the same pressures as smaller towns. Improved roads and automobiles allowed church goers to drive past the small country churches to the larger churches in town, and the radio extended the reach of fundamentalist preachers such as J. Frank Norris of Fort Worth. Meanwhile, the rural population shrank, and croppers replaced farm owners. This decline in number and change in type negatively affected rural churches. Fewer people in the countryside translated into fewer members and reduced donations to the church. Croppers' pattern of moving from place to place every few years made building ties to a church difficult, and even if they joined a rural church their poverty meant smaller financial contributions than the farm owners they replaced. Consequently, denominations with many small rural churches, such as the Baptists and some Pentecostal or Holiness groups, faced severe challenges in the 1920s. The growth of Paris and Texarkana, however, gave competing denominations a chance to win new members.[23]

Changes in church size reflected the pressures and opportunities of the 1920s. During the early part of the decade, the number of black and white Baptists declined slightly. Pentecostal groups such as the Church of the Nazarene, another organization with small rural churches, also declined. Black Methodists, white Methodists, and Presbyterians increased slightly, especially in Bowie and Lamar counties. (The Presbyterians were more traditionally urban than Baptists. Methodists fell somewhere in between.) The highest rate of increase, however, came in the membership of the Churches of Christ and Disciples of Christ (Christian Church). Again, they did best in Bowie and Lamar, the counties with the two largest urban centers in the region. By 1926 the Churches of Christ and the Disciples of Christ both roughly matched the Presbyterians, with each claiming about 5 percent of the region's church members. Baptists, despite their slight decline, still attracted almost 50 percent of all church members, while Methodists made up just over 30 percent.[24]

Both of the fastest growing denominations, the Disciples and the Churches of Christ, shared many common features. In fact, before 1906 they were loosely affiliated, but disputes about the level of organization beyond the local churches and about biblical literalism split the two. Both feared the centralized control found in Methodist and Presbyterian organizations, but the Disciples took the half step of cooperating in the Texas Missionary Society. The Churches of Christ remained extremely zealous in protecting local autonomy, and each church carried on its own evangelical and missionary work. The Churches of Christ also stressed the literal truth of the Bible to a far greater degree than the Disciples. The latter made serious efforts to grapple with evolution and other scientific discoveries, while the Churches of Christ roundly condemned anything not explicitly stated in the Bible. For that reason, they banned the use of instrumental music in their services and in other ways tried to restore the church to the purity of the first century after the death of Jesus. While Disciples often worked with other denominations, especially the Presbyterians, the Churches of Christ avoided contact with those not dedicated to the restoration of Christianity to its original form. Instead, their members concentrated on attracting converts to their local churches.[25]

Subtle social differences existed between the Disciples and the Churches of Christ. The Disciples, as their greater willingness to cooperate with other denominations demonstrated, integrated more easily into the middle-class life of the towns and villages where they built their churches. The Churches of Christ remained more rural, did not depend upon an educated ministry, and drew from those who wanted to follow

TABLE 8.1
Church Membership in Northeast Texas, 1906–1936

opulation:	1900	1910	1920	1930
	220,322	239,341	271,472	256,152

otal church membership and membership as % of population:

	1906	%	1916	%	1926	%	1936	%
	74,689	33.9	100,300	41.9	101,678	37.5	80,295	31.4

enominational members and members as % of total membership:

	1906	%	1916	%	1926	%	1936	%
aptists	38,216	51.8	50,940	50.8	50,495	49.7	42,549	53.0
lethodists	24,553	32.9	32,272	32.9	32,480	32.0	23,291	29.0
resbyterians	4,165	5.6	3,672	3.7	4,481	4.4	3,191	4.0
hurch of Christ	2,168	2.9	4,577	4.6	5,335	5.3	3,545	4.4
isciples	2,096	2.8	3,398	3.4	4,108	4.0	2,268	2.8
atholic	1,396	1.9	1,511	1.5	1,463	1.4	1,176	1.5
piscopal	516	0.7	485	0.5	605	0.6	692	0.9
ther Protestant	1,539	2.1	3,445	3.4	2,711	2.7	3,583	4.5

Source: U.S., *Census: Religious Bodies, 1906,* pt. 1, 358–363; U.S., *Census: Religious Bodies, 1916,* pt. 1, !2–317; U.S., *Census: Religious Bodies, 1926,* vol. 1, 678–691; U.S., *Census: Religious Bodies, 1936,* vol. 1, !4–836.

their own moral code instead of being bound by prohibition laws or other measures that regulated society. While generally regarded as conservative, members of the Churches of Christ as well as some Pentecostal groups were among the most ardent backers of socialism in pre-World War I Texas and Oklahoma. They belonged to the old-time insurgents who resented external efforts that forced conformity to the middle-class rules of town-dwelling Baptists, Methodists, and Presbyterians.[26]

For roughly 10 percent of church members, the Disciples and the Churches of Christ offered relief from a rapidly changing and increasingly complex world. Especially in the case of the Churches of Christ, which grew slightly faster than the Disciples, the emphasis on restoring the original purity of the church and on complete autonomy gave members the same comforts as the culture of localism. As worldly events swirled around them, they found blessed assurance in their holy purpose and unique culture. God set them apart from the world.

Baptists meanwhile adapted to the threat of the 1920s by adopting new technology such as the radio and new methods of advertising their faith. The denomination popularized the chalk talk, which borrowed some of the immediacy of motion pictures and allowed the audience to participate in a dramatic act of artistic creation. In the mid-1920s, William Owens learned about chalk talks at a Baptist convocation in Waco. Before long he began touring the rural Baptist churches near Paris, delivering chalk talks with a minister and gospel singer. As the minister talked, or perhaps with a favorite hymn in the background, he sketched a religious scene before a rapt audience. Working with chalk on paper, Owens tried to capture the spirit of the song and the message of the sermon. Christ on the road to Calvary was a particular favorite, and Owens reported that the audience liked "the feeling that they were sharing in the creation of the picture." Baptists willingly adapted modern media to their services but would not embrace modern notions of greater freedom and equality for women or an ecumenical approach to Christianity. Pulpit messages typically exhorted the congregation to avoid the sins of the flesh all around and follow the doctrine of total immersion baptism. Baptists, like the Disciples and the Churches of Christ, zealously guarded the power and authority of individual congregations. In their own way, they too were set apart. Between 1926 and 1936, as the total population declined, all the major denominations lost members in Northeast Texas. While the Baptists lost their share, they did not lose the same percentage as the Presbyterians and the Methodists, who both went further down the road of accepting modern science and ecumenicalism. By 1936 Baptists dominated the religious scene more completely than ever.[27]

Localism in religion, stories, memories, and monuments—the celebration of the particular and the different in a world of change—mostly offered succor, though sometimes gave pause. Soon after Owens began giving chalk talks, a wealthy citizen of Paris donated a replica of a Greek statue depicting two naked male wrestlers to Paris Junior College. Local preachers protested that the statue might corrupt the young, but eventually everyone accepted the display of nudity. The statue became a part of life in Paris and a demonstration of how the rich truly could change the world around them. Even more than the rich, government could change society. Some sought and some feared this intervention in their lives.

GOVERNMENT ACTION AND MODERN CULTURE

Both the culture of localism and denominational membership connected the past, present, and future. Selecting John Chisum from among past heroes demonstrated the need to develop a local personality worthy of emulation and the gradual replacement of southern fables with western myths. Once selected, Chisum influenced how future citizens of Paris thought about themselves. Attitudes toward government action also drew on the past, were influenced by the present, and changed the future. In 1912 Horace Vaughan, the newly elected congressman, praised a new series of books called *The South in the Building of the Nation*. Vaughan, claiming that he read each volume as it came out, described the series as follows: "It is a work that should be in every southern library and home throughout the country. While there is no narrow sectionalism shown, full justice is done to the Southland; from every point of view." As Morris Sheppard had demonstrated before him, lauding the South brought political benefits, no matter how progressive your record. Besides, it came naturally. Oratorical custom demanded glorification of the South. Identification with a southern past, however, usually limited the role of government because excessive power at the national level threatened white supremacy and threatened to make a distinctive South part of an homogenized whole. Thus, Vaughan balked at extending the reach of the federal government to achieve prohibition, just as other southerners balked at extending the reach of the federal government to achieve woman suffrage. It cost Vaughan his office.[28]

Eugene Black, who defeated Vaughan, did not celebrate the South with as many flourishes as Vaughan and eschewed the florid romanticism that often accompanied talks on the South. His supporters, however, always pointed to his courtly southern manners and in other ways tried to stress his southerness, but during Black's stint in office the importance of a romanticized southern image lessened. Black served as a transitional figure, representing not the Old South or the Confederate South, but the New South of lawyer, merchant, and banker. In that role he deserved deference because of his place in society. Like others among the southern elite, he opposed federally mandated woman suffrage and voted against submitting the Nineteenth Amendment to the states in 1919.[29]

Between 1914 and 1928 political reality and local custom changed dramatically. Women voted. A new set of heroes, World War I veterans, replaced the Confederate heroes. The Civil War grew more distant as the ranks of ancient veterans thinned. World War I, on the other hand, helped form a new generation—Wright Patman's generation. Beginning in 1928, Patman pushed the Bonus Bill for veterans harder than anyone else in Washington. This bill, which passed in 1936, paid veterans a cash bonus at an earlier date and with fewer strings attached than Congress had promised in a 1924 bill. Patman's actions, like the Littlefield Fountain, constructed while he served in the state legislature, spoke more about the current generation than the past. From time to time Patman sounded the obligatory notes about states' rights and southern patriotism. To the end of his life he boasted of his southern origins. Yet, like Neville, his main concern was life in the raw. He even contributed a history of the regional post offices to the drive to remember everyday life.[30]

More than economic instability and strong campaigning brought Patman victory in 1928. Patman fit his time and his place far better than Black. He had an image that appealed to voters. Running a campaign based on the theme "give a young man a chance," he represented a generational shift. The genteel, courtly, traditional, and southern gave way to the energetic, aggressive, modern Texan or American.[31]

Patman's success in 1928 marked one of many signs that the First District had become a more Texas sort of place. While similar changes occurred in much of the South, one thing differed. Texans left behind a good bit of the "defensiveness," the feelings of inferiority, that still trailed behind the Confederate legend. Northeast Texans became less conservative, less tradition bound, and certainly less deferential because of the region's Texas image. While Texas history often bound its audience to a narrow-minded, intolerant view of those who did not fit the pioneer image, it also freed the reader and believer in the myth to strive and acquire, to take action and accept risk. Independent oilmen and ranchers became the archetype Texans. This translated into a more open and entrepreneurial society that accepted change and innovation more quickly. A local editor caught the spirit of this change when he insisted that instead of being conservative, Northeast Texans like other Americans were "nearly the most radical people on earth" because they were "the readiest to follow new paths." Backward glances did not necessarily make everyone forward looking. Most faced change with a trace of reluctance and a hint of deference to tradition. A new history, however, made an active government all the more appealing.[32]

Typically, calls for government action focused on a few key pieces of legislation. In 1922 much of the criticism of Black centered on the Esch-Cummings bill and his support for a hands-off approach to major railroad companies. In fact, Black grew increasingly inactive, and when he lost in

1928, even his friends admitted he received more recognition for the bills he opposed than for those he supported.[33]

In 1928 regional newspapers quoted Patman as saying that since World War I, "Mr. Black has turned the back of his hand to the cause of the plain people including the farmers, laborers, and soldiers who are my friends and has favored big wealth and Wall Street bankers." As in 1922, his opponent linked Black with "profit puffed plutocrats."[34]

While railroad issues resurfaced in 1928, the key questions concerned federal support for agricultural commodity prices. The McNary-Haugen bill, vetoed twice by President Calvin Coolidge, drew the most attention. The bill set up a two-price system in which cotton, wheat, and other commodities not needed domestically would be sold on the international market at a lower price. Tariffs would protect producers from imported commodities. An equalization fee paid by producers insured the government against loss. This bill did not receive universal support from cotton growers, especially larger cotton growers, because the high volume of cotton already exported raised fears about the cost of equalization fees. By 1927, however, more southerners accepted the scheme. After years of opposing the bill, Eugene Black made a rare speech on its behalf that year.[35]

Given the trying market conditions of the previous two years, Black could not afford to remain silent. In the fiscal year beginning August 1, 1926, cotton spot prices hit their lowest point since 1920 (see Figure 5.3). The carryover from the huge 1925 crop initially dragged down the market, and once it became clear that the 1926 crop was also large, the price fell dramatically. Prices improved in the summer of 1927 but fell back again in the summer of 1928. Luckily, the 1927 crop surpassed the previous year's, and farmers sold more cotton at a slightly higher price. Still, by July 1928 the uncertain cotton market worried those dependent upon cotton. Directly or indirectly, that meant a large majority of the citizens of the First District. They remained an "agricultural people," but that now required an active government and aggressive representation.[36]

By 1928 preserving the viability of local communities also demanded an active federal government. Only the federal government could control the federal agencies and the major corporations that now played such a large role in the South. Perhaps the best example of this was the intense interest in Northeast Texas in the questioning of Will Clayton by a Senate subcommittee in March 1928. Northeast Texans, already angered by what they perceived as the negative impact of USDA crop forecasts on cotton prices, appeared ready to blame Anderson, Clayton as well as the government for the price declines of 1926. Animosity against Clayton's company eased after Clayton skillfully explained that he held 200,000 bales in New York in 1926 and 1927 not to rig prices but to lessen the expense of futures transactions, and thereby raise the price dealers could offer growers. Clayton told those who purchased cotton futures on the New York market they could either accept delivery of cotton for which they had no storage facilities and no ready market or stop charging a transportation charge on cotton that never came through New York. Southerners appreciated Clayton's anti-Wall Street biases, but they also appreciated the Senate's effort to do something about a serious problem that affected every town in the South.[37]

Taking action, even if it did little, brought admiration. A do-nothing government favored the status quo—it favored Wall Street not the main street of Paris. Thus, in 1928 the charge that Eugene Black did nothing and thereby aided the rich resonated with a broader audience than in 1922. Middle-class merchants as well as railroad workers and tenant farmers responded.[38]

At a time when the culture of localism celebrated John Chisum and E. L. Dohoney as resolute men of action who changed the world around them, having a reputation for opposing legislation instead of proposing legislation cost Black votes. Doing nothing while the economy seemed to demand doing something cost more votes. As one local commentator put it, "American prizes go to the doers." Voters sought a more activist congressman, and they found one in Wright Patman. As an added bonus, he fit the eccentric, flamboyant, and even outrageous mold of a western hero.[39]

WRIGHT PATMAN

Three basic reasons explained Wright Patman's victory in 1928. The growing coalition between factions opposed to social or economic conservatives let Patman preach to the choir when he charged Black with being the tool of Wall Street. When preaching, he displayed a mastery of modern campaign techniques, and he repeatedly found effective ways to get his message across. As a good Baptist, Patman used the devices of the modern world without becoming completely of that world, and his image, personality, and ideology better fit a people concerned both with restoration and prosperity.

Patman's image, personality, and ideology sprang from his own history. He was born in rural Cass County on August 6, 1893. His father farmed, traded livestock, and repaired cotton gins. A stubborn man of deeply felt religious convictions, John Patman split with his local Primitive Baptist Church when it began using a piano in its services, a move he opposed because scripture never mentioned the use of instruments in the early church. This marked him as part of the strong Northeast Texas trend to restore religion to its first-century purity. Wright's mother, Emma Patman, worked on the farm and helped instill strict religious principles in her children. After church each Sunday, she questioned her children about the content of the sermon, and through the week she set an example of daily Bible reading. Both parents displayed remarkable ingenuity in rising above the level of poor farmers. Patman's father, for example, toured the countryside with an early-day motion picture projector—taking the movies to the customers in a wagon. His son had the same determination to get ahead.[40]

Patman attended elementary school near Patman's Switch and later rode a horse to Hughes Springs, where he graduated as valedictorian of his high school in 1912. Since he did not live in the district served by the Hughes Spring school, he paid his own way by working as a janitor. After high school Patman worked as a cropper and at other occupations, carefully saving money for college. In 1915, with a hard-earned $100, he entered Cumberland University in Lebanon, Tennessee. He received a degree in law in 1916 and passed the Texas bar exam that year. Once the United States entered World War I, he volunteered for service, but health problems slowed his advancement in the army. His congressman, Eugene Black, helped arrange a transfer to the Coast Guard, and he served the remainder of the war in the United States as a member of that service.[41]

Returning home in 1919, Patman married Merele Connor and established a prosperous law practice in Linden. Elected to the Texas House of Representatives in 1920, Patman strongly opposed the Ku Klux Klan. After making threatening calls and throwing bricks through his windows, the Klan fielded a candidate that opposed his re-election in 1922. Patman won easily and returned the favor Eugene Black had done him during the war by aiding his cause in Cass and Bowie counties. He, more than any other, turned the election in those counties into a referendum on the Klan—insisting that the Klan's secrecy, violence, and willingness to operate outside the law made it both un-American and undemocratic. During his second term, he devoted much of his attention to education reform and aid to rural schools. He also pressed to shift the funding of schools and other programs from property taxes to occupational taxes and introduced a large number of bills in the regular session and the three called sessions.[42]

In early 1924 Governor Pat Neff appointed Patman to fill an unexpired term as district attorney for Cass and Bowie counties. Patman won the election for the post later that year and was re-elected in 1926. He quickly established a reputation as a flamboyant crime fighter, but one who fit within the traditional parameters of shooting black prisoners first and asking questions later. In March 1924 Patman and the deputy sheriff were transporting a black prisoner accused of murder from jail in Texarkana to trial in New Boston. On the way the prisoner attempted to escape, forcing the car's driver to crash into an embankment. The deputy shot and killed the prisoner, leading to a legal investigation of both Patman and the deputy. Patman also led a campaign against drunk driving and aggressively pursued convictions for several murder cases. He was best known, however, for closing down the saloons and whorehouse in Texarkana's red-light district. To the delight of the local Ministerial Alliance, landlords in the red-light district soon faced the choice of having their buildings padlocked and losing a year's rent or finding tenants other than those engaged in prostitution and bootlegging. Patman also aggressively enforced all prohibition laws, to the point of locking up the guests at a local Chamber of Commerce function where liquor was served. Such vigorous attacks on the liquor trade in a town that, because of its good railroad connections, served as an important distribution point for bootleggers led to repeated threats on his life—out of which he secured maximum publicity. Fears that he might be assassinated by a mob hit man led Governor Dan Moody to send two Texas Rangers to guard Patman. During the 1928 campaign, Patman repeatedly used his image as a vigorous crime fighter willing to risk death for prohibition, public morality, and the enforcement of all laws.[43]

Patman's vigor extended to his study of what it took to be a member of Congress. He began reading the *Congressional Record* at age fifteen. By 1928 he believed he knew more about Congress than the incumbent Eugene Black and was ready to take his place. Patman knew his district well and honed his message to fit the times. Taking advantage of his mastery of the *Congressional Record*, he attacked Black's voting history at every opportunity.[44]

While Patman later called himself the last of the Populists, he did not run as a Populist in 1928. True, former Populist Cyclone Davis spoke for him. He also made much of his intention to help the little man. He unseated Black, however, by charging that the incumbent was the tool of Wall Street, an ideological note that played as well in town as in the country. His list of supporters included lawyers, bankers, merchants, and prosperous, large-scale landowning farmers, all groups usually outside the ranks of the Populists. It was the same theme sounded by Jesse

Jones, the Houston millionaire and close friend of Woodrow Wilson who won the admiration of Northeast Texans for bringing the 1928 National Democratic Convention to Texas.[45]

As the similarity between Patman and Jones suggested, the future congressman more nearly matched a World War I era progressive than a Populist. Certainly his call for increased government activism better suited a rapidly changing district than Black's slow and cautious approach to legislation. Black represented the country merchants, largest landowners, and cotton brokers of his district. In his lengthy appraisal of the First District published in April 1928, Dabney White declared that Black "has many staunch supporters among the conservative interests of his district." In contrast, the "brilliant and aggressive" Patman spoke for the emerging economy of large-scale mechanized cotton farmers, producers of other specialized commodities, industrial workers, and the merchants and professionals dependent upon their trade. They needed good farm-to-market roads, government-backed loans, stable prices, and limited, predictable business regulation. Patman, the activist, promised all four. When Black spoke for economy in government and morality, he spoke for bygone times.[46]

In other ways, however, Patman evoked bygone times. Calling on a traditional vote-getter, he said that Black went against the principle of states' rights when he voted for the Esch-Cummings Bill, which limited the power of Texas to regulate railroads. He also repeatedly declared that "the same differences that separated Alexander Hamilton and Thomas Jefferson separated Representative Eugene Black" from him. Patman also used Cyclone Davis to strike the chords of the 1890s. He was against "monopolies, trusts, branch banking, and excessive and discriminatory freight rates." He battled for the "plain people" against those like Black who extended "government favoritism" to the rich.[47]

In striking a blow for the plain people, Patman evoked the symbols and rhetoric of restoration theology, a part of his childhood and that of most of his voters. For Patman the 1920s meant the creation of millionaires, even billionaires, while the average person struggled to keep up. The gap between the very wealthy and the rest of the nation had widened too much for the health of the country. He insisted that "no one objects to the accumulation of wealth by honest methods and by one's own effort." Following his own advice, over the following decades he grew wealthy through shrewd real estate investments. Yet in 1928 he argued that Congress violated the intent of the American system of government by favoring the rich and the Northeast over the plain people and the South. Black "allowed the concentration of wealth and the building up of great monopolies and trusts without taking decided action." Black "favored big wealth, Wall Street bankers and foreigners in preference to the true, liberty loving, hard pressed Americans of his own district." In contrast, Patman sought to restore the doctrine of "equal rights to all and special privileges to none."[48]

While some of these themes recalled Populist campaigns of the 1890s or Cyclone Davis's 1922 campaign, crucial differences separated Patman's 1928 run for Congress from these earlier campaigns. For Patman, the foe of the plain people did not live next door. It was not a case of town versus country. Instead, Wall Street was the enemy, and this meant he avoided the charge of inciting class antagonisms that had always dogged Cyclone Davis. Further, Patman labeled Black as a weak prohibitionist, a slacker when it came to pushing for stronger enforcement laws. By linking prohibition and woman suffrage and insisting that Black opposed giving the vote to women, he paid his respects to the female voters and promised to listen to their requests on an equal basis with men. Indeed, in rounding up campaign workers, he went out of his way to enlist the help of women. Attacks on Black's record on prohibition and woman suffrage opened the way for the most avid supporters of prohibition and public morality, who usually opposed the Populists, to vote for Patman. Finally, by pressing for an enhanced bonus for World War I veterans, Patman again underscored that his campaign targeted liberty lovers and freedom fighters. None could charge the man who stood up for the common soldier with Bolshevism. No matter how strident his attacks on wealth and privilege might sound, his stubborn insistence on paying a larger bonus at an earlier time than promised by the government sheltered him from accusations of radicalism.[49]

Despite differences with Davis, Patman sought Cyclone's help in 1928. Davis spoke for Patman throughout the district and helped organize his campaign in Hopkins, Delta, and Franklin counties. He advised Patman on what issues to stress and what rhetoric to use. Given Patman's repeated attacks on the Klan and Davis's close association with it in 1922, this must have struck some voters as odd. Patman's introduction into the state legislature of laws aimed at achieving the social morality the Klan deemed proper, however, suggested Patman agreed with the Klan's effort to restore old-time morality but opposed their methods and their role in politics. For him restoration worked on two levels. Encouraging morality was fine, but not at the cost of violating the rule of law and the tradition of equal opportunity in politics. Thus for him, restoration could easily include giving women the right to vote because it extended the tradition of equal opportunity in politics. (Besides, Patman clearly understood the lesson of the past few years. The votes of women could make or break a candidate.)[50]

Seeking restoration also meant that the Klan, just like Wall Street or a Republican party manipulated by trusts and monopolies, threatened the ability of the plain people to elect virtuous candidates who would pass beneficial legislation. Restoring a society that respected the rule of law meant enforcing not only laws governing prohibition, but also laws against assault and murder. While the leaders of the Klan probably still held a grudge against Patman, the rank-and-file members, many of whom had left the organization by 1928, probably did not. That added to the value of having Davis campaign for Patman.[51]

While Davis built support among his traditional followers, Patman toured the district talking of helping World War I veterans. He explained in great detail his plan to fix the McNary-Haugen Bill. His campaign systematically used Black's record to defeat him. With many votes over a long career and few bills to his credit, Black seemed stale. In contrast Patman appeared youthful, vigorous, and colorful. He was a local boy made good, a role model for others who sought to rise in the world. In that sense Patman, unlike Black or for that matter unlike Cyclone Davis, represented his time. Yet the essential Patman message was one of restoration. Return to the Jeffersonian ideal of getting ahead by hard work instead of getting ahead by governmental favoritism.

Like the Baptist's use of chalk talks, Patman mixed restoration theology and the culture of localism with modern methods. Patman was an adept, well-organized campaigner but also a showman. A forceful and energetic speaker, Patman toured the district in a new Model A Ford. Some believed the car attracted a bigger crowd than the candidate.[52]

Besides driving a flashy new car, Patman used another notable device in 1928. He began the career-long habit of sending out a calendar of significant dates and a summary of important information on the election process to voters and candidates for local office. A flattering biography and a photograph of Patman included with the political information made this an extremely effective form of advertising. Voters, especially candidates for local office and Democratic party activists, saved the information, and every time they looked up an election law or the last date for filing for office they saw Patman. If it did nothing else, it reminded them of his cleverness and imagination. Learning from the increasingly sophisticated advertising common to the 1920s, he planted the seed that Patman rather than his opponent could better stabilize crop prices, smooth out the uneven prosperity of the 1920s, and meet the other challenges of a modern age.[53]

Patman also anticipated modern efforts to identify likely voters. Believing that supporters of Governor Dan Moody in 1926 would vote for him, he began assembling precinct-level returns in 1927. Moody, a young and energetic candidate with a record of vigorous opposition to the Ku Klux Klan and official corruption, rose to the top of Texas politics faster than any individual in the state's history. Only one year older than Patman, Moody carried every county in Northeast Texas, but using precinct returns let Patman target the areas of each county Moody carried. By targeting his efforts, he soon had a list of key supporters in towns and villages across the district. Incumbents usually had such lists of supporters, but first-time challengers seldom did. Patman overcame this handicap by sound campaign strategy and extensive early preparation.[54]

Patman also sought the support of the American Federation of Labor (AFL) and the Anti-Saloon League of Texas. He used those organizations to gather information on Black's voting record and to discover more likely supporters. Atticus Webb of the Anti-Saloon League, for example, confirmed that Black voted against woman suffrage and missed the final vote on the Volstead Act, the law that enforced prohibition. Webb characterized Black as "a sincere prohibitionist," but observed that "by nature Mr. Black is not a fighter." Through the AFL, Patman gained support from the Twin City Central Labor Union in Texarkana.[55]

Some post-election commentators considered labor's support the key to Patman's 3,000 vote victory in the July primary. Both Bowie and Titus contained strong railroad unions that evidently turned out to vote for Patman. In both counties the total vote in the House race exceeded the tightly contested 1928 Senate race and the 1922 House contest by about a thousand votes. Since none of the major Senate candidates actively sought union votes, those voters likely skipped the Senate race but voted for Patman. The difference between 1928 and 1922 reflected both the continued concentration of rail workers in the Texarkana area and Davis's link with the Klan, whose campaigns against vice and morality often seemed aimed at labor. Union votes alone, however, could not come close to carrying the district. Instead, Patman managed to unite all the labor vote with farmers of all types and small-town merchants in a centrist coalition.[56]

While the system had changed a good bit since the 1890s, Patman benefited from the continued multifactional nature of the Democratic party. Aided by two former candidates for the district's seat in Congress, Cyclone Davis and B. B. Sturgeon, he drew votes from the reform and insurgent-labor factions. Earlier Black, stressing propriety and respectability, built a coalition of economic conservatives, elite reformers, and the more-prosperous, upwardly mobile farmers. His very narrow victories in 1914 and 1922 demonstrated Black's ability to draw from all three factions. Yet 1922 also pinpointed an obvious weakness. Black's growing conservatism in using the full force of government in the economy and his willingness to harness government to force right behavior made keeping all the reform vote difficult. In 1928, Sturgeon, an ardent foe of Populists in the 1890s and candidate for Congress in 1912, for once agreed with Davis and backed Patman. As happened repeatedly, the winning candidate benefited from a variant of Jim Hogg's strategy in 1892—seize the middle ground and push opponents to the fringes. Because of his obsessive enforcement of prohibition laws and efforts to restore traditional morality, Patman appealed to some moderate former supporters of the Klan and to middle-of-the-road social reformers in general. His law-and-order record and World War I patriotism insulated him from charges of radicalism, even as he reached out to organized labor. Meanwhile all those interested in economic reform supported Patman —including middle-class, small-town businessmen and businesswomen, farmers, labor, and whatever remained of partisan Populists and Farm-Labor groups.[57]

Essentially, Black drifted too far from his original political base. While his vote against woman suffrage in 1919 did not seem to hurt him in 1922, it demonstrated the limits of his willingness to harness the power of the federal government in the interest of reform. As the perceived threat of socialism and the labor unrest of 1919 to 1922 turned those like Black into reactionaries, they adopted an increasingly negative attitude toward government's economic initiatives. This divided them from reformers primarily interested in building a more prosperous and more equitable economy and from those who defended the modern role of women in uplifting society. Since the cotton price shocks of 1926 still reverberated through the local economy, Sturgeon and those like him had little use for a congressman unwilling to harness the full power of the government.[58]

In practical political terms, Patman's campaign strategy, rhetoric, style, image, and cultural resonance maximized the vote of the most likely groups or factions to vote for him and minimized the vote of the most likely groups or factions likely to vote for Black. Patman carried the countryside, kept Klan voters at home in Sulphur Springs and Paris, did even better than Davis at attracting votes from counties with a strong insurgent tradition, and demolished Black in the small towns and villages of the region. With the help of Sturgeon and other traditional leaders, he even picked up a few votes in the larger cities. He won easily among the economic reform and insurgent groups, split the social reformers, and possibly picked off a few stray conservative votes with his strong law-and-order record.[59]

In building this coalition, Patman benefited from the anti-Klan and antilynching movements and from the economic and demographic changes in the district. The movement of landowners out of the country-side and the decline of small towns and villages, discussed in previous chapters, created a sense of desperation among those most interested in building up places like Naples in Morris County. These communities were part of an agricultural economy and depended heavily on the trade generated by the movement of the cotton crop. The leaders of these communities joined farmers in expressing concern about the concentration of the cotton trade in fewer hands and agreed that without something like McNary-Haugen or some other type of federal-level price stabilization program, conditions would grow worse. Landowners and residents of small towns and villages would continue leaving. Croppers might replace them, but croppers could not buy as much as landowners or town dwellers. Likewise in places where sweet potatoes or dairy farming already offered an alternative to cotton, the need for stable prices, good roads, and access to markets all argued for an active government. The business communities of smaller towns and villages became economic reformers, and that weakened the conservative faction. It was a faction already weakened by its abandonment of the traditional argument against prohibition and other measures that restricted individual freedom. After the Klan demonstrated what could happen when one group took it upon itself to limit behavior, reformers looked twice at this new conservatism, and insurgents saw no reason for any alliance with someone like Eugene Black.[60]

In fact, only in the larger, more-prosperous towns where the Klan had been strongest could Black hope to put together the coalition of conservatives and reformers responsible for past victories. Black carried the largest towns, Texarkana, Paris, and Sulphur Springs, but he lost the next tier of towns, Mount Pleasant, Cooper, and Pittsburg. Mayfield, the Klan candidate for re-election to the Senate, led in the same boxes as Black, indicating that lingering support for the Klan as well as the vote of conservatives hurt Patman.[61] In Mount Pleasant, however, Patman won all four boxes, suggesting that he drew votes from railroad workers and the business community. Even in Paris and Sulphur Springs, Black's total fell below normal levels. Mayfield's vote also fell greatly from that of six years earlier, and he badly trailed the combined total of the second- and third-place candidates for the Senate. Disillusionment with the Klan, Patman's mix of attacking the Klan but supporting its objectives, and the intense criticism of Mayfield by all five of the other candidates for the Senate influenced those on the fringe of the Klan to vote for Patman or not to vote.[62]

At the same time, the old insurgent faction, for which Davis so long spoke, delivered for Patman. In that sense, at least, he could legitimately claim to be an old-time Populist. Patman received over 60 percent of the vote in counties carried by Davis in the 1922 congressional election. Because of the small-town vote, Patman won by bigger margins than Davis countywide, but he won by about the same percentage in rural precincts.[63]

In the end, Patman won seven of eleven counties, captured 54 percent of the total vote, and enjoyed a comfortable 3,000 vote margin of victory.[64] Perhaps no county better explained this result than Hopkins. Because of the ban on black voting in the Democratic primary, Hopkins generally polled the second-highest total vote in that key election. It had the second-largest white population in the district, ranking behind Lamar and ahead of Bowie, and its largest town, Sulphur Springs, had a population of 5,417 in 1930, meaning it ranked third in size among the district's cities. At the time of the election, the county had just begun a major economic transformation from cotton farming to dairying, and improved transportation and a stable market allowed a 45 percent increase in the county's milk production from 1925 to 1930.[65]

Hopkins, the home of Cyclone Davis, also had a long tradition of political rivalry between Sulphur Springs and the rest of the county. In the race for governor in 1894, the Populists carried the county but lost the town, with the Democrats getting 59 percent of the vote in Sulphur Springs. In 1914 Vaughan won the county but lost the town, with Black getting 54 percent of the vote in Sulphur Springs. In 1928 Patman won the county but lost the town, with Black getting 56 percent of the vote in Sulphur Springs. No other town in the county had a population of more than 500, but in 1930 the county population was still almost six times the population of Sulphur Springs.[66]

What changed in 1928 was that Patman, unlike Davis or the Populists, carried the majority of the district's towns between 500 and 5,000 and almost all the villages of 500 or less. Hopkins suggested a reason for this change. Dairying created a different political economy than cotton. It required less land but more capital investment per acre. Milk processing created new industries in nearby towns and villages that added more money to the local economy than cotton processing. Above all, the dairy industry required improved transportation. Milk spoiled if not transported, processed, and stored quickly, and government provided transportation. In towns, villages, and the countryside where milk production mattered, Patman did well. Economic incentives still meant votes for the more-moderate candidate.[67]

Patman lost in Cumby in Hopkins County and in a few other towns and villages between 500 and 5,000 in population. Still, if the hometown effect in Clarksville is disregarded, the trend seems clear: Patman unlike Davis, Vaughan, and the Populists, did well in most small towns and villages, and those votes brought victory. As Hopkins County indicated, much of that success derived from a changing economy that swelled the ranks of economic reformers and encouraged their alliance with insurgents. In Cooper, a center of the move against the Klan, Patman's unequivocal stand against that organization also clearly helped. Davis lost Cooper in 1922, but Patman won by a large margin in 1928. Yet more than a changing economy and a reaction against the excessive coercion and the political maneuvering of the Klan created the new coalition between reformers, insurgents, and labor.[68]

In 1920, Wright Patman won the first time he ran for public office. In 1974 he won the last time he ran for public office. During those fifty-four years he ran for office every two years and never lost; he never even faced a runoff. No one better practiced the art of politics on the local level. While never venturing out of his native Northeast Texas, in that familiar arena he was unmatched in giving the voters what they wanted. He also gave opponents a very difficult target to hit even when he leaned further left on some issues than many in his district. Yet, instead of chalking up his many victories, including his defeat of Black in 1928, to his one-of-a-kind political skill, we should recognize that Patman won because he reflected the culture and articulated the ideology of the majority in the First District. It was more than the economy, for the economy was worse in 1922 when Black won than in 1928 when he lost. Instead, Patman's image and words gave him victory in Hopkins and Delta counties and brought him closer to winning than any of Black's previous opponents in Lamar and Red River counties. Thus, Patman gives us an unusual opportunity to gauge just what the citizens of Northeast Texas wanted and identified with in 1928, and in what ways they had changed over the previous decades.

During the 1928 campaign, one of Patman's stock speeches included this passage: "When the Civil War was over the Northern soldiers were put on the pension list of the Government and the Southern soldiers were upon crutches. Over $5,000,000,000.00 have been spent for the soldier of the North. After the world's war we had an opportunity to redistribute wealth by paying all ex-service men reasonable compensation for their services. Such a law would have brought much wealth to the South and enabled our soldiers to get a new start in life and would have been doing for them no more than they were entitled to." As Patman quickly pointed out, Black repeatedly voted against such a bill.[69]

This was no Lost Cause speech, celebrating the war and glorifying southern generals. It highlighted the difficulty of the common soldier, the continued poverty of the South, and the unfair treatment of World War I veterans. It spoke of the government redistributing wealth to bring the South up to the level of the rest of the country. Instead of building a wall around the South and rejecting government action that might alter southern culture and race relations, Patman spoke for an active government. In another message to the voters he argued, "The prosperity and happiness of the people is almost wholly dependent upon what is done in Congress." Patman did not hide his positions in 1928, nor did he change much over the ensuing years. While he insisted that the economic benefits of an active government go to white and black in rough parity, Patman never assumed a leadership role in civil rights and in general opposed each halting step toward political equality for blacks. In most other respects, including support for the minimum wage, Patman was and remained a classic New Deal liberal.[70]

Patman's success in 1928 revealed the boundaries of a modern South in Northeast Texas, for he, like Owens, Humphrey, Neville, and most others of the region, still thought of himself as southern. Outside of politics, blacks made modest advances toward equitable treatment. Lynching lost favor with whites as merchants realized that minimal legal safeguards kept black consumers in the district. Instead of celebrating the glories of the Confederacy, the everyday people, especially if they were eccentric, rose to the level of hero. When Patman told farmers and laborers that his "every pulse beat and heart throb will be sympathetic to their interest," he spoke in words colorful enough to attract attention, but words that also articulated a pervasive cultural bias. The farmers and laborers built the region. They, not the Ku Klux Klan, not conservatives, and not Wall Street bankers, deserved a voice in government. Besides, in the emerging new economy such a voice would prove crucial.[71]

Patman added to this his own blend of politics and restoration theology. Mixing quotes from the Bible and allusions to Thomas Jefferson in a style reminiscent of Cyclone Davis, Patman declared: "Our country is getting into the hands of and under the control of a small group of people and will soon become a country of absentee landlords, and the plain people, who furnish the manpower to die for our country in the event of war will become mere vassals." For a people who remembered slavery and understood the implications of white supremacy, the idea of being a vassal carried a potent political message. Modernity meant remembering a particular history—"the doctrine of Equal Rights for all and Special Privilege to none should be impressed upon our minds again and our representatives should re-dedicate themselves to this great principle." Patman's message rang out—rededicate, rebaptize, come back to the faith of the fathers.[72]

Even Patman's use of states' rights took a particular twist. In voting for Esch-Cummings, Black allowed the national government to take away the power of Texas to protect its citizens from large corporations. According to Patman, historically the Railroad Commission protected the common man—a far different use of history and states' rights than commonly found.[73]

Patman realized that the government in Washington could do harm as well as good. He insisted that the quality of the people elected to office and their ability to craft beneficial legislation mattered. Yet, unlike most conservatives, he remained basically confident in the ability of the people to elect talented individuals and in the ability of government to make a difference. The dyspeptic Clarence Wharton, the darling of the conservatives who controlled the textbook-selection process in Texas, closed his 1935 high school text *History of Texas* with these words: "We have come far since the days of the Spanish gold hunters but we yet have far to go before we demonstrate that human integrity is sufficient for self-government." Patman never would have agreed. By then the man whose frequent trips home to his district inspired the same adulation as "the second coming of Christ" was proving that if government could not do everything and do it well, it was not for his lack of effort.[74]

Patman became, like John Chisum, a legend worthy of emulation. Such legends tell us what a society wanted to be, and in this case tell us why Texas distanced itself from the rest of the South. Patman, like so many others from his state, eagerly used the government to redistribute wealth to Texas.[75]

STARS AND BARS AND THE LONE STAR

Memory, Texas, and the South

This book focuses on a specific time, 1887 to 1930, and a specific place, Northeast Texas. The goal of this study, however, has never been simply to recount the story of a region and a time, no matter how interesting or valuable that might be. Instead, this work suggests new ways of understanding, or at least beginning to understand, the relationship between being southern and modern and the relationship between the most southern parts of Texas and the least southern. Ultimately it connects the present with the past.

By 1930 Northeast Texans were reaching for a new identity, an identity that continues to develop to the present day. They increasingly used the lessons, symbols, and myths of triumph at San Jacinto, not defeat at Gettysburg. Different memories and different histories supplemented a distinctive political system and a more fluid economy and society in bonding all Texans together and separating them from other southerners. With that came greater convergence with the rest of the United States, but greater has never meant total convergence.

Separation from the South and convergence with the rest of the United States began with the multifactional political system of the Populist era. By 1905 this system excluded black voters, but it never completely excluded poor whites. In fact, because the system remained divided into three or more persistent and competitive factions, white voters gradually returned to the polls. Debates about how government should improve public morality and increase prosperity often defined these factions, but these debates rarely proved conclusive because no coalition lasted for long and no faction obtained a majority on its own. Instead, the process demanded compromise and conciliation. In a limited way, the system remained receptive to the interests of poorer whites, and at least in 1911 it allowed blacks to play a role.

A more receptive legal and political system aided the quickening of the pre–World War I economy. The impact of oil, lumber, urban growth, and more-mechanized and more-efficient agriculture carried the entire state to new levels of prosperity. Even residents of Northeast Texas, a traditional cotton-growing region, entertained hopes of better times.

Hopes of a better time instigated and propelled an ideological revolution. By the start of World War I, increasing numbers of Northeast Texans accepted an activist government. They expected state and local governmental action to sustain economic growth and correct any temporary economic downturn. If they failed, Northeast Texans turned to the federal government. Of course, as in the rest of the South, national acceptance of the Jim Crow system assuaged fear of the federal government, and for some the drive for prohibition and woman suffrage transformed that government into a force for good. As evidenced by their striking affinity for Woodrow Wilson, these Texans increasingly accepted an active federal government.[1]

A new economy and evolving ideology indicated that Northeast Texans viewed the world differently in 1914 than they had in 1887. The change was not over. Erratic price swings in cotton followed wartime prosperity and led to repeated calls for government aid. Consolidation of landholding allowed greater agricultural efficiency but created a huge nonlandholding class of croppers and farmworkers. Small towns and villages declined as farm owners and the middle class left for brighter opportunities in other parts of Texas.

Not surprisingly, cultural change accompanied and contributed to political, economic, and social change. In particular, an increased devotion to Texas history and new conceptions about the roles of women moved Texas further from the southern orbit. In these two related examples lay the most obvious connections between the present and the past—between the traditional South and a more modern South.

In *Southern Strategies,* Elna C. Green pondered the question of why Texas, Kentucky, Tennessee, and Arkansas approved the Nineteenth Amendment, which gave women the right to vote, while the other southern states did not. After rejecting the notion that these were "border" states and therefore set apart, she argued that the four states did have slightly more open political systems. She then suggested: "Planters and industrialists were most successful in defeating woman suffrage when they could combine the racial fears of white southerners with conservative views on gender and family, and wrap it all in the evocative rhetoric of the

Lost Cause."[2] This study supports Green's argument and supplements it by adding an economic dimension to an equation that stresses politics, race, gender roles, and the rhetoric of the Lost Cause.

A more open political arena characterized by three or more factions that combined in numerous ways offered women opportunities lacking in other southern states. Among those opportunities was the chance for women to vote in the Democratic primary before they could vote in the general election. In the 1918 Democratic primary when Annie Webb Blanton ran for statewide office and won, she toured Northeast Texas with speakers for gubernatorial candidate William P. Hobby. They ran against Jim Ferguson, who opposed woman suffrage and prohibition. Ferguson drew the votes of conservatives and insurgents. Hobby and Blanton, who carried most counties in Northeast Texas, drew the votes of a unified and energized group of reformers. When the Nineteenth Amendment came before the state legislature in June 1919, the victorious reformers realized women could vote them out of, as well as into, office and quickly repaid their debt to women activists by ratifying the amendment.[3]

Yet the fact that Blanton ran for office confirmed a far earlier and more-profound change in attitudes about gender and the family. Because women could already vote in the Democratic primary, the threat of retaliation more than chivalrous courtesy moved the legislature to ratify the suffrage amendment. Prohibition led women into politics as early as 1887 and contributed greatly to the drive to give them the right to vote and hold office. In Northeast Texas women won the office of county clerk even before they voted in the primaries. Birthrates declined, and outspoken successful businesswomen like Birdie Taylor campaigned for a more active political role for women.[4]

In part, women achieved greater political success and changed their roles more quickly because the planters and industrialists never controlled Texas or Northeast Texas with the same death grip as in North Carolina, Virginia, and other southern states. Perhaps Texas was too large, too diverse, and its economic development too recent for such control. Yet even in Northeast Texas, an older, less diverse, and more distinctively southern region, planters and industrialists never exerted the same level of economic, social, and political control as elsewhere in the South. Instead, nationwide business trends such as the expansion of cash-only retailing rapidly appeared, creating successful competitors for the planter-merchants. Capitalists followed their capital into the area and challenged white supremacy, the Democratic party, and a do-nothing legislature. In contrast, Paul Escott closed his study of North Carolina from 1850 to 1900 with this comment: "Undemocratic attitudes and practices more fundamental even than racism were also deeply rooted in the state's history. They, too must be overcome if the Old North State is to become, as its official toast proclaims, a place where 'the weak grow strong and the strong grow great.'"[5]

Undemocratic attitudes and practices existed in Northeast Texas and in the state as a whole, but a more hostile environment stunted their growth. Because restrictions on white suffrage were less severe and dynamic candidates attracted less-prosperous voters, conservatives typically lost the three-way elections that characterized most contests for governor after 1892. Especially after Jim Ferguson became the dominant political figure in Texas, winning candidates went out of their way to appeal to tenants and small-scale farmers.

Race played an important part in why more whites voted and why undemocratic attitudes, such as those embodied by the Ku Klux Klan in the 1920s, eventually lost out. Many sections of Texas contained few blacks and large numbers of whites jealous of their political rights. That explained why the poll tax took longer to arrive in Texas. Yet, thanks in part to linkages with prohibition, it eventually arrived in Texas—followed quickly by the all-white Democratic primary. Still, white Texans pushed to ease restrictions in the first primary law, and within a decade a larger percentage of eligible voters participated in primary elections. Contested primary elections like those of 1924 brought out white voters in nearly the same percentages as the 1890s.

In the years leading up to 1924, however, whites in Texas lynched blacks at a stunning rate and in a gruesome style. In a profoundly southern mix of the profane and the sacred, whites justified lynching as necessary protection of their homes and their families. For similar reasons, white Protestants ended the corruption of saloons, gambling, and prostitution, and they took up the holy cause of ritual killing.[6] Economic needs played a role as well. Newly arrived blacks or blacks that whites believed needed to be taught to stay on the farm became frequent targets of violence. Yet, when the rise of the Ku Klux Klan made parallels between lynching and Klan activity obvious, criticism of lynching swelled along with criticism of the Klan. Lynching slowed dramatically in Texas. In comparison, in Mississippi, opponents of lynching lost elections, and while reported lynchings also slowed, lynching probably just went underground. One reason for this difference was that Texas merchants needed black customers and realized that blacks and whites could easily leave.[7]

The rise of new cities and industries in Texas after 1887 and the conversion of western ranches to farms after 1905 meant most had an alternative to remaining in Northeast Texas. The poorest sharecroppers with no skills and families to feed surely remained tied to the region. The rest could leave. Lynching drove blacks away. Conservative politics and policy did the same for whites. To save their towns and their livelihoods, even small-town merchants in Northeast Texas voted for more-liberal candidates like Wright Patman. Few wanted to return to the days in which speeches about the Confederacy substituted for concrete steps toward greater prosperity.

In that sense, change in the region occurred from the bottom up instead of awaiting some top-down, federally mandated program stimulated by the Great Depression or World War II. After 1920 as conservatives united around the goal of limited government intervention in the economy and increased government restriction of individual behavior, their opponents coalesced into the precursor of the New Deal coalition. The ebbing influence of the Confederacy and the increased emphasis on the plain people, on local culture, and on restoration theology provided a healthy environment for the growth of this anticonservative group. The presence of this coalition of economic reformers, moderate social reformers, insurgents, and labor before 1928 not only indicated the continuation of multifactional politics, it demonstrated that the majority in the region already possessed the mindset, the economic and cultural incentives, and the mechanism for achieving power that would allow them to take full advantage of the opportunities provided by the federal government during the New Deal and World War II.

Perhaps in this political reality, Northeast Texans differed from other southerners, but in their ability to leave, they differed little from those in Southeast Oklahoma, Southwest Arkansas, and Northwest Louisiana, where most counties also lost population in the 1920s.[8] Testimony to kinship went beyond numbers. In 1928 when Dabney White toured Northeast Texas for the *Houston Post,* he insisted that only "an imaginary line" divided the region from its neighbors in Arkansas. Yet that imaginary line—indeed, imagination—nurtured a modern society and culture.[9]

William Humphrey, in his stories of Northeast Texas, offered both an example of how imagination created a new identity and a parable on the ambiguity of being Texan and southern.[10] In *No Resting Place,* Humphrey described how in 1936 he along with the other school children of Clarksville first reenacted the battles of the Texas Revolution. Humphrey remembered:

> For us schoolchildren that year it was hard to believe that Texas had begun in 1836; to us it seemed more as though it had stopped then, for the study of that *annus mirabilis* all but preempted the curriculum and turned back the clock. With school out, on Saturdays, in vacant lots all over town, the

Battle of the Alamo was refought weekly, and the following day, in Sunday school, there was a deliberate confounding of that exodus led by Moses of Egypt with the one of Moses Austin, and of Sam Houston at San Jacinto with Joshua at Jericho.

School-sponsored reenactments became an annual event, with onlookers mouthing the words they said a half century before while watching their grandchildren carry on the tradition.[11]

Humphrey was too young to realize that this continuous and cantankerous celebration of Texas took until 1936 to fully form. It reached maturity in 1936 because Texans sought relief from the Depression. The slight upturn in the economy in 1936 combined with the celebration of the 100-year anniversary of Texas independence from Mexico created a welcome sense of joy and hope. It started in 1936 because of the federal government. As Humphrey noted, "The W.P.A. was being employed that centennial year to put up monuments all over the place." Goaded by Jesse Jones, who through the Reconstruction Finance Corporation controlled their purse strings, the Works Progress Administration and other federal agencies provided two-thirds of the funding for the construction of the San Jacinto Monument and funded scores of smaller commemorative structures. These visible and public structures helped institutionalize Texas patriotism, but just as economic change did not entirely await the spark of federal spending and federal policy, outside intervention alone did not cause the rise of Texas patriotism.[12]

Commemoration of the Texas Revolution in 1936 culminated a two-decade old process—the conscious and unconscious distancing of a people from the South of defeat and poor expectations. Vestiges of the Old South remained. Humphrey always described himself "as a southerner." Southern songs and southern stories never entirely vanished.[13] Yet Northeast Texans turned around the statues of their Confederate heroes so that they "now faced northeast, as though setting off for war," instead of forlornly facing southwest as though "back on foot all the way from Appomattox."[14]

Defeatism and complete opposition to innovation, if not apprehension of change, evaporated with the increased importance of the Texas myth and the decreased importance of the Lost Cause. Northeast Texans abandoned the limited possibilities implicit in the Lost Cause and adopted the mantle of progress of the Texas Revolution. As Humphrey noted, southerners "had a separate history from that of most of my fellow countrymen." The shift from southern to Texan erased that sense of not sharing the prosperous destiny of the rest of the country, easing hostility to innovation and to governmental activism. When Humphrey returned after a long absence, he noted a key feature of modernity, "Red River County had ceased to be Old South and become Far West."[15]

Texans did not stand alone in celebrating their particular past, and a reborn interest in local history appeared in other southern states during the 1920s. In Virginia, concentration on the colonial past increased throughout the decade. After extensive restoration efforts funded by John D. Rockefeller, Jr., Colonial Williamsburg became the focal point for this celebration of the colonial past. Virginians spent considerable energy through the 1920s contesting the right to call their state the first place of American settlement and in other ways sought to reestablish the preeminent place of Virginia in the American past. All of this tended to push aside or at least cloud celebration of the Confederacy, but it did not end the special appeal of Confederate heroes. Instead, as Washington and Lee University symbolized, the image of George Washington and Robert E. Lee combined to define the ideal Virginian. Virginia's failure to ratify woman suffrage suggested that the tradition of the Lost Cause remained strong enough to stifle innovation and change.[16]

History, memory, and tradition worked in different ways in Texas than they did in Virginia or other parts of the South. In much of the South, reverence of tradition and abhorrence of innovation had a symbiotic relationship—each reinforced the other. Scientific history, subject to periodic revision, stood in contrast to tradition. In Texas during the 1910s and 1920s, historians and folklorists set Texas within the current of the American move west, helping to remake Texans' sense of history and their understanding of their traditions. Ironically, in the 1930s and 1940s Texans froze their history and stopped the process of cyclical revision characteristic of the discipline. Modern Texans insist, for example, that Davy Crockett died fighting in the Alamo, despite reliable evidence that he surrendered and was executed. To this extent Texans, like other southerners, became as historian Richard N. Current put it "more taken with tradition" and "less interested in history than New Englanders or Midwesterners." If Texans seem different from other Americans, if they seem less tolerant of change, if convergence with statistical norms for the nation remains incomplete, this freezing of the past after 1936 offers at least a partial explanation of why.[17]

Distinctions between history and tradition, however, may be artificial. Even the strictest practitioners of scientific history find themselves ensnared in the myths, dreams, hopes, and politics of their society. John Bodnar, in his study of public memory and history, observed, "The shaping of a past worthy of public commemoration in the present is contested and involves a struggle for supremacy between advocates of various political ideas and sentiments." While that may ring true for the nation as a whole, to expand on Current's point, the difference in North and South was not between history and tradition, it was between a contested history and a fixed history. In turn, a fixed history, as Elna Green pointed out, blocked innovation.[18]

From roughly 1910 to 1936, when Texans contested history and culture, they bowed to progress, struck a blow to the Lost Cause, and reached out to the rest of the United States. As much as anything else, this allowed woman suffrage and other reform movements to flourish in Texas. The rise of local history in the 1920s and 1930s only confirmed the pattern. John Chisum replaced Robert E. Lee as the model citizen. An innovative westerner took the place of the chivalrous medieval knight.

Altered heroes, and the momentary tolerance for innovation and change their emergence symbolized, allowed the acceptance of other changes. A more open political system, an already evolving economy, a society in which women played a more nearly equal role—all these made Texans more receptive to the momentous transformation of the southern countryside unleashed by the New Deal and perpetuated by World War II. Indeed, within Northeast Texas the economic transformation in particular originated before the New Deal.

Thus, all that came after World War II—the remarkable surge in the Texas economy, the more-rapid and less-violent acceptance of desegregation, the growing convergence in most statistical forms of measurement with the nonsouthern states—has links back to the period of 1887 to 1930. Not just Dallas, the Texas South Plains, and other less-southern areas, but even Northeast Texas, a most southern place, began their transformation before 1930.

In the end, however, Texans did not simply remake their state from southern to western. In their use of history, memory, and tradition in everyday life, Texans remained profoundly southern. Citizens of the state could not view history with the academic detachment Richard Current found outside the South, because their history served a function.

The questions become: Did other southern states—particularly those with significant urban centers—eventually follow a path in some ways similar to that taken by Texas? Did they retool history, open up politics ever so slightly, and eagerly accept the federal government as a source for the redistribution of the nation's wealth, or did federal legislation and federal bureaucracies bludgeon and cajole them toward modernity?[19] Were there multiple paths to a modern South?

NOTES

INTRODUCTION

1. Although marked by less violence and less overt white opposition to change than in other southern states, patterns of racial discrimination and resistance to integration were the most persistent southern characteristics in Texas after World War II. See Lewis L. Gould and Melissa R. Sneed, "Without Pride or Apology: The University of Texas at Austin, Racial Integration, and the Barbara Smith Case," *Southwestern Historical Quarterly* (*SHQ*) 103 (July 1999): 67–87; Interview with Wright Patman by Joe B. Frantz, August 11, 1972 (typescript p. 1–2 side one, p. 3–4 side two), Oral History Collection, Lyndon Baines Johnson Library, Austin.

2. On the relationship between Texas and the South, see Walter L. Buenger, "Texas and the South," *SHQ* 103 (January 2000): 309–326; Walter L. Buenger, *Secession and the Union in Texas* (Austin: University of Texas Press, 1984); Randolph B. Campbell, *An Empire for Slavery: The Peculiar Institution in Texas, 1821–1865* (Baton Rouge: Louisiana State University Press, 1989); Randolph B. Campbell, *Grass-Roots Reconstruction in Texas, 1865–1880* (Baton Rouge: Louisiana State University Press, 1997); Neil Foley, *The White Scourge: Mexicans, Blacks, and Poor Whites in Texas Cotton Culture* (Berkeley: University of California Press, 1997), 17–91; Lawrence Goodwyn, *Democratic Promise: The Populist Movement in America* (New York: Oxford University Press, 1976); Dewey W. Grantham, *Southern Progressivism: The Reconciliation of Progress and Tradition* (Knoxville: University of Tennessee Press, 1983), 1–108; William A. Owens, "Regionalism and Universality," in Don Graham, James W. Lee, and William T. Pillkington (eds.), *The Texas Literary Tradition: Fiction, Folklore, History* (Austin: University of Texas and Texas State Historical Association, 1983), 69–79; Ted Ownby, *Subduing Satan: Religion, Recreation, and Manhood in the Rural South, 1865–1920* (Chapel Hill: University of North Carolina Press, 1990), 103–166.

3. The numbers used in Figure 0.1 are for the calendar year and are not a multiyear economic cycle average. For a discussion of the many problems in

arriving at an accurate estimate of per capita income and for those estimates, see Richard Easterlin, "Interregional Differences in Per Capita Income, Population, and Total Income, 1840-1950," in National Bureau of Economic Research, *Trends in the American Economy in the Nineteenth Century* (Princeton: Princeton University Press, 1960), 73-140; Maurice Levin, *Income in the Various States, Its Sources and Distribution, 1919, 1920, 1921* (New York: National Bureau of Economic Research, 1925), 259-265; Richard A. Easterlin, "State Income Estimates," in Simon S. Kuznets and Dorothy S. Thomas, *Population Redistribution and Economic Growth, United States, 1870-1950* (Philadelphia: American Philosophical Society, 1957), vol. 1, 753; Charles F. Schwartz and Robert E. Graham, Jr., *Personal Income by States since 1929*, supplement to *Survey of Current Business* (Washington: Department of Commerce, 1956); Gavin Wright, *Old South, New South: Revolutions in the Southern Economy since the Civil War* (New York: Basic Books, 1986), 239-240, 299 n. 1; Frank A. Hanna, *State Income Differentials, 1919-1954* (Durham, N.C.: Duke University Press, 1959), 27-58.

4. Grantham and Wright both argued that dynamic growth in West Texas, usually classified as outside the South, explained this economic divergence, but the lack of development in that region before 1910 makes that unlikely. See Grantham, *Southern Progressivism*, 98-99; Wright, *Old South, New South*, 51-60; Nellie Witt Spikes and Temple Ann Ellis, *Through the Years: A History of Crosby County, Texas* (San Antonio: Naylor, 1952), 342-490; Evalyn Parrott Scott, *A History of Lamb County* (Sudan, Texas: privately printed, 1968), 86-268; Mary L. Cox, *History of Hale County, Texas* (Plainview, 1937); Mary Louise McDonald, "The History of Lubbock County, Texas" (master's thesis, University of Texas, Austin, 1942); Vincent Matthew Peterman, *Pioneer Days: A Half-Century of Life in Lamb County and Adjacent Communities* (Lubbock: Texas Tech Press, 1979); Janet M. Neugebauer (ed.), *Plains Farmer: The Diary of William G. DeLoach, 1914-1964* (College Station: Texas A&M University Press, 1991), xv-xxx, 24-115; David B. Gracy, *Littlefield Lands: Colonization on the Texas Plains, 1912-1920* (Austin: University of Texas Press, 1968), 100-138.

5. Bruce J. Schulman, *From Cotton Belt to Sunbelt: Federal Policy, Economic Development, and the Transformation of the South, 1938-1980* (New York: Oxford University Press, 1991), 99. For the ranking of all states in federal agricultural loans and expenditures per farm capita, see Leonard J. Arrington, "Western Agriculture and the New Deal," *Agricultural History* 44 (October 1970): 346-347. In the 1930s the overwhelming majority of Texas farmers still resided in the most southern regions of the state, but Arrington lumped the state with the West, enhancing his point that western farmers received more generous treatment from the federal government than did southern farmers. For why southern states received less per capita, see Lee Alston and Joseph Ferrie, "Labor Costs, Paternalism, and Loyalty in Southern Agriculture: A Constraint on the Growth of the Welfare Sate," *Journal of Economic History* 45 (March 1985): 95-117; Lee Alston and Joseph Ferrie, "Paternalism in Agricultural Labor Contracts in the U.S. South: Implications for the Growth of the Welfare State," *American Economic Review* 83 (September 1993): 852-876; John Joseph Wallis, "Employment, Politics, and Economic Recovery during the Great Depression," *Review of Economics and Statis-*

tics 69 (August 1987): 516–520; John Joseph Wallis, "The Political Economy of New Deal Spending Revisited, Again: With and Without Nevada," *Explorations in Economic History* 35 (April 1998): 140–170.

6. On the literature on Johnson, see Kenneth E. Hendrickson, Jr., "Texas Politics since the New Deal," in Walter L. Buenger and Robert A. Calvert (eds.) *Texas through Time: Evolving Interpretations* (College Station: Texas A&M University Press, 1991), 262–267. Also see Robert Dallek, *Lone Star Rising: Lyndon Johnson and His Times, 1908–1960* (New York: Oxford University Press, 1991); Robert Dallek, *Flawed Giant: Lyndon Johnson and His Times, 1961–1973* (New York: Oxford University Press, 1998). For examples of Johnson's Texas contemporaries who eagerly exploited the advantages presented to them and accepted a changing society, see Joseph A. Pratt and Christopher J. Castaneda, *Builders: Herman and George R. Brown* (College Station: Texas A&M University Press, 1999); Victoria Buenger and Walter L. Buenger, *Texas Merchant: Marvin Leonard and Fort Worth* (College Station: Texas A&M University Press, 1998); Walter L. Buenger, "Between Community and Corporation: The Southern Roots of Jesse H. Jones and the Reconstruction Finance Corporation," *Journal of Southern History* (*JSH*) 66 (August 1990): 481–510; Kenneth E. Hendrickson, Jr., and Michael L. Collins (eds.), *Profiles in Power: Twentieth Century Texans in Washington* (Arlington Heights, Illinois: Harlan Davidson, 1993), 29–174. Contrast these Texans with the portrait of typical southerners in Wright, *Old South, New South*, 78–80, 198–238.

7. Terry G. Jordan, "A Century and a Half of Ethnic Change in Texas, 1836–1986," *SHQ* 89 (April 1986): 385–422; Robin W. Doughty, "Settlement and Environmental Change in Texas, 1829–1900," *SHQ* 89 (April 1986): 423–442; Christopher S. Davies, "Life at the Edge: Urban and Industrial Evolution of Texas: Frontier Wilderness—Frontier Space, 1836–1986," *SHQ* 89 (April 1986): 443–554.

8. In a striking example of ignoring Texas, while histories of slavery appeared decades earlier for all other Confederate states, until 1989 historians did not produce a general history of slavery in the Lone Star state. See Campbell, *An Empire for Slavery*, 1–9; Ann Patton Malone, review of *An Empire for Slavery*, *JSH* 57 (February 1991): 100–102. Also see the discussion of Arrington's use of Texas as a western state, in n.5 above.

9. On state politics, see Alwyn Barr, *Reconstruction to Reform: Texas Politics, 1876–1906* (Austin: University of Texas Press, 1971); Lewis L. Gould, *Progressives and Prohibitionists: Texas Democrats in the Wilson Era* (Austin: University of Texas Press, 1973); Norman D. Brown, *Hood, Bonnet, and Little Brown Jug: Texas Politics, 1921–1928* (College Station: Texas A&M University Press, 1984). Recent publications indicate that concentration on politics may be ending. See Foley, *White Scourge*, 17–202; Rebecca Sharpless, *Fertile Ground, Narrow Choices: Women on Texas Cotton Farms, 1900–1940* (Chapel Hill: University of North Carolina Press, 1999); Judith N. McArthur, *Creating the New Woman: The Rise of Southern Women's Progressive Culture in Texas, 1893–1918* (Urbana: University of Illinois Press, 1998).

10. Edward L. Ayers, *The Promise of the New South: Life After Reconstruction*

(New York: Oxford University Press, 1992), 437. For the view that little changed in the economy before the late 1930s, see Gilbert C. Fite, *Cotton Fields No More: Southern Agriculture, 1865–1980* (Lexington: University Press of Kentucky, 1984), 68–138; Wright, *Old South, New South,* 51–238. For a more nuanced view of change before the late 1930s, see Pete Daniel, *Breaking the Land: The Transformation of Cotton, Tobacco, and Rice Cultures since 1880* (Urbana: University of Illinois Press, 1985), 1–109; Jack Temple Kirby, *Rural Worlds Lost: The American South, 1920–1960* (Baton Rouge: Louisiana State University Press, 1987), 25–333. On Progressivism and the limits of social and cultural change, see Grantham, *Southern Progressivism,* 1–348; William A. Link, *The Paradox of Southern Progressivism, 1880–1930* (Chapel Hill: University of North Carolina Press, 1992); Ownby, *Subduing Satan,* 167–212.

11. Bowie, Camp, Cass, Delta, Franklin, Hopkins, Lamar, Marion, Morris, Red River, and Titus counties made up the Fourth Congressional District until 1902, when they became the First Congressional District. They made up the First District until the early 1930s, when Harrison County replaced Camp County. See *Pittsburg Gazette,* July 15, 1898, p. 2; November 9, 1900, p. 1; November 7, 1902, p. 2; November 11, 1904, p. 1–2. See *Jefferson Jimplecute,* November 12, 1904, p. 1–2; Scrapbook no. 4, Morris Sheppard Papers, Barker Texas History Center, University of Texas at Austin; Political Clippings, Papers of Wright Patman, Lyndon B. Johnson Library, Austin, Texas, Box 72; Interview with Patman by Frantz.

12. On the similarity of the First District to neighboring states, see Interview with Patman by Frantz; Dabney White, "Some Political and Historical Observations about the First Congressional District," *Houston Post,* April 8, 1928, p. 3.

13. Texas Agricultural Experiment Station, *The Soils of Texas,* Extension Service Bulletin no. 431 (College Station, 1931). Also see Terry G. Jordan, "The Imprint of the Upper and Lower South on Mid-Nineteenth-Century Texas," *Annals of the Association of American Geographers* 57 (December 1967): 667–690; *Texas Almanac and State Industrial Guide: A Textbook on Texas* (Dallas: A. H. Belo, 1925), 250–251, 258–259, 316, 324–325. For a close look at a nearby county in the nineteenth century, see Randolph B. Campbell, *A Southern Community in Crisis: Harrison County, Texas 1850–1880* (Austin: Texas State Historical Association, 1983).

14. U.S., *Census: 1890 Population* (Washington: Government Printing Office, 1883), pt. 1, 782–785; U.S., *Census: 1880, Report on Cotton Production in the United States* (Washington: Government Printing Office, 1884): 59–71; U.S., *Census: 1930 Population* (Washington: Government Printing Office, 1932), vol. 3, pt. 1, 965, and pt. 2, 975–990.

15. Texas Agricultural Experiment Station, *Types of Farming in Texas,* Extension Service Bulletin no. 964 (College Station, 1960).

16. U.S., *Census: 1880, Agriculture* (Washington: Government Printing Office, 1883), 88–93; Eugene W. Hilgard, "Report on Cotton Production in the United States (Washington: Government Printing Office, 1884), pt. 1, 59–72; U.S., *Census: 1890, Agriculture,* 182–189; U.S., *Census: 1905, Manufactures* (Washington: Government Printing Office, 1907), pt. 2, 1065–1075; *Texas Almanac and State Industrial Guide, 1904* (Galveston: A. H. Belo, 1904), 92–94, 140–168, 217–374;

Texas Department of Agriculture, Insurance, Statistics and History, *First Annual Report of the Agricultural Bureau* (Austin: State Printing Office, 1889).

17. The Texas Blackland Prairie, a long V-shaped band of fertile soil stretching from east of San Antonio to north of Dallas and Paris, has attracted considerable scholarly attention in the past few years. See Foley, *White Scourge*, 1–140; Sharpless, *Fertile Ground, Narrow Choices*, 69–248; Kyle Grant Wilkison, "The End of Independence: Social and Political Consequences of Economic Change in Texas, 1870–1914" (Ph.D. dissertation, Vanderbilt University, 1995). Also see U.S., *Census: 1890, Population*, pt. 1, 782–785.

18. U.S., *Census: 1930, Population*, vol. 3, pt. 1, 167, and pt. 2, 541, 950–971; *Texas Almanac, 1925*, 269–270, 279, 295–296, 308.

19. U.S., *Census: 1930, Population*, vol. 3, pt. 1, 167, 965, and pt. 2, 541, 941.

20. On the development of towns and small cities in the postwar South, see Ayers, *Promise of the New South*, 3–80.

21. U.S., *Census: 1890, Population*, pt. 1, 329, 335; U.S., *Census: 1930, Population*, vol. 3, pt. 2, 1009; U.S., *Census: 1905, Manufactures*, 1066–1073; *Texas Almanac* for 1914, 1925, and 1929.

22. See *Texas Almanac, 1925*, 250–351; *The Texas Almanac and State Industrial Guide: The Encyclopedia of Texas* (Dallas, 1933): 330–358; U.S., *Census: 1930, Population*, vol. 3, pt. 2, 976, 983; U.S., *Census: 1906, Religious Bodies* (Washington: Government Printing Office, 1910), pt. 1, 357–364; U.S., *Census: 1916, Religious Bodies* (Washington: Government Printing Office, 1919), pt. 1, 311–318; U.S., *Census: 1926, Religious Bodies* (Washington: Government Printing Office, 1930), vol. 1, 678–691.

23. Daniel, *Breaking the Land*, 68–72; Pete Daniel, *Deep'n as It Come: The 1927 Mississippi River Flood* (New York: Oxford University Press, 1977); Nan Elizabeth Woodruff, *As Rare as Rain: Federal Relief in the Great Southern Drought of 1930–31* (Urbana: University of Illinois Press, 1985).

24. Kirby, *Rural Worlds Lost*, 32. This work also offers (pp. 25–50) an excellent description of regional variation in the South.

25. John Steinbeck, *Travels With Charley* (New York: Viking Press, 1962), 201–202. Also see V. O. Key, *Southern Politics in State and Nation* (New York: Knopf, 1949), 254–260, 646–675; Wright, *Old South, New South*, 51–83.

26. Paul D. Escott, *Many Excellent People: Power and Privilege in North Carolina, 1850–1900* (Chapel Hill: University of North Carolina Press, 1985), 241–267. Georgia Democrats used similar tactics. See Barton C. Shaw, *The Wool-Hat Boys: Georgia's Populist Party* (Baton Rouge: Louisiana State University Press, 1984), 194–196.

27. Fite, *Cotton Fields No More*, 101. For conflicting assessments of the impact of World War I, see George B. Tindall, *The Emergence of the New South, 1913–1945* (Baton Rouge: Louisiana State University Press, 1967), 33–69; Wright, *Old South, New South*, 198–216.

28. On religion, rituals, monuments, culture, and the New South, see Gaines M. Foster, *Ghosts of the Confederacy: Defeat, the Lost Cause, and the Emergence of the New South, 1865 to 1913* (New York: Oxford University Press, 1987), 104–198; Charles R. Wilson, *Baptized in Blood: The Religion of the Lost Cause, 1865–*

1920 (Athens: University of Georgia Press, 1980), 161–182. For the view that the pull of the Lost Cause was more permanent, see Thomas L. Connelly and Barbara Bellows, *God and General Longstreet: The Lost Cause and the Southern Mind* (Baton Rouge: Louisiana State University Press, 1982), 107–148; Paul D. Escott, "The Uses of Gallantry: Virginians and the Origins of J. E. B. Stuart's Historical Image," *Virginia Magazine of History and Biography* 103 (January 1995): 47–74.

29. Texas appeared far more dynamic than Georgia, which refused to ratify woman's suffrage and in other ways seemed profoundly conservative from 1896 to 1930. See Numan V. Bartley, *The Creation of Modern Georgia,* 2d ed. (Athens: University of Georgia Press, 1990), 75–178; Grantham, *Southern Progressivism,* 51–55; Shaw, *Wool-Hat Boys,* 183–214. Interestingly, Arkansas, which ratified woman's suffrage and benefited from a more open political process, seemed somewhere between Georgia and Texas. See Carl H. Moneyhon, *Arkansas and the New South, 1874–1929* (Fayetteville: University of Arkansas Press, 1997), 95–150. Also see McArthur, *Creating the New Woman,* 97–149; Elna C. Green, *Southern Strategies: Southern Women and the Woman Suffrage Question* (Chapel Hill: University of North Carolina Press, 1997), 179–183.

30. Wright, *Old South, New South,* 78–80. On Patman, see Nancy Beck Young, "Wright Patman: Congressman to the Nation, 1893–1953" (Ph.D. dissertation, University of Texas at Austin, 1995); Janet Louise Schmelzer, "The Early Life and Early Congressional Career of Wright Patman: 1894–1941" (Ph.D. dissertation, Texas Christian University, 1978); Robert Sherrill, "The Last of the Great Populists," *New York Times Magazine,* March 16, 1969, 24–25, 88, 106–118; *Dallas Times-Herald,* March 11, 1976.

31. On politics see Key, *Southern Politics in State and Nation,* 254–260; Chandler Davidson, *Race and Class in Texas Politics* (Princeton: Princeton University Press, 1990), 3–60; James H. Davis, *Memoir* (Sherman, Texas: *Courier Press,* 1935); Worth Robert Miller, "Building a Progressive Coalition in Texas: The Populist-Reform Democrat Rapprochement, 1900–1907," *JSH* 52 (May 1986): 163–182. For a fuller development of Patman, the economy, and the culture, see chapters 5, 7, and 8.

32. The quote is the subtitle of Grantham, *Southern Progressivism: The Reconciliation of Progress and Tradition.*

33. William Humphrey, *No Resting Place* (New York: Delacorte Press, 1989), 8.

34. Moneyhon, *Arkansas and the New South,* 150. Once Texas myths became more frozen, they too could retard innovation and adaptation. See Walter L. Buenger and Robert A. Calvert, "The Shelf Life of Truth in Texas," in *Texas through Time,* ix–xxxv.

CHAPTER 1: THE FLUID AND THE CONSTANT

1. *Pittsburg Gazette,* August 11, 1887, p. 1. The statewide vote given in *Texas Almanac and State Industrial Guide, 1912* (Galveston: A. H. Belo, 1912), 45, was 129,270 for prohibition and 220,627 against.

2. This description of Henry Smith's lynching is drawn from *Dallas Morning News*, February 1, 2, 3, 1893; *Atlanta Express*, February 2, 1893; *Houston Post*, February 2, 3, 1893; *Paris News*, February 3, 1893, reprinted in *The Facts in the Case of the Horrible Murder of Little Myrtle Vance and its Fearful Expiation at Paris* (Paris: P. I. James, 1893), 246-255. For an introduction to lynching, see Ayers, *Promise of the New South*, 155-159, 495-497; W. Fitzhugh Brundage, "Introduction," in Brundage (ed.), *Under Sentence of Death* (Chapel Hill: University of North Carolina Press, 1997), 1-20; David Thelen (ed.), "What We See and Can't See in the Past, A Round Table," *JAH* 83 (March 1997): 1217-1272.

3. *Pittsburg Gazette*, August 11, 1887, p. 1. The 1887 prohibition election badly needs study and, despite the turmoil it created, is not even mentioned in the best textbook history of Texas. See Robert A. Calvert and Arnoldo De León, *The History of Texas* (Wheeling, Illinois: Harlan Davidson, 1996), 168-306. For the county-level vote in 1887, see *Texas Almanac, 1912*, 42-45. For useful exceptions to the general neglect of prohibition in the 1880s, see Barr, *Reconstruction to Reform*, 85-92; Gregg Cantrell, " 'Dark Tactics': Black Politics in the 1887 Texas Prohibition Campaign," *Journal of American Studies* 25 (April 1991): 85-93. On prohibition in the South before 1900, see Link, *Paradox of Southern Progressivism*, 31-57.

4. *Clarksville Standard*, July 14, 1887, p. 2. On the literature on racism in Texas, see Alwyn Barr, "African Americans in Texas: From Stereotypes to Diverse Roles," in *Texas through Time*, 50-80.

5. Escott, *Many Excellent People*, 241-267; Shaw, *Wool-Hat Boys*, 183-214; Neil R. McMillen, *Dark Journey: Black Mississippians in the Age of Jim Crow* (Urbana: University of Illinois Press, 1989), 224-256; Grantham, *Southern Progressivism*, 36-107; Bartley, *Creation of Modern Georgia*, 75-178. Politics in Arkansas fell somewhere between North Carolina and Texas. See Moneyhon, *Arkansas and the New South*, 77-132.

6. An exception to this is Gould, *Progressives and Prohibitionists*. While the following works do not focus on the party as an institution, Democrats play prominent roles in Barr, *Reconstruction to Reform;* Brown, *Hood, Bonnet, and Little Brown Jug*. For much more focused studies of Whigs, Know-Nothings, Greenbackers, Populists, and Socialists, see Randolph B. Campbell, "Statehood, Civil War, and Reconstruction, 1846-76," in *Texas through Time*, 165-196; Robert Calvert, "Agrarian Texas," in *Texas through Time*, 197-228. Also see Key, *Southern Politics in State and Nation*, 254-260; C. Davidson, *Race and Class in Texas Politics*, 155-271.

7. *Pittsburg Gazette*, March 24, 1887, p. 2. Also see *Pittsburg Gazette*, January 9, 1903.

8. *Pittsburg Gazette*, June 22, 1894, p. 2. Also see *Pittsburg Gazette*, November 4, 1886, p. 3.

9. *Pittsburg Gazette*, March 24, 1887, p. 2. On why southerners felt so strongly about prohibition, see Ownby, *Subduing Satan*, 103-166.

10. Charles DeMorse, one of the founders of the Democratic party in Texas, gave extensive coverage to the impact of the referendum on his party. See *Clarksville Standard*, May 19, August 11, 18, 1887.

11. For a glimpse of the traditional world in eastern Texas, see Thad Sitton, *Backwoodsmen: Stockmen and Hunters along a Big Thicket River Valley* (Norman: University of Oklahoma Press, 1995), 3–274; Deborah Brown and Katherine Gust, *Between the Creeks: Recollections of Northeast Texas* (Austin: Encino Press, 1976); William Humphrey, *Farther off from Heaven* (New York: Knopf, 1977), 61–113.

12. Unlike women in the rest of the South, Texas women played a significant role in the Farmers' Alliance. See Robert C. McMath, *Populist Vanguard: A History of the Southern Farmers' Alliance* (Chapel Hill: University of North Carolina Press, 1975), 67–69.

13. Barr, *Reconstruction to Reform*, 90–92; A. W. Neville, *The History of Lamar County* (Paris: North Texas Publishing, 1937), 182–196.

14. E. L. Dohoney, *An Average American* (Paris, Texas: privately published, 1907), 24–171, 222–254; Ron Tyler, Doug Barnett, and Roy R. Barkley (eds.), *The New Handbook of Texas* (*New HOT*) (Austin: Texas State Historical Association, 1996), vol. 2, 670–671; Buenger, *Secession and the Union*, 119–177; A. W. Neville, *The Red River Valley: Then and Now* (Paris: North Texas Publishing Company, 1948), 198; Neville, *Lamar County*, 182–188; Seth Shepard McKay (ed.), *Debates in the Texas Constitutional Convention of 1875* (Austin: University of Texas, 1930), 142–144.

15. James D. Ivy, " 'The Lone Star State Surrenders to a Lone Woman': Francis Willard's Forgotten 1882 Texas Temperance Tour," *SHQ* 102 (July 1998): 45–61; H. A. Ivy, *Rum on the Run in Texas: A Brief History of Prohibition in the Lone Star State* (Dallas: Temperance Publishing Co., 1910), 19–46; Neville, *Red River Valley*, 262.

16. *Pittsburg Gazette,* July 28, 1911, p. 1.

17. *Pittsburg Gazette,* August 4, 1887, p. 1. For the precinct returns, see *Pittsburg Gazette,* August 11, 1887.

18. *Pittsburg Gazette,* August 4, 1887, p. 1. Also see *Pittsburg Gazette,* August 11, 1887, and November 11, 1898; Election Returns, 1892–1902: Camp.

19. Election Returns, 1887, 1894: Lamar, Hopkins. The link between prohibition and the Alliance and Populism may have been stronger elsewhere in Texas. See McMath, *Populist Vanguard,* 22–24; Roscoe Martin, *The People's Party in Texas: A Study in Third-Party Politics* (Austin: University of Texas, 1933), 80–83.

20. Election Returns, 1886–1894: Secretary of State.

21. For a comparison with 1911, see *Texas Almanac, 1912,* 42–45. Population characteristics are drawn from U.S., *Census: 1880–1910, Population.* Also see Mike Kingston, Sam Attlesey, and Mary G. Crawford, *Texas Almanac's Political History of Texas* (Dallas: *Dallas Morning News,* 1992), 62–69; *Clarksville Standard,* August 11, 1887, p. 3; Martin Leon Edwards, "The Farmers' Movement in Delta County," (master's thesis, East Texas State College, 1964); Marshall L. Williams, "The Political Career of Cyclone Davis," (master's thesis, East Texas State College, 1938); Link, *Paradox of Southern Progressivism,* 51–57.

22. Barr, *Reconstruction to Reform,* 92. Also see *Clarksville Standard,* August 11, 1887; Election Returns, 1887: Secretary of State.

23. *Pittsburg Gazette,* September 28, October 12, 1888; *Galveston Daily News,*

October 14, 31, 1888; Barr, *Reconstruction to Reform*, 93-107; Robert C. Cotner, *James Stephen Hogg: A Biography* (Austin: University of Texas Press, 1959), 147-188.

24. *Pittsburg Gazette*, November 4, 1886, p. 3, and November 9, 16, 1888, pp. 2-3; Kingston, Attlesey, and Crawford, *Political History of Texas*, 62-65.

25. *Clarksville Standard*, September 7, 14, 21, 1888; *Delta Banner*, February 5, 1887, and November 9, 1888; Kingston, Attlesey, and Crawford, *Political History of Texas*, 58-65; Election returns, 1888: Lamar, Hopkins, and Franklin.

26. The Republican candidate for president's total exceeded Martin's vote by a thousand votes in both Lamar and Red River, and none of the minor candidates received those votes. See Election Returns, 1888: Lamar, Secretary of State.

27. On the voting process, see *Pittsburg Gazette*, October 19, 26, 1894; *Jefferson Jimplecute*, November 5, 1904; Worth Robert Miller, "Harrison County Methods: Election Fraud in Late-Nineteenth-Century Texas," *Locus* 7 (spring 1995): 111-128. Between 1881 and 1904 Lamar's citizens regularly voted on local option, but the county went dry permanently only after the poll tax reduced the number of black voters. See Neville, *Lamar County*, 182-183. Older histories of southern states also indicated a strong link between suffrage restrictions and prohibition. See John K. Bettersworth, *Mississippi: A History* (Austin: Steck, 1959), 376-381; James Benson Sellers, *The Prohibition Movement in Alabama, 1702-1943* (Chapel Hill: University of North Carolina Press, 1943), 101-128.

28. J. H. Davis, *Memoir*, 19; Cotner, *Hogg*, 79-104.

29. *Jefferson Jimplecute*, January 22, 1890, p. 2.

30. *Pittsburg Gazette*, November 4, 11, 18, 1892; Kingston, Attlesey, and Crawford, *Political History of Texas*, 58-65; Barr, *Reconstruction to Reform*, 184.

31. *Pittsburg Gazette*, November 9, 1888; *Jefferson Jimplecute*, January 22, 1890; Kingston, Attlesey, and Crawford, *Political History of Texas*, 58-65; McMath, *Populist Vanguard*, 99.

32. Election Returns, 1890, 1892: Hopkins; Election Returns, 1892: Secretary of State; Cotner, *Hogg*, 189-219.

33. Barr, *Reconstruction to Reform*, 120-123; Gerald Nash, "The Reformer Reformed: John H. Reagan and Railroad Regulation," *Business History Review* 29 (June 1955): 189-196; John Stricklin Spratt, *The Road to Spindletop: Economic Change in Texas, 1875-1901* (Dallas: Southern Methodist University Press, 1955), 210-227; Cotner, *Hogg*, 220-249.

34. Barr, *Reconstruction to Reform*, 125-142.

35. For examples of railroad debate, see *Jefferson Jimplecute*, January 22, 1890; *Pittsburg Gazette*, November 4, 11, 18, 1892. Also see Lawrence D. Rice, *The Negro in Texas, 1874-1900* (Baton Rouge: Louisiana State University Press, 1971), 68-82.

36. Dohoney, *Average American*, 232-241; Barr, *Reconstruction to Reform*, 136-139.

37. While Dohoney first belonged to the Cumberland Presbyterian Church, he later became a leader in the First Christian Church of Paris (Disciples of Christ). Davis was a life-long Disciple of Christ. See Dohoney, *Average American*, 132-312; Barr, *Reconstruction to Reform*, 85-86; Neville, *Lamar County*, 182-188; J. H.

Davis, *Memoir,* 54-72, 317-324; Samuel S. Hill, *Encyclopedia of Religion in the South* (Macon: Mercer University Press, 1984), 188-189, 201-205; Ivy, "Francis Willard's Forgotten 1882 Texas Temperance Tour," 48-49 n. 9.

38. *Pittsburg Gazette,* November 4, 11, 1892; Cotner, *Hogg,* 293-296. On the nomination of Martin and Nugent, see *Dallas Morning News,* June 24, 1892.

39. *Dallas Texas Farmer,* November 26, 1892. Also see Robert A. Calvert, "A. J. Rose and the Granger Concept of Reform," *Agricultural History* 51 (January 1977): 181-196; McMath, *Populist Vanguard,* 61, 70-73, 95-96, 99. For an introduction to the vast literature on Populism, see William F. Holmes, "Populism: In Search of Context," *Agricultural History* 64 (fall 1990): 26-58.

40. For the best analysis of the 1892 election, see Barr, *Reconstruction to Reform,* 139-142. Also see Election Returns, 1892: Secretary of State. Official Returns were: Hogg, 190,486; Clark, 133,395; Nugent, 108,483; Houston, 1,322; Pendergrast, 1,592; total vote, 435,278.

41. The 10 percent estimate for conservatives assumes that since vote totals varied by only about 900 votes, most voters cast ballots in all three races. Black Republicans typically voted almost exclusively for the Republican candidate for president, but the black vote was almost certainly split among all three candidates for governor and Congress. Assuming that hard-core black Republicans numbered no more than the total cast for the Republican candidate for Congress, and that this hard core also voted for Clark, conservatives numbered about 3,000, or slightly less than 10 percent of the total number of voters. On black voting habits, see Barr, *Reconstruction to Reform,* 85-142; W. R. Miller, "Harrison County Methods," 111-128.

42. Election Returns, 1890, 1892: Bowie, Cass, Marion, Morris. Also see Gregg Cantrell and D. Scott Barton, "Texas Populists and the Failure of Biracial Politics, *JSH* 55 (November 1989): 661-692; *Pittsburg Gazette,* November 4, 11, 18, 1892.

43. *Dallas Morning News,* November 8, 9, 10, 11, 1892; Election Returns, 1888-1892: Cass.

44. Cotner, *Hogg,* 313. Also see "Special Message to the Texas Legislature on Lynch Law, February 6, 1893," in Robert C. Cotner (ed.), *Addresses and State Papers of James Stephen Hogg* (Austin: University of Texas Press, 1951), 331-334; Maud Cuney Hare, *Norris Wright Cuney* (New York: Crisis Publishing, 1913), 157-163; Harrell Budd, "The Negro in Politics in Texas, 1867-1898" (master's thesis, University of Texas, 1925), 102-112.

45. For a sampling of the themes and issues stressed by Hogg, see Cotner, *Addresses and State Papers of James Stephen Hogg,* 185-288.

46. *Jefferson Jimplecute,* January 22, 1890, p. 2. Also see Traylor Russell, *Carpetbaggers, Scalawags and Others* (Waco: Texian Press, 1973), 87-89; Mrs. Arch McKay and Mrs. H. A. Spelling, *A History of Jefferson, Marion County, Texas, 1836-1936* (Jefferson: privately printed, 1936), 55; *New HOT,* vol. 3, 924-925.

47. Budd, "Negro in Politics in Texas," 97-146; *Jefferson Jimplecute,* January 15, 22, February 5, 1890; *Pittsburg Gazette,* June 15, 1894, p. 2; Kingston, Attlesey, and Crawford, *Political History of Texas,* 58-69; J. A. R. Moseley, "The Citizens White Primary of Marion County," *SHQ* 49 (April 1946): 524-531. For

the best example of co-operation between white and black Populists in Texas, see Gregg Cantrell, *Kenneth and John B. Rayner and the Limits of Southern Dissent* (Urbana: University of Illinois Press, 1993), 191–270.

48. For broadsides used by the Democrats in 1892 and 1894 in Lamar County, see James W. Biard Papers, 1882–1913, American History Center, University of Texas at Austin. On the importance of such issues as taxes and inflation in Lamar, see Dohoney, *Average American*, 232–241. Also compare the vote for president, governor, and congressman in Election Returns, 1892: Lamar.

49. Election Returns: 1892, Delta, Franklin; R. Martin, *People's Party*, 62–63 n. 7.

50. Election Returns, 1892: Hopkins; McMath, *Populist Vanguard*, 68–69; *New HOT*, vol. 2, 129, 467; R. Martin, *People's Party*, 207–208; Mary Jo Wagner, "Farms, Families, and Reform: Women in the Farmers' Alliance and Populist Party" (Ph.D. dissertation, University of Oregon, 1986), 42–43, 318; Marion K. Barthelme, *Women in the Texas Populist Movement* (College Station: Texas A&M University Press, 1997), 6, 63–66.

51. *Atlanta Express*, February 2, 1893.

52. *Dallas Morning News*, February 2, 1893, p. 1; *Atlanta Express*, February 2, 1893.

53. Opposition to secession in Lamar County did not lessen commitment to white supremacy or white reliance on political violence, but the ritualistic violence of the 1890s was new. See William L. Richter, " 'The Revolver Rules the Day!': Colonel DeWitt C. Brown and the Freedmen's Bureau in Paris, Texas, 1867–1868," *SHQ* 93 (January 1990): 303–332; Barry A. Crouch, *The Freedmen's Bureau and Black Texans* (Austin: University of Texas Press, 1992), 69–101.

54. Cotner, *Addresses and State Papers of James Stephen Hogg*, 331. Also see Rice, *Negro in Texas*, 253–254. Because Rice looks only at a four-year period immediately after the passage of the 1897 antilynching law, he is far more sanguine about its beneficial impact.

55. *Dallas Morning News*, February 3, 1893, p. 1. Also see *Dallas Morning News*, January 30, 31, 1893, p. 1; *Paris News*, February 3, 1893; *Atlanta Express*, February 2, 1893.

56. The estimate of the number lynched in Alabama, Arkansas, Florida, Georgia, Kentucky, Louisiana, Mississippi, North Carolina, South Carolina, Tennessee, Texas, and Virginia comes from Brundage, *Under Sentence of Death*, 4. Older states with a stable, highly concentrated black population, such as Virginia, North Carolina, and South Carolina, had fewer lynchings. Only Mississippi and Georgia recorded more lynchings than Texas. For a contemporary count of lynchings by states and a comment on their new style, see James Elbert Cutler, *Lynch-Law: An Investigation into the History of Lynching in the United States* (New York: Longmans, Green, 1905), 183, 191. For other lynching totals, see Monroe Work (ed.), *The Negro Yearbook: An Annual Encyclopedia of the Negro, 1931–1932* (Tuskegee: Negro Year Book Publishing Co., 1931), 293; Stewart Emory Tolnay and E. M. Beck, *A Festival of Violence: An Analysis of Southern Lynchings, 1882–1930* (Urbana: University of Illinois Press, 1995), 259–263. For a word of caution on relying on any lynching total, see Christopher Waldrep, "War of Words: The Con-

troversy over the Definition of Lynching, 1899-1940," *JSH* 66 (February 2000): 75-100.

57. On the gruesome upturn in lynching see Ayers, *Promise of the New South*, 155-159; McMillen, *Dark Journey*, 224-253. Also see the essays in Brundage, *Under Sentence of Death*; Tolnay and Beck, *Festival of Violence*, 239-258; Martha Hodes, *White Women, Black Men: Illicit Sex in the Nineteenth-Century South* (New Haven: Yale University Press, 1997), 125-208.

58. Neville, *Lamar County*, 196; *Atlanta Express*, February 2, 1893; *Dallas Morning News*, February 2, 1893; U.S., *Census: 1896, Religious Bodies*, pt. 1; U.S., *Census: 1906, Religious Bodies*, pt. 1, 357-364; U.S., Census, *Population: 1880*, vol. 1, 410-425; U.S., Census, *Population: 1890*, pt. 1, 335, 555.

59. Daniel T. Williams, *Amid the Gathering Multitude: The Story of Lynching in America: A Classified Listing* (Unpublished: Tuskegee University, 1968). Also see Ownby, *Subduing Satan*, 169.

60. On politically motivated white violence toward blacks, see Cantrell, *Kenneth and John B. Rayner*, 200-270; Barr, *Reconstruction to Reform*, 194-201; Lawrence C. Goodwyn, "Populist Dreams and Negro Rights: East Texas as a Case Study," *American Historical Review (AHR)* 76 (December 1971): 1435-1456. For the best statement of the economic motives of lynchings, see Tolnay and Beck, *Festival of Violence*, 253-257; however, the connection between economic troubles and lynchings is undercut by the case of South Carolina, where cotton was as important as in Texas but lynchings were far fewer. On culture and lynching, see Grace Elizabeth Hale, *Making Whiteness: The Culture of Segregation in the South, 1890-1940* (New York: Pantheon Books, 1998), 199-239.

61. *Dallas Morning News*, February 2, 1893, p. 1. For a description of Paris's churches and map of their locations, see Francis Arnold Ellis and Skipper Steely, *First Church of Paris: First United Methodist Church* (Paris: First United Methodist Church, 1985), 58-60.

62. The numbers and description of lynchings given here are taken from D. T. Williams, *Amid the Gathering Multitude*. Also see the sources given in note 57, above. On social reformers and lynching, see Link, *Paradox of Southern Progressivism*, 58-70.

63. *Pittsburg Gazette*, September 2, 1904, p.4; Joseph David Aldredge, *The Romance of a Growing Boy in Texas: Autobiographical Sketches of His Early Life as a Boy* (Jacksonville, Texas: Pastor's Study, 1923), 108; Joel Williamson, *The Crucible of Race: Black-White Relations in the American South since Emancipation* (New York: Oxford University Press, 1984), 111. DeMorse offered a good example of the tolerant paternalism of older white community leaders and of the power of the belief that blacks opposed prohibition. See *Clarksville Standard*, July 14, 1887, and August 4, 11, 18, 1887; *New HOT*, vol. 2, 144, 591-592.

64. Williamson, *Crucible of Race*, 111; *Paris News*, February 3, 1893. While not explicitly linking lynching and prohibition, Ownby, *Subduing Satan*, 103-193, connects defense of an idealized home life and prohibition. Also see Election Returns, 1892-1896: Lamar; Neville, *Lamar County*, 182-184.

65. Dohoney, *Average American*, 88. Rebecca Latimer Felton has at least a cameo role in most treatments of the New South, but for an introduction to her life

and work, see Williamson, *Crucible of Race*, 124-130; Marjorie Spruill Wheeler, *New Women of the New South: The Leaders of the Woman Suffrage Movement in the Southern States* (New York: Oxford University Press, 1993), 41-54; Bartley, *Creation of Modern Georgia*, 119-123; Ayers, *Promise of the New South*, 424-425. Also see Neville, *Lamar County*, 182-188; Dohoney, *Average American*, 132-254.

66. Walter White, *Rope and Faggot: The Biography of Judge Lynch* (New York: Knopf, 1929), 40; *Dallas Morning News*, February 2, 1893, p. 1. On lynching before the 1880s, see Richard B. McCaslin, *Tainted Breeze: The Great Hanging at Gainesville, Texas, 1862* (Baton Rouge: Louisiana State University Press, 1994). Also see McMillen, *Dark Journey*, 224-253, 399 n. 84; W. White, *Rope and Faggot*, 245, 248; Robert M. Miller, "The Protestant Churches and Lynching, 1919-1939," *Journal of Negro History* 42 (April 1957): 119-126; Jacquelyn Dowd Hall, *Revolt against Chivalry: Jessie Daniel Ames and the Women's Campaign against Lynching* (New York: Columbia University Press, 1979); Neville, *Lamar County*, 188-195; *Paris News*, February 3, 1893; *Atlanta Express*, February 2, 1893.

67. *Pittsburg Gazette*, May 25, November 16, 23, June 15, 1894; Moseley, "Citizens White Primary," 524-531. On Populist attempts to enlist blacks in their cause, see Cantrell, *Kenneth and John B. Rayner*, 200-243.

68. To some extent, white Republicans associated with the lily-white movement emerged as a sixth faction in the mid-1890s, but as Schmitz's vote testified, their numbers were small. See Kingston, Attlesey, and Crawford, *Political History of Texas*, 69; Barr, *Reconstruction to Reform*, 142-160; *New HOT*, vol. 4, 471.

69. Election Returns, 1894: Secretary of State. In Cass, Nugent received 150 more votes from black precincts than in 1892, and he carried the county. See Election Returns, 1892, 1894: Cass; Cantrell, *Kenneth and John B. Rayner*, 215; Cantrell and Barton, "Texas Populists," 667-673.

70. Election returns, 1892, 1894: Lamar, Franklin, Hopkins, Secretary of State. The incorporated area of Paris made up only one voting precinct, and the large unincorporated residential area on the outskirts of town was a second precinct. The following comparison suggests that the almost 500 missing votes were black Republicans:

Paris and Precinct 1	Demo-crat	Repub-lican	Conservative/ Populist	Other	Total
1892 President	1,766	963	235	0	2,964
1892 Governor	1,064	1,633	245	46	2,968
1894 Governor	1,537	461	480	21	2,499

71. Barr, *Reconstruction to Reform*, 157; Election Returns, 1892, 1894: Morris, Cass, Bowie.

72. R. Martin, *People's Party*, 94. Also see R. Martin, *People's Party*, 93 n. 8, 97 n. 17; Election Returns, 1892-1894: Secretary of State; *Pittsburg Gazette*, November 9, 16, 23, 1894.

73. *Pittsburg Gazette*, June 29, 1894, p. 3. Also see *Pittsburg Gazette*, August 3, 24, September 28, 1894; Cantrell and Barton, "Texas Populists," 661–692.

74. Dohoney, *Average American*, 132–254; Barr, *Reconstruction to Reform*, 85–86.

75. *Cooper Review*, July 9, 1909, p. 4. For a fuller discussion of how social and cultural characteristics impacted reformers, see Ownby, *Subduing Satan*, 167–193.

76. For examples of the fence and stock law debate, see *Omaha Breeze*, September 30, 1908; *Pittsburg Gazette*, October 31, 1902; *Atlanta News*, July 23, 1908, and January 14, 1909. For the general decline in stock ownership that accompanied increased cultivation of cotton, see Wilkison, "End of Independence," 55–96.

77. R. Martin, *People's Party*, 93, 221–224; W. R. Miller, "Harrison County Methods," 122–123.

78. J. H. Davis, *Memoir*, 19, 54–71, 270–273, 317–324; Chapin Ross, "A Historical and Critical Study of the Public Address of James Harvey 'Cyclone' Davis [1853–1941] of Texas" (Ph.D. dissertation, University of Southern California, 1969); *New HOT*, vol. 2, 530–531; *Pittsburg Gazette*, May 25, June 22, October 12, November 16, 23, 1894; *Sulphur Springs Gazette*, October 18, 25, 1912.

79. *Dallas Morning News*, May 8, 1900; *New HOT*, vol. 2, 436; *Pittsburg Gazette*, September 7, 14, 21, 28, October 12, 1894; *Jefferson Jimplecute*, May 11, 1900; Leonard Schlup, "Political, Patriarch: David B. Culberson and the Politics of Railroad Building, Tariff Reform, and Silver Coinage in Post-Civil War America," *East Texas Historical Journal (ETHJ)* 34 (spring 1996): 30–39. On Culberson's backing of prohibition and railroad regulation, see *Clarksville Standard*, February 18, April 22, June 23, 30, August 18, 1887.

80. *Pittsburg Gazette*, July 21, 27, 1894, p. 1–3.

81. Each county received a proportion of the delegates for the district convention determined by their vote for the Democratic party in the last election. Thus Camp with relatively few Democratic voters got one delegate and Lamar with many Democrats got fourteen. See *Pittsburg Gazette*, July 27, 1894, p. 3.

82. *Pittsburg Gazette*, June 15, 22, 29, July 13, 20, 27, August 3, 10, 17, 24, September 7, 1894, p. 1–3.

83. *Pittsburg Gazette*, September 7, 1894, p. 2.

84. *Pittsburg Gazette*, June 15, 22, 29, July 13, 20, August 3, 1894, p. 1–4.

85. *Pittsburg Gazette*, November 11, 1892, and May 25, November 23, 1894.

86. Election Returns, 1894: Secretary of State; Cantrell, *Kenneth and John B. Rayner*, 215–216; Cantrell and Barton, "Texas Populists," 667–674; R. Martin, *People's Party*, 185, 221 n. 72.

87. Election Returns, 1894: Secretary of State; R. Martin, *People's Party*, 93–97, 185 n. 72.

88. D. B. Culberson, quoted in *Pittsburg Gazette*, September 28, 1894, p. 3.

89. *Pittsburg Gazette*, June 15, 1894, p. 2. Also see *Pittsburg Gazette*, August 24, September 7, 14, 21, 28, October 12, 19, 26, November 2, 9, 1894; *Dallas Morning News*, October 25, November 7, 8, 9, 1894.

90. *Pittsburg Gazette*, May 25, 1894, p. 2, and November 2, 1894, p. 2. Also see D. B. Culberson in *Pittsburg Gazette*, September 28, 1894, p. 3, and October 26, November 2, 1894; 1894 broadside, Biard Papers.

91. *Pittsburg Gazette,* November 2, 1894, p. 2.

92. Election Returns, 1894: Secretary of State; *Pittsburg Gazette,* February 1, 1895, p. 2.

93. J. H. Davis, *Memoir,* 70. Also see R. Martin, *People's Party,* 93 note 8, 185 n. 72; *Pittsburg Gazette,* November 11, 1892, and November 16, 1894; Election Returns, 1896: Camp.

94. *Pittsburg Gazette,* November 16, 1894, p. 2.

95. Election Returns, 1894: Secretary of State; *Pittsburg Gazette,* January 4, February 15, 1895; *Dallas Morning News,* February 12, 1895.

96. *Dallas Morning News,* April 2, 3, 1893, and April 7, 26, 1895; R. Martin, *People's Party,* 222–224; Goodwyn, "Populist Dreams and Negro Rights," 1435–1456. Camp was mistakenly included in Martin's list of counties where the judicial function was removed after Populist victories in 1892. Actually Camp's judicial functions were removed in 1883 before Populism and the county went Democratic in 1892. See *Pittsburg Gazette,* May 3, 1895.

97. J. H. Davis, *Memoir,* 54–71, 317. Also see U.S., *Census: 1900, Population,* vol. 1, pt. 1, 601–604, 643.

98. *Pittsburg Gazette,* November 2, 9, 16, 1896; *Jefferson Jimplecute,* September 5, 1896.

99. *Pittsburg Gazette,* November 2, 9, 16, 1896; Election Returns, 1896: Secretary of State; Kingston, Attlesey, and Crawford, *Political History of Texas,* 50–69, 72–83.

100. One of the important controversies in the history of Texas politics is the extent to which Populists returned to the Democratic party. What is often missed is that they started returning as early as 1896. Thus any statistical study that bases the Populist voting strength on 1896 or later undercounts the Populists that returned to the Democrats. See W. R. Miller, "Progressive Coalition in Texas," 163–182; M. L. Williams, "Political Career of Cyclone Davis," 32–45.

101. Gold Democrats received a significant vote in Lamar but nowhere else. See Election Returns, 1896, Secretary of State; *Pittsburg Gazette,* November 2, 9, 16, 1896.

102. While the Prohibition party fielded a candidate both in the district and the state, the party drew less than 0.5 percent of the vote. See Election Returns, 1896: Secretary of State; Kingston, Attlesey, and Crawford, *Political History of Texas,* 66–79.

103. Election Returns, 1896: Secretary of State. For a good discussion of voting tendencies, see W. R. Miller, "Harrison County Methods."

104. Election Returns, 1896: Camp, Cass, Secretary of State.

105. Election returns, 1896: Hopkins, Franklin.

106. While population did not grow at a steady rate over the 1890s, adding 60 percent of the gain from 1890 to 1900 to the 1890 total gives a rough approximation of the 1896 voting pool. Lamar's population, including its rural areas, grew more than that of any other county. This high growth rate suggests fraud but raises the possibility that potential voters new to the county simply failed to vote. See Election Returns, 1896: Lamar, Secretary of State; U.S., *Census: 1890, Population,* vol. 1, 782–785; U.S., *Census: 1900, Population,* vol. 2, 203–206.

107. Hale, *Making Whiteness*, 3. Also see Ownby, *Subduing Satan*, 169–174.

108. Grantham, *Southern Progressivism*, 36–107.

CHAPTER 2: COMPETITION, INNOVATION, AND
A CHANGING ECONOMY, 1897–1914

1. For a good starting point on the impact of economic change in this era, see W. A. Owens, *This Stubborn Soil* (New York: Scribner's, 1966). For the literature on the Texas economy, see Buenger, "Flight From Modernity," in *Texas through Time*, 310–341.

2. On world demand for cotton, see U.S. Department of Agriculture (USDA), *Yearbook, 1900* (Washington: Government Printing Office, 1901), 810; Wright, *Old South, New South*, 117–123. On the local economy, see *Pittsburg Gazette*, November 16, December 14, 21, 1900.

3. Charles P. Zlatkovich, *Texas Railroads: A Record of Construction and Abandonment* (Austin: Bureau of Business Research and Texas State Historical Association, 1981), 5; *New HOT*, vol. 2, 767, vol. 5, 759–760, vol. 6, 403.

4. On the impact of the second stage of railroad construction and operation, see Robert S. Maxwell and Robert D. Baker, *Sawdust Empire: The Texas Lumber Industry, 1830–1940* (College Station: Texas A&M University Press, 1983), 34–50; Walter L. Buenger and Joseph A. Pratt, *But Also Good Business: Texas Commerce Banks and the Financing of Houston and Texas, 1886–1986* (College Station: Texas A&M University Press, 1986), 12–63; Interviews with Tom Carter by Walter L. Buenger and Joseph A. Pratt, July 13, 1983, and April 2, 1986, TCB Collection (Carter's family owned both a railroad and a lumber company near the Northeast Texas region). Scholars have long noted the impact of railroads on the post-Reconstruction South but seldom distinguish between the different stages of impact. See Ayers, *Promise of the New South*, 3–33, 437.

5. *New HOT*, vol. 6, 384–386; *Jefferson Jimplecute*, January 22, February 5, 1890.

6. *Pittsburg Gazette*, May 18, June 1, June 15, September 7, 1900, and March 14, July 11, 18, September 12, October 3, 1902; *New HOT*, vol. 2, 767, vol. 5, 759–761, vol. 6, 403; *Texas Almanac and State Industrial Guide, 1904* (Galveston: A. H. Belo & Co., 1904), 164–168.

7. Although almost entirely owned by the Santa Fe, the GC&SF continued to operate under its own name. See *New HOT*, vol. 3, 376–377; Charles S. Potts, "Railroad Transportation in Texas," *Bulletin of the University of Texas* no. 119 (Austin: University of Texas, 1909).

8. Because of Texas law, the T&SF technically continued to exist as a separate system but for all intents and purposes disappeared after the purchase by the KCS. See Zlatkovich, *Texas Railroads*, 61–95; *New HOT*, vol. 3, 1030, vol. 6, 272–273.

9. *Pittsburg Gazette*, October 28, 1904, and January 3, 1913; *Paris News*, April 2, 1922; A. W. Neville, "When the Railroads Came," *The Red River Valley: Then and Now* (Paris: North Texas Publishing, 1948), 197–200; *Texas Alma-*

nac, 1904, 164–168, 217–218, 309–310; *New HOT,* vol. 3, 376–377, vol. 5, 53–54, vol. 6, 363–364; Potts, "Railroad Transportation in Texas," (1909); Arthur H. Lewis, *The Day They Shook the Plum Tree* (New York: Harcourt, Brace, 1963), 87–92.

10. *Pittsburg Gazette,* October 28, 1904; *Cooper Review,* January 22, April 9, October 8, 1909; *Omaha Breeze,* June 7, 1911, and May 29, June 5, 1912; *Paris Morning News,* May 14, 1922; Interstate Commerce Commission, Bureau of Statistics, *Interstate Commerce Commission Activities, 1887–1937* (Washington: Government Printing Office, 1938), 241–242; Maxwell and Baker, *Sawdust Empire,* 48–50; *New HOT,* vol. 2, 566–567, vol. 3, 1030, 1092, vol. 5, 53–54, vol. 6, 272; *Texas Almanac, 1904,* 164–168.

11. *Pittsburg Gazette,* March 14, 1902, p. 4. Also see Zlatkovich, *Texas Railroads,* 42–43, 75–85; *Pittsburg Gazette,* July 11, 18, September 12, 1902.

12. *Omaha Breeze,* June 7, 1911, and May 29, June 5, 1912; Robert H. Ryan, Charles T. Clark, and L. L. Schkade, *Paris, Texas: From Farm to Factory* (Austin: University of Texas Bureau of Business Research, 1963), 2–5; Porter A. Bywaters, Jr., "The Organization and Management of the Bywaters Dry Goods Company," bachelors thesis in business administration, University of Texas, May 20, 1925, vertical file, Barker Texas History Center, University of Texas at Austin.

13. *Jefferson Jimplecute,* July 4, 1912. *Pittsburg Gazette,* August 29, 1902; October 28, 1904; January 3, 1913. *Naples Monitor,* February 20, 1925. *Texas Almanac, 1904,* 164–168. *Texas Almanac and State Industrial Guide, 1914* (Galveston: A. H. Belo & Co., 1914), 137–142. *Texas Almanac and State Industrial Guide, 1925* (Dallas: A. H. Belo & Co., 1925), 250–351. U.S., *Census of Manufactures, 1914* (Washington: Government Printing Office, 1918), vol. 1, 1468.

14. *Omaha Breeze,* June 7, 1911, p. 2. *Jefferson Jimplecute,* May 5, 1911; July 4, 1912; November 13, 1913; May 21, 1914. *Atlanta News,* August 27, 1908. *Cass County Sun,* December 7, 1909. *New HOT,* vol. 3, 929.

15. The best survey on the Texas lumber industry is Maxwell and Baker, *Sawdust Empire,* but it focuses on Southeast Texas. For the changing importance of lumber in Northeast Texas compare the county entries in *Texas Almanac, 1904,* 217–374; *Texas Almanac, 1914,* 246–337; *Texas Almanac, 1925,* 250–351.

16. *Texas Almanac, 1904,* 217–218.

17. Information on black workers in lumber and railroads is scarce, but when racial incidents occurred, they received coverage in the local media. See *Texarkana Texarkanian,* October 6, November 23, 1905; *Pittsburg Gazette,* July 4, 1902. Also see Ruth Alice Allen, *East Texas Lumber Workers: An Economic and Social Picture, 1870–1950* (Austin: University of Texas Press, 1961), 56–87; Thad Sitton and James H. Conrad, *Nameless Towns: Texas Sawmill Communities, 1880–1942* (Austin: University of Texas Press, 1998); Maxwell and Baker, *Sawdust Empire,* 116–135.

18. U.S., *Census of Manufactures, 1914,* vol. 1, 1464. Also see U.S., *Census: 1900, Manufactures* (Washington: U.S. Government Printing Office, 1903), vol. 7, pt. 2, 1066; U.S., *Census of Manufactures, 1905,* pt. 2, (Washington: Government Printing Office, 1907), 1066–1067. By 1914 petroleum refining contributed greatly to

the value of goods manufactured in Texas, but before that lumber led the way. See U.S., *Census of Manufactures, 1914*, vol. 1, 1465-1466. Compare Texas to the story of other southern states given in Wright, *Old South, New South*, 156-197.

19. On wages in the southern states, see Wright, *Old South, New South*, 202; Abraham Bergland, George T. Starnes, and Frank T. De Vyver, *Labor in the Industrial South* (Charlottesville: University of Virginia Institute for Research in the Social Sciences, 1930), 41. Also see Ayers, *Promise of the New South*, 21-22, 453-456 n. 43; *Census of Manufactures, 1914*, vol. 1, 1463-1468; Speech by O. P. Leonard, 1938, Marvin Leonard Papers (author's possession); *Omaha Breeze*, January 22, 1908, p. 2.

20. *Texarkana Texarkanian*, November 26, 1905. Also see Maxwell and Baker, *Sawdust Empire*, 111. When editors started warning blacks of the dangers of moving to cities, it was a sure sign of such movement. See *Pittsburg Gazette*, May 27, June 3, 1904.

21. Maxwell and Baker, *Sawdust Empire*, 118; Interview with Enola Moulton by John David Scott, in John David Scott, "Obie," (typescript, 1983, Leonard Collection), 121-128; Interview with Hugh and Laura Mae Tyree by Walter Buenger, July 1, 1994, Leonard Collection; J. D. Scott, "Obie," 23-26; Speech by O. P. Leonard, 1938.

22. Also see *Cass County Sun*, October 19, December 7, 1909; *Omaha Breeze*, May 17, June 7, 1911; Maxwell and Baker, *Sawdust Empire*, 34-50; Artemesia Lucille Brison Spencer, *The Camp County Story* (Fort Worth: Branch-Smith, 1974), 76-77; Barbara Overton Chandler, "A History of Bowie County" (master's thesis, University of Texas, 1937), 52-67; Myreline Bowman, *People of Cass County: Atlanta and Queen City, Texas* (Queen City: privately published, 1973), 110; Brown and Gust, *Between the Creeks*, xii-xiii.

23. Wright, *Old South, New South*, 14.

24. *Cooper Review*, January 15, 1909, p. 1. Also see *Cooper Review*, May 8, 1908; *Jefferson Jimplecute*, April 7, 1911; Samuel Lee Evans, "Texas Agriculture, 1880-1930" (Ph.D. dissertation, University of Texas, 1960), 347-357; *New HOT*, vol. 3, 1141-1142, vol. 6, 282-283; Robert L. Haney, *Milestones: Marking Ten Decades of Research* (College Station: Texas Agricultural Experiment Station, 1989), 2-8, 89-102.

25. *Jefferson Jimplecute*, May 5, 1911, and July 30, November 12, December 31, 1914; *Atlanta News*, May 28, July 23, August 27, November 12, 1908; *Atlanta News*, December 29, 1910; *Cooper Review*, May 1, December 25, 1908; *Cooper Review*, January 15, 1909; *Omaha Breeze*, June 2, 30, 1909; *Omaha Breeze*, October 11, 1910, and May 29, June 5, 1912; *Pittsburg Gazette*, July 18, 25, November 21, 1902; *Sulphur Springs Gazette*, August 16, September 13, 1912. Also see S. L. Evans, "Texas Agriculture," 7-49, 141-199.

26. Houston perhaps benefited most from the arrival of these energetic entrepreneurs, but they were found throughout the state. See Buenger and Pratt, *But Also Good Business*, 12-64. For nuanced treatments of the ways in which the South's economy was and was not a colonial economy, see Wright, *Old South, New South*, 10-16, 156-197; Ayers, *Promise of the New South*, 104-131. Wright, however, indicates capitalists seldom followed their capital to the South. See Wright,

Old South, New South, 62-64. In the lumber industry, building up an identification with the local inhabitants often brought economic advantages because it slowed the incidence of arson. See Maxwell and Baker, *Sawdust Empire,* 66-69, 111-113.

27. Lewis, *Day They Shook the Plum Tree,* 118. Also see *New HOT,* vol. 3, 312-313, 1141-1142; *Paris Morning News,* May 25, 1922; Lewis, *Day They Shook the Plum Tree,* 74-239. Contrast Green and Knox to the portrait of typical southern power brokers drawn in Wright, *Old South, New South,* 122-123.

28. Lewis, *Day They Shook the Plum Tree,* 74-92.

29. *Pittsburg Gazette,* April 15, 1904; *Sulphur Springs Gazette,* July 5, 1912; *Cooper Review,* October 4, 1912; Joseph M. Grant and Lawrence L. Crum, *The Development of State-Chartered Banking in Texas* (Austin: Bureau of Business Research, University of Texas, 1978), 3-70; Spencer, *Camp County Story,* 161-162.

30. *Pittsburg Gazette,* April 15, May 27, November 25, 1904. A new national bank also was organized in Jefferson in October 1904. See *Jefferson Jimplecute,* October 29, 1904. Also see Buenger and Pratt, *But Also Good Business,* 40-63; "First National Bank, Oldest in Delta County," *Cooper Review,* October 4, 1912.

31. *Pittsburg Gazette,* February 23, 1900; December 27, 1901; February 7, 1902; February 5, April 8, July 15, September 9, November 18, 1904; January 13, 1905; December 18, 1911. Also see Spencer, *Camp County Story,* 180.

32. Grant and Crum, *State-Chartered Banking in Texas,* 47-90; Buenger and Pratt, *But Also Good Business,* 40-63.

33. *Jefferson Jimplecute,* October 24, 1912, p. 3. Also see *Pittsburg Gazette,* November 25, 1904; January 13, 1905; November 15, 1907.

34. *Pittsburg Gazette,* October 25, November 1, 8, 15, 22, 1907. For other examples of the cooperation between banks and businesses during the panic, see *Atlanta Citizens Journal,* October 31, 1907; *Omaha Breeze,* January 8, 15, 1908; *Cooper Review,* January 24, 1908. On the Panic of 1907 and the nature of the American banking system before the creation of the Federal Reserve, see Eugene Nelson White, *The Regulation and Reform of the American Banking System, 1900-1929* (Princeton: Princeton University Press, 1983), 3-125.

35. U.S., *Census: 1910, Population* (Washington, D.C.: Government Printing Office, 1913), vol. 3, 806-846; *Pittsburg Gazette,* August 12, 1904, and December 15, 1911; *Jefferson Jimplecute,* January 20, 1911; H. P. Burford, "Cookville, Texas," in Traylor Russell, *A History of Titus County* (Waco: W. M. Morrison, 1965), 198-204; *Omaha Breeze,* May 1, 1912, p. 1; *Texas Almanac and State Industrial Guide, 1911* (Galveston: A. H. Belo & Company, 1911), 32-34.

36. Grant and Crum, *State-Chartered Banking in Texas,* 37-90; Buenger and Pratt, *But Also Good Business,* 40-63; John Roy Mitchell, "The Limits of Reform: Major Financial Legislation in Texas, 1904-1910" (master's thesis, Texas A&M University, 1989). Kirby, *Rural Worlds Lost,* 22, cites lack of capital as a primary reason for the delayed transformation of the entire South.

37. Also see *Omaha Breeze,* September 30, 1908, and May 1, 29, 1912; Quentin Miller, *The First Sixty Years of the Delta National Bank, Cooper, Delta County Texas, 1900-1960* (Cooper, privately published, 1960), 14-24; *Red River Recollections* (Clarksville, Texas: Red River County Historical Society, 1986), 420-422.

38. *Atlanta Citizens Journal,* December 19, 1907. *Cass County Sun,* January 21,

February 4, April 14, 1908. *Atlanta News,* March 19, 1908. *Cooper Review,* March 26, 1909, and October 4, 1912. *Pittsburg Gazette,* March 2, October 19, December 7, 1917. *Jefferson Jimplecute,* January 13, 20, March 17, 1911; April 10, 1913; July 2, 9, 1914. *Paris Morning News,* April 1, 1912. As late as 1914, T. P. Hanks, the area agricultural agent, complained that banks were not willing to lend on other crops besides cotton. See *Jefferson Jimplecute,* October 28, 1914, p. 1.

39. Walton Peteet, "Farming Credit in Texas," Extension Service Bulletin no. B-34 (College Station: Extension Service of the Agricultural and Mechanical College of Texas, 1917), 5; Lewis H. Haney, "Farm Credit in a Cotton State," *American Economic Review* 4 (March 1914): 51–52. Also see Peteet, "Farming Credit," 11–18; L. H. Haney, "Farm Credit," 47–61; Charles B. Austin, "Co-Operation in Agriculture: Marketing and Rural Credit" (Austin: University of Texas, 1914), 71–95. Haney and Austin completed their studies before the destabilization caused by the start of World War I in August 1914. Peteet waited until the credit markets calmed in 1915 before initiating his study. Also see S. L. Evans, "Texas Agriculture," 329–346.

40. Thomas D. Clark, *Pills, Petticoats and Plows: The Southern Country Store* (Indianapolis: Bobbs-Merrill, 1944), 22. Also see Ayers, *Promise of the New South,* 13–15, 94, 451–452 n. 22; Fite, *Cotton Fields No More,* 22–24; Harold D. Woodman, *King Cotton and His Retainers: Financing and Marketing the Cotton Crop of the South, 1800–1925* (Lexington: University of Kentucky Press, 1968 [reprinted Columbia: University of South Carolina Press, 1990]), 295–314. Piggly Wiggly, which introduced self-service and stressed the advantages of cash only in their advertisements, revolutionized the grocery industry. It began in Memphis in 1916 and soon entered Texas. See Susan Strasser, *Satisfaction Guaranteed: The Making of the American Mass Market* (New York: Pantheon Books, 1989), 202–251; Richard Tedlow, *New and Improved: The Story of Mass Marketing in America* (New York: Basic Books, 1990), 182–258; Buenger and Buenger, *Texas Merchant,* 15–31.

41. *Pittsburg Gazette,* February 13, 1884; June 24, July 8, 1904; December 29, 1911. *Sulphur Springs Gazette,* January 12, 1912. Spencer, *Camp County Story,* 62–63, 180, 183. For a description of the furnishing-merchant system at the end of its life, see Charles S. Johnson, Edwin R. Embree, and W. W. Alexander, *The Collapse of Cotton Tenancy* (Chapel Hill: University of North Carolina Press, 1935), 25–33. For useful historiographic comments, see Harold D. Woodman, "Introduction to Southern Classics Series Edition," *King Cotton* (1990), xiii–xix.

42. *Sulphur Springs Gazette,* January 13, 1911, p. 1. Also see Peteet, "Farming Credit," 3–24; E. V. White and William E. Leonard, "Studies in Farm Tenancy in Texas," *University of Texas Bulletin* no. 21 (Austin: University of Texas, 1915); William Bennett Bizzell, *Farm Tenantry in the United States* (College Station: Experiment Station, Agricultural and Mechanical College of Texas, 1921), 211–221; Spencer, *Camp County Story,* 180.

43. These observations are based on a careful reading of the *Pittsburg Gazette,* 1904–1917; *Jefferson Jimplecute,* 1904–1918; *Cooper Review,* 1908–1918; *Sulphur Springs Gazette,* 1911–1914; *Omaha Breeze,* 1908–1912. These newspapers list bank directors and provide biographical information on many of them. On loan

committees and directors, see Buenger and Pratt, *But Also Good Business*, 40-261; Buenger and Buenger, *Texas Merchant*, 146-156.

44. Peteet, "Farming Credit," 15.

45. For contemporary accounts of the transformation of retailing, see Simon S. Kuznets, *Cyclical Fluctuations: Retail and Wholesale Trade, United States, 1919-1925* (Westport, Connecticut: Hyperion Press, 1926); J. George Frederick, "The Chain Store," *American Review of Reviewers* 70 (September 1924): 297-299; Walter S. Hayward, "The Chain Store and Distribution," *Annals of the American Academy of Political and Social Science* 115 (September 1924): 220-225; Ruel McDaniel, "How Those Amazing Leonard Brothers Gross $8,000,000 A Year," *American Business* 8 (October 1938): 22-24, 48-49. Also see Susan Porter Benson, *Counter Cultures: Saleswomen, Managers, and Customers in American Department Stores, 1890-1940* (Chicago: University of Illinois Press, 1986), 12-74; William Leach, *Land of Desire: Merchants, Power, and the Rise of a New American Culture* (New York: Pantheon Books, 1993); Alan R. Raucher, "Dime Store Chains: The Making of Organization Men, 1880-1940," *Business History Review* 65 (spring 1991): 130-163; Peter Samson, "The Department Store, Its Past and Its Future: A Review Article," *Business History Review* 55 (spring 1981): 26-34; Strasser, *Satisfaction Guaranteed*, 203-251; Tedlow, *New and Improved*, 3-21; Buenger and Buenger, *Texas Merchant*, 15-60.

46. On the new methods of distribution, see Strasser, *Satisfaction Guaranteed*, 58-88. Also see "Monnig Dry Goods Co. Twenty-Third Anniversary Section," *Fort Worth Star-Telegram*, April 7, 1912; Otto Monnig, General Manager of Monnig Dry Goods Company, to Miss Betty Jane Jones, January 11, 1934, in Box 3, no. 7, Business History, Miscellaneous Manuscripts (Local History Division, Forth Worth Public Library); Tedlow, *New and Improved*, 259-343; Leon Joseph Rosenberg, *Sangers': Pioneer Texas Merchants* (Austin: Texas State Historical Association, 1978), 61-92; Boris Emmet and John E. Jeuck, *Catalogues and Counters: A History of Sears, Roebuck and Company* (Chicago: University of Chicago Press, 1950), 23-195.

47. Emmet and Jeuck, *Catalogues and Counters*, 23-84; *Atlanta News*, February 4, 1909, p. 1; *Fort Worth Star-Telegram*, September 30, 1928, p. 1.

48. *Cass County Sun*, February 4, 1908, p. 3. On mail-order houses and the new parcel-post system, see *Jefferson Jimplecute*, November 27, 1913 p. 2; Emmet and Jeuck, *Catalogues and Counters*, 150-195.

49. *Cooper Review*, March 20, 1908 p. 4; *Jefferson Jimplecute*, November 27, 1913, p. 2. Also see *Cass County Sun*, September 1, 1908; *Atlanta News*, Feb 4, 1909; *Omaha Breeze*, September 15, 1909; *Cumby Rustler*, January 12, April 19, 1912.

50. *Atlanta News*, Feb 4, 1909, p. 1.

51. *Atlanta News*, January 7, 1909, p. 1. For the figures to back up Knapp's analysis, see Peteet, "Farming Credit," 7; White and Leonard, "Farm Tenantry in Texas," 49-52.

52. *Atlanta News*, April 9, 1908; *Cass County Sun*, January 12, 1909; *Jefferson Jimplecute*, January 20, 1911, and May 30, September 19, October 17, 1912; *Cumby*

Rustler, April 19, May 31, June 7, July 5, 1912; *Paris Morning News,* January 1, February 16, April 9, 1922. For the obituary of the founder of Perkins Bros., see *Jefferson Jimplecute,* July 19, 1917, p. 1. Also see Peteet, "Farming Credit," 15.

53. *Cooper Review* (Special Edition), March 26, 1909, p. 1. Also see *Jefferson Jimplecute,* December 18, 24, 1914. According to the *Paris Morning News,* July 5, 1922, Penney's had nineteen stores in Texas, including the Paris store established a few years earlier. On the S. H. Kress store in Paris, see William A. Owens, *A Season of Weathering* (New York: Scribner's, 1973), 37-91.

54. *Cass County Sun,* February 18, 1908, p. 4; *Pittsburg Gazette,* January 3, 1919, p. 3. Also see the advertisements and agricultural columns of the following newspapers: *Pittsburg Gazette, Atlanta News, Jefferson Jimplecute, Paris Morning News, Texarkana Texarkanian, Cooper Review, Omaha Breeze.*

55. Peteet, "Farming Credit," 26. Also see Peteet, "Farming Credit," 7-10.

56. *Jefferson Jimplecute,* September 19, 1912; *Cumby Rustler,* January 5, 12, April 19, May 31, July 5, 1912; *Pittsburg Gazette,* January 8, 1904, and August 4, October 6, 1911; *Atlanta News,* January 14, 1909; *Omaha Breeze,* September 29, 1909.

57. *Omaha Breeze,* June 7, 1911, p. 2. Also see *Pittsburg Gazette,* 1901-1910; *Jefferson Jimplecute,* 1901-1910; *Atlanta News,* 1910; *Cass County Sun,* 1908-1909; *Paris Morning News,* 1909-1911; Tedlow, *New and Improved,* 4-21.

58. *Jefferson Jimplecute,* April 20, 1916, p. 1. Also see Interview with Lloyd Shockley and Ruth Shockley by Walter Buenger, June 28, 1995, Leonard Collection. On the limits of change from pre-World War I to the interwar years, see Johnson, Embree, and Alexander, *Collapse of Cotton Tenancy,* 1-69; Bizzell, *Farm Tenantry,* 107-393. On how credit stores competed with cash stores by giving rebates to landlords who instead of cash advances gave their black and Tejano croppers credit allowances at these credit stores, see David Montejano, *Anglos and Mexicans in the Making of Texas, 1836-1986* (Austin: University of Texas Press, 1987), 240-242.

59. Peteet, "Farming Credit," 40; *Chicago Defender,* May 6, 1916.

60. U.S., *Census: 1880, Report on Cotton Production in the United States* (Washington: Government Printing Office, 1884), pt. 1, 59-72; U.S., *Census: 1890, Agriculture* (Washington: Government Printing Office, 1895), vol. 1, xxx; U.S., *Census: 1900, Agriculture* (Washington: Government Printing Office, 1902), vol. 6, pt. 2, 184-187, 260-263, 391-394, 434-435, 573-575, 743-745; U.S., *Census: 1910, Agriculture* (Washington: Government Printing Office, 1913), vol. 7, 680-698; U.S., *Census: 1920, Agriculture* (Washington: Government Printing Office, 1922), vol. 6, pt. 2, 716-735; U.S., *Census: 1930, Agriculture* (Washington: Government Printing Office, 1932), vol. 2, pt. 2, 1468-1569.

61. USDA, *Yearbook, 1900,* 806. Newly harvested cotton began moving on the market in August, and the crop year price came from the average of August through July prices on the spot market. For monthly prices on the major cotton markets, see "Spot Cotton Prices, 1900-1928," *The Texas Almanac and State Industrial Guide, 1929* (Dallas: A. H. Belo, 1929), 106; USDA, *Yearbook, 1900,* 813-814; USDA, *Yearbook, 1905* (Washington, Government Printing Office, 1906), 713; USDA, *Yearbook of Agriculture, 1922* (Washington: Government Printing Office,

1923), 718; USDA, *Yearbook of Agriculture, 1934* (Washington: Government Printing Office, 1934), 466. Fite, *Cotton Fields No More,* 84, claimed that the price surpassed 10 cents in only three of those years and stressed the lack of significant change in agriculture before World War I. Wright, *Old South, New South,* 115-123, provided data indicating that cotton prices went sharply upward from 1903 to 1914. Writers for the *Texas Almanac* sometimes exaggerated their claims in their zeal to promote Texas, but for two reasonably balanced and generally positive appraisals of the state's cotton industry, see *Texas Almanac, 1904,* 92-95; *Texas Almanac and State Industrial Guide, 1926* (Dallas: A. H. Belo, 1926), 135-143.

62. *Texas Almanac, 1904,* 142-143, 249, 291, 309-310; William Bennett Bizzell, *Rural Texas* (New York: Macmillan, 1924), 265-269; U.S., *Census of Manufactures, 1914,* vol. 1, 1464-1465. On the smell and image of a cottonseed mill, see Humphrey, *Farther off from Heaven,* 242.

63. *Pittsburg Gazette,* January 24, 1902, p. 1, and March 29, 1918, p. 2; Ryan, Clark, and Schkade, *Paris, Texas,* 5, 89-97; *Texas Almanac, 1929,* 338-339; Lamar Fleming, Jr., *Growth of the Business of Anderson, Clayton and Co.,* edited by James A. Tinsley (Houston: Texas Gulf Coast Historical Association, 1966), 5-21.

64. "Spot Cotton Prices, 1900-1928," 106.

65. For a description of many of the large cotton firms doing business in Texas, see S. Deane Wasson, *Fifty Years a Cotton Market: Houston Cotton Exchange and Board of Trade Brochure, 1924* (Houston: Houston Cotton Exchange, 1924), 14-106. On the related firms of Neil P. Anderson and Anderson, Clayton, see Fleming, *Anderson, Clayton,* 1-5; Benjamin Clayton, *Notes on Some Phases of Cotton Operations, 1905-1929* (Houston: privately printed, 1966), 17-50; Interview with James Blair by Walter Buenger, July 6, 1995, Leonard Collection (Blair worked for Neil Anderson in the 1920s); Interview with S. M. McAshan by Walter L. Buenger and Joseph A. Pratt, January 4, 1985, Texas Commerce Bank Collection (McAshan married the daughter of Will Clayton and served as president of Anderson, Clayton). Also see J. R. Killick, "The Transformation of Cotton Marketing in the Late Nineteenth Century: Alexander Sprunt and Son of Wilmington, N.C., 1884-1956," *Business History Review* 55 (summer 1981): 143-169; Kenneth J. Lipartito, "The New York Cotton Exchange and the Development of the Cotton Futures Market," *Business History Review* 57 (spring 1983): 50-72.

66. Wasson, *Fifty Years a Cotton Market,* 87; Woodman, *King Cotton,* 288-294; Killick, "Transformation of Cotton Marketing," 143-150.

67. Fleming, *Anderson, Clayton,* 1-21; Woodman, *King Cotton,* 288-294; Buenger and Pratt, *But Also Good Business,* 64-73; Interview with McAshan by Buenger and Pratt. On the general principles of hedging, see Peter S. Rose, *Money and Capital Markets: The Financial System in the Economy* (Plano, Texas: Business Publications, 1983), 330-333. Also see Lipartito, "The New York Cotton Exchange," 50-72.

68. Peteet, "Farming Credit," 11. Also see Bizzell, *Farm Tenantry,* 219-220. For the memories of one Lamar County planter, ginner, and cotton buyer, see Interview with C. R. McClure by Corrine E. Crow, November 7, 1973, typescript, Cotton History Project, East Texas State University. (McClure began working at his father's gin in 1903.)

69. *Pittsburg Gazette,* July 1, 1904, p. 5; August 23, 1907; August 11, 1911. Fite, *Cotton Fields No More,* 62–65. Robert L. Hunt, *A History of Farmer Movements in the Southwest, 1873-1925* (College Station: Texas A&M, 1935), 41–143.

70. On post–Civil War changes in cotton marketing, see Woodman, *King Cotton,* 243–360. Also see Interview with McClure by Crow, 10–13, 23–38.

71. *Pittsburg Gazette,* January 5, 1900, p. 1; December 9, 16, 23, 1904; January 6, 13, 1905.

72. *Omaha Breeze,* January 24, 1912, p. 2. For extensive quotes from Will Clayton on how this process worked, see Ellen Clayton Garwood, *Will Clayton: A Short Biography* (Austin: University of Texas Press, 1958), 95–101.

73. *Omaha Breeze,* September 27, October 18, 1911. On communicating the latest changes in cotton prices, see *Pittsburg Gazette,* July 25, 1902 p. 1.

74. First quote in *Omaha Breeze,* January 8, 1908, p. 2; *Sulphur Springs Gazette,* August 7, 1914, p. 2. Also see *Jefferson Jimplecute,* July 9, 1914.

75. *Omaha Breeze,* February 7, 1912, p. 2. Also see *Pittsburg Gazette,* October 13, 1911, p. 2; *Jefferson Jimplecute,* February 29, 1912, p. 2; U.S., *Census: 1920. Agriculture,* vol. 6, pt. 2, 664–684. Comparisons are in 1991 dollars according to the consumer price index provided in John J. McCusker, *How Much Is That in Real Money? A Historical Price Index for Use as a Deflator of Money Values in the Economy of the United States* (Worcester: American Antiquarian Society, 1992), 312, 329–332.

76. *Sulphur Springs Gazette,* August 7, 1914, p. 2.

77. J. T. Sanders, "Farm Ownership and Tenancy in the Black Prairie of Texas," *USDA Bulletin* no. 1068 (Washington: Government Printing Office, 1922), 5–9; Owens, *Stubborn Soil,* 31–37; Fite, *Cotton Fields No More,* 109–110, 150–158; Interview with McClure by Crow, 15–17.

78. C. O. Brannen, "Relation of Land Tenure to Plantation Organization," *USDA Bulletin* no. 1269 (Washington: Government Printing Office, 1924), 24. Also see Kirby, *Rural Worlds Lost,* 1–6; Wright, *Old South, New South,* 51–70. Kirby and Wright included eastern Texas in the portion of the South in which industrialization and agricultural mechanization worked at cross purposes, and in which low acreage per farm operator limited income and efficiency. Wright indicated that large ranches in West Texas explained the higher ratio of land to labor in the state, but as Brannen understood, this also characterized eastern Texas. The census confirms this. For the ratio of land to labor in 1910, 1920, and 1925, see U.S., *Census of Agriculture, 1925* (Washington: Government Printing Office, 1927), pt. 2, 1110–1139.

79. *Cumby Rustler,* January 26, 1912, p. 6. Also see Wright, *Old South, New South,* 14. R. L. Bennet, *A Method of Breeding Early Cotton to Escape Bollworm Damage, USDA Bulletin* no. 314 (Washington: Government Printing Office, 1908). *Pittsburg Gazette,* April 12, 1912, July 10, 1914. *Jefferson Jimplecute,* October 24, 1912; May 8, 15, 22, 1913; January 15, 22, March 26, July 9, 30, 1914; October 28, 1915. *Omaha Breeze,* January 18, 1911. *Sulphur Springs Gazette,* August 16, 1912, and August 21, September 4, 11, 18, 1914. S. L. Evans, "Texas Agriculture," 3–49, 301–367. R. L. Haney, *Milestones,* 2–8. Bizzell, *Rural Texas,* 360–367. As discussed in chapter 4, Texas had the first county agents in the United States. See

Henry C. Dethloff, *A Centennial History of Texas A&M University, 1876-1976* (College Station: Texas A&M University Press, 1975), vol. 2, 382-396.

80. *Cooper Review*, March 6, 1908, and July 2, 1909; *Jefferson Jimplecute*, June 25, 1914, p. 3; Interview with McClure by Crow, 27-28. Also see J. Douglas Helms, "Just Lookin' for a Home: The Cotton Boll Weevil and the South" (Ph.D. dissertation, Florida State University, 1977); S. L. Evans, "Texas Agriculture," 50-74; W. D. Hunter, "Methods of Controlling the Boll Weevil," *USDA Bulletin* no. 163 (Washington: Government Printing Office, 1903); W. D. Hunter and W. B. Pierce, "The Mexican Cotton Boll Weevil: A Summary of the Investigations of This Insect up to December 31, 1911," *USDA Bulletin* no. 114 (Washington: Government Printing Office, 1912).

81. This is a point made in a more general way in Daniel, *Breaking the Land*, 7-18. Also see Fite, *Cotton Fields No More*, 68-90.

82. On the complexities of the tenant system, see Rex E. Willard, "A Farm Management Study of Cotton Farms of Ellis County, Texas," *USDA Bulletin* no. 659 (Washington: Government Printing Office, 1918), 2-3, 15. Ellis County closely resembled Hopkins, Lamar, and Delta counties. Also see S. L. Evans, "Texas Agriculture," 316-346; Bizzell, *Farm Tenantry*, 107-224; USDA, *Agricultural Yearbook, 1923* (Washington: Government Printing Office, 1924), 507-600; White and Leonard, "Farm Tenantry in Texas."

83. Willard, "Cotton Farms of Ellis County," 9, 21. Also see Sanders, "Ownership and Tenancy in the Black Prairie," 31-60; Earl Bryan Schwulst, *Extension of Bank Credit: A Study in the Principles of Financial Statement Analysis as Applied in Extending Bank Credit to Agriculture, Industry, and Trade in Texas* (Boston and New York: Houghton Mifflin, 1927), 98-103; Harold D. Woodman, "Sequel to Slavery: The New History Views the Postbellum South," *JSH* 43 (November 1977): 523-54; Cecil Harper, Jr., "Farming Someone Else's Land: Farm Tenancy in the Brazos River Valley, 1850-1880" (Ph.D. dissertation, University of North Texas, 1988); Kirby, *Rural Worlds Lost*, 140-141; Johnson, Embree, and Alexander, *Collapse of Cotton Tenancy*, 4-11.

84. Humphrey, *Farther off from Heaven*, 54-57.

85. Interview with Shockleys by Buenger; Interview with Moulton by J. D. Scott; Willard, "Cotton Farms of Ellis County," 14-54. For further testimony that conditions for prosperous tenants, especially those in the blacklands, were improving, see L. H. Haney, "Farm Credit," 51-54.

86. Reprinted in the *Omaha Breeze*, May 24, 1911, p. 1. For other cases of the varied status of tenants, see Foley, *White Scourge*, 64-91.

87. In 1920 there were more share croppers in Arkansas and Louisiana than share tenants. In Texas share tenants outnumbered croppers two to one, and this was about the same ratio as counties in Northeast Texas. See U.S., *Census: 1920, Agriculture*, vol. 6, pt. 2, 560, 596, 664-686.

88. Because the census did not divide croppers from share tenants until 1920, tenants in Figure 2.4 includes both types. The first mid-decade census of agriculture was in 1925. See U.S., *Census: 1920, Agriculture*, vol. 6, pt. 2, 664-686; U.S., *Census of Agriculture, 1925* (Washington: Government Printing Office, 1927), pt. 2, 1240-1263.

89. George Luther Vaughan, *The Cotton Renter's Son* (Wolfe City, Texas: Henington Publishing, 1967), 142. Land consolidation remains a difficult question to analyze because farm operators listed in the census were often not farm owners. A few studies indicate that concentration of landownership did not occur before World War I. See Sanders, "Ownership and Tenancy in the Black Prairie," 3, 15–30. As discussed later, consolidation of land ownership in Northeast Texas began during World War I and continued through the mid-1920s. See U.S., *Census of Agriculture, 1925*, pt. 2, 1110–1139.

90. See the summary of questionnaires collected in 1919 in Sanders, "Ownership and Tenancy in the Black Prairie," 19–22; and the 1915 questionnaires in Peteet, "Farming Credit," 25–79. Also see L. H. Haney, "Farm Credit," 51–54; Willard, "Cotton Farms of Ellis County," 14–40.

91. Robert A. Calvert, "Agrarian Texas," 220–224; Wright, *Old South, New South*, 81–123.

92. Quoted in the *Omaha Breeze*, February 19, 1908, p. 2. Also see *Jefferson Jimplecute*, August 26, 1915, p. 4; Peteet, "Farming Credit," 5–24; L. H. Haney, "Farm Credit," 49–50.

93. *Pittsburg Gazette*, December 29, 1911, p. 1. Also see *Pittsburg Gazette*, February 13, 1884, and June 24, July 8, 1904; *Sulphur Springs Gazette*, January 12, 1912; Spencer, *Camp County Story*, 62–62, 180, 183.

94. Sanders, "Ownership and Tenancy in the Black Prairie," 15–30; Bizzell, *Rural Texas*, 376–417.

95. Peteet, "Farming Credit," 24–79; Brannen, "Relation of Land Tenure to Plantation Organization," 19–38; Foley, *White Scourge*, 64–91.

96. *Naples Monitor*, March 13, June 12, 1925; *Paris Morning News*, January 1, February 8, 1928; *Pittsburg Gazette*, May 31, August 11, 18, 25, October 6, 13, 1911, and March 9, 16, 1928; U.S., *Census: 1920. Agriculture*, vol. 6, pt. 2, 655–56; Interview with McClure by Crow, 4–16, 35–37; L. H. Haney, "Farm Credit," 54; Brannen, "Relation of Land Tenure to Plantation Organization," 60–67.

97. In the 1914 Democratic primary, Ferguson carried the rural boxes in most Northeast Texas counties. See *Jefferson Jimplecute*, July 30, 1914; *Sulphur Springs Gazette*, July 24, 1914; *Pittsburg Gazette*, July 31, 1914. Also see Hunt, *Farmer Movements in the Southwest*, 132–142; Gould, *Progressives and Prohibitionists*, 120–221; James R. Green, "Tenant Farmer Discontent and Socialist Protest in Texas, 1901–1917," *SHQ* 81 (October 1977): 133–154. Also see the answer to question 16, "Cause of increase in tenancy?" in Peteet, "Farming Credit," 24–79.

98. For a detailed analysis of changes in wealth in neighboring Hunt County, see Wilkison, "End of Independence," 55–96. Wilkison uses 1870 as a point of comparison, but does not adjust for the impact of very rapid population growth on wealth holding. As J. T. Sanders noted eighty years ago, "The inflow of immigrants during the decade 1870 to 1880 greatly influenced the agriculture of the region, reducing stock raising to secondary place in farm enterprises, decreasing the average size of farms to about one-fifth of the average of 1860, and developing tenancy." Sanders, "Ownership and Tenancy in the Black Prairie," 7. Not surprisingly, Sanders's evaluation of changes in wealth tended to emphasize the rise of the middle and upper middle class in the early twentieth century, but he agreed that

the bottom group slid downward in the 1910s. See Sanders, "Ownership and Tenancy in the Black Prairie," 15-60. Much of the improved position of the middle and upper middle class came from the almost fivefold increase in the value of land between 1890 and 1914. See *Pittsburg Gazette*, August 5, 1904; Wilkison, "End of Independence," 61; Sanders, "Ownership and Tenancy in the Black Prairie," 28-29. Also see the summary of interviews done with farmers in 1915 in Peteet, "Farming Credit," 24-79.

99. Peteet, "Farming Credit," 27. Also see Sanders, "Ownership and Tenancy in the Black Prairie," 15-30; Willard, "Cotton Farms of Ellis County," 14-20; Bizzell, *Farm Tenantry*, 359.

100. Southerners' influence and instrumentality in the process of modernization deserves further debate. For the view that southerners lacked agency and tended to be acted upon by mechanization and government policy instead of acting themselves, see Daniel, *Breaking the Land*, xi-xvi. For a more nuanced view, see Kirby, *Rural Worlds Lost*, 1-22.

CHAPTER 3: A NEW POLITICAL ORDER, 1897-1912

1. *Pittsburg Gazette*, January 22, 1904, p. 3.

2. For a standard defense of racism and the violent elimination of black political influence, including reference to "hordes of carpetbaggers," see Moseley, "Citizens White Primary," 524-531.

3. Barr, *Reconstruction to Reform*, 186-189; *New HOT*, vol. 2, 446; Rice, *Negro in Texas*, 34-52.

4. For a fuller explanation of the link between "reform," prohibition, lynching, and religion, see chapter 1. Also see Ownby, *Subduing Satan*, 167-212.

5. W. R. Miller, "Progressive Coalition in Texas," 180-182.

6. Moseley, "Citizens White Primary," 524-531; W. R. Miller, "Harrison County Methods," 122-128; Barr, *Reconstruction to Reform*, 194-195; Darlene Clark Hine, *Black Victory: The Rise and Fall of the White Primary in Texas* (Millwood, N.Y.: KTO Press, 1979), 3-71. On whitecapping in Titus County at about the same time, see H. P. Burford, "The Race Riots in Cookville, Texas in 1898," in Russell, *Titus County*, 205-206. The spelling and word order of the Marion County primary varied. Moseley called it the Citizens White Primary. The *Jefferson Jimplecute* often referred to it as the White Citizens' Primary but sometimes reversed white and citizen and dropped the possessive. See *Jefferson Jimplecute*, November 5, 1904, and July 9, 1914.

7. Report of the spring 1898 meeting of the White Citizens in the *Jefferson Jimplecute*, quoted in Moseley, "Citizens White Primary," 526-527.

8. Moseley, "Citizens White Primary," 524-531, identifies about twenty leaders of the original White Citizens primary. He gives biographical information on a few, and additional information is found in McKay and Spelling, *History of Jefferson*. On similar Jaybird organizations, see Barr, *Reconstruction to Reform*, 193-201.

9. Moseley, "Citizens White Primary," 524-531; Cantrell and Barton, "Texas

Populists," 687–692; Bernice Rash Fine, "Agrarian Reform and the Negro Farmer in Texas, 1886–1896" (master's thesis, University of North Texas, 1971); Budd, "Negro in Politics in Texas." Between 1890 and 1902, similar events happened in other Texas counties with a black majority or where blacks were the deciding vote between two political parties. See Goodwyn, "Populist Dreams and Negro Rights," 1435–1456; Gilbert Cuthbertson, "The Jaybird Woodpecker War," *Texana* 10 (fall 1972): 297–309; W. R. Miller, "Harrison County Methods," 122–126; R. Martin, *People's Party*, 89–112; *Dallas Morning News*, November 15, 18, 22, 1894.

10. *Jefferson Jimplecute*, November 5, 1904, p. 1; *Jefferson Jimplecute*, quoted in Moseley, "Citizens White Primary," 526. On Todd, see *Pittsburg Gazette*, November 9, 1900.

11. *Jefferson Jimplecute*, quoted in Moseley, "Citizens White Primary," 527. Also see *Jefferson Jimplecute*, November 5, 12, 19, 1904. Election Returns, 1898–1904: Secretary of State, show a steady downward trend in the vote in the general election in all races and a decline in the vote for the Republican candidate for Congress.

12. *Pittsburg Gazette*, July 20, 1894, p. 3. Also see *Pittsburg Gazette*, August 17, 24, 1894.

13. *Pittsburg Gazette*, July 8, 1898, p. 3; February 16, 1900, p. 4. Also see *Pittsburg Gazette*, June 24, July 1, 8, 15, August 19, 1898; February 9, 1900; January 24, 1902. On E. A. King see *Pittsburg Gazette*, February 13, 1884; June 24, July 8, 1904; December 29, 1911. On King, also see Spencer, *Camp County Story*, 62–63, 180, 183.

14. W. R. Miller, "Progressive Coalition in Texas," 165–169; *Pittsburg Gazette*, February 16, 1900.

15. Election Returns, 1896: Secretary of State.

16. *Pittsburg Gazette*, August 12, 1898, p. 2. Also see *Pittsburg Gazette*, July 15, August 5, 19, November 2, 11, 25, 1898; Election Returns, 1898: Secretary of State.

17. Election Returns, 1900: Cass, Hopkins, Lamar, Morris, Secretary of State.

18. In Marion, Sayers received 1,752 votes, while the Democratic candidates for president and Congress received only about 400 votes. Total vote for Congress and president equaled about 1,200, but total vote for governor equaled about 2,000. In Camp, Sheppard outdrew all Democrats by about 100 votes. See Election Returns, 1900: Secretary of State; Kingston, Attlesey, and Crawford, *Political History of Texas*, 66–83, 272–279; *Pittsburg Gazette*, November 9, 1900.

19. J. P. Talkington to J. W. Biard, June 15, 1900, Biard Papers. Also see *Pittsburg Gazette*, November 11, 1898; November 9, 1900; November 7, 21, 1902; November 11, 1904.

20. *Pittsburg Gazette*, October 19, 1900, p. 4. The quote from the *Hopkins County Echo* is in the *Dallas Morning News*, June 19, 1902. On Biard see Joe Eagle to J. W. Biard, July 3, 1899; J. P. Talkington to J. W. Biard, June 15, 1900; H. S. P. Ashby to My Dear Biard, July 14, 1900; James A. Parker to J. W. Biard, December 24, 1902; James W. Biard to Dear Wife, July 28, 1903; all in James W. Biard Papers, American History Center, University of Texas at Austin.

21. F. A. and Burt Lockhart were good examples of moderate Democrats who supported Sayers but still encouraged numerous reforms. See *Pittsburg Gazette*, January 5, February 23, March 9, April 20, June 29, October 29, November 9, 16, 1900. Little has been done on Sayers, but he was a former law partner with George W. Jones. Since Jones was a maverick politician beloved by Greenbackers, Populists, and black Republicans, it seems unlikely that Sayers was an extreme conservative. See *New HOT*, vol. 5, 906-907; Barr, *Reconstruction to Reform*, 193-208; W. R. Miller, "Progressive Coalition in Texas," 163-171. Also see Cantrell, *Kenneth and John B. Rayner*, 242-243.

22. Cantrell, *Kenneth and John B. Rayner*, 244-250; *Southern Mercury*, January 17, 1901; W. R. Miller, "Progressive Coalition in Texas," 172-174.

23. Joe Eagle to J. W. Biard, July 3, 1899; H. S. P. Ashby to My Dear Biard, July 14, 1900; John A. Parker to J. W. Biard, December 24, 1902; all in Biard Papers. Also see *Pittsburg Gazette*, November 9, 1900.

24. Election Returns, 1892-1904: Secretary of State.

25. For an introduction to Morris Sheppard, often called the father of prohibition, see Richard Bailey, "Morris Sheppard," in Hendrickson and Collins, *Profiles in Power*, 29-42. Also see W. R. Miller, "Progressive Coalition in Texas," 172-173; Election Returns, 1902: Secretary of State.

26. For the earliest expression of this "fait accompli" theory of disfranchisement, see Key, *Southern Politics in State and Nation*, 533-539. On the poll tax, see J. Morgan Kousser, *The Shaping of Southern Politics: Suffrage Restriction and the Establishment of the One-Party South, 1880-1910* (New Haven: Yale University Press, 1974); Barr, *Reconstruction to Reform*, 195-205. On the intricacies of Texas elections, see William Fletcher Garner, "The Primaries in Texas" (master's thesis, University of Texas, 1920); Henry M. Laughlin, "The Election Laws of Texas, 1876-1828" (master's thesis, University of Texas, 1928); Howard Mell Greene, "Legal Regulation of Political Parties in Texas" (master's thesis, University of Texas, 1923); Dale Brown Wood, "The Poll Tax as a Requirement for Voting" (master's thesis, University of Texas, 1942); Laura Snow, "The Poll Tax in Texas: Its Historical, Legal, and Fiscal Aspects" (master's thesis, thesis, University of Texas, 1936). For evidence that reformers designed the poll tax to limit the power of conservatives and build a Populist-Progressive coalition, see W. R. Miller, "Progressive Coalition in Texas," 172-174.

27. Kousser, *Shaping of Southern Politics*, 205.

28. W. R. Miller, "Progressive Coalition in Texas," 163-182.

29. The poll tax generally did best in precincts and counties where Hogg did best in 1892. See Election Returns, 1892, 1902: Camp, Cass, Franklin, Hopkins, Lamar, Morris, Secretary of State. Also see comments on the poll tax in *Atlanta Citizen*, November 4, 18, 1904; *Cass County Sun*, June 23, 1908; J. H. Davis, *Memoir*, 54-60, 70-71, 317-324; Barr, *Reconstruction to Reform*, 193-208.

30. For some indication of the return of Populists to the Democratic party, see the precinct-level election returns in *Pittsburg Gazette*, November 11, 1898; November 9, 1900; November 7, 21, 1902; November 11, 1904.

31. On the link between prohibition and suffrage restrictions in other south-

ern states, see Bettersworth, *Mississippi*, 376–381; Sellers, *Prohibition Movement in Alabama*, 101–102. Also see Barr, *Reconstruction to Reform*, 203–206; Gould, *Progressives and Prohibitionists*, 32–57; Ivy, *Rum on the Run*, 30–35.

32. On Neff, see Gould, *Progressives and Prohibitionists*, 271–276. On the link between the poll tax and prohibition in counties with few blacks, see Conrey Bryson, "El Paso and the Poll Tax," *Password* 4 (1959): 46; Abner V. McCall, "Introduction," *Vernon's Civil Statues of Texas* (Kansas City: Vernon Law Book Company, 1952), vol. 9, xxii.

33. Election Returns, 1887–1896: Secretary of State.

34. Neville, *Lamar County*, 182–183; W. R. Miller, "Progressive Coalition in Texas," 163–174.

35. Neville, *Lamar County*, 183; *Omaha Breeze*, March 25, June 28, July 19, 26, 1911; *Jefferson Jimplecute*, July 21, 28, 1911. Pittsburg also put local option back into play immediately after the passage of the poll tax. See *Pittsburg Gazette*, January 23, 1903.

36. Election Returns, 1887, 1902: Secretary of State.

37. *Pittsburg Gazette*, June 13, 1902, p. 4.

38. Ballots for the poll tax appeared on separate pieces of white paper from other elections, and in Marion, Democrats probably removed at least 200 of these ballots. Another thousand or more Marion County blacks either gave up on politics or were intimidated into not voting. See Election Returns, 1892, 1894, 1902: Marion, Franklin; W. R. Miller, "Progressive Coalition in Texas," 181–182.

39. The Morris County pattern repeated itself in Cass and Hopkins. Election Returns, 1894, 1896, 1902: Morris, Hopkins, Cass. In particular, see the returns for the small, largely white villages of Avinger, Bryans Mill, Dalton, Galloway, Hollingsworth, and Marietta, in Cass County. For the state as a whole, Cantrell and Barton argue that 48 percent of those who voted for the Populist candidate in 1894 did not vote in the 1902 poll tax election. See Cantrell and Barton, "Texas Populists," 691.

40. The vote for the poll tax in the eleven counties was 13,741 for and 7,647 against, or 64.3 to 35.7 percent. In comparison, the state bank amendment of 1904 carried the region by 4,752 to 3,725, or 56.1 to 43.9 percent. See Election Returns, 1902, 1904: Secretary of State. Also see *Pittsburg Gazette*, June 13, October 17, November 7, 14, 1902.

41. For positive reactions to the passage of the poll tax, see *Pittsburg Gazette*, November 14, 1902; January 9, 30, 1903; January 22, 1904. Some did not agree. See *Jefferson Jimplecute*, November 19, 1904.

42. Grantham, *Southern Progressivism*, 36–107; McMillen, *Dark Journey*, 35–253; Escott, *Many Excellent People*, 171–267.

43. *Pittsburg Gazette*, July 29, 1904, p. 4. Also see *Pittsburg Gazette*, July 22, 1904.

44. *Dallas Morning News*, April 19, 1904, p. 1. Also see *Pittsburg Gazette*, January 22, April 22, 29, 1904; *General Laws of the State of Texas, Twenty-Eighth Legislature*, regular session, 1903 (Austin: Von Boeckmann-Jones, 1904), chapter 101, section 93; Garner, "Primaries in Texas," 73–93; Hine, *Black Victory*, 25–53; Bruce A. Glasrud, "Black Texans, 1900–1930: A History" (Ph.D. dissertation,

Texas Technological College, 1969), 57-59. Blacks in counties where they were few in number sometimes continued to vote in local Democratic primaries until the 1920s. See Conrey Bryson, *Dr. Lawrence A. Nixon and the White Primary* (El Paso: Texas Western Press, 1974), 6-17.

45. *New HOT,* vol. 2, 814-815, vol. 6, 258-259; *Sulphur Springs Gazette,* September 13, 1912, p. 1; *Jefferson Jimplecute,* November 12, 19, 1904; Kousser, *Shaping of Southern Politics,* 201-209. For the election laws that the Terrell law replaced, see H. P. N. Gammel, *The Laws of Texas, 1822-1897* (Austin: Gammel Book Co., 1898), vol. 8, 1419-1420; Laughlin, "Election Laws of Texas," 63-165.

46. *Pittsburg Gazette,* February 12, 1904, p. 4, and July 22, 1904, p. 5; *Jefferson Jimplecute,* November 19, 1904, p. 8.

47. *General Laws of the State of Texas, Twenty-Ninth Legislature,* first called session, 1905 (Austin: Von Boeckmann-Jones, 1906), chapter 11; *House Journal, 1905,* 329-338; Garner, "Primaries in Texas," 51-55; Snow, "Poll Tax in Texas"; W. R. Miller, "Progressive Coalition in Texas," 172-174.

48. *Omaha Breeze,* April 22, 1908, p. 2. Also see *General Laws of the State of Texas, Thirtieth Legislature,* regular session, 1905 (Austin: Von Boeckmann-Jones, 1908), chapter 84; *Texas House Journal,* Thirtieth Legislature, 177; *Omaha Breeze,* August 5, 1908; *Cass County Sun,* June 23, 1908; *Atlanta News,* July 16, 30, October 22, 1908.

49. *Texas House Journal,* Twenty-Eighth Legislature, 1903 Regular Session, 814-815; *Texas Senate Journal,* Twenty-Eighth Legislature, 1903 Regular Session, 806-807; *Texas House Journal,* Twenty-Ninth Legislature, 1905 First Special Session, 92, 297; *Texas Senate Journal,* Twenty-Ninth Legislature, 1905 First Special Session, 274; *Texas House Journal,* Thirtieth Legislature, 1907 Regular Session, 1220-1222; *Texas Senate Journal,* Thirtieth Legislature, 1907 Regular Session, 1010-1013, 1100. Also see *Members of the Texas Legislature, 1846-1962* (Austin: State Printing Office, 1962), 198-220.

50. *Pittsburg Gazette,* January 1, March 11, March 25, July 22, 29, 1904; *Atlanta Citizen,* July 21, 28, November 4, 1904; *Jefferson Jimplecute,* July 23, 30, August 6, 1904.

51. *Pittsburg Gazette,* January 30, 1903, and July 22, 1904; *Texarkana Four States Press,* January 7, 1912; Easterlin, "Interregional Differences in Per Capita Income," 97-140; Hanna, *State Income Differentials,* 248-264; McCusker, *How Much Is That,* 329-332.

52. Jerrold G. Rusk and John J. Stucker, "The Effect of the Southern System of Election Laws on Voting Participation: A Reply to V. O. Key, Jr.," in Joel H. Silbey, Allan G. Bogue, and William H. Flanigan (eds.), *The History of American Electoral Behavior* (Princeton: Princeton University Press, 1978), 219; Kousser, *Shaping of Southern Politics,* 63-72, 196-209. Also see Gould, *Progressives and Prohibitionists,* 3-27.

53. *Dallas Morning News,* August 4, 5, 13, 1906; W. R. Miller, "Progressive Coalition in Texas," 178-180.

54. *Dallas Morning News,* August 5, 13, 1906. For a balanced sketch of Colquitt, see Gould, *Progressives and Prohibitionists,* 86-91. Also see *Pittsburg Gazette,* February 13, 1884.

55. *Dallas Morning News,* February 28, 1906. Also see W. R. Miller, "Progressive Coalition in Texas," 178-179; James R. Green, *Grass Roots Socialism: Radical Movements in the Southwest, 1865-1943* (Baton Rouge: Louisiana State University Press, 1978), 53-125; *Cass County Sun,* February 4, 1908, and April 27, June 29, November 9, November 30, 1909.

56. For voting returns, see *Dallas Morning News,* August 5, 13, 1906. Also see *Texarkana Texarkanian,* February 7, 14, 21, 1906; *Atlanta Citizens Journal,* July 20, 27, August 4, 11, 1906; *Sulphur Springs Gazette,* June 1, 8, 1906; *Pittsburg Gazette,* March 2, 9, July 20, 27, August 3, 11, 1906.

57. *Pittsburg Gazette,* June 24, 1904, and February 13, 1934; Gould *Progressives and Prohibitionists,* 45, 86-91.

58. *Cooper Review,* July 31, 1908, p. 1. Primary returns for 1904 are difficult to find. Local newspapers give returns for Camp, Cass, and Marion. See *Pittsburg Gazette,* July 22, 29, 1904; *Atlanta Citizen,* July 21, 1904; *Jefferson Jimplecute,* July 23, 30, 1904. For primary returns collected from the *Dallas Morning News* and the *Texas Almanac* and for a comment on sources, see Kingston, Attlesey, and Crawford, *Political History of Texas,* 200-271, 331-334. Also see *Dallas Morning News,* August 5, 13, 1906.

59. *Cass County Sun,* June 23, 1908, p. 4.

60. For a comparison of state-level politics and politicians, see Grantham, *Southern Progressivism,* 36-107. Also see Gould, *Progressives and Prohibitionists,* 48-50.

61. *Omaha Breeze,* April 8, 1908, p. 2, and March 11, 1908, p. 2. For other protests against white brutality toward blacks, see *Pittsburg Gazette,* October 17, 1902; *Cass County Sun,* May 4, 1909; *Texarkana Texarkanian,* November 23, 25, 29, 1905; *Dallas Morning News,* July 24, 1912.

62. *Pittsburg Gazette,* September 2, 1904, p.4.

63. *Cass County Sun,* April 27, 1909, p. 2.

64. Grantham, *Southern Progressivism,* 99. Also see *Pittsburg Gazette,* July 4, 1902; *Jefferson Jimplecute,* November 12, 1904; *Omaha Breeze,* April 8, 1908, and May 12, 1909.

65. *Texas Almanac, 1912,* 42-45; Election Returns, 1900: Secretary of State; *Jefferson Jimplecute,* July 28, 1911; *Pittsburg Gazette,* July 28, August 4, 1911; *Omaha Breeze,* August 2, 1911; *Sulphur Springs Gazette,* July 28, August 4, 1911; *Paris Morning News,* July 23, 25, 28, 1911.

66. Quoted in *Pittsburg Gazette,* April 1, 1904, p. 4. Also see *Pittsburg Gazette,* July 29, 1904.

67. *Cass County Sun,* November 23, 1909, p. 4. Also see W. R. Miller, "Progressive Coalition in Texas," 163-182.

68. *Cumby Rustler,* January 5, 12, 1912; *Pittsburg Gazette,* January 8, 1904, and August 4, October 6, 1911; J. R. Green, *Grassroots Socialism,* 53-57; W. R. Miller, "Progressive Coalition in Texas," 176-178; Barr, *Reconstruction to Reform,* 229-234; Hunt, *History of Farmer Movements in the Southwest,* 41-143; Charles Simon Barrett, *The Mission, History and Times of the Farmers' Union: a Narrative of the Greatest Industrial-Agricultural Organization in History and Its Makers* (Nashville: Marshall & Bruce, 1909).

69. *Pittsburg Gazette,* July 1, 1904; *Cumby Rustler,* January 5, 1912; *Omaha Breeze,* January 15, 22, February 5, 1908; *Cooper Review,* January 24, February 14, March 6, 13, 20, 1908.

70. *Pittsburg Gazette,* August 4, 1911, p. 2. *Cumby Rustler,* January 12, 19, 26, 1912. *Omaha Breeze,* January 15, August 19, 1908; March 24, 1909; August 3, 1910; February 28, 1912.

71. *Cumby Rustler,* January 19, 1912, p. 4. Also see *Cumby Rustler,* April 5, 1912; *Pittsburg Gazette,* January 29, 1904.

72. *Cumby Rustler,* February 9, 1912, p. 4. Also see *Cooper Review,* April 3, 1908; *Cumby Rustler,* January 19, April 12, 1912; *Pittsburg Gazette,* January 29, 1904.

73. On Colquitt, see the feature article in the *Pittsburg Gazette* 50th Anniversary Edition, February 13, 1934; Gould, *Progressives and Prohibitionists,* 86–91. Also see *Cumby Rustler,* July 19, August 9, 1912; *Pittsburg Gazette,* February 13, 20, 1884, June 21, 28, July 5, August 2, 1912.

74. *Sulphur Springs Gazette,* July 19, August 2, 1912, and June 6, July 11, 18, 25, August 1, 1913; *Omaha Breeze,* June 5, 1912; *Pittsburg Gazette,* June 21, 28, 1912.

CHAPTER 4: "OLD IDEAS" AND "IMPROVED CONDITIONS"

1. *Omaha Breeze,* January 22, 1908, p. 1, and April 1, 1908, p. 2. For additional evidence of optimism, see the county entries written by local citizens in *Texas Almanac, 1904,* 217–374. Also see *Pittsburg Gazette,* August 4, 1905, and January 2, 1907; *Sulphur Springs Gazette,* June 21, July 5, September 6, 1912; *Paris Advocate* in the *Omaha Breeze,* January 8, 1908.

2. *Omaha Breeze,* May 8, 1912, p. 2.

3. Barr, *Reconstruction to Reform,* 155–211; Grant and Crum, *State-Chartered Banking in Texas,* 23–36.

4. *Austin Statesman,* March 14, 15, 1903; *Proceedings of the Fifth Annual Convention of the Texas Bankers' Association, Held at Dallas, Texas, May 8, 9, and 10, 1889* (Dallas: privately published, 1889), 14–20; *Austin Statesman,* March 14, 15, 1903; Texas, *State Bank Law of the State of Texas As Passed by the 29th Legislature, Effective August 14, 1905* (Austin: State Printing Company, 1905); Mitchell, "Limits of Reform."

5. *Pittsburg Gazette,* January 5, 1900, p. 4. Also see R. A. Morris, "To the People of Camp County," *Pittsburg Gazette,* August 12, 1904, p. 1. For a discussion of the creation and early days of the state banking system by an active participant in the process, see Thomas B. Love, "Some East Texas Banking History," in T. C. Richardson, *East Texas: Its History and Its Makers,* edited by Dabney White (New York: Lewis Historical Publishing Co., 1940): 1337–1384. Also see Buenger and Pratt, *But Also Good Business,* 40–63.

6. *Pittsburg Gazette,* November 4, 18, 1904; *Atlanta Citizens Journal,* November 17, 1904; *Jefferson Jimplecute,* October 29, November 5, 12, 1904; "State Banks," *Texas Banker* 3 (December 1904): 11; Grant and Crum, *State-Chartered Banking in Texas,* 23–46.

7. *Pittsburg Gazette,* May 18, 1900, and February 26, April 15, 1904; Election Returns, 1904: Secretary of State.

8. *Pittsburg Gazette,* November 4, 1904; Election Returns, 1904: Secretary of State.

9. *Atlanta Citizen's Journal,* July 21, November 4, 1904; April 23, 1908; March, 1929, Special Issue.

10. Election returns, 1894, 1904: Secretary of State.

11. *Cass County Sun,* July 20, 1909, p. 1. Also see *Omaha Breeze,* January 8, 15, March 4, 1908; *Pittsburg Gazette,* April 15, 22, 1904; *Pittsburg Gazette,* October 25, November 15, 22, 1907; *Atlanta Citizens Journal,* October 31, November 7, 1907; *Cass County Sun,* November 9, 1909.

12. *Omaha Breeze,* September 13, 1911.

13. For Lindsey's estimate, see his letter quoted in Bizzell, *Farm Tenantry,* 357–358. Also see Bizzell, *Rural Texas,* 286–294; Johnson, Embree, and Alexander, *Collapse of Cotton Tenancy,* 71–72; David G. McComb, *Houston: A History* (Austin: University of Texas Press, 1981), 82–83; *Houston Post-Dispatch,* October 3, 1924.

14. *Pittsburg Gazette,* July 18, 1902, p. 4.

15. *Atlanta Citizens Journal,* November 21, 1907, p. 1. Also see Calvert, "Agrarian Texas," 226–228; Carl H. Moneyhon, "Public Education and Texas Reconstruction Politics, 1871–1874," *SHQ* 92 (January 1989): 393–416; Frederick Eby, *Education in Texas: Source Materials* (Austin: University of Texas, 1918), 802–835; Frederick Eby, *The Development of Education in Texas* (New York: Macmillan, 1925), 193–262.

16. Even under the law of 1884 and the county superintendent law of 1887, some community schools continued to operate in Northeast Texas and were largely unsupervised and unregulated. Governor Campbell pushed legal changes that ended community schools by 1908. See Eby, *Education in Texas: Source Materials,* 809, 829–835; Eby, *Development of Education in Texas,* 193–211.

17. *Cass County Sun,* March 17, 1908, p. 4; *Omaha Breeze,* September 14, 1910, p. 2. Also see *Cass County Sun,* February 25, 1908. *Atlanta News,* June 25, 1908. *Omaha Breeze,* May 12, 19, August 25, September 8, 22, 1909. *Cooper Review,* February 14, May 29, June 19, September 11, 18, October 16, 1908; March 26, April 19, May 21, August 13, October 1, 22, November 5, 1909; May 23, June 20, 1913. *Jefferson Jimplecute,* January 20, 1911, and July 6, 1916. Eby *Development of Education in Texas,* 206–218. Buenger and Buenger, *Texas Merchant,* 21–26.

18. For a list of incorporated places, see U.S., *Census: 1910, Population,* vol. 3, 795–796. Also see Eby, *Development of Education in Texas,* 260–262; *Sulphur Springs Gazette,* June 7, 1912; *Cumby Rustler,* Feb 16, 1912; *Jefferson Jimplecute,* May 14, 21, 1914, and February 11, 1915.

19. *Cumby Rustler,* February 16, 1912 p. 4. Also see Eby, *Development of Education in Texas,* 260.

20. Hazel Beauton Riley, *Washing on the Line* (Wichita Falls: Nortex Offset Publications, 1973), 18. On the limited effect of school reforms in rural areas, see Eby, *Development of Education in Texas,* 304–321. For first-hand accounts of rural schools in Northeast Texas early in the century, see Lula Kathryn Peacock Jones,

Recollections of the Life of Lula Kathryn (Kate) Peacock Jones (Amarillo: Coltharp Printing, 1979), 1–42; Riley, *Washing on the Line*, 1–51.

21. Owens, *Stubborn Soil*, 213.

22. James A. Tinsley, "The Progressive Movement in Texas," (Ph.D. dissertation, University of Wisconsin, 1953); Eby, *Development of Education in Texas*, 304–321.

23. *Cooper Review*, July 9, 1909, p. 4. Also see *Cooper Review*, June 18, July 2, 9, 1909; *Pittsburg Gazette*, January 15, 1904.

24. *Texas Almanac, 1904*, p. 94. R. L. Haney, *Milestones*, 2–7, 90–91; S. L. Evans, "Texas Agriculture," 50–52; Dethloff, *History of Texas A&M*, vol. 2, 382–396.

25. *Pittsburg Gazette*, October 19, 1906, p. 4. Also see *Pittsburg Gazette*, January 1, April 8, September 30, 1904; *Cass County Sun*, September 1, 1908; *The Texas Almanac, 1926*, 135–137; *The Texas Almanac, 1929*, 99; *New HOT*, vol. 1, 628–629. Fite, *Cotton Fields No More*, 81, doubts that efforts to combat the boll weevil improved cultivation practices in the entire South.

26. Establishing that different classes reacted differently to the boll weevil is difficult, but some hint of this comes from *Pittsburg Gazette*, June 24, July 8, September 30, 1904, and August 11, December 29, 1911; Bizzell, *Rural Texas*, 166–167, 387–395.

27. *Cooper Review*, May 28, June 18, July 2, 1909.

28. *Cooper Review*, May 28, 1909, p. 2.

29. *Jefferson Jimplecute*, January 15, 1914, p. 1. Also see *Jefferson Jimplecute*, May 22, 1911; "Boll Worm," notice from Horace W. Vaughan, *Jefferson Jimplecute*, April 16, 1914, p. 1; *Atlanta News*, December 29, 1910; "A Premium on Industry," *Omaha Breeze*, January 22, 1908, p.2; *Omaha Breeze*, October 14, 1908, and April 19, 1911; *Cooper Review*, May 8, 1908; Dethloff, History of *Texas A&M*, 382–394.

30. Gould, *Progressives and Prohibitionists*, 28–57; Grantham, *Southern Progressivism*, 160–177; Jeannie M. Whayne, "The Significance of Race, Class, and Family in the Battle for Prohibition in Small Town Arkansas," *Locus* 7 (spring 1995): 129–149.

31. *Cooper Review*, July 3, 10, 17, 1908; "Prohibition Rally A Big Success!" *Sulphur Springs Gazette*, July 23, 1911, p. 1; *Jefferson Jimplecute*, March 3, 10, 17, 1911; *Pittsburg Gazette*, March 24, August 4, 11, 1887, and March 25, June 24, 1904; *Omaha Breeze*, February 12, July 15, 1908. For the antiprohibition view that all true Jeffersonians opposed statewide prohibition, see *Omaha Breeze*, July 22, 1908.

32. *Omaha Breeze*, June 28, 1911, p. 2. Also see Election Returns, 1887, 1911: Secretary of State.

33. Election Returns, 1887, 1894, 1911: Lamar.

34. *Paris Morning News*, July 21, 22, 23, 25, 28, 1911.

35. Election Returns, 1887, 1902, 1911: Secretary State, Cass, Lamar; *Jefferson Jimplecute*, July 28, 1911.

36. Election Returns, 1887, 1894, 1902, 1904, 1911, 1912: Secretary of State; *Sulphur Springs Gazette*, February 3, 1911. For precinct-level returns, see *Pittsburg*

Gazette, July 28, 1911; *Omaha Breeze,* August 2, 1911; *Sulphur Springs Gazette,* July 28, 1911; *Paris Morning News,* July 23, 25, 1911; *Jefferson Jimplecute,* July 28, 1911.

37. *Sulphur Springs Gazette,* July 23, 1911, p. 1. For an example of white opposition to prohibition, see Thad Sitton, *Backwoodsmen,* 124–133.

38. *Pittsburg Gazette,* July 28, 1911, p. 1.

39. *Pittsburg Gazette,* July 14, 21, 28, August 4, 1911; *Jefferson Jimplecute,* July 14, 21, 28, 1911; *Omaha Breeze,* February 11, March 15, June 28, July 12, 19, 26, August 2, 9, 16, 23, 1911; *Sulphur Springs Gazette,* July 16, 23, 30, August 6, 1911; *Cumby Rustler,* July 11, 18, 25, 1911.

40. This point is forcefully made in Gould, *Progressives and Prohibitionists,* 28–57.

41. *Jefferson Jimplecute,* June 16, p. 3.

42. On stock laws and other similar elections, see *Pittsburg Gazette,* September 29, 1911, and May 17, December 20, 1912; *Cumby Rustler,* February 4, 11, March 24, 31, 1916; *Omaha Breeze,* September 30, 1908, and May 19, 1909. For a discussion of class-based divisions in a nearby county, see Wilkison, "End of Independence," 275–342.

43. Peteet, "Farming Credit," 46 (quote), 32–52. On Ferguson, see Gould, *Progressives and Prohibitionists,* 120–149; Ralph W. Steen, "The Political Career of James E. Ferguson, 1914–1917," (master's thesis, University of Texas, 1929).

44. Kousser, *Shaping of Southern Politics,* 209; J. R. Green, *Grass Roots Socialism,* 12–269.

45. *Cass County Sun,* January 26, 1910, p. 1. Also see *Omaha Breeze,* August 17, 1910; John A. Parker to J. W. Biard, December 24, 1902, Biard Papers. Wright, *Old South, New South,* 117–118, stresses that the lack of labor unrest in the South as a whole indicated a slowing in the growth of tenancy, but the reverse was true of Texas and Oklahoma. See J. R. Green, *Grass Roots Socialism,* 12–269.

46. Sanders, "Ownership and Tenancy in the Black Prairie," 2. Also see Interview with George Mathena by Corrine E. Crow, April 25, 1974, transcript (Texas A&M, Commerce); Foley, *White Scourge,* 64–140.

47. News of the start of World War I pushed official precinct-level election returns for the 1914 primary out of the newspapers, but for reasonably reliable returns, see *Cumby Rustler,* July 27, 1914; *Mount Vernon Optic Herald,* July 31, 1914; *Omaha Breeze,* August 5, 1914; *Sulphur Springs Gazette,* August 7, 1914; *Pittsburg Gazette,* July 31, 1914; *Jefferson Jimplecute,* July 30, 1914. Also see *Dallas Morning News,* July 27, 28, 29, 30, 31, 1914; *Houston Post,* July 28, 30, 31, 1914. Statewide, the total vote in the 1914 gubernatorial primary was 428,620, while the vote in the 1911 prohibition referendum totaled 468,489. See *Texas Almanac, 1912,* 45; *Dallas Morning News,* July 31, 1914; *Houston Post,* July 31, 1914.

48. *Texarkana Daily Texarkanian,* February 21, 1914. In Hopkins, for example, Ball carried *Sulphur Springs* by impressive margins, but Ferguson carried many rural precincts, including those carried by the Populists in the 1890s. See *Sulphur Springs Gazette,* August 7, 1914; Election Returns, 1890–1914: Hopkins, Cass, Camp, Lamar, Morris.

49. *Jefferson Jimplecute*, July 2, 30, 1914, p. 2, and July 30, 1914, p. 2. Also see *Jefferson Jimplecute*, November 5, 1914.

50. Ferguson has proved very difficult for historians to categorize. Some call him a demagogue, others a liberal. See Gould, *Progressives and Prohibitionists*, 132 n. 29; Robert S. Maxwell, "Texas in the Progressive Era, 1900–1930," in Donald W. Whisenhunt (ed.) *Texas: A Sesquicentennial Celebration* (Austin: Eakin Press, 1984), 173–200; Larry D. Hill, "Texas Progressivism: A Search for Definition," in *Texas through Time*, 248–249; Lewis L. Gould, "The University Becomes Politicized: The War with Jim Ferguson, 1915–1918," *SHQ* 86 (October 1982): 255–276.

51. *Mount Pleasant Times Review*, quoted in the *Omaha Breeze*, January 27, 1909, p. 3.

52. Gould, "The University Becomes Politicized," 261; *Jefferson Jimplecute*, April 22, 1915, p. 4.

53. Ferguson in general supported Texas A&M, and in some ways his disputes with the University of Texas were part of a long-standing turf war between the state's two leading institutions of higher education. See Larry D. Hill and Robert A. Calvert, "The University of Texas Extension Services and Progressivism," *SHQ* 86 (October 1982): 231–244; Gould, "The University Becomes Politicized," 259–274.

54. *Jefferson Jimplecute*, August 1, 1912, p. 1; *Pittsburg Gazette*, June 8, 1917, p. 2. Also see Hill and Calvert, "University of Texas Extension Services," 235–242. *Jefferson Jimplecute*, October 6, 1911; September 3, 1914; June 24, July 15, 1915; July 16, 1916; June 7, 14, 1917; February 6, May 24, 1919. *Omaha Breeze*, January 22, 1908; September 8, 15, 1909; February 11, 1911. *Atlanta News*, December 29, 1910. *Cooper Review*, July 6, 1917.

55. Brannen, "Relation of Land Tenure to Plantation Organization," 22, 24, 26, 27, 64. Bowie was one of the approximately sixty counties that Brannen intensely examined. See Appendix B, p. 69. Also see Johnson, Embree, and Alexander, *Collapse of Cotton Tenancy*, 71–72; Bizzell, *Farm Tenantry*, 212–221, 354–362; Sanders, "Ownership and Tenancy in the Black Prairie," 12–15. For a comparison of the southern states in the Progressive Era that in general supports the argument that Texas was somewhat different but still southern, see Grantham, *Southern Progressivism*, 36–108.

56. *Omaha Breeze*, October 4, 1911, p. 1.

57. For different views on Texas nationalism, see Gould, *Progressives and Prohibitionists*, 30–31; Mark W. A. Nackman, *A Nation within a Nation: The Rise of Texas Nationalism* (Port Washington, N.Y.: Kennikat Press, 1975); Joseph Leach, *The Typical Texan: Biography of an American Myth* (Dallas: Southern Methodist University Press, 1952). Also see Emma Jean Walker, "The Contemporary Texan: An Examination of Major Additions to the Mythical Texan in the Twentieth Century" (Ph.D. dissertation, University of Texas, 1966); Laura Lyons McLemore, "Creating a Mythhistory: Texas Historians in the Nineteenth Century" (Ph.D. dissertation, University of North Texas, 1998), 83–261; Buenger, *Secession and the Union*, 159–182; Buenger and Calvert, "Shelf Life of Truth in Texas," ix–xxxv;

Susan Prendergast Schoelwer, *Alamo Images: Changing Perceptions of a Texas Experience* (Dallas: Southern Methodist University Press, 1985), 163-173.

58. David Thelen noted that "Since politicians must by trade find memories that still have private resonance for large numbers of voters, politics opens many ways for exploring how individuals connected (or failed to connect) their private memories with the defining memories of larger groups and associations." See David Thelen, "Memory and American History," *JAH* 75 (March 1989): 1124. This insight and others in the two issues focused on memory have aided my work. See *JAH* 75 (March 1989); *JAH* 85 (September 1998): 409-446. For a national perspective on altered uses of history that examines the changing place of the Alamo in popular culture, see Michael G. Kammen, *Mystic Chords of Memory: The Transformation of Tradition in American Culture* (New York: Knopf, 1991), 93-298. Also see Schoelwer, *Alamo Images*, 18-60; Martha Anne Turner, *Clara Driscoll: An American Tradition* (Austin: Madrona Press, 1979), 43-48.

59. *Paris Advocate* quoted in the *Omaha Breeze*, January 8, 1908, p. 2; *Pittsburg Gazette*, September 9, 1898, p. 1. Perhaps because of focusing on the ministerial elite, one perceptive analyst missed the more mixed impact of the Spanish-American War. See Wilson, *Baptized in Blood*, 161-163. Also see Foster, *Ghosts of the Confederacy*, 145-159; Connelly and Bellows, *God and General Longstreet*, 107-148.

60. Traylor Russell, "The Confederate Monument on the Courthouse Square of Titus County and the History of Dudley W. Jones," in *History of Titus County*, 187-189; *Houston Post*, July 26, 1914, Sunday Section, p. 8; *Jefferson Jimplecute*, April 2, 1914, p. 4. For an interesting study of monuments, see Kirk Savage, *Standing Soldier, Kneeling Slaves: Race, War, and Monument in Nineteenth-Century America* (Princeton: Princeton University Press, 1997).

61. Emily Fourmy Cutrer, *The Art of the Woman: The Life and Work of Elisabet Ney* (Lincoln: University of Nebraska Press, 1988); Charles P. Roland, *Albert Sidney Johnston: Soldier of Three Republics* (Austin: University of Texas Press, 1964).

62. Jacquelyn Dowd Hall, "'You Must Remember This': Autobiography as Social Critique," *JAH* 85 (September 1998): 449. Also see *Cass County Sun*, May 26, September 8, 1908; *Atlanta News*, May 21, August, 27, 1908; *Atlanta Citizens Journal*, May 21, 28, 1908.

63. *Omaha Breeze*, February 10, 1910, p. 3.

64. Eugene W. Bowers and Evelyn Oppenheimer, *Red River Dust: True Tales of an American Yesterday* (Waco: Word Books, 1968), 47. Also see *Texarkana Texarkanian*, January 29, 1906; *Cooper Review*, June 5, 1908, and July 12, 1912.

65. *Atlanta Citizens Journal*, April 23, 1908. p. 2. Also see Fred Arthur Bailey, "The Textbooks of the 'Lost Cause': Censorship and the Creation of Southern State Histories," *Georgia Historical Quarterly* 75 (fall 1991): 507-533.

66. "Southern History Facts to Be Kept, George W. Littlefield, Terry Ranger, Presents History Fund to the University of Texas," *Jefferson Jimplecute*, July 9, 1914, p. 5. Also see Foster, *Ghosts of the Confederacy*, 197-198; *New HOT*, vol. 4, 230-231; Fred Arthur Bailey, "Free Speech and the 'Lost Cause' in Texas: A Study of Social Control in the New South," *SHQ* 97 (January 1994): 453-479.

67. *Omaha Breeze*, August 3, 1910, p. 3.

68. On this point, see Hall, "Autobiography as Social Critique," 448–449.

69. *Omaha Breeze*, January 15, 1908 p. 2.

70. *Omaha Breeze*, May 8, 1912, p. 2. Also see Foster, *Ghosts of the Confederacy*, 163–198; Wilson, *Baptized in Blood*, 161–182; Connelly and Bellows, *God and General Longstreet*, 107–148. A fascinating study of school textbooks used in Texas provides evidence both of the power of the Lost Cause in pre-1930 Texas and the subtle differences between Texas and other southern states. Textbooks used in Texas included glorification of the Ku Klux Klan of the 1870s as the savior of the white South, but these texts also were rejected by other southern states as not being southern enough. The state textbook committee also rejected some texts for general adoption because they were too prejudiced toward the South. See F. A. Bailey, "Free Speech and the 'Lost Cause' in Texas," 452–477.

71. For the history of Confederate organizations in the area, see Bowers and Oppenheimer, *Red River Dust*, 44–48; Russell, "Confederate Monument," 187–192; *Atlanta Citizens Journal*, 50 Year Anniversary Edition, 1929. For an introduction to the growing literature on celebrating the Confederate experience after 1890, see Wilson, *Baptized in Blood*, 139–182; Foster, *Ghosts of the Confederacy*, 79–159; Connelly and Bellows, *God and General Longstreet*, 1–38; Thomas L. Connelly, *The Marble Man: Robert E. Lee and His Image in American Society* (New York: Knopf, 1977), 27–140; Hall, "Autobiography as Social Critique," 439–465.

72. R. Bailey, "Morris Sheppard," 29–42. *Jefferson Jimplecute*, November 5, 1904; May 26, 1911; July 18, August 1, 8, 1912. *Pittsburg Gazette*, October 31, 1902; January 1, March 11, 25, July 29, 1904; August 23, 1907; November 17, 1911; May 3, June 7, 1912. *Omaha Breeze*, January 22, March 11, 18, May 13, October 7, 28, 1908.

73. *Cass County Sun*, August 17, 1909, p. 4. This newspaper's editor never lauded the South in the same way as other editors. See *Cass County Sun*, August 18, 1908.

74. *Dallas Morning News*, July 24, 25, 26, 27, 28, 29, 30, 31, 1912. *Pittsburg Gazette*, August 23, 1907. *Jefferson Jimplecute*, May 26, 1911, and August 8, 1912. *Omaha Breeze*, October 7, 1908; March 24, April 7, May 12, 1909; April 13, May 4, 1910; September 27, 1911; February 28, 1912. *New HOT*, vol. 5, 1016–1017.

75. *New HOT*, vol. 4, 230–231; *Pittsburg Gazette*, May 9, 16, 1919.

76. Lela McClure, *Captain Rosborough and the Confederate Memorial* (Texarkana: United Daughters of the Confederacy, Chapter 568, 1961), 1. Also see McClure, *Captain Rosborough*, 2–10.

77. *Jefferson Jimplecute*, July 1, 1920, p. 3.

78. *Jefferson Jimplecute*, October 25, 1917, p. 2.

79. *Paris Morning News*, April 19, 1922, p. 2. Compare this with the much more tepid announcement of Texas Independence Day in *Jefferson Jimplecute*, February 28, 1914, p. 2.

80. *Sulphur Springs Gazette*, August 7, 1914, p. 10. For the limits placed on one southern reform movement by the Lost Cause, see Wheeler, *New Women of the New South*, 3–37.

CHAPTER 5: AN ECONOMIC ROLLER COASTER, 1914–1930

1. For examples of prosperity and confidence in the future of the economy, see *Pittsburg Gazette*, February 17, 1928; *Paris Morning News*, February 21, 1928; *Naples Monitor*, March 9, 1928. For the opposite, see Wilkison, "End of Independence," 275–350.

2. *Jefferson Jimplecute*, October 4, 1917, p. 1. Also see *Pittsburg Gazette*, December 7, 1917.

3. *Cass County Sun*, June 23, 1908, and December 14, 1909; U.S., *Census: 1890, Agriculture*, 182–189; U.S., *Census: 1920, Agriculture*, vol. 6, pt. 2, 664–686; Robert L. Martin, *The City Moves West: Economic and Industrial Growth in Central West Texas* (Austin: University of Texas Press, 1969), 50–95; Ayers, *Promise of the New South*, 3–26.

4. *Cooper Review*, March 29, 1908, p. 4; Jan Blodgett, *Land of Bright Promise: Advertising the Texas Panhandle and South Plains, 1870–1917* (Austin: University of Texas Press, 1988); second quotation is from the title of Blodgett's book. Also see *Pittsburg Gazette*, August 11, 1911; January 3, 1913; October 12, 26, 1917; January 24, June 20, 1919. *Sulphur Springs Gazette*, July 31, 1914. *Omaha Breeze*, February 26, 1908; November 2, 1910; June 28, 1911. *Jefferson Jimplecute*, August 30, September 27, 1917.

5. *Omaha Breeze*, February 26, 1908, p. 2.

6. *Jefferson Jimplecute*, July 3, 1913; July 30, 1914; May 27, 1915. *Pittsburg Gazette*, November 25, December 2, 1904, and October 12, 1917. *Omaha Breeze*, February 2, 1910. U.S., *Census: 1900, Agriculture*, vol. 5, pt. 2, 184–187, 260–263, 391–394, 434–435, 573–575, 743–745. U.S., *Census: 1910, Agriculture*, vol. 7, 680–698. U.S., *Census: 1920, Agriculture*, vol. 6, pt. 2, 717–735. *Texas Almanac, 1914*, 209–212.

7. For a good summary of oil's impact, see Roger M. Olien and Diana Davids Olien, *Oil Booms: Social Change in Five Texas Towns* (Lincoln: University of Nebraska Press, 1982), 1–18. Also see *Texas Almanac, 1904*, 153–160; *The Texas Almanac and State Industrial Guide, 1933* (Dallas: A. H. Belo, 1933), 204–208; Bennett H. Wall (ed.), *Louisiana: A History* (Arlington Heights: Forum Press, 1990), 280–285. There is no mention of petroleum production in a Northeast Texas county in the extensive county entries of the *Texas Almanac, 1925*, 250–351. Nor is a Northeast Texas county listed among the major producing counties in the *Texas Almanac and State Industrial Guide, 1929* (Dallas: A. H. Belo, 1929), 180.

8. *Pittsburg Gazette*, November 30, 1917, and January 10, 24, 1919; *Jefferson Jimplecute*, December 4, 1919; "Petroleum," *Fort Worth* (Fort Worth: Chamber of Commerce, 1924), 5–8.

9. *Fort Worth Star-Telegram*, December 15, 1918, p. 1. Also see *Pittsburg Gazette*, March 23, October 19, November 30, 1917, and January 10, 24, 1919; "Petroleum," *Fort Worth*, 5–8; *Fort Worth Star Telegram*, February 22, December 1, 15, 17, 1918; *The Story of Fort Worth from Outpost to Metropolis* (Fort Worth: Fort Worth National Bank, 1973); Roger Olien and Diana Davids Olien, *Easy Money: Oil Promoters and Investors in the Jazz Age* (Chapel Hill: University of North Carolina Press, 1990), 73–103.

10. Francis Benton Burdine, "Regional Economic Effects of Petroleum Industry Development in Texas, 1900-1970" (Ph.D. dissertation, University of Texas at Austin, 1976); R. B. Johnson, "The Petroleum Industry and the Southwest," *Monthly Business Review of the Federal Reserve Board* 32 (March 1947): 33-39; Maxwell and Baker, *Sawdust Empire,* 181-202.

11. Olien and Olien, *Oil Booms,* 21-40; Joseph A. Pratt, *The Growth of a Refining Region* (Greenwich, Conn.: JAI Press, 1980), 33-87; Harold L. Platt, "Energy and Urban Growth: A Comparison of Houston and Chicago," *SHQ* 91 (July 1987): 1-18; Arthur M. Johnson, "The Early Texas Oil Industry: Pipelines and the Birth of an Integrated Oil Industry, 1901-1911," *JSH* 32 (November 1966): 516-528. Also see Interview with Herbert Allen by Walter L. Buenger and Joseph A. Pratt, August 7, 1985, Texas Commerce Bank Archives. (Allen began working for Cameron Iron Works in 1928.)

12. *Jefferson Jimplecute,* July 12, August 1, 23, September 27, 1917; June 27, 1918; March 20, August 14, 21, September 11, November 13, 27, December 4, 1919; January 1, 8, 29, February 5, March 4, 11, 18, April 1, 29, May 20, June 17, 24, July 22, August 19, 26, September 9, October 7, November 25, 1920. *Pittsburg Gazette,* February 14, 1919. *Paris News,* February 19, 1922.

13. U.S., *Census of Manufacture, 1914,* vol. 1, 1468; U.S., *Census: Manufactures, 1919,* vol. 9, 1449-1450, 1462; U.S., *Biennial Census of Manufactures, 1925,* 1467; *Jefferson Jimplecute,* May 18, 1916; *Pittsburg Gazette,* April 18, 1919.

14. Owens, *Stubborn Soil,* 183. Also see U.S., *Census of Manufactures, 1914,* vol. 1, 1468; U.S., *Census: Manufactures, 1919,* vol. 9, 1449-1450, 1462; U.S., *Biennial Census of Manufactures, 1925,* 1467; *Jefferson Jimplecute,* May 18, 1916; Thomas Elliot Born, "Goobers, Ground Pease, and Peanuts: The Transformation of the Texas Peanut Culture, 1890-1990" (master's thesis, Texas A&M University, 1992), 55-81. On the Paris fire, see *Jefferson Jimplecute,* March 23, 1916; Herbert L. Hollis, *Paris Fire of 1916* (Wolfe City, Texas: Henington Publishing, 1982); Neville, *Lamar County,* 158-170, 223-229; Interview with Maitland Mayer Truby by Anna May Curtis, April 23, 1980, transcript (Aikin Regional Archives, Paris Junior College).

15. For a sketch of manufacturing in area cities, see *Texas Almanac, 1925,* 250-351. Also see Humphrey, *Farther off from Heaven,* 56-57.

16. For spot cotton prices, see *Texas Almanac, 1929,* 106. Also see *Jefferson Jimplecute,* January 21, May 6, 1915; U.S., *Census: 1910, Agriculture,* vol. 7, 655-700; U.S., *Census: 1920, Agriculture,* vol. 6, pt. 2, 716-735.

17. U.S., *Census: 1910, Agriculture,* vol. 7, 680-698; U.S., *Census: 1920, Agriculture,* vol. 6, pt. 2, 717-735; U.S., *Census of Agriculture, 1925,* pt. 2, 1208-1236; *Pittsburg Gazette,* March 15, 22, 1918.

18. Brown and Gust, *Between the Creeks,* xii-xiv; Russell, *Titus County,* 142-152; *Jefferson Jimplecute,* August 30, 1917, and January 16, 1919.

19. U.S., *Census: 1900, Agriculture,* vol. 5, pt. 1, 124-130, 298-301; U.S., *Census: 1910, Agriculture,* vol. 7, 634-675; U.S., *Census: 1920, Agriculture,* vol. 6, pt. 2, 665-684; Sanders, "Ownership and Tenancy in the Black Prairie," 6-12. U.S., *Census: 1920, Agriculture,* vol. 6, pt. 2, 655, defines improved acres as "all land regularly tilled or mowed, land in pasture which has been cleared or tilled,

land lying fallow, land in gardens, orchards, vineyards, and nurseries, and land occupied by farm buildings." In 1925 and 1930 "improved acres" was obtained by combining the categories "total cropland" and "plowed pasture." (Total cropland equals cropland harvested, crop failure, and cropland idle or fallow.) See U.S., *Census of Agriculture, 1925*, pt. 2, 914, 982, 1110-1139; U.S., *Census of Agriculture, 1935*, vol. 1, pt. 2, 670, 696, 742-763.

20. Sanders, "Ownership and Tenancy in the Black Prairie," 1-30. Also see Wilkison, "End of Independence," 275-350; Kirby, *Rural Worlds Lost*, 44-50; Fite, *Cotton Fields No More*, 68-150.

21. *Pittsburg Gazette*, June 14, 1918; Sanders, "Ownership and Tenancy in the Black Prairie," 13, 28-30; Willard, "Cotton Farms of Ellis County," 10-20; Peteet, "What Texas Farmers Pay for Credit," 24-79.

22. *Jefferson Jimplecute*, May 24, June 7, August 7, November 8, 1917; February 14, 1918; January 23, July 24, 31, August 14, September 4, December 18, 1919. *Pittsburg Gazette*, April 20, June 8, October 19, 1917; August 9, 1918. For the consumer price index, see McCusker, *How Much Is That*, 330.

23. *Pittsburg Gazette*, July 6, 1917, p. 2. Also see *Jefferson Jimplecute*, April 17, 1913; October 4, 1917; February 14, 1918. U.S., *Census: Agriculture, 1920*, vol. 6, pt. 2, 658, 738-745. Studies done at the time include Henderson H. Donald, "The Negro Migration of 1916-1918," *Journal of Negro History* 6 (October 1921): 338-498; Thomas Jackson Woofter, Jr., *Negro Migration: Changes in Rural Organization and Population of the Cotton Belt* (New York: W. D. Gray, 1920); Emmett Scott, *Negro Migration during the War* (New York: Oxford University Press, 1920). For more recent studies of migration, see James R. Grossman, *Land of Hope: Chicago, Black Southerners, and the Great Migration* (Chicago: University of Chicago Press, 1989), 6-19; Daniel M. Johnson and Rex Campbell, *Black Migration in America: A Social Demographic History* (Durham: Duke University Press, 1981), 71-89; Neil Fligstein, *Going North: Migration of Blacks and Whites from the South, 1900-1950* (New York: Academic Press, 1981), 61-136; Robert Higgs, "The Boll Weevil, the Cotton Economy, and Black Migration, 1910-1930," *Agricultural History* 50 (April 1976): 335-350; Flora Gill, *Economics and the Black Exodus: An analysis of Negro Emigration from the Southern United States, 1910-1970* (New York: 1979).

24. Wright, *Old South, New South*, 205; Brannen, "Relation of Land Tenure to Plantation Organization," 19-38; *Jefferson Jimplecute*, April 11, 1918. On Red River County, see Interview with Mathena by Crow, p. 11; Steven A. Reich, "Soldiers of Democracy: Black Texans and the Fight for Citizenship, 1917-1921," *JAH* 82 (March 1996): 1487-1488.

25. *Jefferson Jimplecute*, April 11, July 11, 25, 1918; Brannen, "Relation of Land Tenure to Plantation Organization," 24; Lawrence A. Cardoso, *Mexican Emigration to the United States, 1897-1931* (Tucson: University of Arizona Press, 1980), 38-70; Paul S. Taylor, *A Mexican-American Frontier: Nueces County, Texas* (Chapel Hill: University of North Carolina Press, 1934), 98-146; Manuel Gamio, *Mexican Immigration to the United States* (Chicago: University of Chicago Press, 1930), 1-50; George O. Coalson, *The Development of Migratory Farm Labor in Texas, 1900-1954* (San Francisco: Rand E Research Associates, 1977).

26. U.S., *Census: 1906, Religious Bodies*, pt. 1, 357-364; *Pittsburg Gazette*,

March 4, 1904. This early presence of Mexicans in the Texarkana area reenforces Terry G. Jordan's point that significant Mexican immigration to Texas began in the 1890s instead of taking off from a standing start after 1910. See Jordan, "A Century and a Half of Ethnic Change in Texas," 393-400.

27. Quoted in *Pittsburg Gazette*, June 21, 1918, p. 3. Also see *Pittsburg Gazette*, March 4, 1904; May 11, 1917; August 2, 1918.

28. Foley, *White Scourge*, 40-91; Cardoso, *Mexican Emigration*, 38-70; P. S. Taylor, *Mexican-American Frontier*, 98-146.

29. *Pittsburg Gazette*, April 20, 1917, and March 1, 1918; *Jefferson Jimplecute*, November 1, 1917; Born, "Transformation of the Texas Peanut Culture," 55-81.

30. *Pittsburg Gazette*, December 7, 1917, p.1. For the argument that the impact of World War I was temporary, see Wright, *Old South, New South*, 200-207. Also see *Jefferson Jimplecute*, September 27, October 4, 1917. On the value of farm implements, see U.S., *Census: 1920, Agriculture*, vol. 6, pt. 2, 664-686; U.S., *Census of Agriculture, 1925*, pt. 2, 1140-1170. Comparisons are in 1991 dollars according to McCusker, *How Much Is That*, 312, 329-332.

31. *Pittsburg Gazette*, December 26, 1919, p. 1. On land consolidation and mechanization during and at the close of World War I, also see Interview with Mathena by Crow, April 25, 1975. George Mathena came to Red River County in 1919 to manage a large farm for Richard Taylor, who brought ten families of black sharecroppers from Mississippi to work the land (see p. 11 of the transcript).

32. Garwood, *Will Clayton*, 93. Also see Garwood, *Will Clayton*, 100; Schwulst, *Extension of Bank Credit*, 165-181; Fleming, *Anderson, Clayton*, 16-18; Clayton, *Phases of Cotton Operations*, 51-128; Interview with McAshan by Buenger and Pratt; Interview with McClure by Crow, 10-13; Woodman, *King Cotton* (1990 ed.), xv-xviii, 288-289; Killick, "Transformation of Cotton Marketing," 143-169.

33. *Pittsburg Gazette*, October 11, 1918, p. 4. Also see Gladys Annelle St. Clair, "A History of Hopkins County, Texas" (master's thesis, University of Texas, 1940), 97-99.

34. On price volatility, see Robert E. Snyder, *Cotton Crisis* (Chapel Hill: University of North Carolina Press, 1984), xiii-xvii, 3-16.

35. *Texas Almanac, 1929*, 106.

36. *Paris Morning News*, March 14, 15, 16, 20, 30, 31, 1928; *Naples Monitor*, December 6, 1929; Garwood, *Will Clayton*, 97-111; Schwulst, *Extension of Bank Credit*, 165-181; Fleming, *Anderson, Clayton*, 16-18; Clayton, *Phases of Cotton Operations*, 51-128; Interview with McAshan by Buenger and Pratt; Interview with McClure by Crow, 10-13; Woodman, *King Cotton*, 288-289; John Chamberlain, "Will Clayton and His Problem," *Life*, May 19, 1947, 114-126.

37. Alonzo B. Cox, "Cotton Prices and Markets," *USDA Bulletin* no. 1444 (December 1926): 44. Cox (pp. 39-48) cites Paris as one of the largest markets and describes the buying and selling of cotton in such markets. Also see *Paris Morning News*, July 9, 1922.

38. U.S., *Census: 1920, Agriculture*, vol. 6, pt. 2, 665-684; U.S., *Census: 1930, Agriculture*, vol. 2, pt. 2, 1424-1445. Also see Russell, *Titus County*, 114-115.

39. Spot cotton prices and bales ginned in each county were recorded and pub-

lished by the USDA and reprinted in the *Texas Almanac*. See Milton S. Eisenhower (ed.), *Yearbook of Agriculture, 1934* (Washington: Government Printing Office, 1934), 466; *Texas Almanac, 1926*, 139-142; *Texas Almanac and State Industrial Guide, 1936* (Dallas: A. H. Belo, 1936), 239-242. The fiscal year ran from August 1 of the year depicted on the graph to July 31 of the next calendar year. Figure 5.3 illustrates prices and bales ginned from August 1, 1916, to July 31, 1933.

40. *Pittsburg Gazette*, January 31, April 11, September 19, 26, December 19, 1919; *Jefferson Jimplecute*, January 23, February 6, September 4, October 16, December 18, 1919, and January 22, February 19, April 29, May 13, July 29, August 26, October 28, December 2, 1920.

41. For contemporary accounts of the impact of prices and boll weevils, see Bizzell, *Rural Texas*, 276-283. Harriet Smith and Darthula Walker, *The Geography of Texas* (Boston: Ginn and Co., 1923), 90-134. *Paris Morning News*, January 12, 1922. *Jefferson Jimplecute*, September 2, October 7, 28, 1920; December 1, 1921; February 16, 1922. Also see Snyder, *Cotton Crisis*, xiii-xvii; Fite, *Cotton Fields No More*, 91-119; U.S., *Census: 1920, Agriculture*, vol. 6, pt. 2, 664-686; U.S., *Census: 1930, Agriculture*, vol. 2, pt. 2, 1382-1401; *Texas Almanac, 1929*, 99-106.

42. U.S., *Census: 1920, Agriculture*, vol. 6, pt. 2, 664-686; U.S., *Census of Agriculture, 1925*, pt. 2, 1110-1139. On land as an investment, see Sanders, "Ownership and Tenancy in the Black Prairie," 23-30.

43. Spikes and Ellis, *Crosby County, Texas*, 342-490; E. P. Scott, *Lamb County*, 86-268; M. L. Cox, *Hale County*; McDonald, "The History of Lubbock County, Texas"; Peterman, *Lamb County and Adjacent Communities*.

44. Hazel Cobb Wiseman, "Thomas C. Wiseman Family," in E. P. Scott, *Lamb County*, 267. Also see Neugebauer, *Diary of William G. DeLoach*, 24-115; Wright, *Old South, New South*, 17-50; Owens, *Season of Weathering*, 26-37. The South Plains is represented by the six counties surrounding Lubbock. For land prices represented in Figure 5.4, see U.S., *Census: 1900, Agriculture*, pt. 1, 125-131; U.S., *Census: 1910, Agriculture*, vol. 7, 655-675; U.S., *Census: 1920, Agriculture*, vol. 6, pt. 2, 664-686; U.S., *Census of Agriculture, 1925*, pt. 2. 1140-1170; U.S., *Census of the United States: 1930, Agriculture*, vol. 2, pt. 2, 1424-1445.

45. U.S., *Census of Religious Bodies, 1916*, pt. 1, 312-317; U.S., *Census of Religious Bodies, 1926*, vol. 1, 679-691, shows a similar percentage of white Baptists and Methodists in the South Plains and Northeast Texas but almost no members of black denominations. Also see Gary L. Nall, "The Farmer's Frontier in the Texas Panhandle," *Panhandle-Plains Historical Review (PPHR)* 45 (1972): 1-20; Nall, "Panhandle Farming in the 'Golden Age' of American Agriculture," *PPHR* 46 (1973): 94-112; Donald E. Green, *Land of the Underground Rain: Irrigation on the Texas High Plains, 1910-1970* (Austin: University of Texas Press, 1973), 100-144; Richard Wilson Arnold, "A History of Adaptation of Cotton to the High Plains of Texas, 1890-1974" (master's thesis, Texas Tech University, 1975); William Morris Holmes, "An Historical Geography of Dry Farming on the Northern High Plains of Texas" (Ph.D. dissertation, University of Texas at Austin, 1975). On problems faced by blacks in Oklahoma, see *Pittsburg Gazette*, June 3, August 5, 1904. Also see Interview with Dave M. Thompson by Walter L. Buenger,

December 1999 (author's possession). Thompson, born in the South Plains in the early 1920s, recalled using four-mule teams on his family's farm until he went off to World War II.

46. U.S., *Census: 1920, Agriculture*, vol. 6, pt. 2, 664–686; U.S., *Census of Agriculture, 1925*, pt. 2, 1140–1170; U.S., *Census: 1930, Agriculture*, vol. 2, pt. 2, 1422–1447; Sanders, "Ownership and Tenancy in the Black Prairie," 16–17.

47. For the value of machines and implements per improved acre, see Table 5.2. On how Americans conceptualized modern agriculture in the 1920s and the impact of those concepts on the South, see Kirby, *Rural Worlds Lost*, 1–22.

48. As noted in 1920, "The census classification of farm land as 'improved land' . . . is one not always easy for the farmers or enumerators to make, and statistics, therefore, must be considered at best a close approximation." Improved acres typically meant harvested cropland, failed cropland, fallow cropland, pasture that has been or can be plowed, gardens, orchards, nurseries, and vineyards. By 1935 this category had become "land available for crops." See U.S., *Census: 1920, Agriculture*, vol. 6, pt. 2, 655; U.S., *Census of Agriculture, 1935* (Washington: Government Printing Office, 1936), vol. 1, pt. 2, 742. According to U.S., *Census: 1920, Agriculture*, vol. 6, pt. 2, 664–686; U.S., *Census of Agriculture, 1925*, pt. 2, 1110–1139; U.S., *Census of Agriculture, 1935*, vol. 1, pt. 2, 742–763. Improved acres in Northeast Texas changed as follows: 1910 acreage 1,605,398; 1920 acreage 1,852,513 (+14.4 percent change); 1925 acreage 1,694,981 (-8.5 percent change); 1930 acreage 1,814,115 (+7 percent change).

49. *Paris Morning News*, June 23, 1928; U.S., *Census: 1920, Agriculture*, vol. 6, pt. 2, 664–686; U.S., *Census of Agriculture, 1925*, pt. 2, 1140–1170; U.S., *Census: 1930, Agriculture*, vol. 2, pt. 2, 1422–1447.

50. On implements, see Table 5.2 and U.S., *Census: 1920, Agriculture*, vol. 6, pt. 2, 664–686; U.S., *Census of Agriculture, 1925*, pt. 2, 1110–1139; U.S., *Census of Agriculture, 1935*, vol. 1, pt. 2, 742–763. On the decline in total population and rural population, see U.S., *Census: 1930, Population*, vol. 1, "Population of Counties by Minor Civil Divisions: 1930, 1920, and 1910," 1063–1086. In his 1924 work C. O. Brannen commented that in Texas "the acreage per tenant is higher than in other regions." See Brannen, "Relation of Land Tenure to Plantation Organization," 24.

51. U.S., *Census: 1920, Agriculture*, vol. 6, pt. 2, 664–686; U.S., *Census: 1930, Agriculture*, vol. 2, pt. 2, 1382–1401; Brannen, "Relation of Land Tenure to Plantation Organization," 29–32, 44–46; Sanders, "Ownership and Tenancy in the Black Prairie," 19–22.

52. Fligstein, *Going North*, 61–136; Wright, *Old South, New South*, 193–207; Brannen, "Relation of Land Tenure to Plantation Organization," 44–52.

53. From 1920 to 1930, share tenants, both black and white, decreased by about 10 percent in the county. Croppers increased by about 40 percent. See U.S., *Census: 1920, Agriculture*, vol. 6, pt. 2, 664–686; U.S., *Census: 1930, Agriculture*, vol. 2, pt. 2, 1382–1401. Children under age seven of all races declined by 34 percent in the county, too large a figure to be accounted for by changes in birth control. Young couples with small children of all races probably left. For that and other age, gender, and race data, see U.S., *Census: 1920, Population*, vol. 3, 991–

1012; U.S., *Census: 1930, Population,* vol. 3, pt. 2, 976-989. On black croppers moving from Mississippi, see Interview with Mathena by Crow, April 25, 1974, p. 11.

54. U.S., *Census: 1920, Agriculture,* vol. 6, pt. 2, 669; U.S., *Census: 1930, Agriculture,* vol. 2, pt. 2, 1428; U.S., *Census: 1920, Population,* vol. 3, 996, 1018; U.S., *Census: 1930, Population,* vol. 1, 1069, vol. 3, pt. 2, 954, 978, vol. 6, 1305; *Texas Almanac, 1925,* 269-270; Paul Garland Hervey, "A History of Education in Delta County, Texas" (master's thesis, University of Texas, 1951); Brannen, "Relation of Land Tenure to Plantation Organization," 24.

55. *Paris Morning News,* May 23, 25, 1922.

56. Schwulst, *Extension of Bank Credit,* 118. Also see Schwulst, *Extension of Bank Credit,* 86-118; *Pittsburg Gazette,* March 9, 16, 23, 1928; *Naples Monitor,* March 20, 1925; Brannen, "Relation of Land Tenure to Plantation Organization," 32.

57. *Texas Almanac, 1929,* 97-106; *Yearbook of Agriculture, 1934,* 466; *Texas Almanac, 1936,* 239-242; *Paris Morning News,* January 1, 1928; Fite, *Cotton Fields No More,* 150. It is useful here to recall the distinction between dynamic and "retrograde cotton counties" in Kirby, *Rural Worlds Lost,* 30.

58. *Texas Almanac, 1929,* 320-321; *The Texas Almanac and State Industrial Guide, 1931* (Dallas: A. H. Belo, 1931), 328. Also see Buenger and Pratt, *But Also Good Business,* 46-47; Michael Quinley Hooks, "The Struggle for Dominance: Urban Rivalry in North Texas, 1870-1910" (Ph.D. dissertation, Texas Tech University, 1979); William N. Black, "Empire of Consensus: City Planning, Zoning and Annexation in Dallas, 1900-1960" (Ph.D. dissertation, Columbia University, 1982).

59. On the impact of roads, see *Paris Morning News,* January 28, March 21, 25, 1928; Howard Lawrence Preston, *Dirt Roads to Dixie: Accessibility and Modernization in the South, 1885-1935* (Knoxville: University of Tennessee Press, 1991); John David Huddleston, "Good Roads for Texas: A History of the Texas Highway Department, 1917-1947" (Ph.D. dissertation, Texas A&M University, 1981); Kirk Kite, "A History of the Texas State Department of Highways and Public Transportation, 1917-1980" (Ph.D. dissertation, University of New Mexico, 1981).

60. U.S., *Census: 1910, Population,* vol. 2, 779; U.S., *Census: 1930. Population,* vol. 3, pt. 1, 980.

61. *Jefferson Jimplecute,* January 23, 1913; April 23, 1913; November 13, 1913. *Pittsburg Gazette,* November 15, 1912.

62. *Texas Almanac, 1925,* 269. Also see *Jefferson Jimplecute,* July 4, 1912. *Pittsburg Gazette,* June 15, 1917; July 27, 1917; July 11, 18, 1919, p. 1; August 1, 1919.

63. *Atlanta News,* quoted in *Cass County Sun,* July 20, 1909, p. 4. Also see *Cumby Rustler,* June 21, 1912, and February 4, 18, March 24, 31, 1916. *Jefferson Jimplecute,* March 10, 1911; May 23, December 19, 1912; July 2, 1914; September 9, December 2, 1915; February 17, 1916; July 12, December 6, 1917. *Naples Monitor,* April 10, August 25, 1925, and September 29, 1929. *Paris Morning News,* June 23, 30, 1928. Ina McAdams, "A Study of the Mt. Vernon *Optic-Herald,* 1906-1931, and its Community" (master's thesis, University of Texas, 1960).

64. U.S., *Census of Agriculture, 1925*, pt. 2, 1174-1203; U.S., *Census: Agriculture, 1930*, vol. 2, 1550-1561; *Texas Almanac, 1914*, 217-373; *Texas Almanac, 1925*, 250-351; *Texas Almanac, 1933*, 328-61; *The Texas Almanac and State Industrial Guide, 1941-42* (Dallas: A. H. Belo, 1941), 408-523; *Paris Morning News*, January 1, February 8, 9, 10, March 29, 1928; *Cooper Review*, March 29, 1908; St. Clair, "History of Hopkins County," 101-108.

65. U.S., *Census of Agriculture, 1925*, pt. 2, 1208-1236; U.S., *Census: 1930, Agriculture*, vol. 2, pt. 2, 1468-1470; *Pittsburg Gazette*, March 28, 1919; Spencer, *Camp County Story*, 70-80; Bureau of Business Research, *An Economic Survey of Camp County, Prepared for the Texas and Pacific Railroad Company* (Austin: University of Texas, 1949), 4.0101-4.0107. Also see interviews with area farmers in *Naples Monitor*, June 12, 1925.

66. U.S., *Census: 1910, Agriculture*, vol. 7, 680-698; U.S., *Census: 1920, Agriculture*, vol. 6, pt. 2, 717-735; U.S., *Census of Agriculture, 1925*, pt. 2, 1208-1236; U.S., *Census: 1930, Agriculture*, vol. 2, pt. 2, 1469-1485, 1562-1563; *Paris Morning News*, February 19, March 1, 1928; *Texas Almanac, 1925*, 250-351; Fite, *Cotton Fields No More*, 68-119; Robert A. Calvert, "Nineteenth-Century Farmers, Cotton, and Prosperity," *SHQ* 73 (April 1970): 509-21.

67. For the problems with substitutes for cotton, see *Jefferson Jimplecute*, July 30, 1914; *Pittsburg Gazette*, Anniversary Edition, February 16, 1934; Fite, *Cotton Fields No More*, 12-15; Spencer, *Camp County Story*, 70-80.

68. *Pittsburg Gazette*, August 18, 1922, and March 23, November 23, December 14, 1928; Fite, *Cotton Fields No More*, 13-18; "Commercial Crops of Texas," *Texas Almanac, 1929*, 85-96; Bureau of Business Research, *Economic Survey of Camp County*, 4.0107, 4.06.

69. For a thoughtful commentary on economic change and the lack thereof, see *Old South, New South*, 51-60. For statistics, including the addition of more than 11 million acres of improved acres available for crops, that indicate Texas was different, see U.S., *Census of Agriculture, 1925*, pt. 2, 1110; *Texas Almanac, 1926*, 135-141.

70. U.S., *Census: 1930, Population*, vol. 1, 1063-1094.

71. *Texas Almanac, 1914*, 217-218, 300-301, 319; *Jefferson Jimplecute*, September 19, October 24, 1912; Neville, *Lamar County*, 94; *Worley's Directory of Paris and Lamar County, Texas* (Dallas: J. F. Worley, 1908), 217-238.

72. Ayers, *Promise of the New South*, 55-80; U.S., *Census: 1930, Population*, vol. 1, 1064-1091; *Texas Almanac, 1904*, 217-374; *Texas Almanac, 1914*, 246-337.

73. *The Whisper, The Official Mouthpiece of Leonard Bros. Department Store* (Fort Worth: Leonard Brothers, 1929); Interview with Marty Leonard by Victoria L. Buenger and Walter L. Buenger, July 14, 1994; Interview with Hugh Tyree and Laura Tyree by Walter L. Buenger, July 1, 1994; Neil M. Clark, "Brother Act," *Saturday Evening Post*, June 24, 1944, 14-15, 59-63; Buenger and Buenger, *Texas Merchant*, 15-60. Members of William A. Owens's family also moved to Dallas in these years. See Owens, *Stubborn Soil*, 118-307. Also see *Jefferson Jimplecute*, October 23, 1919; January 20, 1920.

74. Francine Carraro, *Jerry Bywaters: A Life in Art* (Austin: University of

Texas Press, 1994), 1–8; Porter A. Bywaters, Jr., "The Organization and Management of the Bywaters Dry Goods Company" (bachelor's thesis in Business Administration, University of Texas, May 10, 1925, vertical file, Barker Texas History Center, University of Texas at Austin); *The Whisper.* Also see Larry H. Long, "Migration to, from and within Texas and its Metropolitan Areas for Selected Periods of Time between 1930 and 1960" (master's thesis, University of Texas at Austin, 1968).

75. *Pittsburg Gazette,* October 5, 1928, p. 1.

76. *Naples Monitor,* February 20, 1925, p. 2 (first quotation); September 20, 1929, p. 1 (second quotation); March 9, 1928, p. 1 (third quotation). For an example of how retailing in a large rural area concentrated in one Texas city, see Buenger and Buenger, *Texas Merchant,* 32–87.

77. *Paris Morning News,* February 16, 1928; *Fort Worth Star-Telegram,* January 1, September 28, 30, 1928; Emmet and Jeuck, *Catalogues and Counters,* 338–357.

78. U.S., *Census: 1930, Population,* vol. 1, 1063–1086.

79. U.S., *Census: 1930, Population,* vol. 1, 1003–1091.

80. U.S., *Census: 1930, Population,* vol. 1, 1087–1091; Buenger and Pratt, *But Also Good Business,* 64–91; Schwulst, *Extension of Bank Credit,* 41–118; Texas Historical Commission, "Delta County Centennial," marker file for Delta County, 1970, Austin; Texas Historical Commission, "First National Bank," marker file for Delta County, 1965, Austin.

81. *Pittsburg Gazette,* August 18, 1922; November 23, 1928; March 23, 1928; December 14, 1928. *Naples Monitor,* June 12, 1925. *Paris Morning News,* February 8, 10, 16, April 8, 19, 1928. U.S., *Census: 1920, Agriculture,* vol. 6, pt. 2, 717–735. U.S., *Census of Agriculture, 1925,* pt. 2, 1208–1236. U.S., *Census: 1930, Agriculture,* vol. 2, pt. 2, 1469–1485, *Texas Almanac, 1925,* 257–259. "Cotton," *Texas Almanac, 1926,* 135–143. "Cotton Growing Industry of Texas," *Texas Almanac, 1929,* 97–107.

82. *Paris Morning News,* May 8, 1928, p. 4, and February 16, 1928, p. 5. Also see *Texas Almanac, 1925,* 308; *Texas Almanac, 1933,* 345; Neville, *Lamar County,* 158–70, 223–29; *Paris Morning News,* January 1, 20, 28, February 16, March 20, 22, 25, 29, 31, April 1, 3, 5, 8, 10, 18, July 26, 1928.

83. U.S., *Census: 1930, Population,* vol. 1, 1063–1091.

84. *Texas Almanac, 1931,* 324; Bureau of Business Research, *Economic Survey of Camp County.* On elites and labor, see Wright, *Old South, New South,* 78–80.

85. U.S., *Census: 1920, Population,* vol. 3, 1017–1021; U.S., *Census: 1930, Population,* vol. 3, pt. 2, 1009–1013.

86. Owens, *Season of Weathering,* 258.

87. For a good description of the many subregions in the South of the 1920s, see Kirby, *Rural Worlds Lost,* 25–50. For an expanded discussion of the theme of connectedness, see Buenger, "Texas and the South," 310–314. Also see Grossman, *Land of Hope,* 40.

88. The closeness of urban centers was a fundamental difference between Texas and other southern states. See Fite, *Cotton Fields No More,* 113.

CHAPTER 6: WORLD WAR I AND A SHIFTING CULTURE

1. For the best argument that the war was the beginning point of significant change, see Kirby, *Rural Worlds Lost*, 51–79. For the best argument for the war's limited consequences, see Wright, *Old South, New South*, 198–238.

2. Wright, *Old South, New South*, 52, 206.

3. *Pittsburg Gazette*, July 6, 1917, p. 2; June 8, 1917, p. 2. Also see *Jefferson Jimplecute*, April 17, 1913; September 2, 1915; October 4, 1917; February 14, 1918. *Pittsburg Gazette*, April 11, May 31, June 21, 1918. Wright, *Old South, New South*, 201–203.

4. *Jefferson Jimplecute*, September 2, 1915.

5. For the list of lynchings in Texas, see D. T. Williams, *Amid the Gathering Multitude*. Also see U.S., *Census: 1920, Population*, vol. 3, 990–1014.

6. *Pittsburg Gazette*, August 24, 31, 1917, and July 18, 1919; *Jefferson Jimplecute*, August 30, 1917, and July 24, 1919; James M. SoRelle, "The 'Waco Horror': The Lynching of Jesse Washington," *SHQ* 86 (April 1983): 517–536; Kenneth R. Durham, "The Longview Race Riot of 1919," *ETHJ* 18 (spring 1980): 13–24; William Tuttle, "Violence in a 'Heathen' Land: The Longview Race Riot of 1919," *Phylon* 33 (winter 1972): 324–333; Robert V. Haynes, *Night of Violence: The Houston Race Riot of 1917* (Baton Rouge: Louisiana State University Press, 1976).

7. Tolnay and Beck, *Festival of Violence*, 202–238; McMillen, *Dark Journey*, 394–396 n. 30–33.

8. *Paris Morning News*, July 7, 1920; *Jefferson Jimplecute*, July 8, 1920; *Dallas Morning News*, July 3, 1920.

9. In 1980 Vernon Jarrett, a journalist, interviewed Ervin Hill, Herman and Ervin Arthur's nephew. Portions of that interview were quoted in Vernon Jarrett, "An Old Photo Comes to Life," in the column "Remembering Black Chicago." This column appeared in several newspapers that year, and I am indebted to Albert S. Broussard for a clipping.

10. *Paris Morning News*, July 7, 1920, p. 1; *Dallas Morning News*, July 7, 1920, p. 1.

11. *Dallas Morning News*, July 8, 1920, p. 1. Also see *Paris Morning News*, July 8, 9, 10, 1920; *Dallas Morning News*, July 9, 1920; Jarrett, "An Old Photo Comes to Life." For a photo of the Arthur family upon their arrival in Chicago, see Allan N. Spear, *Black Chicago: The Making of a Negro Ghetto, 1890–1920* (Chicago: University of Chicago Press, 1967), photo no. 11.

12. *Paris Morning News*, July 10, 1920, p. 1. Compare this with the refusal of ministers in the Waco area to condemn the brutal lynching of Jesse Washington in 1916. See SoRelle, "Lynching of Jesse Washington," 528–536. For biographical information on Shuler, see *Bob Shuler's Free Lance*, January 1919, 8; Ellis and Steely, *First Church of Paris: First United Methodist Church*, 128–132.

13. *Paris Morning News*, July 10, 1920, p. 1. Also see *Paris Morning News*, February 3, 1893.

14. On the black veterans of Paris, see Reich, "Soldiers of Democracy," 1499.

15. On the use of ritualized violence before a large audience as a form of race

control, see W. Fitzhugh Brundage, *Lynching in the New South: Georgia and Virginia, 1880-1930* (Urbana and Chicago: University of Illinois Press, 1993), 17-49. Also see U.S., *Census: 1910, Population,* vol. 3, 804-847; U.S., *Census: 1920, Population,* vol. 3, 990-1014; U.S., *Census: 1930, Population,* vol. 3, pt. 2, 975-990; U.S., *Census: 1920, Agriculture,* vol. 6, pt. 2, 664-686; U.S., *Census of Agriculture, 1925,* pt. 2, 1110-1139.

16. *Paris News,* July 7, 8, 9, 10, 1920; *Jefferson Jimplecute,* September 2, 1915. Also see U.S., *Census: 1910, Population,* vol. 3, 804-847; U.S., *Census: 1920, Population,* vol. 3, 990-1014. For a discussion of the relationship between cotton and lynching and a brief review of several attempts to explain lynching, see Tolnay and Beck, *Festival of Violence,* 119-165, 253-257.

17. *Pittsburg Gazette,* September 19, 26, October 17, December 19, 1919; *Jefferson Jimplecute,* November 6, 1919, and January 22, 29, February 4, March 4, 1920.

18. *Jefferson Jimplecute,* April 11, 1918, p. 2. Also see *Jefferson Jimplecute,* May 14, 21, August 21, November 5, 1914; January 7, 1915; April 20, 1916; August 26, September 9, 1920. *Omaha Breeze,* August 24, 1910. Moseley, "Citizens White Primary," 524-531.

19. *Jefferson Jimplecute,* November 27, 1913; August 27, 1914; February 3, April 20, 1916; February 14, April 11, 1918. *Pittsburg Gazette,* August 5, 1904; May 25, June 22, July 6, 13, 1917; May 3, 31, June 21, 1918; April 11, 1919. *Cass County Sun,* February 11, 1908. *Omaha Breeze,* August 24, 1910, and June 5, 1912. On the Great Migration and the ebbing of lynching, see Tolnay and Beck, *Festival of Violence,* 202-238. Texas, which is not included in their statistical study, seemed to be slightly ahead of the downward curve in lynching in the mid-1920s.

20. U.S., *Census: 1910, Population,* vol. 3, 854-857; U.S., *Census: 1920, Population,* vol. 3, 1017-1021. Part of Texarkana is in Arkansas. Taken as a whole it was slightly larger than Paris by 1920.

21. U.S., *Census: 1920, Population,* vol. 3, 1017-1021; U.S., *Census: 1930, Population,* vol. 3, pt. 2, 1009-1013; U.S., *Sixteenth Census of the United States: 1940, Population* (Washington: Government Printing Office, 1943), vol. 2, 995-1002, 1015-1016; *Jefferson Jimplecute,* September 9, 1920.

22. U.S., *Census: 1910, Agriculture,* vol. 7, 655-675; U.S., *Census: 1920, Agriculture,* vol. 6, pt. 2, 664-686; U.S., *Census of Agriculture, 1925,* pt. 2, 1110-1139.

23. *Pittsburg Gazette,* June 21, 1918, p. 3. Also see D. T. Williams, *Amid the Gathering Multitude; Jefferson Jimplecute,* April 11, July 11, 25, 1918; Foley, *White Scourge,* 40-91; P. S. Taylor, *Mexican-American Frontier,* 98-146.

24. On counting Mexican immigrants, see Mark Reisler, *The Sweat of Their Brow: Mexican Immigrant Labor in the United States, 1900-1940* (Westport, Conn.: Greenwood Press, 1976), 265-270; Lawrence A. Cardoso, "Labor Emigration to the Southwest, 1916 to 1920: Mexican Attitudes and Policy," *SHQ* 79 (April 1976): 400-416; Cardoso, *Mexican Emigration,* 83, 129-130; R. Reynolds McKay, "Texas Mexican Repatriation during the Great Depression" (Ph.D. dissertation, University of Oklahoma, 1982), 66; Arnoldo De León and Kenneth L. Stewart, *Tejanos and the Number Game: A Socio-Historical Interpretation from the Federal Census* (Albuquerque: University of New Mexico Press, 1989).

25. U.S. *Census: 1930, Population,* vol. 3, pt. 2, 975-990.

26. U.S., *Census: 1916, Religious Bodies*, pt. 1, 311–318; U.S., *Census: 1926, Religious Bodies*, vol. 1, 678–691.

27. Church membership typically ranged between 32 percent and 40 percent of the total population. See U.S., *Census: 1906, Religious Bodies*, pt. 1, 357–364; U.S., *Census: 1916, Religious Bodies*, pt. 1, 311–318; U.S., *Census: 1926, Religious Bodies*, vol. 1, 678–691; U.S., *Census: 1936, Religious Bodies*, vol. 1, 824–836. Also see *Pittsburg Gazette*, March 4, 1904; May 11, 1917; August 2, 1918. *Paris Morning News*, May 19, 1922. Montejano, *Anglos and Mexicans in the Making of Texas*, 157–256. Foley, *White Scourge*, 44–50. Foley, *White Scourge*, 57, quotes Eugene Black, the congressman from Northeast Texas as saying in the mid-1920s that large-scale Mexican immigration would "pull down the pillars of our whole economic structure on our heads."

28. For an excellent discussion of responses to discrimination, see Emilio Zamora, *The World of the Mexican Worker in Texas* (College Station: Texas A&M University Press, 1993), 10–109.

29. *Sulphur Springs Gazette*, May 31, 1912, p. 2. Also see *Sulphur Springs Gazette*, June 21, 1912; *Pittsburg Gazette*, September 5, 1919. For comparison with Georgia, where World War I made at least a limited difference in the nature of lynching, see Brundage, *Lynching in the New South*, 215–244. Lynching remained a force in Georgia, however, far longer than it did in Texas. See Brundage, *Lynching in the New South*, 245–259.

30. *Pittsburg Gazette*, March 8, 1918, p. 7. Also see *Pittsburg Gazette*, May 31, 1918.

31. R. Douglas Brackenridge, *Voices in the Wilderness: A History of the Cumberland Presbyterian Church in Texas* (San Antonio: Trinity University Press, 1968), 130–131; Ivy, "Francis Willard's Forgotten 1882 Texas Temperance Tour," 48–50. E. L. Dohoney and his wife were members of the Cumberland Presbyterian Church. See Dohoney, *Average American*, 190–231.

32. *Omaha Breeze*, August 5, 1908, p. 2, and January 26, 1910, p. 2; *Cass County Sun*, June 29, 1909, p. 2. Also see *Omaha Breeze*, May 1, 1912. *Pittsburg Gazette*, January 18, 25, 1910; May 10, 1912; April 5, 1918; August 2, 9, 1918. *Jefferson Jimplecute*, October 1, 1914. *Sulphur Springs Gazette*, August 7, 1914.

33. *Jefferson Jimplecute*, June 19, 1913; November 5, 1914; September 2, 1915; December 29, 1918. Russell, *Carpetbaggers, Scalawags and Others*, 87–89. McKay and Spelling, *History of Jefferson*, 55.

34. *Jefferson Jimplecute*, July 26, 1917, p. 1, and April 4, 1918, p. 2. For a mid-nineteenth-century Marion County woman who also demonstrated considerable autonomy and business skill, see Judith N. McArthur, "Myth, Reality, and Anomaly: The Complex World of Rebecca Hagerty," *ETHJ* 24, no. 2 (1986): 18–32.

35. *Pittsburg Gazette*, May 31, 1918; June 21, 1918; August 2, 1918. *Jefferson Jimplecute*, January 27, 1912, and January 22, 1914. *Cass County Sun*, May 18, 1909. McArthur, *Creating the New Woman*, 97–150.

36. *Houston Post*, July 24, 1916; *Jefferson Jimplecute*, July 20, 27, August 3, 1916; *Pittsburg Gazette*, July 19, 1918; Gould, *Progressives and Prohibitionists*, 194–199, 222–248.

37. On Northeast Texas women in politics, see *Jefferson Jimplecute*, April 4, July 18, 1918, and February 28, March 13, 20, May 15, 22, 29, 1919; *Pittsburg Gazette*, May 31, 1918, and May 2, 9, 16, June 6, 1919; *Cooper Review*, July 12, 1918. For an elaboration of which women voted and why women got the vote in the Texas primary, see McArthur, *Creating the New Woman*, 137-139; E. C. Green, *Southern Strategies*, 179-183; Susan E. Marshall, *Splintered Sisterhood: Gender and Class in the Campaign against Woman Suffrage* (Madison: University of Wisconsin Press, 1997), 17-57, 223-235.

38. *Pittsburg Gazette*, May 3, 1918, p. 6.

39. *Pittsburg Gazette*, July 5, 1918, p. 8.

40. *Pittsburg Gazette*, August 2, 9, 30, 1918.

41. *Pittsburg Gazette*, August 2, 30, 1918.

42. *Pittsburg Gazette*, June 7, 14, 21, July 19, August 2, 1918; *Jefferson Jimplecute*, June 12, 27, July 11, 18, 25, August 1, 1918; *Cooper Review*, August 2, 9, 1918; *Mount Vernon Optic Herald*, July 19, 26, August 2, 1918; *Omaha Breeze*, August 7, 1918; Debbie Mauldin Cottrell, *Pioneer Woman Educator: The Progressive Spirit of Annie Webb Blanton* (College Station: Texas A&M University Press, 1993); Judith N. McArthur, "Motherhood and Reform in the New South: Texas Women's Political Culture in the Progressive Era" (Ph.D. dissertation, University of Texas at Austin, 1992), 552-555.

43. *Jefferson Jimplecute*, July 18, 25, August 1, 1918; *Pittsburg Gazette*, May 10, 24, June 7, July 5, 19, 26, August 2, 1918.

44. *Jefferson Jimplecute*, June 12, July 11, 18, 25, 1918; Gould, *Progressives and Prohibitionists*, 222-248.

45. *Cooper Review*, July 12, August 9, 16, 1918; *Paris Morning News*, July 9, 10, 23, 24, 25, 26, 27, 28, 1918; *Pittsburg Gazette*, June 14, July 12, 19, 26, 1918.

46. *Jefferson Jimplecute*, April 4, June 14, 1918; *Pittsburg Gazette*, June 14, July 5, 1918. In 1916 Ferguson faced a weak and disorganized opponent. See *Dallas Morning News*, July 23, 24, 1916; *Houston Post*, July 23, 124, 25, 26, 1916.

47. *Omaha Breeze*, May 12, 1909, and August 7, 1918; *Pittsburg Gazette*, August 2, 1918; *Texarkana Four States Press*, July 28, 29, 1918; *Dallas Morning News*, July 28, 31, 1918; *Houston Post*, August 11, 19, 1918.

48. *Pittsburg Gazette*, March 8, 1918, p. 7. Also see McArthur, *Creating the New Woman*, 97-150.

49. *Jefferson Jimplecute*, October 21, 1920, p. 1; November 8, 1917, p. 2; January 15, 1920, p. 3. Also see *Jefferson Jimplecute*, June 16, 23, July 28, 1911; January 22, October 1, 1914; April 13, 1916; October 2, 1919. *Omaha Breeze*, May 12, 1909. Wheeler, *New Women of the New South*, 38-99. Link, *Paradox of Southern Progressivism*, 124-159.

50. *Sulphur Springs Gazette*, November 8, 1912; Bowers and Oppenheimer, *Red River Dust*, 56-58, 73-75; Stroud, *Gateway to Texas*, 307-385; Humphrey, *Farther off from Heaven*, 26-29, 198-200.

51. *Texas Almanac, 1925*, 308. Also see Hollis, *Paris Fire of 1916*; Neville, *Lamar County*, 223-229; Interview with Maitland Mayer Truby by Anna May Curtis, April 23, 1980; Interview with Mutt Cross by Corrine Crow, December 5, 1972;

Interview with Mutt Cross by Steve Burgin, 1985 (transcriptions of all three interviews are available in the Aikin Regional Archives, Paris Junior College).

52. *Omaha Breeze*, July 28, 1909, p. 2. Also see *Pittsburg Gazette*, April 5, 12, May 24, 31, June 14, July 5, 12, 19, August 2, 1918.

53. *Jefferson Jimplecute*, January 16, May 29, 1919; *Pittsburg Gazette*, May 30, 1919; Gould, *Progressives and Prohibitionists*, 253–257; A. Elizabeth Taylor, "The Woman Suffrage Movement in Texas," *JSH* 17 (May 1951): 194–215; Election Returns: 1919, Secretary of State.

54. *Jefferson Jimplecute*, May 7, 1919, supplement. Also see *Jefferson Jimplecute*, May 15, 23, 30, 1919.

55. *Pittsburg Gazette*, May 16, 23, 30, June 6, 1919; *Jefferson Jimplecute*, May 29, June 5, 1919; *Paris Morning News*, May 29, 30, 1919; Election Returns: 1919, Secretary of State.

56. *Jefferson Jimplecute*, May 22, June 5, 12, 19, 26, 1919; *Pittsburg Gazette*, June 17, 1919.

57. For poll tax receipts divided by gender, see *Jefferson Jimplecute*, February 5, 1920, p. 3. Also see *Jefferson Jimplecute*, January 15, 22, 29, 1920. For comments on women and newspaper readership, see Owens, *Season of Weathering*, 177–192.

58. *Jefferson Jimplecute*, January 1, 1920, p. 3; *Pittsburg Gazette*, May 2, 1919, p. 8. Also see *Pittsburg Gazette*, February 6, 1920; *Jefferson Jimplecute*, January 15, 1920.

59. *Naples Monitor*, February 20, May 15, 1925; *Jefferson Jimplecute*, May 15, 1919, and February 15, 1923; *Pittsburg Gazette*, June 6, 13, 1919; *Paris Morning News*, July 26, 27, 1922, and April 5, 6, 1928. Also see Brown, *Hood, Bonnet, and Little Brown Jug*, 129–167, 340–373; Emma Louise Moyer Jackson, "Petticoat Politics: Political Activism among Texas Women in the 1920s," (Ph.D. dissertation, University of Texas at Austin, 1980).

60. On changes in family structure and fertility, see Steven Ruggles, *Prolonged Connections: The Rise of the Extended Family in Nineteenth-Century England and America* (Madison: University of Wisconsin Press, 1987), 3–105; Lee L. Bean, Geraldine P. Mineau, and Douglas L. Anderton, *Fertility Change on the American Frontier: Adaptation and Innovation* (Berkeley: University of California Press, 1990), 9–108; James Reed, *From Private Vice to Public Virtue: The Birth Control Movement and American Society since 1830* (New York: Basic Books, 1978), 37–142; Stewart E. Tolnay and Avery M. Guest, "American Family Building Strategies in 1900: Stopping or Spacing?" *Demography* 21 (1984): 9–18.

61. Before 1910 the census does not give totals for women 21 and older or children under 5. It also does not break down women 21 and older into subcategories, preventing a more targeted look at women of child-bearing age—roughly 18 to 45. The rate of growth of the under-5 population before 1910 was determined by using the following formula. Population under 5 = (total population) − (males 21 and over) − [(all females/all males) × (males 21 and over)] − (age 5 to 20). See U.S., *Census: 1890, Population*, pt. 1, 782–785; U.S., *Census: 1900, Population*, vol. 1, pt. 1, 520–524, and vol. 2, pt. 2, 203–206. The 1910 census gives the

6 to 20 population instead of 5 to 20. See U.S., *Census: 1910, Population,* vol. 3, 804–847. The following formulas yield a rough equivalent. Population under 6 = (total population) − (males 21 and over) − [(all females/all males) × (males 21 and over)] − (age 6 to 20). Population under 5 = (under 6) − (under 6/6). Also see U.S., *Census: 1920, Population,* vol. 3, 991–1012; U.S., *Census: 1930, Population,* vol. 3, pt. 2, 976–989. For the conversion method used to make the 1910 figures compatible with 1920 and 1930, see note 74 in this chapter.

62. U.S., *Census: 1910, Population,* vol. 3, 806–847; U.S., *Census: 1920, Population,* vol. 3, 991–1012. For an example of a much more sophisticated examination of changes in fertility made possible by a wealth of data, see Bean, Mineau, and Anderton, *Fertility Change on the American Frontier,* 109–254.

63. There are also other possible methods for determining change in birth rates, including using the birth records collected by the State Health Department. Before the 1930s, however, these records were incomplete and varied from county to county. If doctors and midwives did not send in birth notification, the Health Department had no record of birth. Blacks in particular were under reported. In 1927 only one black birth was reported for Camp County, yet blacks made up 40 percent of the population. See Texas, *Biennial Report of the State Department of Health,* 1916–1918, p. 16; 1927–1928, p. 72–76. Thus, while admittedly a rough gauge of change, the school-age divisions provided in the *Census* offer the best available long-term measurement of a changing birth rate.

64. Local newspapers in 1918 reveal no disproportionate number of deaths due to influenza among the young. See *Jefferson Jimplecute; Naples Monitor; Paris Morning News; Pittsburg Gazette; Sulphur Springs Gazette; Texarkana Four States Press.* Also see Texas, *Biennial Report of the State Health Officer of Texas,* 1900–1927 (Austin); Owens, *Stubborn Soil,* 199–204.

65. U.S., *Census: 1910, Population,* vol. 3, 806–847; U.S., *Census: 1920, Population,* vol. 3, 991–1012; U.S., *Census: 1930, Population,* vol. 3, pt. 2, 976–989.

66. U.S., *Census: 1910, Population,* vol. 3, 806–847; U.S., *Census: 1920, Population,* vol. 3, 991–1012; U.S., *Census: 1930, Population,* vol. 3, pt. 2, 976–989.

67. The more detailed 1930 census shows that for whites the ratio of children under 10 to women between 15 and 44 was 0.96:1 and for blacks the ratio was 1.08:1. A *t*-test for paired samples indicates that the difference between white and black ratios was not random. See U.S., *Census: 1930, Population,* vol. 3, pt. 2, 951–969.

68. The 1925 *Census of Agriculture* gives figures for children under 10 and women 10 and older by race and tenure. Using these figures the child to women ratio was 0.764:1 for the entire farm population and 0.769:1 for the white farm population. The figure for all farm owners was 0.579:1. For white owners it was 0.576:1. For black owners it was 0.588:1. The figure for the entire black farm population was 0.02 lower than for the entire white farm population. This may have been the result of some black agricultural workers' having families that lived in town. See U.S., *Census of Agriculture, 1925,* pt. 2, 1241–1262.

69. U.S., *Census: 1910, Population,* vol. 3, 806–847; U.S., *Census: 1920, Population,* vol. 3, 991–1012; U.S., *Census: 1930, Population,* vol. 3, pt. 2, 976–989. Also see Calvert, "Agrarian Texas," 225–228.

70. The correlation coefficient of low percentage black and high percentage decline of the under-seven population of the ten counties that lost population is 0.709. See U.S., *Census: 1910, Population*, vol. 3, 806-847; U.S., *Census: 1920, Population*, vol. 3, 991-1012; U.S., *Census: 1930, Population*, vol. 3, pt. 2, 976-989.

71. *Jefferson Jimplecute*, April 4, 1918, p. 2.

72. For a review of the debate on family structure, see Tamara K. Hareven, "The History of the Family and the Complexity of Social Change," *American Historical Review (AHR)* 96 (February 1991): 95-124. Also see Bean, *Fertility Change*, 29-33; Reed, *From Private Vice to Public Virtue*, 197-210; Ruggles, *Prolonged Connections*, xvii-xix, 58-135; Steven Ruggles, "The Transformation of American Family Structure," *AHR* 99 (February 1994): 103-128.

73. On public interest in education, see *Pittsburg Gazette*, February 26, September 9, 1904, and January 3, 1913. *Jefferson Jimplecute*, January 15, May 14, 21, September 24, 1914. *Omaha Breeze*, August 3, 24, 31, 1910; February 11, 1911; February 14, 1912. *Cass County Sun*, Feb 25, March 17, 1908. Also see John C. Caldwell, *Theory of Fertility Decline* (London and New York: Academic Press, 1982), 3-8, 301-330.

74. U.S., *Census: 1910, Population*, vol. 3, 806; U.S., *Census: 1920, Population*, vol. 3, 991-1012; U.S., *Census: 1930, Population*, vol. 3, pt. 2, 976-989; U.S., *Census: 1940, Population*, vol. 2, 793-805. The 1910 figures were converted to age groups used in the later censuses as follows. Under 7 = (total population) - (males 21 and older) - [(all females/all males) × (males 21 and older)] - (age 6 to 20) + [(age 6 to 9)/4]. Age 7 to 13 = (age 6 to 9) - [(age 6 to 9)/4] + (age 10 to 14) - (age 10 to 14)/5. Age 14 to 15 = [(age 10 to 14)/5] + [(age 15 to 17)/3]. Age 16 to 17 = (age 15 to 17) - [(age 15 to 17)/3].

75. Ruggles, *Prolonged Connections*, xix.

76. *Omaha Breeze*, May 8, 1912, p. 2. Link, *Paradox of Southern Progressivism*, 160-199, 296-321, considers Texas an exception to widespread southern resistance to changes in family life.

77. *Atlanta Citizens Journal*, May 7, 1908; *Omaha Breeze*, October 4, 1911; *Pittsburg Gazette*, September 29, 1911, and February 2, May 17, 1912; *Sulphur Springs Gazette*, February 2, July 26; *Jefferson Jimplecute*, February 15, July 25, 1912; Francis W. Johnson, *A History of Texas and Texans* (Chicago: American Historical Society, 1914), 5: 2555-2556; *Members of the Texas Legislature, 1842-1962* (Austin: State Printing Office, 1962), 233.

78. *Sulphur Springs Gazette*, February 2, March 1, 1912; *Members of the Texas Legislature*, 223; *Omaha Breeze*, March 24, 1909, and March 8, 1911.

79. *Sulphur Springs Gazette*, March 29, July 19, 1912; *Omaha Breeze*, May 1, 1912; *Members of the Texas Legislature*, 223.

80. *Pittsburg Gazette*, July 19, p. 7. Also see *Sulphur Springs Gazette*, May 31, 1912; *Pittsburg Gazette*, July 12, 19, 1912.

81. *Sulphur Springs Gazette*, April 5, 1912.

82. For the best analysis of regionalism within the district, see *Sulphur Springs Gazette*, July 19, 1912. For precinct returns, see *Sulphur Springs Gazette*, August 9, 1912, p. 9; *Jefferson Jimplecute*, August 1, 1912, p. 2; *Pittsburg Gazette*, August 2, 1912, p. 1; *Cooper Review*, August 2, 9, 1912, p. 1.

83. *Pittsburg Gazette*, August 2, 9, 1912; *Jefferson Jimplecute*, August 1, 8, 1912; *Sulphur Springs Gazette*, July 26, August 2, 9, 1912.

84. For information on the candidates and the campaign, see *Pittsburg Gazette*, February 2, July 26, 1912; *Jefferson Jimplecute*, February 15, June 13, July 25, August 1, 1912; *Omaha Breeze*, March 16, May 1, August 31, 1910, and April 24, May 1, 1912; *Dallas Morning News*, July 29, 1912; Texas Senate, *Journal of the Called Session of the Senate of the Thirty Second Legislature*, 609; F. W. Johnson, *Texas and Texans* 5: 2555–2556.

85. *Omaha Breeze*, April 5, 1911, p. 2. Also see *Omaha Breeze*, March 8, October 4, 1911, and June 5, 1912; *Jefferson Jimplecute*, August 1, 1912.

86. *Cumby Rustler*, February 9, 1912, p. 4. Also see *Sulphur Springs Gazette*, June 14, 21, 28, July 5, 12, 19, 26, 1912; *Jefferson Jimplecute*, May 26, June 2, 9, 16, 23, 30, July 7, 14, 21, 28, August 11, 1912.

87. *Sulphur Springs Gazette*, August 2, 1912, p. 2, and November 29, 1912, p. 6. Also see *Pittsburg Gazette*, September 29, 1911, and February 2, May 17, July 26, 1912; *Sulphur Springs Gazette*, February 2, July 26, 1912; *Cumby Rustler*, August 23, 1912.

88. *Sulphur Springs Gazette*, July 24, 1914 p. 6.

89. *Pittsburg Gazette*, June 26, 1914, p. 4; *Sulphur Springs Gazette*, July 24, 1914, p. 6.

90. *Jefferson Jimplecute*, February 19, 1914, p. 1. Also see *Washington Post*, May 27, 1975.

91. *Jefferson Jimplecute*, February 19, April 23, July 30, 1914; *Sulphur Springs Gazette*, July 24, 1914; *Pittsburg Gazette*, June 26, July 24, August 14, 1914; *Houston Post*, July 26, 1914.

92. *Pittsburg Gazette*, July 31, 1914, and August 4, 1922.

93. *Jefferson Jimplecute*, August 1, 1912, p. 2.

94. This is a point discussed in Link, *Paradox of Southern Progressivism*, xi–xii, 10–16.

95. *Sulphur Springs Gazette*, June 21, 1912, p. 2. Also see *Omaha Breeze*, April 17, 1912; Gould, *Progressives and Prohibitionists*, 283–291.

96. *Jefferson Jimplecute*, June 14, 1917, p. 1.

97. *Jefferson Jimplecute*, September 18, 1919 p. 2; November 6, 1919, p. 3.

98. *Jefferson Jimplecute*, November 6, 1919, p. 3. Also see *Pittsburg Gazette*, May 16, June 6, July 18, August 15, November 14, 21, December 12, 1919.

99. *Pittsburg Gazette*, February 28, 1919, p. 2.

100. Owens, *Stubborn Soil*, 191. Also see Vaughan, *Cotton Renter's Son*, 148–193; Clyde L. Emby, *Our Good Old Days* (Laird Hill, Texas: n.p., 1970), 170–212.

101. Wright Patman to Eugene Black, May 30, 1918, Wright Patman Papers (WPP), LBJ Library, Austin; Eugene Black to Wright Patman, July 28, 1918, WPP; Nancy Beck Young, "Wright Patman: Congressman to the Nation"; "Opponent and Champion of the KKK," *Austin Statesman*, August 14, 1921; Schmelzer, "Wright Patman," 20–24.

102. *Paris Morning News*, January 4, 10, 1922.

103. *Paris Morning News*, January 10, 1922, p. 2.

104. Compare the status of women in Northeast Texas with those in Wheeler, *New Women of the New South,* 72–187.
    105. Emby, *Our Good Old Days,* 212.
    106. *Paris Morning News,* March 16, 1922, p. 1.

CHAPTER 7: WOMEN, THE KU KLUX KLAN, AND
FACTIONAL IDENTITY, 1920–1927

1. *Jefferson Jimplecute,* November 6, 1919, p. 2.
    2. *Jefferson Jimplecute,* January 22, 1920, p. 3. Also see Owens, *Stubborn Soil,* 186–187; *Jefferson Jimplecute,* January 23, March 13, April 17, 24, May 29, June 12, 19, September 18, October 9, 16, 23, 30, November 13, December 4, 1919, and March 24, 1921; *Pittsburg Gazette,* January 10, Feb 14, May 9, 16, 23, July 18, December 12, 1919; *Paris Morning News,* May 25, 27, 1919.
    3. Election Returns: 1916, Secretary of State.
    4. Interview with Mathena by Crow, April 25, 1974, p. 34. Also see J. R. Green, *Grass-Roots Socialism,* 228–344.
    5. *Cooper Review,* July 19, 1918, p. 4.
    6. *Pittsburg Gazette,* January 10, 1919, p. 2. Also see Eugene Black to Wright Patman, February 24, 1922, WPP; Eugene Black to the people of Morris County, *Naples Monitor,* March 30, 1928, p. 1; *Cooper Review,* August 9, 1918; *Pittsburg Gazette,* January 10, February 14, May 9, 16, 23, 1919; *Jefferson Jimplecute,* January 23, February 13, April 24, June 19, July 3, August 28, 1919.
    7. Gould, *Progressives and Prohibitionists,* 16–27, 249–277; Bob Charles Holcomb, "Senator Joe Bailey: Two Decades of Controversy" (Ph.D. dissertation, Texas Tech University, 1969).
    8. *Jefferson Jimplecute,* July 15, 22, 29, 1920; *Pittsburg Gazette,* December 19, 1919, and February 6, July 16, 23, 30, 1920.
    9. *Jefferson Jimplecute,* July 15, 22, 29, 1920; *Pittsburg Gazette,* December 19, 1919, and February 6, July 16, 23, 30, 1920; Gould, *Progressives and Prohibitionists,* 271–272.
    10. *Jefferson Jimplecute,* July 15, 22, 29, 1920; *Pittsburg Gazette,* December 19, 1919, and February 6, July 16, 23, 30, 1920; *Dallas Morning News,* July 26, 1920; Gould, *Progressives and Prohibitionists,* 271.
    11. *Jefferson Jimplecute,* June 17, July 29, 1920; *Pittsburg Gazette,* July 30, 1920; *Dallas Morning News,* July 26, 27, 1920; *Houston Post,* July 26, 27, 1920.
    12. *Jefferson Jimplecute,* August 26, September 2, 1920; *Pittsburg Gazette,* August 27, September 3, 1920; *Dallas Morning News,* August 28, 29, 30, 1920.
    13. *Jefferson Jimplecute,* January 20, 1920, p. 3.
    14. *Paris Morning News,* February 5, August 26, 27, 28, 29, 30, 1920; *Dallas Morning News,* August 30, 1920; *Jefferson Jimplecute,* February 5, August 26, 1920; *Pittsburg Gazette,* February 6, August 27, 1920.
    15. Dohoney, *Average American,* 87. The most avid upper-class advocates of the Confederate myth probably also led the antisuffrage movement and may not

have voted in 1920. See Marshall, *Splintered Sisterhood,* 17–57, 223–235; E. C. Green, *Southern Strategies,* 30–55, 78–126, 179–183.

16. *Jefferson Jimplecute,* September 22, 1921, p. 1.

17. *Jefferson Jimplecute,* February 19, 1914, p. 1.

18. Owens, *Stubborn Soil,* 40.

19. Owens, *Stubborn Soil,* 305, but see throughout. For further information on education in the 1910s and 1920s in Northeast Texas, see Owens, *Season of Weathering;* Interview with Corener Dean by Corrinne Crow, June 1973, East Texas State University Library; Riley, *Washing on the Line,* 18–51; Jones, *Recollections,* 1–42; John Marion Ellis II, *The Way It Was: a Personal Memoir of Family Life in East Texas* (Waco: Texian Press, 1983), 17–79. Also see *Jefferson Jimplecute,* February 6, 28, 1919; July 22, September 23, October 14, 21, 1920; May 21, 26, 1926.

20. *Jefferson Jimplecute,* August 1, 1912, p. 2; *Cooper Review,* March 26, 1909 (special issue), p. 1. Also see *Omaha Breeze,* September 8, 1909; *Atlanta News,* December 29, 1910; *Sulphur Springs Gazette,* December 6, 1912; *Jefferson Jimplecute,* April 4, 1918.

21. Owens, *Season of Weathering,* 4–11, 182–257; Thad Sitton and Milam C. Rowold, *Ringing the Children In: Texas Country Schools* College Station: Texas A&M University Press, 1988); *Sulphur Springs Gazette,* December 6, 1912.

22. *Paris Morning News,* March 26, 30, 31, July 6, 7, 12, 19, 1922; Brown, *Hood, Bonnet and Little Brown Jug,* 49–87.

23. Shawn Lay, "Conclusion: Toward a New Historical Appraisal of the Ku Klux Klan of the 1920s," in Shawn Lay (ed.), *The Invisible Empire in the West: Toward a New Historical Appraisal of the Ku Klux Klan of the 1920s* (Urbana: University of Illinois Press, 1992), 222. Also see Charles C. Alexander, *Crusade for Conformity: The Ku Klux Klan in Texas, 1920-1930* (Houston: Texas Gulf Coast Historical Association, 1962), 1–14; Charles C. Alexander, *The Ku Klux Klan in the Southwest* (Lexington: University of Kentucky Press, 1965), 1–54; Leonard J. Moore, "Historical Interpretations of the 1920s Klan: The Traditional View and Recent Revisions," in Lay (ed.), *The Invisible Empire in the West,* 17–38; Reich, "Soldiers of Democracy," 1478–1504; Kathleen M. Blee, *Women of the Klan: Racism and Gender in the 1920s* (Berkeley: University of California Press, 1991), 1–8.

24. For a notable exception to the paucity of records, see Nancy MacLean, *Behind the Mask of Chivalry: The Making of the Second Ku Klux Klan* (New York: Oxford University Press, 1994). She argues that in Athens, Georgia, half the Klansmen were small proprietors or white-collar workers who were born into farm families that owned a few acres and rented a few more. Having climbed a rung up from their parents, they feared slipping back. Thus the Klan appealed to those determined not to fall back to the status of their parents. Also see Buenger and Buenger, *Texas Merchant,* 63–66.

25. Quoted in Reich, "Soldiers of Democracy," 1478–1479.

26. Fred McKenzie, "The Kellyville Incident," *ETHJ* 37 (spring 1999): 39–41.

27. *Jefferson Jimplecute,* August 12, 1920; McKenzie, "The Kellyville Incident," 40–41.

28. Owens, *Season of Weathering,* 22. Some evidence indicates that the Klan

took up the cause of white supremacy a few years earlier. According to the *Fort Worth Record*, April 5, 1917, "German agents are trying to incite southern negroes to riot. Whites are forming KKK to protect against uprisings." Also see Reich, "Soldiers of Democracy," 1500-1504.

29. *Paris Morning News*, February 10, 22, 25, 26, 28, May 20, 1922; Reich, "Soldiers of Democracy," 1503.

30. *Paris Morning News*, January 7, February 1, 13, March 3, 14, 23, 30, April 6, 11, May 7, July 21, 1922.

31. *Paris Morning News*, January 7, March 3, 14, 23, 30, 1922.

32. *The Holy Bible*, New Revised Standard Version (Nashville: Thomas Nelson, 1989), New Testament, 161. Also see David Chalmers, "Ku Klux Klan," in S. S. Hill, *Encyclopedia of Religion in the South*, 396-397.

33. *Pittsburg Gazette*, June 13, 1924, p. 3; *Paris Morning News*, February 13, 1922, p. 8. Also see Interview with Patman by Frantz, 5; Walter N. Vernon, *Methodism Moves across North Texas* (Dallas: North Texas Conference of the Methodist Church, 1967), 250-253. Vernon was present when the Klan in full regalia marched into a Methodist church in Howland in Lamar County, and he recalled that they gave the minister an envelope full of money.

34. For an introduction to a complex topic, see Randall M. Miller, "Restoration Christianity," in Charles Reagan Wilson and William Ferris (eds.), *Encyclopedia of Southern Culture* (Chapel Hill: University of North Carolina Press, 1989), 1303-1306; Paul K. Conkin, *American Originals: Homemade Varieties of Christianity* (Chapel Hill: University of North Carolina Press, 1997), 1-56. Also see Vernon, *Methodism Moves across North Texas*, 132-266; David Edwin Harrell, Jr., *The Sources of Divisions in the Disciples of Christ, 1865-1900* (Atlanta: Publishing Systems, 1973); Dohoney, *Average American*, 190-205; John W. Storey, *Texas Baptist Leadership and Social Christianity, 1900-1980* (College Station: Texas A&M University Press, 1986), 108-110, 132-133; Stephen Daniel Eckstein, Jr., *History of the Churches of Christ in Texas, 1824-1950* (Austin: Firm Foundation Press, 1963), 84-153, 229-295; Alexander, *Crusade for Conformity*, 27-32; Robert M. Miller, "A Note on the Relationship between the Protestant Churches and the Ku Klux Klan," *JSH* 22 (August 1956): 257-266.

35. Ownby, *Subduing Satan*, 167-212.

36. *Pittsburg Gazette*, July 13, 1924, p. 3. Evidence on women in the Klan in Texas is even scarcer than evidence on men. As Charles Alexander pointed out, "the Women of the Klan never possessed the strength in the southwestern states it did in Indiana," yet Kathleen Blee probably is correct that "their activities and ideologies differed" from men in the Klan. See Alexander, *Ku Klux Klan in the Southwest*, 104; Blee, *Women of the Klan*, 2.

37. *Jefferson Jimplecute*, June 14, 1922, p. 1. Also see U.S., *Census: 1920, Population*, vol. 1, 304. For an example of the role of women in an influential local church, see J. A. R. Moseley, *The Presbyterian Church in Jefferson* (Austin: Texas State Historical Association, 1946).

38. *Fort Worth Press*, June 5, 9, 1923, and June 28, 30, July 1, 5, 8, September 8, 1924; Alexander, *Ku Klux Klan in the Southwest*, 102-106.

39. *Paris Morning News*, August 1, 1922; J. H. Davis, *Memoir*, 14-325; Chapin

Ross, "Public Address of James Harvey 'Cyclone' Davis." Also see D. White, "Observations about the First Congressional District," 3, for the claim that Cyclone Davis was a paid speaker for the KKK before he ran for Congress in 1922.

40. *Pittsburg Gazette,* January 31, April 11, September 19, 26, December 19, 1919; *Jefferson Jimplecute,* January 23, February 6, September 4, October 16, December 18, 1919, and January 22, February 19, April 29, May 13, July 29, August 26, October 28, December 2, 1920. On the cotton market in the 1920s, see Snyder, *Cotton Crisis,* xiii–xvii; Fite, *Cotton Fields No More,* 91–119.

41. *Paris Morning News,* March 29, 1922, p. 1.

42. Morris Sheppard to William Atkinson, October 2, 1924, Morris Sheppard Papers, University of Texas Archives; Brown, *Hood, Bonnet, and Little Brown Jug,* 78–87, 226; George Clifton Edwards, "Texas: The Big Southwestern Specimen," *Nation* 116 (March 21, 1923): 334–335. For examples of the lingering bitterness of some areas toward industrial concentration and high freight rates, see *Naples Monitor,* June 12, July 17, 1925.

43. *Pittsburg Gazette,* July 14, 21, 28, August 4, 11, 18, 1922; *Paris Morning News,* July 21, 22, 23, 25, 26, 27, 1922; *Jefferson Jimplecute,* March 9, April 6, July 20, 27, 1922; Brown, *Hood Bonnet, and Little Brown Jug,* 81–87; Paul D. Casdorph, "The Texas National Guard and the 1922 Railroad Strike at Denison," *Texas Military History* 3 (winter 1963): 211–218; Colin J. Davis, *Power at Odds: The 1922 National Railroad Shopmen's Strike* (Urbana: University of Illinois Press, 1997), 64–100.

44. *Paris Morning News,* June 6, 1922, p. 2. Also see *Dallas Morning News,* July 24, 27, 1922; *Paris Morning News,* March 26, 30, 31, July 6, 7, 12, 19, 23, 27, 1922; Brown, *Hood, Bonnet, and Little Brown Jug,* 49–87.

45. *Jefferson Jimplecute,* March 9, 1922, p. 1.

46. *Pittsburg Gazette,* August 4, 1922, p. 2.

47. Election returns for the district are in the *Pittsburg Gazette,* August 4, 1922, p. 1. Also see *Jefferson Jimplecute,* June 1, 1922; Wright Patman to Eugene Black, March 8, 1922, WPP.

48. "Democratic Election Returns," *Jefferson Jimplecute,* July 27, 1922, p. 1.

49. *Paris Morning News,* February 16, June 4, July 13, 25, 1922; *Dallas Morning News,* July 24, 1922; *Pittsburg Gazette,* July 31, 1914, and August 4, 1922. After the election Delta County Democrats tried to get an anti-Klan plank passed at the 1922 Democratic State Convention. See Brown, *Hood, Bonnet, and Little Brown Jug,* 119–122.

50. *Paris Morning News,* July 25, 27, 1922, and May 12, 1928; Neville, *Lamar County,* 1–20.

51. *Paris Morning News,* February 23, 1922, p. 2. Also see *Paris Morning News,* July 23, 25, 26, 27, 1922.

52. *Paris Morning News,* July 23, 27, 1922; *Pittsburg Gazette,* August 4, 1922.

53. *Paris Morning News,* August 27, 1922, p. 4. On the record turnout, see Brown, *Hood, Bonnet, and Little Brown Jug,* 211–239. Also see *Pittsburg Gazette,* April 6, 1922.

54. According to the *Dallas Morning News,* record numbers of women voted in the 1922 Democratic primary. See *Dallas Morning News,* July 24, 1922.

55. *Pittsburg Gazette*, June 13, July 18, 1924; Brown, *Hood, Bonnet, and Little Brown Jug*, 211–252.

56. *Pittsburg Gazette*, July 18, 1924, p. 6. Also see *Paris Morning News*, July 28, 29, 30, 31, 1924.

57. *Pittsburg Gazette*, June 13, 1924; *Jefferson Jimplecute*, July 3, 10, 17, 24, 31, 1924; Alexander, *Ku Klux Klan in the Southwest*, 192–199; T. Whitfield Davidson, *The Memoirs of T. Whitfield Davidson* (Waco: Texian Press, 1972), 23–25.

58. *Paris Morning News*, February 22, 1922, p. 1.

59. *Jefferson Jimplecute*, 3, 10, 17, 24, 1924; Shelley Sallee, " 'The Woman of It': Governor Miriam Ferguson's 1924 Election," *SHQ* 100 (July 1996): 1–16.

60. Kingston, Attlesey, and Crawford, *Political History of Texas*, 204–207.

61. V. A. Collins, another member of the Klan who openly sought its support, received few votes in Northeast Texas except in Bowie County. Including his vote with that of Robertson pushed the total number of Klan voters to about 30 percent in Bowie—what you would expect in a county with a city the size and type of Texarkana. See *Jefferson Jimplecute*, July 3, 10, 17, 24, 31, 1924; Kingston, Attlesey, and Crawford, *Political History of Texas*, 204–207.

62. *Dallas Morning News*, August 15, 23, 1924; *Jefferson Jimplecute*, July 31, 1924; T. W. Davidson, *Memoirs*, 4–30; Brown, *Hood, Bonnet, and Little Brown Jug*, 227–242.

63. While the total vote in Texas or the region did not match that of 1924 during the rest of the decade, it also remained well above the 1922 level. Since the white adult male population of Northeast Texas declined, women continued voting or the level would have fallen below 1922. See Alexander Heard, *Southern Primaries and Elections, 1920–1949* (Freeport, N.Y.: Books for Libraries, 1950), 134–148.

64. *Paris Morning News*, August 24, 26, 1924; *Jefferson Jimplecute*, August 28, 1924; *Pittsburg Gazette*, August 27, 1924. Texas Germans and Czechs played a dominant role in about a dozen central and southeastern counties. In Comal County, a traditional center of German Texas, Robertson received only 48 votes, while Ferguson garnered over 2,000. See *Dallas Morning News*, August 24, 1924.

65. *Pittsburg Gazette*, June 13, July 18, August 1, 29, 1924; Shelley Sallee, " 'The Woman of It,' " 1–16.

66. Brown, *Hood, Bonnet, and Little Brown Jug*, 66–67.

67. *Paris Morning News*, February 24, 1922. Also see *Paris Morning News*, February 22, 25, 1922. On the possibility that whites simply stopped printing accounts of lynchings in newspapers or in other sources, see McMillen, *Dark Journey*, 251–253. On a similar role played by Rotary Clubs in Georgia, see Brundage, *Lynching in the New South*, 227–244.

68. McMillen, *Dark Journey*, 233–253; *Dallas Morning News*, May 10, 1930; *Paris Morning News*, May 10, 1930; Arthur F. Raper, *The Tragedy of Lynching* (Chapel Hill: University of North Carolina Press, 1933), 319–355. For another example of Texas business leaders acting to improve local race relations, see Buenger and Buenger, *Texas Merchant*, 141–146.

69. *Paris Morning News*, February 23, 1922, p. 2. For other variations of the

quote, see *Paris Morning News,* January 10, 17, February 3, 10, 22, 23, 24, 26, March 2, 3, 17, 22, 25, April 4, 5, 8, 11, 12, 13, 21, 30, May 7, 26, July 2, 1922.

70. *New York Evening Post* quoted in Brown, *Hood, Bonnet, and Little Brown Jug,* 338. Also see Kingston, Attlesey, and Crawford, *Political History of Texas,* 208-211; *Paris Morning News,* July 24, 25, 26, 1926; *Naples Monitor,* July 9, 16, 23, 30, August 6, 1926.

71. *Naples Monitor,* May 2, June 8, July 9, 16, 23, 30, August 6, 13, September 3, 1926; *Jefferson Jimplecute,* May 18, June 25, 1926.

72. *Paris Morning News,* August 30, 1926; *Dallas Morning News,* August 30, 1926; Kingston, Attlesey, and Crawford, *Political History of Texas,* 208-219.

73. *Paris Morning News,* April 19, 1922 p. 2.

CHAPTER 8: POLITICS AND CULTURE, 1928

1. *Pittsburg Gazette,* August 3, 1928; *Paris Morning News,* May 29, 1956.

2. Neville borrowed this phrase from Wordsworth. See Neville, *Red River Valley,* 143. Also see *Dallas Morning News,* May 29, 1956; *Paris Morning News,* May 29, 1956, and July 12, 1970.

3. On Texas cultural life, see Ronald L. Davis, "Modernization and Distinctiveness: Twentieth-Century Cultural Life in Texas," in *Texas through Time,* 3-19; William A. Owens, *Tell Me a Story, Sing Me a Song* (Austin: University of Texas Press, 1983); Graham, Lee, and Pilkington, *Texas Literary Tradition;* Clifford Craig and Tom Pilkington (eds.), *Range Wars: Heated Debates, Sober Reflections, and Other Assessments of Texas Writings* (Dallas: Southern Methodist University Press, 1989); Owens, "Regionalism and Universality," 69-79; Don Graham, *Giant Country: Essays on Texas* (Fort Worth: Texas Christian University Press, 1998).

4. William Humphrey, *The Ordways* (New York: Knopf, 1964), 36. Also see James W. Lee, "The Old South in Texas Literature," *Texas Literary Tradition,* 46-57.

5. Henry Nash Smith, "Culture," *Southwest Review* 13 (January 1928): 255; Owens, *Stubborn Soil,* 4.

6. See, for example, Humphrey, *No Resting Place;* Cecilia Elizabeth O'Leary, " 'Blood Brotherhood': The Racialization of Patriotism, 1865-1918," in John Bodnar (ed.), *Bonds of Affection: Americans Define Their Patriotism* (Princeton: Princeton University Press, 1996), 53-81. On the growing importance of tangling and untangling history and memory, see Tamara Plakins Thornton, "Timely Reminders," *Reviews in American History* 26 (December 1998): 793-798; Thomas P. Slaughter, "Ahanagran's Loss," *Reviews in American History* 26 (September 1998): 475-481; *JAH* 85 (September 1998): 409-465. Also see Buenger, "Texas and the South"; John Bodnar, *Remaking America: Public Memory, Commemoration, and Patriotism in the Twentieth Century* (Princeton: Princeton University Press, 1992), 13-20; Kammen, *Mystic Chords of Memory;* "A Special Issue Focusing on the Theme Historians and the Public(s)," *Perspectives* 38 (May 2000): 15-49.

7. Foley also suggested that, like memories of the past, definitions of white-

ness changed with time. See Foley, *White Scourge,* 203–213. Also see Humphrey, *No Resting Place,* 10–21; Interview with Dean by Crow, 18–25.

8. Owens, "Regionalism and Universality," 71.

9. Neville, *Red River Valley,* vii; *Paris Morning News,* May 8, 1928, p.4. Also see *Paris Morning News,* April 12, 1928; Gould, "The University Becomes Politicized," 256–259. Dobie published his first book, *Coronado's Children,* and began his legendary course "Life and Literature of the Southwest" in 1930. Webb published *The Great Plains* in 1931. Work on both began in the 1920s. For an introduction to Dobie and Webb, see Don Graham, "J. Frank Dobie: A Reappraisal," *SHQ* 92 (July 1988): 1–15; Joe B. Frantz, "Remembering Walter Prescott Webb," *SHQ* 92 (July 1988): 17–30.

10. On this point see Foster, *Ghosts of the Confederacy,* 97–98; Daniel Joseph Singal, *The War Within: From Victorian to Modernist Thought in the South, 1919–1945* (Chapel Hill: University of North Carolina Press, 1982), 3–36.

11. *Paris Morning News,* April 12, 1928, p. 4; Eugene C. Barker, *The Life Of Stephen F. Austin: Founder of Texas, 1793–1836* (Nashville and Dallas: Cokesbury Press, 1926), vii; *Paris Morning News,* April 10, 1928, p. 4. Also see Neville, *Red River Valley,* vii–xiii; Barker, *Stephen F. Austin,* 3–12.

12. For a starting point in understanding Texas fiction, see Larry McMurtry, "Ever a Bridegroom: Reflections on the Failure of Texas Literature," *Range Wars,* 13–42; Tom Pilkington, "Herding Words: Texas Literature as Trail Drive," *Range Wars,* 155–172.

13. Singal, *War Within,* xiii.

14. *Cooper Review,* July 9, 1909, p. 4.

15. On Blind Lemon Jefferson, see *New HOT,* vol. 3, 924. Also see Bill C. Malone, *Country Music, USA,* rev. ed. (Austin: University of Texas Press, 1985), 31–92; Alan B. Govenar, *Meeting the Blues* (Dallas: Taylor, 1988); Kammen, *Mystic Chords,* 375–443.

16. *Paris Morning News,* January 1, 1922, p. 3. Also see *Naples Monitor,* June 12, October 23, 1925; April 30, 1926; July 1, August 26, December 9, 1927; March 9, August 17, 1928. *Jefferson Jimplecute,* March 19, 26, April 6, 1926.

17. Neville, *Red River Valley,* 278.

18. Dohoney, *Average American,* 1–7.

19. Neville, *Lamar County,* 190–194; Chamber of Commerce of Lamar County, *Paris, Texas Style* (San Diego: Watermark Publishers, 1996), 12–13.

20. Spencer, *Camp County Story,* 161–162. *Pittsburg Gazette,* April 15, November 4, 1904; May 30, 1919; July 18, 1924.

21. Interview with Truby by Curtis; Neville, *Lamar County,* 216–235; J. L. Wees Papers, Center for American History, University of Texas at Austin.

22. David S. Evans and J. Derral Mulholland, *Big and Bright: A History of McDonald Observatory* (Austin: University of Texas Press, 1986), 165–169. Also see Laura Wimberley, "Cooperative Science: Origins of the William Johnson McDonald Observatory, 1926–1939," *ETHJ* 35 (spring 1997): 54–56.

23. On Texas churches in the 1920s, see J. Wayne Flynt, "Southern Protestantism and Reform, 1890–1920," in Samuel S. Hill (ed.), *Varieties of Southern Religious Experience* (Baton Rouge: Louisiana State University Press, 1988), 135–157;

Storey, *Texas Baptist Leadership,* 39-69; Vernon, *Methodism Moves across North Texas,* 218-266.

24. Changes in denominational structure also impacted the size of these denominations. The Cumberland Presbyterians, the largest Presbyterian group in Northeast Texas in 1906, merged with the Presbyterian Church, U.S.A. (Northern), later that year. After 1906 many Cumberland Presbyterians shifted to the Disciples, including E. L. Dohoney. The 1906 Census marked the first time the Churches of Christ and the Disciples were enumerated separately. See S. S. Hill, *Encyclopedia of Religion in the South,* 188-189, 201-205; Dohoney, *Average American,* 190-205; George H. Paschal, Jr., and Judith A. Banner, *One Hundred Years of Challenge and Change: A History of the Synod of Texas of the United Presbyterian Church in the U.S.A.* (San Antonio, Trinity University Press, 1968), 37-72.

25. Howard Miller, "Texas," in Sam S. Hill (ed.), *Religion in the Southern States* (Macon: Mercer University Press, 1983), 327-333; Carter E. Boren, *Religion on the Texas Frontier* (San Antonio: Naylor, 1968), 73-163; Conkin, *American Originals,* 1-56.

26. Stephen Daniel Eckstein, *History of the Churches of Christ in Texas;* J. R. Green, *Grass-Roots Socialism,* 169-172; Garin Burbank, *When Farmers Voted Red: The Gospel of Socialism in the Countryside, 1910-1924* (Westport, Conn.: Greenwood Press, 1976), 14-43.

27. Owens, *Season of Weathering,* 96-114.

28. *Jefferson Jimplecute,* November 21, 1912, p. 4. Also see *Sulphur Springs Gazette,* November 29, 1912; E. C. Green, *Southern Strategies,* 78-184.

29. See the description of Black in *Pittsburg Gazette,* April 6, 1928; *Paris Morning News,* February 26, 1928. Also see *Jefferson Jimplecute,* June 5, 1919; E. C. Green, *Southern Strategies,* 127-150; Atticus Webb to Wright Patman, April 14, 1927, Box 77A, WPP.

30. Wright Patman, *Post Offices of the First District; New York Times,* May 8, July 29, 30, 1932; *Jefferson Journal,* November 3, 1928.

31. For numerous statements of this theme, see Patman's Political File, Special Correspondence, 1928, Box 77A, WPP; *Pittsburg Gazette,* April 6, August 3, 1928.

32. *Paris Morning News,* April 8, 1928, p. 4. On the mystique of the independent oilman, see Lawrence Goodwyn, *Texas Oil, American Dreams: A Study of the Texas Independent Producers and Royalty Owners Association* (Austin: Texas State Historical Association, 1996).

33. Webb to Patman, April 14, 1927; *Dallas Morning News,* July 29, 1928; *Pittsburg Gazette,* August 3, 1928.

34. *Naples Monitor,* July 27, 1928, p. 3; *Paris Morning News,* March 29, 1922, p. 1. Also see Nancy Beck Young, "Change and Continuity in the Politics of Running for Congress: Wright Patman and the Campaigns of 1928, 1938, 1962, and 1972," *ETHJ* 34 (fall 1996): 52-64.

35. For Black's own explanation of why he changed his mind on McNary-Haugan, see Eugene Black to Judge Hugh Carney, February 25, 1929, Box 77A, WPP; *Naples Monitor,* July 27, 1928; "Great Crowd Hears Congressman Black in Sulphur Springs," clipping from the *Hopkins County Echo,* March 1928, WPP.

Also see *Congressional Record*, 69 Congress, 2 session, 1927, 3906-3909, 3877-3878, 3874-3875, 4094; Fite, *Cotton Fields No More*, 110-111; Philip A. Grant, Jr., "Southern Congressmen and Agriculture, 1921-1932," *Agricultural History* 53 (January 1979): 338-351; Young, "Politics of Running for Congress," 52-55.

36. For prices and the volume of the crop, see Figure 5.3. For an overview of the problem, see Fite, *Cotton Fields No More*, 106-114. For local reaction, see *Paris Morning News*, January 1, 1928.

37. *Paris Morning News*, March 3, 4, 6, 8, 14, 15, 30, 1928; *Pittsburg Gazette*, 16, 23, 30, 1928; Fleming, *Anderson, Clayton*, 14 n. 5; Garwood, *Will Clayton*, 97-101.

38. *Paris Morning News*, March 4, 14, 1928.

39. *Paris Morning News*, April 12, 1928, p. 4.

40. Interview with Patman by Frantz; Interview with Wright Patman by Michael L. Gillete, February 4, 1976, LBJ Library; Sherrill, "Last of the Great Populists," 24-118.

41. Young, "Politics of Running for Congress," 52-55; Schmelzer, "Wright Patman," 10-24.

42. *Austin Statesman*, July 24, 25, 27, 1921; Max Bentley, "A Texan Challenges the Klan," *Collier's*, November 3, 1923, p. 12, 22; Schmelzer, "Wright Patman," 25-43.

43. *Texarkana Evening News*, January 6, 11, September 2, 16, 1927; *Paris Morning News*, May 10, 1928.

44. On Patman's campaign tactics, see the type of supporters he targeted in "List of Supporters, 1928," Box 39C, WPP. Also see Eugene Black to Wright Patman, July 6, 1928, Box 77A, WPP.

45. Interview with Patman by Frantz; Sherrill, "Last of the Great Populists." On Jones, see *Paris Morning News*, May 15, June 5, 1928; *Naples Monitor*, January 20, March 23, May 25, 1928; *Pittsburg Gazette*, May 25, 1928.

46. D. White, "Observations about the First Congressional District." Contrast Black's opening speech in the *Hopkins County Echo*, June 3, 1928, with "Wright Patman Opens Campaign for Congress," broadside, Box 82B, WPP.

47. *Paris Morning News*, July 19, 1928, p. 3; "Patman Opens Campaign," broadside. Also see Wright Patman to J. H. "Cyclone" Davis, July 25, 1927, and Wright Patman to J. H. "Cyclone" Davis, January 5, 1928, Box 45A, WPP.

48. "Patman Opens Campaign," broadside.

49. "Patman Opens Campaign," broadside; *Paris Morning News*, July 19, 1928; *Naples Monitor*, May 25, July 20, 27, August 3, 1928.

50. D. White, "Observations about the First Congressional District"; *Dallas Morning News*, July 25, 1928; Wright Patman Diary, 1928, Box 1705, WPP.

51. Interview with Patman by Frantz; Mary Jimerieff, "Opponent and Champion of the KKK," *Austin Statesman*, August 14, 1921, p. 4.

52. *Paris Morning News*, May 10, 1928.

53. Interview with Patman by Frantz; "Important Political Information," Box 72A, WPP.

54. Wright Patman to J. D. More, December 15, 1927; Wright Patman to J. W. Middleton, December 15, 1927; Wright Patman to T. H. Bomar, December 15,

1927; R. H. Good to Wright Patman, December 30, 1927; T. H. Bomar to Wright Patman, December 20, 1927; W. T. Mauldin to Wright Patman, December 17, 1927; all in Box 79A, WPP. Also see *New HOT*, vol. 4, 810–811.

55. Webb to Patman, April 14, 1927. Also see Wayne B. Wheeler to Wright Patman, April 16, 1927; Francis Scott McBride to Wright Patman, July 6, 1928; Frank Morrison to Wright Patman, August 1, 1927; all in Box 77A, WPP.

56. *Pittsburg Gazette*, August 6, 1928. Patman repaid the support of labor by consistently voting in their favor even when labor played a less prominent roll at the polls. See Young, "Politics of Running for Congress," 56–62.

57. *Naples Monitor*, March 30, 1928; "List of Supporters, 1928"; Black to Carney, February 25, 1929.

58. *Paris Morning News*, February 4, 1928; Wright Patman to Russell Chaney, July 7, 1928, WPP; *Naples Monitor*, July 27, 1928; "Hon. Eugene Black's Prohibition Record," notes to a 1928 speech, WPP.

59. For precinct-level voting returns, see *Pittsburg Gazette*, August 3, 1928; *Lamar County Echo*, August 10, 1928; *Delta County Banner*, July 31, 1928; *Texarkana Gazette*, August 12, 1928; "Vote By Boxes-1928," Box 82B, WPP.

60. For a fuller discussion of economic and demographic change, see chapter 5. For changes in factional alignment, see chapter 7.

61. Mayfield won each of the Paris voting boxes by a large margin, as did Black. In Lamar County, Black won 20 of 49 boxes. Mayfield led in 19 of those 20. Patman led in 29 of the 49 boxes and carried the county outside of Paris. Mayfield led in only 15 of the 29 boxes carried by Patman. In Texarkana Black carried all but 2 of the city's 11 boxes, but Patman swamped him in the rest of the county. He won the county by 1,000 votes. Mayfield again led in the same boxes as Black but usually trailed in the boxes carried by Patman. In Sulphur Springs, Black won all 4 boxes, and again Mayfield also led those boxes. Patman carried almost every other box in Hopkins County, and in the few he did not carry, Mayfield again led the field of six candidates for the Senate. See "Vote By Boxes—1928."

62. *Pittsburg Gazette*, August 4, 1922; *Paris Morning News*, July 27, 1922; *Jefferson Jimplecute*, July 27, 1922; *Dallas Morning News*, July 24, 25, 26, 1922; "Vote by Boxes—1928."

63. *Pittsburg Gazette*, August 4, 1922; *Paris Morning News*, July 27, 1922; *Jefferson Jimplecute*, July 27, 1922; *Dallas Morning News*, July 24, 25, 26, 1922; "Vote By Boxes—1928."

64. "Vote By Boxes—1928," gives the following:

	Black	Patman	Total
Bowie	2,910 (43.0%)	3,847 (57.0%)	6,757
Camp	729 (37.5%)	1,157 (62.5%)	1,852
Cass	1,450 (39.0%)	2,266 (61.0%)	3,716
Delta	1,220 (47.4%)	1,356 (52.6%)	2,576
Franklin	611 (31.0%)	1,364 (69.0%)	1,975
Hopkins	2,205 (45.2%)	2,671 (54.8%)	4,876

	Black	Patman	Total
Lamar	3,924 (56.7%)	2,997 (43.7%)	6,921
Marion	277 (54.7%)	229 (45.3%)	506
Morris	588 (32.8%)	1,205 (67.8%)	1,793
Red River	2,964 (64.9%)	1,602 (35.1%)	4,566
Titus	1,099 (33.4%)	2,190 (66.6%)	3,289
Total	17,943 (46.2%)	20,884 (53.8%)	38,827

65. U.S., *Census: 1925: Agriculture*, 1174-1202; U.S., *Census: 1930: Agriculture*, vol. 2, pt. 2, 1562-1573; St. Clair, "History of Hopkins County" 97-108.

66. U.S., *Census: Population, 1930*, vol. 1, 1074; Election Returns, 1894: Secretary of State; *Sulphur Springs Gazette*, August 7, 1914; "Vote By Boxes—1928."

67. "Vote By Boxes—1928."

68. "Vote by Boxes—1928."

69. "Soldiers Compensation Speech, 1928" Box 77A, WPP.

70. "Patman Opens Campaign," broadside.

71. "Patman Opens Campaign," broadside.

72. "Patman Opens Campaign," broadside.

73. "Patman Opens Campaign," broadside.

74. Clarence R. Wharton, *History of Texas* (Dallas: Turner Company, 1935), 459; Young, "Politics of Running for Congress," 56.

75. On other Texans in Washington at about the same time, see Buenger, "Jesse H. Jones and the Reconstruction Finance Corporation," 481-510; Hendrickson and Collins, *Profiles in Power*. Some Texans, most notably Hatton Sumners, did not completely fit this pattern, but even Sumners used the government to build up Texas. See Lionel V. Patenaude, "Garner, Sumners, and Connally: The Defeat of the Roosevelt Court Bill in 1937," *SHQ* 74 (July 1970): 36-51; *New HOT*, vol. 6, 149-150.

EPILOGUE

1. Gould, *Progressives and Prohibitionists*, 58-119; Buenger, "Jesse H. Jones and the Reconstruction Finance Corporation," 492-498. For a useful comparison of the southern states in this period, see Grantham, *Southern Progressivism*, 36-108. Grantham notes the ambiguous nature of Texas but in general sees it as slightly more diverse, more open to innovation, more prosperous, and more liberal than most other southern states. Also see Buenger, "Texas and the South," 306-324.

2. E. C. Green, *Southern Strategies*, 179, 182.

3. For the argument that women took advantage of factionalism within the Democratic party to achieve reform, see McArthur, *Creating the New Woman*, 97-150. Also see Grantham, *Southern Progressivism*, 98-103; C. Davidson, *Race and Class in Texas Politics*, 3-62.

4. For a statewide view, see McArthur, *Creating the New Woman*, 5-134.

5. Escott, *Many Excellent People*, 267.

6. Ownby, *Subduing Satan*, 167-212.

7. McMillen, *Dark Journey*, 245-253.

8. U.S., *Census: 1930, Population*, vol. 1, 103-1098; Gregory, *American Exodus*, 3-35.

9. D. White, "Observations about the First Congressional District."

10. Compare Northeast Texas with descriptions of the South in Daniel, *Breaking the Land*, 1-61; Kirby, *Rural Worlds Lost*, 25-50.

11. Humphrey, *No Resting Place*, 9.

12. Humphrey, *No Resting Place*, 18. Also see Bascom Timmons, *Jesse H. Jones* (New York: Henry Holt, 1956), 269-272; Kenneth B. Ragsdale, *The Year America Discovered Texas: Centennial '36* (College Station: Texas A&M University Press, 1987), 111-114; Tom C. King, *Report of an Examination of the Texas Centennial* (Austin: Office of the State Auditor and Efficiency Expert, 1939).

13. Humphrey, *No Resting Place*, 16. Also see *Paris News*, February 17, 1922.

14. Humphrey, *Farther off from Heaven*, 242.

15. Humphrey, *No Resting Place*, 16; Humphrey, *Farther off from Heaven*, 239.

16. For an introduction to Lee, see Emory M. Thomas, *Robert E. Lee: A Biography* (New York: W. W. Norton, 1995). Also see Kammen, *Mystic Chords*, 342-443; Connelly, *Marble Man*, 99-140; Emory M. Thomas, "Review Essay: Civil Warriors in Memory and Memoir, Lee Remembered," *Georgia Historical Quarterly* 75 (fall 1991): 534-541; Connelly and Bellows, *God and General Longstreet*, 39-106; Wilson, *Baptized in Blood*, 119-182; Escott, "Uses of Gallantry," 47-74. On the general conservatism of Virginia, see Allen Wesley Moger, *Virginia: Bourbonism to Byrd, 1870-1925* (Charlottesville: University Press of Virginia, 1968).

17. Richard N. Current, *Northernizing the South* (Athens: University of Georgia Press, 1983), 14. Also see Current, *Northernizing*, 85-105; Paul D. Lack, "In the Long Shadow of Eugene C. Barker: The Revolution and the Republic," in *Texas through Time*, 134-164; Buenger and Calvert, "Shelf Life of Truth in Texas," ix-xxv. For how history was taught when Bill Moyers was growing up in Texas, see Moyers, "The Big Story: A Journalist Looks at Texas History," *SHQ* 101 (July 1997): 1-16. On Crockett, see James E. Crisp, "The Little Book That Wasn't There: The Myth and Mystery of the de la Peña Diary," *SHQ* 98 (October 1994): 261-296.

18. Bodnar, *Remaking America*, 15. Also see Walter L. Buenger and Robert A. Calvert, *Texas History and the Move into the Twenty-First Century* (Austin: Texas Committee for the Humanities, 1990).

19. On the role of government, see Kirby, *Rural Worlds Lost*, 25-111; Daniel, *Breaking the Land*, 63-151; Foley, *White Scourge*, 163-213.

A COMMENT ON
PRIMARY SOURCES

As the notes indicate, many secondary sources informed my work. To a large degree, however, this study rests upon primary source material. Explaining that source material probably requires more than simply letting each reader dig citations out of the notes.

Election returns contributed a great deal to my understanding of the region. Since there were only eleven counties, more formal statistical methods of analysis seemed useless, but I compensated for the small-number problem by relying as much as possible on precinct-level returns. Each county filed official returns from the general election with the Texas Secretary of State, and these can be found in Election Returns, Secretary of State Papers, Texas State Archives, Austin. Precinct-level returns are sometimes available from local newspapers and in other cases in each county's Records of Election Returns. These Records of Election Returns are available in the county clerk's office or in regional archives. Once the primary became the key election, returns grew more difficult to discover. Primary returns are available only from the *Texas Almanac* or from newspapers. For a convenient and usually accurate source of election returns by county in gubernatorial and presidential elections, see Mike Kingston, Sam Attlesey, and Mary G. Crawford, *Texas Almanac's Political History of Texas* (Dallas: *Dallas Morning News,* 1992), 50–315. Unfortunately there are several gaps in this study, and it does not include congressional elections.

Newspapers offered more than simply election returns. I read more than twenty Northeast Texas newspapers and three statewide papers. They sometimes did not get the facts straight, they reflected the biases of their owners and editors, and they tended to ignore the poor and minorities. Still, nothing else offered a year-by-year view of the region. Nothing else told what people cared about, or described in detail the grassroots struggle for prohibition and other reforms.

Northeast Texans left behind few large-scale manuscript collections, but they compensated for that by writing numerous memoirs and autobiographical works. Local histories written by people who lived through this period also added to my store of information and understanding of what happened in the region.

Like memoirs, oral interviews offer problems for researchers. Memories of distant days become clouded and an editing process often goes on. Still, several oral interviews aided this project. They were particularly useful in pinpointing changes in agricultural methods and population shifts.

Several Northeast Texas counties or counties adjacent to the region became objects of study for early-day agricultural scientists, and these too offered information on economic and social change. Particularly useful were those studies that included surveys of the citizens of the region. These works supplemented information from U.S. censuses and from the *Agricultural Yearbook.*

Photographs added a visual dimension to my understanding of the past. The Jenkins Garret Postcard Collection and reproductions of postcards in the American History Center at Austin proved especially useful. Simply understanding that whites turned photographs of black victims of lynching into postcards reveals a disregard for human life that is difficult to comprehend.

Throughout the writing and researching of this book, I wished for more primary sources. I particularly regret that black voices appeared so seldom, but they did show up in some newspaper accounts, in oral interviews, and in local histories. Two recent articles let blacks in Northeast Texas speak—Fred McKenzie, "The Kellyville Incident," *East Texas Historical Journal* 37 (spring 1999): 39–41; Steven A. Reich, "Soldiers of Democracy: Black Texans and the Fight for Citizenship, 1917–1921," *Journal of American History* 82 (March 1996): 1478–1504. Despite gaps, the works summarized below offered a secure base for understanding Northeast Texas and what its history meant for our understanding of Texas and the South.

TEXAS NEWSPAPERS

Atlanta Citizens Journal
Atlanta Express
Atlanta News
Bonham Daily Favorite
Cass County Sun
Red River County Review
Clarksville Standard
Clarksville Times
Cooper Review
Cumby Rustler
Dallas Morning News
Fort Worth Star-Telegram
Hopkins County Echo
Houston Post
Jefferson Jimplecute
Lamar County Echo
Mount Vernon Optic-Herald
Naples Monitor

Omaha Breeze
Paris Morning News
Pittsburg Gazette
Sulphur Springs Gazette
Texarkana Four States Press
Texarkana Texarkanian

ORAL INTERVIEWS

Dean, Corener, by Corrinne E. Crow, June 1973, Texas A&M University at Commerce.

Leonard, Marty, by Victoria L. Buenger and Walter L. Buenger, July 14, 1994, Garrett Library, University of Texas at Arlington.

McAshan, S. M., by Walter L. Buenger and Joseph A. Pratt, January 4, 1985, Texas Commerce Bank Archives.

McClure, C. R., by Corrinne E. Crow, November 7, 1973, Texas A&M University at Commerce.

Mathena, George, by Corrinne E. Crow, April 25, 1974, Texas A&M University at Commerce.

Moulton, Enola, by John David Scott, 1983, Garrett Library, University of Texas at Arlington.

Patman, Wright, by Joe B. Frantz, August 11, 1972, Lyndon Baines Johnson Library, Austin.

Patman, Wright, by Michael L. Gillette, February 4, 1976, Lyndon Baines Johnson Library, Austin.

Truby, Maitland Mayer, by Anna May Curtis, April 23, 1980, Aikin Regional Archives, Paris Junior College.

Tyree, Hugh, and Laura Tyree by Walter L. Buenger, July 1, 1994, Garrett Library, University of Texas at Arlington.

MANUSCRIPT COLLECTIONS

James Biard Papers, American History Center, University of Texas at Austin.
Wright Patman Papers, Lyndon Baines Johnson Library, Austin.
J. L. Wees Papers, American History Center, University of Texas at Austin.

PUBLISHED MEMOIRS AND AUTOBIOGRAPHICAL WORKS

Aldredge, Joseph David, *The Romance of Growing a Boy in Texas: Autobiographical Sketches* (Jacksonville, TX: Pastor's Study, 1923).

Bourne, Emma Guest. *A Pioneer Farmer's Daughter of Red River Valley, Northeast Texas* (1950).

Colquitt, Oscar B., "Governor Oscar B. Colquitt Tells of Early Life and of his Newspaper and Political Experiences" (*Pittsburg Gazette,* February 13, 1934).

Davidson, T. Whitfield, *The Memoirs of Judge T. Whitfield Davidson* (Waco: Texian Press, 1972).

Davis, James Harvey "Cyclone," *Memoir* (Sherman, Texas: Courier Press, 1935).

Dohoney, E. L., *An Average American* (Paris, Texas: privately published, 1907).

Ellis, John Marion, II (b. 1917), *The Way it Was: A Personal Memoir of Family Life in East Texas* (Waco: Texian Press, 1983).

Embry, Clyde L. (b. 1900), *Our Good Old Days* (Laird Hill, Texas: n.p., 1970. 241 pp. illus. and ports).

Humphrey, William, *The Ordways* (New York: Knopf, 1964).

——, *Farther off from Heaven* (New York: Knopf, 1977).

——, *No Resting Place* (New York: Delacorte Press, 1989).

Jones, Lula Kathryn Peacock, *Recollections of the Life of Lula Kathryn (Kate) Peacock Jones* (1979).

Owens, William A., *This Stubborn Soil: A Frontier Boyhood* (New York: Scribner's, 1966).

——, *A Season of Weathering* (New York: Scribner's, 1973).

Riley, Hazel Beauton, *Washing on the Line* (Wichita Falls, Texas: Nortex Offset Publications, 1973).

Vaughan, George Lester, *The Cotton Renter's Son* (Wolfe City, Texas: Henington Publishing, 1967).

NORTHEAST TEXAS LOCAL HISTORIES

Bowers, Eugene, and Evelyn Oppenheimer, *Red River Dust* (Waco: Word Books, 1968).

Bowman, Myreline, *People of Cass County: Atlanta and Queen City, Texas* (Queen City: Privately published, 1973).

Brown, Deborah, and Katherine Gust, *Between the Creeks: Recollections of Northeast Texas* (Austin: Encino Press, 1976).

Chandler, Barbara Overton, "A History of Bowie County" (master's thesis, University of Texas, 1936).

Hollis, Herbert L., *Paris Fire of 1916* (Wolfe City, Texas: Henington Publishing, 1982).

McKay, Mrs. Arch, and Mrs. H. A. Spelling, *A History of Jefferson, Marion County, Texas, 1836-1936* (Jefferson: privately published, 1936).

Moseley, J. A. R., "The Citizens White Primary of Marion County," *Southwestern Historical Quarterly* 49 (April 1946).

Neville, Alexander White, *The History of Lamar County* (Paris: North Texas Publishing, 1937).

——, *The Red River Then and Now* (Paris: North Texas Publishing, 1948).

Ressler, Mary, "Bad Roads and Good Memories: An Oral History of 'East End,' Delta County, Texas, 1918-1940," Texas A&M University at Commerce.

Russell, Traylor, *History of Titus County, Texas* (Waco: W. M. Morrison, 1965).

Spencer, A. L. B., *The Camp County Story* (1974).

Stroud, Martha Sue, *Gateway to Texas: History of Red River County* (Austin: Nortex Press, 1997).

AGRICULTURAL STUDIES

Austin, Charles B., "Co-Operation in Agriculture: Marketing and Rural Credit" (Austin: University of Texas, 1914).

Bizzell, William Bennett, *Farm Tenantry in the United States* (College Station: Experiment Station, Agricultural and Mechanical College of Texas, 1921).

Brannen, C. O., "Relation of Land Tenure to Plantation Organization," *USDA Bulletin* no. 1269 (Washington: Government Printing Office, 1924).

Cox, Alonzo B., "Cotton Prices and Markets," *USDA Bulletin* no. 1444 (Washington, December 1926).

Haney, Lewis H., "Farm Credit in a Cotton State," *American Economic Review* 4 (March 1914): 47–67.

Hunter, W. D., "Methods of Controlling the Boll Weevil," *USDA Bulletin* no. 163 (Washington: Government Printing Office, 1903).

Hunter, W. D., and W. B. Pierce, "The Mexican Cotton Boll Weevil: A Summary of the Investigations of This Insect up to December 31, 1911," *USDA Bulletin* no. 114 (Washington: Government Printing Office, 1912).

Peteet, Walton, "Farming Credit in Texas," Extension Service Bulletin no. B-34 (College Station: Extension Service of the Agricultural and Mechanical College of Texas, 1917).

Potts, Charles S., "Railroad Transportation in Texas," *Bulletin of the University of Texas* no. 119 (Austin: University of Texas, 1909).

Sanders, J. T., "Farm Ownership and Tenancy in the Black Prairie of Texas," *USDA Bulletin* no. 1068 (Washington: Government Printing Office, 1922).

White, E. V., and William E. Leonard, "Studies in Farm Tenancy in Texas," *University of Texas Bulletin* no. 21 (Austin: University of Texas, 1915).

Willard, Rex E., "A Farm Management Study of Cotton Farms of Ellis County, Texas," *USDA Bulletin* no. 659 (Washington: Government Printing Office, 1918).

INDEX

8686